What We Owe to Each Other

What We Owe to Each Other

T. M. SCANLON

The Belknap Press of Harvard University Press

Cambridge, Massachusetts, and London, England   1998

Third printing, 2000

First Harvard University Press paperback edition, 2000

Library of Congress Cataloging-in-Publication Data

Scanlon, Thomas.
    What we owe to each other / T.M. Scanlon.
      p. cm.
    Includes bibliographical references and index.
    ISBN 0-674-95089-5 (cloth)
    ISBN 0-674-00423-x (pbk.)
    1. Right and wrong. 2. Judgment (Ethics). I. Title.
BJ1411.S36 1998
170—dc21   98-23318

For my father

and in memory of my mother

Acknowledgments

In September 1979, I set out to write a book in moral philosophy. I had leave from Princeton for the year and a Visiting Fellowship at All Souls College in Oxford, and I expected, quite unrealistically as it turned out, to complete a draft of the book that year. Now, more than eighteen years later, I have finally finished the task. In the interval I have received more help than anyone could possibly expect, from my family, colleagues, and students, as well as from various institutions. Innumerable family activities during these years fell under the shadows of these chapters and their many revisions. My wife, Lucy, and our daughters, Sarah and Jessie, helped by providing these diversions as well as by understanding and accepting my need to work. I am grateful to them, and especially to Lucy for her endless support and understanding.

The influence of John Rawls and Thomas Nagel on the ideas presented in the following chapters will, I trust, be obvious. Their suggestions and encouragement have also made an enormous difference. Perhaps less obvious to the reader, but at least as pervasive, are the contributions that Derek Parfit has made. From that first year at All Souls through the seminar we gave together at Harvard in the fall of 1997, he has provided a constant flow of the most trenchant and detailed comments, combined with the friendliest encouragement and advice. These have led to significant improvements in every part of the book. Ronald Dworkin and Amartya Sen also provided great help in the form of comments on many chapters and stimulating conversations about the issues they deal with. I have also benefited from conversations about these matters with Frances Kamm, Christine Korsgaard, Joseph Raz, Judith Thomson, and Bernard Williams.

Many other friends, students, and colleagues have read drafts of all or part of the book and offered comments that helped me to improve it. I thank all of them, including, in particular, Robert Audi, Carla Bagnoli, Michael Bratman, George Boolos, Talbot Brewer, G. A. Cohen, Joshua Cohen, Peter de Marneffe, Samuel Freeman, Gilbert Harman, Pamela Hieronymi, Aaron James, Shelly Kagan, Leonard Katz, Erin Kelly, Arthur Kuflik, Rahul Kumar, Sebastiano Maffettone, Richard Moran, Hilary Putnam, Sophia Reibetanz, Faviola Rivera-Castro, Larry Temkin, Dennis Thompson, Dietmar von der Pfordten, and Yoshiki Wakamatsu. I also owe thanks to the two anonymous readers for Harvard University Press for their helpful comments.

Agnieszka Jaworska and Tamar Schapiro provided research assistance, as did Angela Smith, whom I also thank for her critical comments and her marvelous copy editing.

Most of the ideas in this book were developed in material that was presented and discussed at meetings of the Society for Ethical and Legal Philosophy. I am extremely grateful to all the members of that group for the help and stimulation they provided over the years. Many chapters were also presented at the New York University Colloquium on Law, Philosophy, and Political Theory. These were wonderful sessions, and I benefited enormously from them. I thank the participants in the Colloquium, as well as the members of many other audiences at various universities to whom parts of the book were presented.

Several chapters of the book draw on previously published material. An earlier version of Chapter 3 appears as "The Status of Well-Being," in *The Tanner Lectures on Human Values*, vol. 19 (1998); and Chapter 6 is derived from "The Significance of Choice," in *The Tanner Lectures on Human Values*, vol. 8 (1988). Both are used with the permission of the Tanner Lectures on Human Values and the University of Utah Press. Much of Chapter 7 is taken from "Promises and Practices," *Philosophy and Public Affairs* 19 (1990), and is used with the permission of Princeton University Press. Finally, parts of Chapter 8 are taken from "Fear of Relativism," which appeared in R. Hursthouse, G. Lawrence, and W. Quinn, eds., *Virtues and Reasons: Philippa Foot and Moral Theory* (Oxford: Oxford University Press, 1995). This material is used with the permission of Oxford University Press.

Princeton University, Harvard University, and All Souls College have at various times provided both financial support and wonderfully congenial environments in which to work. I am grateful to the Guggenheim Foundation for support in the spring of 1990 and, especially, to The John D. and Catherine T. MacArthur Foundation for a fellowship that gave me the freedom to make the last push to complete the book.

This book is dedicated to my parents, Thomas and Grace Scanlon, who first inspired my interest in philosophy and have supported it in every possible way.

Contents

Introduction

We all believe that some actions are morally wrong. But when we claim that an action is wrong, what kind of judgment are we making? Judgments about right and wrong cannot be straightforwardly understood as factual claims about the empirical world or about our own psychology. Yet they do seem to make claims about some subject matter, claims which are capable of being true or false. Moreover, while certain kinds of experience can be important in putting us in a position to make moral judgments, making these judgments themselves does not seem to be a matter of observation. Rather, we arrive at the judgment that a certain kind of action would be wrong simply by thinking about the question in the right way, sometimes through a process of careful assessment that it is natural to call a kind of reasoning. But what kind of reasoning is it? Finally, the fact that a certain action would be morally wrong seems to provide a powerful reason not to do it, one that is, at least normally, decisive against any competing considerations. But it is not clear what this reason is. Why should we give considerations of right and wrong, whatever they are, this kind of priority over our other concerns and over other values? The aim of this book is to answer these questions.

In one sense, the question of the subject matter of judgments of right and wrong has an obvious answer: they are judgments about morality or, more specifically, about what is morally right. Moral judgments have the form of ordinary declarative sentences and obey the usual laws of logic. Why not just take them at face value, as making claims about what they say they are about? I believe that we should take these judgments at face value, as making claims about their apparent subject matter, right and wrong. But we also have reasons for wanting a fuller characterization of this subject matter. One possible reason arises from a metaphysical concern. If judgments of right and wrong can be said to be true or false, this must be because there is some realm of facts that they are meant to describe, and to which they can correspond, or fail to correspond. It might therefore seem that an adequate answer to the question of subject matter should, first and foremost, make clear what part of "the world" these judgments make claims about.

But this metaphysical question is not, for me at least, the primary issue. What drives me to look for a characterization of the subject matter of judgments of right and wrong that goes beyond the trivial one I mentioned above, is not a concern about the metaphysical reality of moral facts. If we could characterize the method of reasoning through which we arrive at judgments of right and wrong, and could explain why there is good reason to give judgments arrived at in this way the kind of importance that moral judgments are normally thought to have, then we would, I believe, have given a sufficient answer to the question of the subject matter of right and wrong as well. No interesting question would remain about the ontology of morals—for example, about the metaphysical status of moral facts.

This is because, in contrast to everyday empirical judgments, scientific claims, and religious beliefs that involve claims about the origin and control of the universe, the point of judgments of right and wrong is not to make claims about what the spatiotemporal world is like. The point of such judgments is, rather, a practical one: they make claims about what we have reason to do. Metaphysical questions about the subject matter of judgments of right and wrong are important only if answers to them are required in order to show how these judgments can have this practical significance. It may be said that we need a metaphysical characterization of the subject matter of morality in order to establish that moral judgments are about something "real," but it is worth asking what kind of reality is at issue and why it is something we should be worried about.

One worry would be that there may be no right answer to questions of right and wrong. This is a serious challenge, and it may seem that in order to answer it we must provide a metaphysical account of the subject matter of judgments of this kind. I believe that this is not what is necessary, however. The question at issue is not a metaphysical one. In order to show that questions of right and wrong have correct answers, it is enough to show that we have good grounds for taking certain conclusions that actions are right or are wrong to be correct, understood as conclusions about morality, and that we therefore have good grounds for giving these conclusions the particular importance that we normally attach to moral judgments.

A second interpretation of the charge that judgments of right and wrong are not about anything "real" would take it as the claim that they should not have this importance. This is a charge that any account of the reason-giving force of judgments of right and wrong needs to meet. But it is again not clear that an adequate response requires an account of the metaphysical status of the subject matter of such judgments, because it does not seem that the reason-giving force of facts about right and wrong derives from their metaphysical status. This is shown by the fact that it is not clear how an account of this status—for example, one showing that judgments of right and wrong are about some aspect of physical and psychological reality—would, simply in virtue of the "reality" it would give to the subject matter of judgments of right and wrong, bolster their reason-giving force.

The view I will defend takes judgments of right and wrong to be claims about reasons—more specifically about the adequacy of reasons for accepting or rejecting principles under certain conditions. It might be objected that this is to explain right and wrong in terms of something else—the idea of a reason—that is equally in need of philosophical explanation. As I will argue in Chapter 1, I do not believe that we should regard the idea of a reason as mysterious, or as one that needs, or can be given, a philosophical explanation in terms of some other, more basic notion. In particular, the idea of a reason should not be thought to present metaphysical or epistemological difficulties that render it suspect. As long, therefore, as we have suitable ways of determining whether there would or would not be good reasons for rejecting a principle under the relevant circumstances, and as long as we have reason to care about this result, a characterization of judgments right and wrong in terms of such reasons provides a satisfactory account of the subject matter of these judgments.

Thus, of the three questions about right and wrong with which I began—the questions of subject matter, method of reasoning, and reason-giving force—it is the second and especially the third which I take to be of primary concern. Accordingly, I take the reason-giving force of judgments of right and wrong as the starting point of my inquiry. I begin by offering a characterization of the reason-giving force of such judgments, and then take that characterization as the basis for an account of their subject matter.

When I ask myself what reason the fact that an action would be wrong provides me with not to do it, my answer is that such an action would be one that I could not justify to others on grounds I could expect them to accept. This leads me to describe the subject matter of judgments of right and wrong by saying that they are judgments about what would be permitted by principles that could not reasonably be rejected, by people who were moved to find principles for the general regulation of behavior that others, similarly motivated, could not reasonably reject. In particular, an act is wrong if and only if any principle that permitted it would be one that could reasonably be rejected by people with the motivation just described (or, equivalently, if and only if it would be disallowed by any principle that such people could not reasonably reject).

This description characterizes moral wrongness in a way that is appropriate for our purposes. First, it bears the right relation to our first-order moral beliefs. Those actions, such as wanton killings, that strike us intuitively as obviously wrong are also clearly wrong according to this account, since any principles that permitted these things could reasonably be rejected. More generally, it is plausible to take our intuitive judgments of right and wrong to be judgments about the subject matter just described. But this description of the subject matter of our judgments of right and wrong also has the appropriate degree of independence from our current first-order beliefs, since it leaves open the possibility that some of these beliefs are mistaken and that the authority that we now attach to those beliefs in fact belongs to others instead.

Second, this characterization describes wrongness in a way that provides plausible answers to the philosophical questions I mentioned at the outset. It describes judgments of right and wrong as judgments about reasons and justification, judgments of a kind that can be correct or incorrect and that we are capable of assessing through familiar forms of thought that should not strike us as mysterious. In addition, as I have just suggested and will argue at greater length in Chapter 4, these judgments are ones that we have reason to care about and to give great weight in deciding how to act and how to live.

Many people might agree that an act is wrong if and only if it could not be justified to others on grounds that they could not reasonably reject. But they might say that this is true only because what people could or could not reasonably reject is determined by facts about what is right or wrong in a deeper sense that is independent of any idea of reasonable rejection. So, for example, some acts are wrong because they are acts of wanton killing or acts of deception, and because they are wrong it would be reasonable to reject any principle permitting them. But this last fact is to be explained in terms of the former ones, not the other way around.

My view denies this. It holds that thinking about right and wrong is, at the most basic level, thinking about what could be justified to others on grounds that they, if appropriately motivated, could not reasonably reject. On this view the idea of justifiability to others is taken to be basic in two ways. First, it is by thinking about what could be justified to others on grounds that they could not reasonably reject that we determine the shape of more specific moral notions such as murder or betrayal. Second, the idea that we have reason to avoid actions that could not be justified in this way accounts for the distinctive normative force of moral wrongness.

In the article in which I first presented this view, I referred to it as "contractualism."[1] I will continue to use this name, despite the fact that it has certain disadvantages. There are a number of other views, differing in various ways from the one I present, which are commonly called contractualist.[2] In addition, 'contract' and its cognates seem to many people to suggest a process of self-interested bargaining that is foreign to my account. What distinguishes my view from other accounts involving ideas of agreement is its conception of the motivational basis of this agreement. The parties whose agreement is in question are assumed not merely to be seeking some kind of advantage but also to be moved by the aim of finding principles that others, similarly motivated, could not reasonably reject. The idea of a shared willingness to modify our private demands in order to find a basis of justification that others also have reason to accept is a central element in the social contract tradition going back to Rousseau. One of the main reasons for calling my view "contractualist" is to emphasize its connection with this tradition.

The account of right and wrong presented in Part II is likely to strike many as a Kantian theory, and the idea that the rightness of an action is determined by whether it would be allowed by principles that no one would reasonably reject does have an obvious similarity to Kant's Categorical Imperative. In addition, my overall strategy resembles Kant's argument in the *Groundwork* in that it begins by characterizing the distinctive reason-giving force of judgments of right and wrong and takes this characterization as the key to understanding the content of these judgments and the kind of reasoning through which we arrive at them. But my account of the reasons supporting our concern with the rightness of our actions is very different from Kant's. My strategy is to describe these reasons in substantive terms that make clear why we should find them compelling. While Kant sought to explain the special authority of moral requirements by showing how they are grounded in conditions of our rational agency, I try to explain the distinctive importance and authority of the requirements of justifiability to others by showing how other aspects of our lives and our relations with others involve this idea. The result is an account of right and wrong that is, in Kant's terms, avowedly heteronomous.

In "Contractualism and Utilitarianism," I described my project as an investigation of the nature of *morality,* and I identified, as the motivational basis of my account, a *desire* to be able to justify one's actions to others on grounds that they could not reasonably reject. The structure of this book reflects the fact that both of these claims now seem to me to be mistaken.

The range of moral criticism, as most people understand it, is very broad. Various forms of behavior, such as premarital sex, homosexuality, idleness, and wastefulness, are often considered immoral even when they do not harm other people or violate any duties to them. Whether or not these forms of behavior are in fact open to serious objection, what those who believe that they are immoral have in mind is clearly not that they are wrong in the sense I described above. What I have presented is thus most plausibly seen as an account not of morality in this broad sense in which most people understand it, but rather of a narrower domain of morality having to do with our duties to other people, including such things as requirements to aid them, and prohibitions against harming, killing, coercion, and deception. This domain is the subject that has been most discussed (often under the name "morality") in contemporary moral philosophy. But while it is an important part of morality, as generally understood, it is only a part, not the whole.

It is not clear that this domain has a name. I have been referring to it as "the morality of right and wrong," and I will continue to use this label. But 'right' and 'wrong' are also commonly used in a broader sense, as when it is said that certain forms of sexual conduct or conduct that leads to the destruction of animal species is wrong. The part of morality that I have in mind is broader than justice, which has to do particularly with social institutions. 'Obligation' also picks out a narrower field, mainly of requirements arising from specific actions or undertakings. So I have taken the phrase "what we owe to each other" as the name for this part of morality and as the title of this book, which has this domain as its main topic. I believe that this part of morality comprises a distinct subject matter, unified by a single manner of reasoning and by a common motivational basis. By contrast, it is not clear that morality in the broader sense is a single subject that has a similar unity.

I originally identified the motivational basis of "what we owe to each other" as a *desire* to act in a way that can be justified to others, because I took the idea of a desire to be clearer and less controversial than that of a reason. It seemed to me unproblematic (perhaps the least problematic claim about reasons) to say that a person who has a desire has a reason to do what will promote its fulfillment. I was inclined to believe that not all reasons are based on desires in this way, but defending this more controversial thesis did not seem necessary for my purpose, which was, primarily, to identify the reason-giving force that considerations of right and wrong have for those of us who are moved by them. I therefore characterized the source of this reason-giving force as a desire to act in ways that can be justified to others, thinking that I could leave aside such questions as what to say about those who lacked this desire and whether the fact that an act was wrong would give such people any reason to avoid it.

This strategy proved untenable, however. Many people pressed me to say whether, on my view, a person who lacked this desire would have any reason to avoid acting wrongly, and to explain how I would account for the fact that lacking this desire is a particularly serious fault. In addition, it became clear that the accounts I wanted to offer of the structure of reasoning about right and wrong, and of the relation between this part of morality and other values, were much more naturally put in terms of reasons. It was very difficult, perhaps even impossible, to present these accounts adequately within a conception of practical reasoning that took it to be a matter of figuring out how to fulfill various desires and how to balance these desires against one another. This forced me to undertake a deeper examination of reasons and rationality, which led to the conclusion that my initial assumption about reasons and desires got things almost exactly backward. Desire is not a clearer notion in terms of which the idea of having a reason might be understood; rather, the notion of a desire, in order to play the explanatory and justificatory roles commonly assigned to it, needs to be understood in terms of the idea of taking something to be a reason. Nor do desires provide the most common kind of reasons for action; rather, it is almost never the case that a person has a reason to do something because it would satisfy a desire that he or she has. I argue for these conclusions in Chapter 1, where I also set out the ideas of rationality, irrationality, and reasonableness that are relied on in subsequent chapters.

Chapters 2 and 3 take up the notions of value and well-being. It is commonly supposed that value (or "the good") and individual well-being are notions that are independent of the part of morality that is my main concern. They can thus provide grounds on which the requirements that make up this part of morality can be justified, but they also constitute a potential source of difficulty for it, since its requirements may conflict with the promotion of well-being and other forms of value. To be valuable, or "good," on this common view, is to be something that is to be brought about or promoted. The things that are valuable are thus states of affairs, or components of states of affairs, and one of the main things that contribute to the value of a state of affairs is the well-being of the individuals in it. Most other things are valuable because of the contribution they make to individual well-being. In Chapter 3 I argue that this common view of well-being as a "master value" is mistaken, and I argue against the idea that there is a single notion of well-being that should play a central role both in individual decision-making and in the justification of moral principles. Chapter 2 attacks the more general idea that to be valuable is to be "to be promoted." My argument proceeds by examining some of the things that are generally held to be valuable, such as friendship and intellectual and artistic accomplishment. Recognizing these things as valuable does involve seeing some states of affairs as "to be promoted," but I argue that not all the reasons that are involved in recognizing these values or most others are reasons to promote certain states of affairs. In particular, I argue that to recognize human life as valuable is, first and foremost, to see the reasons we have for treating others in ways that accord with principles that they could not reasonably reject. This connects the sphere of value, or "the good," with "what we owe to each other" in a way that reduces the apparent conflict between them.

Chapter 4 presents my account of the motivational basis of what we owe to each other and shows how this account can explain the priority and importance that moral considerations are generally thought to have. Chapter 5 then describes the structure that moral justification takes on this account, examining and elaborating the idea of principles that no one can reasonably reject.

The idea of responsibility, and the notions of freedom and voluntariness that it involves, play important roles in the content of these principles and also in the process of justifying them, since the force of a person's reasons for rejecting a principle that would require him to bear a certain burden can be reduced by the fact that this burden is one he could have avoided by choosing appropriately. The idea of responsibility is also relevant to moral assessment in another, equally familiar, way as a condition for attributing an action to an agent as one for which he or she can be morally assessed. The aim of Chapter 6 is to show how my version of contractualism explains these two notions of responsibility, and to argue for the importance of distinguishing between them. Chapter 7 considers the duty to keep a promise, duties not to lie, and related duties concerning the expectations we lead others to form. The arguments for these duties provide examples of the process of justification described in Chapter 5. In addition, since the validity of a promise depends on its being made voluntarily, these arguments illustrate points made in Chapter 6 about the ways in which ideas of freedom and voluntariness figure in the justification of moral principles.

Promises as I describe them do not, however, provide the only ostensibly moral reasons for keeping one's word, and at the end of Chapter 7 I will discuss some other reasons, such as those arising from oaths and ideals of personal honor. These provide useful examples for the discussion of moral relativism in Chapter 8. My account of the morality of right and wrong is not a form of relativism, but it allows for considerable variability in what is morally required, both because a variety of requirements can be justified within my account of what we owe to each other, and because of the plurality of values that morality in the broader sense can include. I argue that this is as much variability as a reasonable relativist could require. The range of actual disagreement about right and wrong is broader than this, however, and in the last part of Chapter 8 I will consider how this disagreement should be understood and what conclusions we should draw from it.

The possibility of such disagreement raises a question about the kind of claim I am making in Part II of this book. I argue that contractualism provides the best interpretation of what at least many of us are claiming when we say that an action is morally wrong. But I am not offering it as an account of the meaning of the word 'wrong' or of the expression 'morally wrong'. These terms can be used by people who hold noncontractualist accounts of morality, such as utilitarian or divine command theories, and it would not be plausible to claim that in such cases these words are being misused or have a different meaning. People who hold noncontractualist views about moral wrongness would agree with contractualists that to call an action morally wrong is to say that it violates important standards of conduct and is therefore open to serious criticism. Perhaps this much is part of the meaning of these terms. But holders of these different views disagree about what these standards are and about what it is that makes them authoritative. As a result, when they claim that actions are wrong the claims they are making have overlapping but divergent content. I will sometimes say in such cases that people have in mind different "senses" of moral wrongness. This is not, however, to say that the words involved have multiple meanings but rather that, with their ordinary meanings, they are used to express different claims.

It might be said that the holders of such views disagree about what makes acts wrong, and that this is what I am offering a particular account of in this book. This description is plausible in at least two respects. First, part of what I am offering is a characterization of certain standards by which, I argue, the rightness or wrongness of actions should be judged; so it seems appropriate to call this an account of what makes acts wrong. Second, in order for different moral views (contractualist, utilitarian, divine command, and so on) to be actually disagreeing, they have to be talking about the same thing and making competing claims about it. One natural way to describe the situation is thus to say that they agree about what wrongness is, and are disagreeing about what gives acts this property.

Two considerations count against this way of describing things, however. The first is that giving an account of what makes acts wrong, on the most natural understanding of that phrase, is a matter of identifying the relevant wrong-making properties, such as being an intentional killing or the breaking of a promise. The view just suggested is that being disallowed by any principles that no one could reasonably reject should be understood simply as a more general property of this kind, a property which, like these more specific wrong-making properties, brings with it the (separate) property of being morally wrong. This further property then provides reasons to avoid acting in the way specified, to criticize those who so act, and so on. But, while one aim of my contractualist account is to give a general criterion of wrongness that explains and links these more specific wrong-making properties, this is not its only, or even its chief, aim. It also aims to characterize wrongness in a way that makes clear what reasons wrongness provides, and this aim goes beyond saying "what makes acts wrong," at least on the most natural reading of these words.

A second problem with this description emerges when we ask what the property of moral wrongness is supposed to be on this account. If the views I have mentioned agree about what wrongness is and disagree only about what makes acts wrong, what is the property about which they agree? Since these views disagree both about the content of moral standards and about the ground of their authority, it would seem that the property that is the shared object of their disagreement must either be an unanalyzable normative property of wrongness (akin to the simple, unanalyzable, non-natural property of goodness that G. E. Moore believed he had identified) or else the higher-order property of violating (some or other) important standards of conduct and therefore being open to (some or other) serious objection.

As I argue in Chapter 2, I believe that a formal, or "buck-passing," analysis of the latter kind is correct in the case of goodness and value. Goodness is not a single substantive property which gives us reason to promote or prefer the things that have it. Rather, to call something good is to claim that it has other properties (different ones in different cases) which provide such reasons. But wrongness seems different. In at least a wide range of cases, the fact that an act is wrong seems itself to provide us with a reason not to do it, rather than merely indicating the presence of other reasons (although it may do that as well).

A Moorean account of the kind just mentioned would be in accord with this intuition, since it would identify wrongness as a specific unanalyzable, non-natural property that provides us with reasons. The problem with such an account is not that this property would be "non-natural." (I am quite willing to accept that "being a reason for" is an unanalyzable, normative, hence non-natural relation.) The difficulty is rather that an account that simply points to an unanalyzable property of wrongness leaves unexplained the reasons we have to avoid actions that are wrong and to criticize those who engage in them. I believe that it is possible to say more about what these reasons are, and one of the main aims of my contractualist theory is to do this. Many utilitarian theories, divine command theories, and other accounts are best understood as offering alternative explanations. It therefore seems to me that contractualism and these other views are better described as rival accounts of the property of moral wrongness itself, rather than as differing accounts of the conditions under which actions have that property.[3]

It may be helpful here to consider an analogy between the distinction I have just been discussing and the distinction between our concept of a natural kind, such as gold, and the property of being gold.[4] Whatever our concept of gold may be, the property of being gold is the property of having the physical constitution that is typical of that substance and underlies its observed characteristics, such as being yellow, malleable, and resistant to certain acids. It was an empirical discovery, not a conceptual truth, that, for example, gold has a certain atomic structure. Similarly, whatever our concept of a tiger may be, the property of being a tiger is the property of having the physical nature that is typical of creatures belonging to that species. Unlike gold and tiger, moral wrongness is not a natural kind; but it is what might be called a normative kind. That is to say, the property of moral wrongness can be identified with a certain normatively significant property which is shared by actions that are wrong and which accounts for their observed normative features, such as the fact that we have reason to avoid such actions, to criticize those who perform them, and so on.

Adopting this analogy for the moment, one of the claims I will argue for in Chapter 4 can be put as the claim that the actions that are commonly taken to merit moral disapproval in the very broadest sense of the term 'moral' do not, in fact, form a single normative kind. That is to say, there is no single normatively significant property which they all have and which provides the main reason not to perform them. (This does not mean that there may not be, in each case, good reason not to do these things, and hence that they may all have the higher-order property of being actions which there is good reason to avoid and which are therefore open to serious criticism.) But the contractualist theory that I will set out in Chapters 4 and 5 provides an account of the normative kind to which a large and central class of the things we normally call "morally wrong" belong. Because this class is both large and central, I will refer to what I am offering as an account of the morality of right and wrong even though, as I will note below, the expression 'morally wrong' is also used in the broader sense just mentioned. Similarly, if the stuff we normally call gold turned out not all to be examples of the same substance, we would still refer to a characterization of the substance that most, although not all, of the stuff we have called gold is as an account of the nature of gold.

This example shows the limits of the analogy between wrongness and natural kinds, however. If gold has a certain physical structure, then people who believe that it has some other structure, or who call stuff that does not have this structure gold, are simply mistaken. In the case of morality, however, there may be more room for differing views. Suppose that contractualism offers a satisfactory account of at least a large and central class of our judgments of right and wrong. Suppose that it identifies a property that many actions that we call morally wrong seem in fact to have; that this property seems to be connected in the right way with our reasons for thinking those actions to be wrong; and that it provides a plausible interpretation of reasons for avoiding such actions and criticizing those who perform them. If a competing account of moral wrongness cites, as the reason for avoiding actions that is given by the fact that they are wrong, some consideration that is not a good reason at all, or is not a reason of the right kind, then that view is simply mistaken. But even if the contractualist account is fully satisfactory in the ways I have described (and even if it is the most satisfactory such account), there may still be other reasons for avoiding some of the actions commonly held to be morally wrong. Alternative accounts of wrongness that emphasize these other reasons, and which may therefore pick out a different subset of the actions that people think of as morally wrong than contractualism does, may therefore deserve to be taken seriously in certain ways, even if they cannot claim to be the best account of wrongness. I will consider the possibility of such accounts in Chapter 8.

What began as an investigation of "the nature of morality" has ended as a book dealing with three concentric and successively narrower normative domains: reasons, values, and what we owe to each other. Chapter 1 provides a general account of reasons and rationality; Chapters 2 and 3 give an analysis, in terms of reasons, of the general idea of value and of ideas of individual well-being; and Chapters 4 through 7 examine what we owe to each other, seen as an aspect of one central value, the value of human, or rational, life.

PART I

REASONS AND VALUES

1

Reasons

1. Introduction

I will take the idea of a reason as primitive. Any attempt to explain what it is to be a reason for something seems to me to lead back to the same idea: a consideration that counts in favor of it. "Counts in favor how?" one might ask. "By providing a reason for it" seems to be the only answer. So I will presuppose the idea of a reason, and presuppose also that my readers are rational in the minimal but fundamental sense that I will presently explain.

The idea of a reason does not seem to me to be a problematic one that stands in need of explanation. I will say something in Section 11 about why various attempts—dispositional, expressivist, and so on—to explain this notion strike me as unsatisfactory. I doubt whether any general account of this kind could succeed, but it is not my present purpose to argue that this is the case, since nothing that I will go on to say depends on it. The claims about value and morality that I will be making in later chapters would be compatible with any deeper account of reasons which left the contours of our ordinary notions of reasons and rationality undisturbed. The main aim of this chapter is to describe what I take those contours to be, and to do so in a way that will, I hope, lend support to my claim that the idea of a reason should not be seen as problematic. I will also try to present the matter in such a way as to make it plausible that if there is a problem about reasons it is a general one about reasons of all kinds. There is no particular problem about practical reasons, or reasons for action. If the kind of reasons that we respond to when we decide that a certain action is morally wrong stand in need of explanation, what needs explaining is the notion of moral wrongness, not the general idea of a reason for action.

My strategy will be to locate reasons, in the sense I will be concerned with, as the central element in a familiar form of reflection, and to call attention to structural features which I argue are common to thinking about reasons of all kinds: reasons for belief, for action, and for such attitudes as fear, resentment, and admiration. Since reasons for action have been thought to bear a distinctively close relation to, and perhaps even to be dependent on, desires, I will discuss the relation between reasons and desires. I will argue that desires, insofar as they are distinguished from the recognition of reasons, have a much less fundamental role in practical thinking than is commonly supposed. Indeed, I have become convinced that insofar as "having a desire" is understood as a state that is distinct from "seeing something as a reason," it plays almost no role in the justification and explanation of action. My aim in all of this will be to make clear the role that I take reasons to play in our own thinking and in argument with each other, thus providing a basis for my discussion of values and well-being in Chapters 2 and 3, and for the discussion, in the chapters that follow, of the structure and motivational basis of our ideas of right and wrong.

2. Judgment-Sensitive Attitudes

The rudimentary observation that a reason is a consideration that "counts in favor of" something points toward a question, "In favor of what?" and hence toward an important distinction, between those things for which reasons, in the sense I have in mind, can sensibly be offered or requested and those for which they cannot. It makes no sense to demand a reason, in this sense, for an event in the world that is unconnected with any intentional subject. I might ask, "Why is the volcano going to erupt?" But what I would be understood to be asking for is an explanation, a reason why the eruption is going to occur, and this would not (at least among most contemporary people) take the form of giving the volcano's reason for erupting.

I might also ask, "Why do *you think* that the volcano is going to erupt?" and there are at least two things that I might be asking. First and most naturally, I might be taken to be asking you to give a justification for this belief. "Why should one think that the volcano will erupt? What reason is there to think this?" This is the sense of "reason" that I will be concerned with. I will call it the standard, normative sense. I have just illustrated this sense by citing reasons for belief, but reasons in the same sense can be asked for and given for other attitudes such as intentions and fears.

In offering a justification for the belief that the volcano will erupt you may also be explaining how you came to have that belief: you have it because you have taken it to be supported by these reasons. As I will emphasize in a moment, it is characteristic of attitudes like belief that there is a close tie between justification and this kind of explanation. Nonetheless, the two can come apart. There is a difference between asking what reason there is for believing that P and asking what a given person's reason for believing it was. (I will refer to the latter as the person's *operative* reason.) Both of these questions have to do with what I am calling "reasons in the standard normative sense." The first asks for an assessment of the grounds for taking P to be the case, while the second asks what, as a matter of biographical fact, Jones took to be a reason for believing it. So, while both questions deal with the idea of a reason in the standard normative sense, it is the first question that is primary: the second is concerned with what an individual takes to be reasons in this primary sense.

What I am concerned with, then, are reasons in the "standard normative sense." So when I say that something is or is not a reason I will not be concerned with whether it is or could be someone's operative reason but with whether it is a *good* reason—a consideration that really counts in favor of the thing in question. It may seem that in simply assuming the notion of a reason in a fully normative sense, and by assuming that rational agents are capable of making and being moved by judgments about reasons in this sense, I am begging an important question in contemporary debates about reasons. But I do not think that these matters are really in dispute in the contemporary discussion of these issues.

To begin with, it is difficult to see how they could be in dispute. Genuine skepticism about reasons—skepticism about whether anything ever "counts in favor of" anything else in the sense typical of reasons, or about whether we are actually capable of making judgments about when this is the case—would be a very difficult position to hold. Perhaps one could hold such skepticism just about reasons for action, holding that although various states in fact move us to act, there is no sense to the question of when we have good reason for these actions. But even this view strikes me as awkward and unstable. To hold it consistently one would need to regard all one's actions as things that merely happen, and to abstain from taking at face value any thought about what could be said for or against performing them.

Hume may have held such a view, but I do not believe that most modern-day "Humeans" follow him in this. When Bernard Williams, for example, says that a person has a reason to ϕ if ϕ-ing would advance some aim that he or she has, it seems clear that he intends this claim in a fully normative sense. This is indicated, I think, by his emphasis on the idea that the claim that such a person has a reason is something that could be offered to him or her as *advice*.[1] The very idea of offering such advice presupposes that the agent in question is capable of thinking about what he or she has reason to do—that is, capable of understanding judgments about reasons in a normative sense. So I take the contemporary controversy (at least that between Williams and defenders of "external" reasons) to be not about the intelligibility or reality of "taking something to be a reason" but rather about when people really do have reasons in this sense and about the role of such reasons in explaining their actions.

What is the range of things for which reasons in the standard normative sense can be asked for or offered? States or occurrences that are independent of any conscious agent are clearly excluded. Most, perhaps even all, of the things that are included are attitudes of rational agents such as beliefs, intentions, hopes, fears, and attitudes such as admiration, respect, contempt, and indignation. These must be distinguished, however, from mere feelings such as hunger (as distinguished from taking oneself to have a reason for seeking food) or tiredness or distraction. These are states for which no reason in the standard normative sense can be demanded. They may affect our judgment about the reasons we have (when one is tired it may seem that nothing is worth doing), but they need not depend on any judgment about reasons.

The class of attitudes for which reasons in the sense I have in mind can sensibly be asked for or offered can be characterized, with apparent but I think innocent circularity, as the class of "judgment-sensitive attitudes." These are attitudes that an ideally rational person would come to have whenever that person judged there to be sufficient reasons for them and that would, in an ideally rational person, "extinguish" when that person judged them not to be supported by reasons of the appropriate kind. Hunger is obviously not a judgment-sensitive attitude; but belief is, and so are fear, anger, admiration, respect, and other evaluative attitudes such as the view that fame is worth seeking.

Having a judgment-sensitive attitude involves a complicated set of dispositions to think and react in specified ways. For example, a person who believes that P will tend to have feelings of conviction about P when the question arises, will normally be prepared to affirm P and to use it as a premise in further reasoning, will tend to think of P as a piece of counterevidence when claims incompatible with it are advanced, and so on. Similarly, a person who intends to do A will not only feel favorably disposed, on balance, to that course of action, but will also tend to be on the lookout for ways of carrying out this intention (finding means, looking for ways of fitting it in with other plans, and so on), and will think of this intention as a prima facie objection when incompatible courses of action are proposed. An attitude is judgment-sensitive if it is part of being the attitude it is that this complex of dispositions should be sensitive to a particular kind of judgment. But having such an attitude involves not only being disposed to judge in certain ways but also being disposed to various patterns of unreflective thought, such as being disposed to *think* of the proposition believed or the course of action intended at the relevant moments.

I have said that judgment-sensitive attitudes constitute the class of things for which reasons in the standard normative sense can sensibly be asked for or offered. Actions might be cited as a class of glaring exceptions to this claim, on the ground that they are not themselves attitudes yet are clearly things for which standard normative reasons can be given. But they are only an apparent exception. Actions are the kind of things for which normative reasons can be given only insofar as they are intentional, that is, are the expression of judgment-sensitive attitudes. Against this, it might be pointed out that (at least in normal cases) in order to intend to do something I must take myself to have a reason for *doing* that thing. So it might seem that reasons for action are, after all, primary, and reasons for intending are dependent upon them. But there is no real disagreement here. A reason for doing something is almost always a reason for doing it intentionally, so "reason for action" is not to be contrasted with "reason for intending." The connection with action, which is essential to intentions, determines the kinds of reasons that are appropriate for them, but it is the connection with judgment-sensitive attitudes that makes events actions,[2] and hence the kind of things for which reasons can sensibly be asked for and offered at all.

The idea of judgment sensitivity helps to isolate the sense in which attitudes can be things we are "responsible for" even when, unlike most voluntary actions, they are not the result of choice or decision. Not only perceptual beliefs, but many other attitudes as well arise in us unbidden, without conscious choice or decision. Nonetheless, as continuing states these attitudes are "up to us"—that is, they depend on our judgment as to whether appropriate reasons are present. Because of this dependence on judgment, these are things we can properly be "held responsible" for in several central senses of that phrase: they can be properly attributed to us, and we can properly be asked to defend them—to justify the judgment they reflect. On the other hand, it is not open to us to adopt, modify, or reject judgment-sensitive attitudes in any way we choose. For while it is up to us to judge whether appropriate reasons for that attitude are or are not present, it is not generally within our power to make it the case that these reasons are or are not there; this depends on facts outside us. But these limits on our power and freedom do not undermine our responsibility for our attitudes in the senses listed above.

In some cases judgment-sensitive attitudes can be "up to us" in a further sense, since there may be reasons that support but do not require these attitudes. This is commonly true of intentions: there may be sufficient reason for following one course of action even though it would not be irrational to pass it up and do something else instead. As I will argue in Chapter 6, however, this additional degree of "freedom" is not required in order for a person to be properly held responsible for an action. Because "being responsible" is mainly a matter of the appropriateness of demanding reasons, it is enough that the attitude in question be a judgment-sensitive one—that is, one that either directly reflects the agent's judgment or is supposed to be governed by it. For this reason, one can be responsible not only for one's actions but also for intentions, beliefs, and other attitudes.[3] That is, one can properly be asked to defend these attitudes according to the canons relevant to them, and one can be appraised in the light of these canons for the attitudes one holds. The "sting" of finding oneself responsible for an attitude that shows one's thinking to be defective by certain standards will be different in each case, depending on our reasons for caring about the standards in question. But the basic idea of responsibility is the same.

3. Rationality

This discussion of judgment-sensitive attitudes has already brought us close to several ideas of rationality: the idea of a rational creature and the ideas of what it is rational or irrational to do. This section sets out a few basic points about how I will understand these important notions. I will argue that we should construe the notion of irrationality more narrowly than is sometimes done, and my understanding of rationality will in this respect be more permissive. The result will be that some theses that have been put forward as claims about rationality must be considered instead as substantive claims about what reasons there are. Making this shift does not settle the question of what we have reason to do, but I believe that it allows important issues about reasons and rationality to be considered in a fairer light.

A rational creature is, first of all, a reasoning creature—one that has the capacity to recognize, assess, and be moved by reasons, and hence to have judgment-sensitive attitudes. In line with what I have said in the preceding section, I am drawing no distinction here between theoretical and practical reasoning. The capacities I am attributing to a rational creature include both the capacities to recognize, assess, and be moved by reasons for belief and the capacities to recognize, assess, and be moved by reasons for other attitudes such as intention, fear, and admiration. These reflective capacities set us apart from creatures who, although they can act purposefully, as my cat does when she tries to get into the cabinet where the cat food is kept, cannot raise or answer the question whether a given purpose provides adequate reason for action. We have this capacity, and consequently every action that we take with even a minimum of deliberation about what to do reflects a judgment that a certain reason is worth acting on.[4]

This is not to say that intentional actions are always based on conscious reflective judgments, at the time of acting, that certain reasons are worth acting on; nor is it to claim, more generally, that all judgment-sensitive attitudes arise immediately from such judgments of adequacy. Judgment-sensitive attitudes can arise spontaneously, without judgment or reflection, but they are responsive to the agent's judgments about the adequacy of reasons in a number of looser and more general ways. Let me mention three such ways.

First, when a rational creature does make a conscious reflective judgment that a certain attitude is warranted, she generally comes to have this attitude. For example, if she judges there to be good grounds for a belief that P, then she generally has this belief. That is to say, unless she revises this judgment or takes it to be undermined, she has feelings of conviction about P when the question arises, and she is prepared to affirm that P and to use it as a premise in further reasoning.

Similarly, if she judges there to be compelling grounds for forming a certain intention, then she adopts that intention and it is manifest in her further behavior: unless or until she revises this judgment, she looks for ways to implement this intention, takes herself to have reason to avoid incompatible intentions, and acts on it when the occasion presents itself.

Second, when a rational creature judges that the reasons she is aware of count decisively against a certain attitude, she generally does not have that attitude, or ceases to have it if she did so before—ceases to feel conviction in regard to the belief or to use it as a premise, or ceases to look for ways to implement the intention, and is not inclined to act on it.

Third, although rational creatures commonly form beliefs, intentions, and other attitudes unreflectively, the formation of these attitudes is generally constrained by general standing judgments about the adequacy of reasons. For example, if a person holds that a certain class of putative evidence is not good grounds for forming beliefs, or that certain reasons are not good grounds for action of a given kind, then she generally does not unreflectively form beliefs on the basis of such evidence or unreflectively take action of the given kind on the basis of those reasons.

I have said several times that an agent's judgment about the adequacy of certain reasons normally makes a difference (where it is relevant) to his or her thought and action unless that judgment is overruled by a later one. The possibility of overruling and being overruled is a distinctive characteristic of judgments and judgment-sensitive attitudes. Desires can conflict in a practical sense by giving incompatible directives for action. I can want to get up and eat and at the same time want to stay in bed, and this kind of conflict is no bar to having both desires at the same time. Judgments about reasons can conflict in this same way. I can take my hunger to be a reason for getting up and at the same time recognize my fatigue as a reason not to get up, and I am not necessarily open to rational criticism for having these conflicting attitudes. But judgments can also conflict in a deeper sense by making incompatible claims about the same subject matter, and attitudes that conflict in this way cannot, rationally, be held at the same time. This is true not only of judgments about "the external world" but equally of judgments of other kinds, for example about the adequacy of certain reasons. I cannot simultaneously judge that certain considerations constitute good reason to get up at six and that they do not constitute good reason to do this. If I first hold one of these opinions and then shift to the second I have to overrule my former judgment, by holding, for example, that circumstances have changed, or that there is new information, or that the earlier judgment "got it wrong," perhaps by failing to take note of some relevant fact or by giving one consideration more weight than it deserves.

4. Irrationality Narrowly Construed

Rationality involves systematic connections between different aspects of a person's thought and behavior. But it is sufficient for rationality in the general sense I am describing—sufficient for being a rational creature—that these connections be systematic, not merely accidental or haphazard. They need not hold in every case: rational creatures are sometimes irrational. Irrationality in the clearest sense occurs when a person's attitudes fail to conform to his or her own judgments: when, for example, a person continues to believe something (continues to regard it with conviction and to take it as a premise in subsequent reasoning) even though he or she judges there to be good reason for rejecting it, or when a person fails to form and act on an intention to do something even though he or she judges there to be overwhelmingly good reason to do it. These are clear cases of irrationality because the thought or action they involve is in an obvious sense "contrary to (the person's own) reason": there is a direct clash between the judgments a person makes and the judgments required by the attitudes he or she holds.

Irrationality in this sense occurs when a person recognizes something as a reason but fails to be affected by it in one of the relevant ways. Beyond this, are there also more substantive standards that it is irrational to violate? Is it sometimes irrational to fail to accept certain considerations as reasons? It seems to me that philosophical usage, but perhaps not "ordinary" usage, is divided on this point. Some philosophers may confine the term 'irrational' to what I have called the clearest sense, in which a person fails to respond to what he or she acknowledges to be relevant reasons, but many others extend the term more broadly.[5] I myself will confine 'irrational' to the narrower sense in both theoretical and practical domains. As I will now argue, this fits better with ordinary usage and has other important advantages.

Consider first the question of irrationality in the theoretical realm. Not every mistaken belief is one that it is irrational to hold, even when the reasons for taking it to be mistaken are entirely available to the believer. Suppose, for example, that I am convinced by a fallacious proof of Fermat's Last Theorem. This might happen because the proof is very complicated, or because the proof proceeds at a certain point by an enumeration of the possible cases and I simply fail to see that a certain possibility has been left out. This would be a mistake on my part, but more would be required to support a charge of irrationality. This charge might seem more plausible in the case of a believer in extrasensory perception, who denies that controlled experiments by established scientists cast doubt on the reality of psychokinesis, and who points instead to allegedly confirming experiments by its supporters. But it is worth asking what difference between this case and that of the person who accepts the fallacious proof makes the charge of irrationality warranted. Let us stipulate that the person who believes in extrasensory perception is clearly mistaken; his conclusions violate the relevant standards of statistical reasoning and good scientific procedure. This alone does not seem to me to make these conclusions instances of irrationality. We might call them irrational if certain further things were true: if, for example, the person admitted that the established scientists' experiments would, if valid, count against psychokinesis, and admitted that he could see no flaw in the methods used, but still kept insisting that there must be some flaw, without being able to cite any reason for this conclusion. But if the person was simply hasty, or not very good at statistics, or at weighing evidence, or at thinking of possible sources of bias in the experiments that are supposed to demonstrate the possibility of psychokinesis, then the charge of irrationality would seem no more warranted than in the case of the fallacious proof.

Derek Parfit considers this same issue in the case of practical thinking and makes the opposite terminological choice. He writes:

> The charge 'irrational' is at one end of a range of criticisms. It is like the charge 'wicked'. We may claim that some act, though not so bad as to be wicked, is still open to moral criticism. We may similarly claim that some desire, though not deserving the extreme charge 'irrational', is open to rational criticism. To save words, I shall extend the ordinary use of 'irrational'. I shall use this word to mean 'open to rational criticism'. This will allow 'not irrational' to mean 'not open to such criticism'.[6]

It may seem that nothing of substance hinges on the choice of terminology here, as long as one is clear about what one takes 'irrational' to mean. I believe, however, that there are good reasons for restricting 'irrational' to the narrower of the two senses Parfit describes. As he indicates in calling this "the ordinary use," and as I have argued above in discussing the case of belief, this sense has the stronger claim to be in accord with our ordinary intuitions. I believe that we normally draw a distinction between an attitude's being irrational and its being mistaken or "open to rational criticism." We need not take ordinary usage as authoritative on this point, but I believe that it is helpful to preserve this distinction and to mark it clearly. 'Irrational' is certainly sometimes used in the broader sense that Parfit describes, and we could stipulate that we were going to use it in this sense. Even if we were to make this stipulation, however, the intuitive resonance of the stronger, narrow sense of 'irrational' would remain, and would be likely to have a distorting effect on our thinking. .

This effect can be seen in defenses of subjectivism about reasons which appeal to the oddness of applying the term 'irrational' to a person who has desires that we regard as mistaken. Bernard Williams, for example, observes that there are many things that we can say about a person who does not behave as we think he ought to, such as "that he is inconsiderate, or cruel, or selfish or imprudent." Williams says that his opponent (the defender of reasons that do not depend on an agent's subjective motivational set) would add that there are reasons for acting differently that this man is not seeing the force of. (Indeed, this seems to many of us to be entailed by the epithets just listed—cruel, heartless, and so on.) But Williams also says that the defender of such "external reasons" wants to claim that the man just described is *irrational*.[7] Williams is quite right that this claim would be implausible, but wrong, I think, to hold that his opponent is committed to making it.

To the extent that the narrow sense of irrationality that Parfit calls "the ordinary use" is in fact ordinary, or is at least *one* of the senses of the term in common use, it will sound odd to call this man irrational (whatever stipulation we may have made about the use of that term), since he is clearly not irrational in that sense. But insofar as this oddness depends on the narrower understanding of 'irrational' it is not germane to the point at issue in Williams' argument, since the question is not whether the desire is irrational in this narrower sense but whether it is open to rational criticism as, for example, mistaken or misguided. Someone who wishes to defend the latter claim need not (and should not) go on to make the former, stronger claim as well.

Confining 'irrational' to the narrower use circumvents this dialectical tangle and lets us confront the main issue directly, with less danger of being misled by semantic resonances that are in fact irrelevant. We should appeal to intuitions about whether a person does or does not have a reason, not to intuitions about irrationality.

In her essay "Reasons for Action and Desires," Philippa Foot appears to deny what I am here suggesting, that we can hold that a person makes a mistake in failing to appreciate the force of a reason, yet refrain from saying that he is therefore irrational. I believe that her argument is like Williams' in turning on an appeal to intuitions about irrationality in the narrow sense, so it is relevant to examine it here. Some people hold, she says, that "the cool calculating man is not to be called irrational, but [they] nevertheless say that he has reason to act morally whatever his interests and desires." She goes on to say that this seems to be an inconsistent position. Her argument is the following.

Suppose a man to assert these propositions:

A1. I have a reason to do action *a*.
A2. I have no reason not to do *a*.
A3. I am not going to do *a*.

From which he must conclude

A4. I am going to act irrationally.

On the other hand, the following are admitted to be consistent:

B1. I shall act immorally unless I do *a*.
B2. I have no reason not to do *a*.
B3. I am not going to do *a*.
B4. I am not going to act irrationally.

But, Foot says, "We can show by a simple argument that when B1–B4 are true, A1 is false; from which it follows that B1 cannot entail A1."[8]

This argument seems to me to be faulty. At least it is so if my view of irrationality is accepted. For on that view what forces the conclusion A4 is not the *truth* of A1–A3 but the fact that the person has assented to them, in particular the fact that the person has assented to A1. This can easily be seen by translating A1–A4 into the second or third person or into the past tense. So transformed, A1–A3 could clearly be true while A4 was false. But someone might assent to B1 without assenting to A1. (Indeed, this is just the attitude that the "cool calculating man" is likely to have.) So from the consistency and truth of B1–B4 we cannot conclude that A1 is false but only that it is false that the person has asserted (or accepts) it.

Stating the argument in the first person and present tense binds together the truth of the statement that the agent has a reason and the acceptance of this judgment by the agent. It thus converts the claim that a person has a reason even though he may not recognize it into a charge of irrationality in the narrow sense. Like Williams' argument, Foot's can be resisted if we attend more carefully to the idea of irrationality that is being appealed to.

As Parfit mentions, the price of confining the term 'irrational' to the narrow use I have described may seem to be that we are barred from applying it to even extreme cases of consistent but substantively senseless behavior. He gives the example of a person who expresses "future Tuesday indifference." This person, while concerned in general with what may happen to him in the future, does not care about what happens to him on Tuesdays. He would therefore be willing to accept excruciating pain occurring on a future Tuesday in order to avoid a minor ache on some other day of the week. Certainly this attitude is "open to rational criticism," and there is certainly a temptation to go farther and say that it is irrational, as Parfit suggests.[9]

One problem with this case is that there are several different ways of understanding the position that this man is supposed be in. If, as suggested, he is concerned with his future interests in general, what reason can he have for thinking that it makes a difference whether something happens to him on a Tuesday rather than on some other day of the week? If he has some positive reason for this (even a very implausible one, such as some strange theory of well-being), then I have no hesitation in saying that he is not irrational, just seriously mistaken in his assessment of the reasons that he has. In the example as given, however, he is not said to have any such further reason: he just does not care what happens to him on Tuesdays. If he believes that he has a reason to avoid pain on Tuesdays (because it is just as bad as pain on any other day) but does not care about this, then he is irrational on my account, since he is failing to respond to a reason that he judges himself to have. The case in which Parfit and I would disagree, then, is one in which, although the person may have views about what he has reason to do from which it follows that he should avoid pain on Tuesdays, he has not drawn this conclusion, and he will not do anything to avoid such pain. It is difficult to imagine attributing this view to someone, absent further explanation. Taking the description to be correct, however, I am prepared to say that such a person would not be irrational, but only substantively mistaken. But it is certainly an extreme case.

5. The (Most) Rational Thing to Do

It is particularly tempting to classify this version of future Tuesday indifference as a case of irrationality because the connection between the judgments that the agent accepts (that all future pains are bad) and the conclusion that he fails to accept (that he has reason to avoid pains on future Tuesdays) is so close that it is difficult to see how he could accept one without accepting the other. There is little room for confusion, for failure to follow the steps of an argument, or for substantive disagreement. The same would be true of a person who purports to believe that A and that if A then B, but denies that this gives any reason to believe B (or denies that it gives such a reason on Tuesdays). But there is also a more general tendency to lump together, as "requirements of rationality," two kinds of requirements that should, I believe, be kept distinct. Requirements of the first kind specify the form that our thinking must take if we are to avoid the charge of irrationality. Requirements of the second kind specify what we have most reason to do, hence what we would do if we were "ideally rational."[10] Accounts of the latter kind are often referred to as "conceptions of rationality," but I believe that they are more appropriately seen as substantive conceptions of the reasons that we have.[11]

The distinction between the two is well illustrated by the idea that there is a rational requirement to give weight to one's future interests. There certainly are some cases in which a person's failure to give weight to his or her future interests is irrational. These are cases in which a person judges that these considerations are reasons but then fails to take them into account in deciding what to do, or fails to give them the weight that he or she judges them to have. This is what is usually going on when we fail to floss our teeth, to fasten our seat belts, or to do other things that we can see we have reason to do because they will promote our present or future aims. Cases of this kind are extremely common, and this may explain the widespread tendency to cite failure to give weight to considerations of one's own well-being as the prime example of irrationality.

But not every failure to give weight, or to give proper weight, to one's future interests is an instance of irrationality. It is, for example, a matter of controversy how one's future interests should be taken into account in present decisions—whether these interests should be "discounted" because of their remoteness in time and if so at what rate. This may be called a debate about "rationality," but this label is appropriate only if what is meant is that it is a debate about what we have most reason to do, or what we would do if ideally rational. A person who believes, on general theoretical grounds, that her future interests should be sharply discounted, and who acts accordingly, may be making a mistake about the reasons that she has, but this does not make her irrational, any more than it does a person who accepts a fallacious argument or makes some other mistake about reasons. One might of course stipulate that "irrationality" simply means acting contrary to one's interests. But such a stipulation has the effect of giving one class of reasons special status as far as rationality and irrationality are concerned. Given that there are reasons for action other than those provided by an agent's own interests, I see no justification for giving this one class of interests such special status.

Another area in which "requirements of rationality" in the two senses just distinguished are often run together is in claims made for axiomatic theories of rational choice.[12] People often violate these axioms by making mistakes in probabilistic reasoning, or by failing to see that the complex gamble they have chosen is dominated by another alternative (that is to say, that this alternative would be better from their point of view, no matter which of the uncertain states turns out to be realized).[13] But these mistakes do not deserve the name of irrationality any more than accepting a fallacious proof or making some other error in calculation does. Decision theory should thus be understood as presenting requirements of rationality in the second sense I distinguished: that is to say, as offering a partial account of what one has most reason to prefer, and hence would prefer if one were "ideally rational." More specifically, the axioms of such a theory state consistency conditions that our choices, and judgments of desirability and probability, would meet if we were perfectly rational, just as a system of deductive logic states consistency conditions that would be fulfilled by the beliefs of an ideally rational person. Violating conditions of either of these kinds leaves one open to rational criticism: criticism that is of a particularly clear and uncontroversial kind since it does not depend on any substantive claims about the truth of particular statements or the desirability or probability of particular outcomes. But this relatively uncontroversial character is not accurately described by saying that although other mistakes leave one open to criticism, violating these conditions amounts to irrationality. It is not, after all, always irrational to have inconsistent beliefs or to reject a claim that (although one does not realize it) follows logically from other things one holds.

The axioms of rational choice theory provide only a partial account of ideal rationality, since they state only conditions of consistency and since these conditions apply only to reasons for promoting certain states of affairs or for wanting them to occur. A full account of what an "ideally rational" agent would do could involve at least three possible dimensions of idealization, in the directions of (1) possession of full information about one's situation and the consequences of possible lines of action, (2) awareness of the full range of reasons that apply to someone in that situation, and (3) flawless reasoning about what these reasons support. The most fully ideal notion of "the (most) rational thing to do" would thus be "the course of action that is best supported by all the relevant reasons given a full and accurate account of the agent's actual situation." Given the great variety of reasons for action, it seems to me very unlikely that there could be such a thing as a theory of reasons in this sense—that is to say, a systematic, substantive account of what we have most reason to do.[14]

6. Reasonableness

In between the minimum standards marked out by the idea of irrationality and the ideal of what it would be (most) rational to believe or do, there are the notions of what is reasonable and unreasonable. I will later be relying on these ideas in the context of moral argument, but they have a wider use, and I want to say a few things here about how I understand this use, as a basis for that later discussion.

Recalling the three dimensions of idealization that I have just mentioned in discussing "the (most) rational thing to do," I suggest that judgments about what it is or is not reasonable to do or think are relative to a specified body of information and a specified range of reasons, both of which may be less than complete. For example, the reasonableness of a belief or action may be assessed relative to the agent's beliefs at the time and the reasons he sees as relevant. But the grounds of assessment may be broader than this, provided that the reasons and information in question are available to the agent. When we urge a person, "Be reasonable!" or complain, "Don't be unreasonable!" we may be objecting to the way that person is reasoning from a shared body of information and conception of the relevant considerations, but we may also be urging him to take into account facts or reasons that he is presently ignoring. We can say, for example (insisting on a broader range of information), "That was not a reasonable conclusion. You should have noticed that the boat was gone and that I was therefore almost certainly not on the island any longer," or (insisting on a broader range of reasons) "It was unreasonable of me to refuse to consider the possibility that Smith's experiment revealed a fundamental problem with the theory," or "That was not a reasonable thing to do. You should have realized that telling that joke was quite out of place at a funeral."

In each of these cases a certain general aim or concern is presupposed—scientific progress or a concern with other people's feelings—and a claim is made about what reasons there are given this general concern. The same is true in most everyday situations in which the charge of unreasonableness is made. When we say, in the course of an attempt to reach some collective decision, that a person is being unreasonable, what we often mean is that he or she is refusing to take other people's interests into account. What we are claiming is that there is reason to take these interests into account *given* the supposed aim of reaching agreement or finding a course of action that everyone will be happy with. It is in this sense that I am using the term when I say that an action is wrong if it would be excluded by any principles that no one could reasonably reject given the aim of finding principles that others, similarly motivated, could also accept. I will say more in Chapter 5 about the idea of reasonableness as it figures in moral argument.

7. Reasons and Motivation

Rationality involves systematic connections between a person's judgments and his or her subsequent attitudes. A rational person who judges there to be sufficient grounds for believing that P normally has that belief, and this judgment is normally sufficient explanation for so believing.[15] There is no need to appeal to some further source of motivation such as "wanting to believe." Similarly, a rational person who judges there to be compelling reason to do A normally forms the intention to do A, and this judgment is sufficient explanation of that intention and of the agent's acting on it (since this action is part of what such an intention involves). There is no need to invoke an additional form of motivation beyond the judgment and the reasons it recognizes, some further force to, as it were, get the limbs in motion.[16]

These claims follow from the account of rationality that I have been presenting. I will argue in this section and the next that they are also supported by consideration of the phenomenology of judgment and motivation. These are not, of course, independent sources of support, since my account of rationality would not be plausible unless it seemed to fit the facts about what it is like to be a rational creature. It may seem that these facts support the opposing view, that reasons by themselves do not motivate, because it is clear from our experience that recognizing something as a reason and being motivated by it are two quite different things. So I need to consider what this experience actually shows.

It is a familiar fact that recognizing a consideration as a reason (and as a reason with the very same significance) can have different effects on our thought and behavior under different circumstances or when that consideration is presented in different ways. I may decide, before going to a party, that the pleasures of drinking and the conviviality it brings are not sufficient reasons for having more than two glasses of wine. Once at the party, however, these very same reasons may have a stronger effect on me, and I may act on them even though my judgment as to their sufficiency does not change. In other cases, changes in experience and circumstance can strengthen rather than undermine the effects of one's judgments about reasons. I recognize the dangers of driving while intoxicated as providing a strong reason not to drink, but my response to this judgment may be different before and after seeing an accident caused by a drunk driver. In each of these cases my judgment of the reason-giving force of certain considerations is held constant, but changes in my circumstances lead to changes in the motivational effects of these considerations, partly by changing the degree to which these considerations, rather than others, are vividly before my mind at the time of acting.

It is an obvious and familiar fact that one's state of mind, the state of one's body, and the content of one's immediate experiences strongly affect the reasons one attends to: when I have not eaten for some time I just can't keep my mind off food; when I am lonely I keep hoping that a friend will call and keep looking for an excuse to telephone someone. Of course, I can also directly address the question of which considerations to attend to. This reflection may lead to my feeling more fully the force of those considerations I deem to be relevant reasons, while others remain unremarked or "in the background," but it does not, unfortunately, always have this effect.

These examples show that there is clearly a distinction between a person's recognizing something as a reason and the effect that this has on the person's subsequent thought and action. What they do not show, it seems to me, is that when a person not only recognizes something as a reason but also is moved to act this is due to the presence of some further motivating element in addition to that recognition—something appropriately called a desire. On the contrary, when I examine these cases it seems to me that in all of them the only source of motivation lies in my taking certain considerations—such as the pleasures of drinking, of eating, of hearing from a friend—as reasons. The strength of this motivation varies depending on what happens—for example, on the degree to which I attend to a given consideration, focus on it, and ignore others—but these reasons remain the only motivating factors. Just as in the case of belief, there is no need to appeal to a further source of motivation to explain how a rational creature can be led to act.

It may seem that the very fact that there is a distinction between recognizing something as a reason for action and being motivated by it disrupts the parallel between reasons for belief and reasons for action, since there is no room for a comparable distinction where reasons for belief are concerned. One reason for thinking this—for thinking that there can be no "*akrasia* of belief"[17]—is the idea that judging P to be supported by the best evidence is so immediately connected with believing P that there is no room for slippage of the kind that can occur between judgment and action. To take P to be supported by the best evidence just *is* to believe it. But this seems to me a mistake. Belief is not merely a matter of judgment but of the connections, over time, between this judgment and dispositions to feel conviction, to recall as relevant, to employ as a premise in further reasoning, and so on. Insofar as akrasia involves the failure of these connections, it can occur in the case of belief as well as in that of intention and action.[18] I may know, for example, that despite Jones's pretensions to be a loyal friend, he is in fact merely an artful deceiver. Yet when I am with him I may find the appearance of warmth and friendship so affecting that I find myself thinking, although I know better, that he can be relied on after all.

The contrary position derives some of its plausibility from the appeal of what might be called the unity of reasons for belief. This is the idea that since believing is believing to be *true*, the only kind of reason one can have for believing something—for feeling conviction, employing it as a premise in further thinking, and so on—is a reason for thinking it true. So any judgment that undermines a consideration's status as evidence for the truth of P deprives it of the only kind of force that it can have as a reason for believing P. Reasons for action, on the other hand, are plural. The fact that it would be more pleasant to go for a walk than to meet with a job candidate is not a good reason to do that. But even if I accept this judgment, the pleasure of the walk could still serve as my reason for taking it and leaving the candidate waiting.[19]

But this idea is mistaken. Even if it is true that in order to believe something one must take there to be a reason for thinking it true (so there can be no such thing as believing something *simply* because one would like it to be true), this would not rule out "akratic belief." For example, in the case of the false friend, mentioned above, there is something that I take to be a reason for believing in his genuineness, namely his *appearance* of genuineness. Given all that I know about him, of course, I know that this is not a good reason in this case, but it can serve as my reason nonetheless. In this respect the situation is quite parallel to some examples of akratic action: even though I accept the judgment that the pleasure of going for a walk is not a good reason for missing my appointment, I act on it nonetheless. In each of these examples a consideration of the kind that can sometimes serve as a good reason (for action or for belief) is known not to be such a reason in the case at hand, but is nonetheless taken as the basis for belief or intentional action.

In the case of both belief and action, then, there is a distinction between an agent's assessment of the reason-giving force of a consideration and the influence that that consideration has on the agent's thought and action. I have argued that this distinction should not be explained, in either case, in terms of the need for some additional motivating factor separate from the recognition of a consideration as a reason. In the case of action it is common, however, to describe this as a distinction between seeing something as a reason and having a desire. I will argue in the following section that while there is something right about this familiar idea it is also seriously misleading. In order to assess it, however, we need a clearer idea of what is meant by desire.

8. Reasons and Desires: Motivation

Desires are commonly understood in philosophical discussion to be psychological states which play two fundamental roles. On the one hand, they are supposed to be motivationally efficacious: desires are usually, or perhaps always, what move us to act. On the other hand, they are supposed to be normatively significant: when someone has a reason (in the standard normative sense) to do something this is generally, perhaps even always, true *because* doing this would promote the fulfillment of some desire which the agent has.

That there is a psychological state of "having a desire" that plays this dual role seems like common sense, at least philosophical common sense. But I have come to believe that this apparent truism is in fact false. To explain why, I will begin by examining some of the different senses in which the term 'desire' may be used. I will then go on to consider the motivational role of desires in these various senses.

'Desire' is sometimes used in a broad sense in which the class of desires is taken to include any "pro-attitude" that an agent may have toward an action or outcome, whatever the content or basis of this attitude may be. Desires in this sense include such things as a sense of duty, loyalty, or pride, as well as an interest in pleasure or enjoyment. It is uncontroversial that desires in this broad sense are capable of moving us to act, and it is plausible to claim that they are the only things capable of this, since anything that moves us (at least to intentional action) is likely to count as such a desire. But many elements of this class are what Nagel calls "motivated desires"; that is to say, they do not seem to be *sources* of motivation but rather the motivational consequences of something else, such as the agent's recognition of something as a duty, or as supported by a reason of some other kind.[20]

A substantial thesis claiming a special role for desires in moving us to act would have to be based on some narrower class of desires, which can be claimed to serve as independent sources of motivation and perhaps also of reasons to act. Natural candidates for this role are what Nagel calls "unmotivated desires" (that is to say, desires that are not dependent on some other state for their motivating and reason-giving force). He cites thirst as an example, and it does seem that when we speak of desires in the narrow sense (not meaning to include just any form of motivation, such as a sense of duty) the prime examples seem to be desires which are like thirst in being for, or prompted by, experiential states. So let us consider this case.

Suppose I am thirsty. What does this involve? First, there is the unpleasant sensation of dryness in my mouth and throat. Also, there is the thought that a cool drink would relieve this sensation and, in general, feel good. I take this consideration, that drinking would feel good, to count in favor of drinking, and I am on the lookout for some cool drink. This description includes three elements: a present sensation (the dryness in my throat), the belief that some action would lead to a pleasant state in the future, and my taking this future good to be a reason for so acting. It is this future good—the pleasure to be obtained by drinking—that makes it worth my while to look for water. The present dryness in my throat, and the fact that this condition is not about to go away on its own, give me reason to believe that a drink of water in the near future will give this particular pleasure. But the motivational work seems to be done by my taking this future pleasure to count in favor of drinking.

It may seem, however, that this account of the matter leaves out the crucial element. In addition to the dryness in my throat, the future pleasure brought about by drinking, and my judgment that this pleasure is desirable, there is the fact that I feel an urge to drink. This, it might be said, is what my desire consists in. But when we focus on this idea of a mere urge to act, separated from any evaluative element, it does not in fact fit very well with what we ordinarily mean by desire. Here we may consider Warren Quinn's example of a man who feels an urge to turn on every radio he sees. It is not that he sees anything *good* about radios' being turned on; he does not want to hear music or news or even just to avoid silence; he simply is moved to turn on any radio that he sees to be off. Quinn's point is that such a functional state lacks the power to rationalize actions, and I will return to this point in the next section. But as he also points out, although we may sometimes have such urges, the idea of such a purely functional state fails to capture something essential in the most common cases of desire: desiring something involves having a tendency to see something good or desirable about it.[21] This is clear from the example of thirst. Having a desire to drink is not merely a matter of feeling impelled to do so; it also involves seeing drinking as desirable (because, for example, it would be pleasant). The example of the urge to turn on radios is bizarre because it completely lacks this evaluative element.

I might seem to be saying here that there is no such thing as an unmotivated desire. Taken in Nagel's sense this would entail that all desires arise from prior evaluative judgments of some kind, a claim which seems clearly false. What I am claiming, however, is not that all desires arise from prior judgments but rather that having what is generally called a desire involves having a tendency to see something as a reason. Even if this is true, however, this is not all that desire involves. Having a desire to do something (such as to drink a glass of water) is not just a matter of seeing something good about it. I might see something good about drinking a glass of foul-tasting medicine, but would not therefore be said to have a desire to do so, and I can even see that something would be pleasant without, in the normal sense, feeling a desire to do it. Reflection on the differences between these cases leads me to what I will call the idea of desire in the directed-attention sense. A person has a desire in the directed-attention sense that P if the thought of P keeps occurring to him or her in a favorable light, that is to say, if the person's attention is directed insistently toward considerations that present themselves as counting in favor of P.

This idea seems to me to capture an essential element in the intuitive notion of (occurrent) desire. Desires for food, for example, and sexual desires are marked by just this character of directed attention. And this character is generally missing in cases in which we say that a person who does something for a reason nonetheless "has no desire to do it," as when, for example, one must tell a friend some unwelcome news. As my first examples indicate, we most commonly speak of "having a desire" in this sense for things that involve the prospect of pleasant experiences (or the avoidance of unpleasant ones). But while it seems to be a fact about us that pleasure and pain are particularly able to attract our attention, they are not the only things that can do so. People can "have a great desire" in the directed-attention sense to succeed in some endeavor, to achieve fame (even posthumous fame), to provide for their children after their death, or even, in the case of some compulsives, to wash their hands.[22] Since the definition I have given leaves the possible objects of a "desire in the directed-attention sense" entirely open, it is just as appropriate on this account to say that someone with a very active conscience "has a strong desire to do the right thing" as it is to say of a person who is utterly unscrupulous that he "has a strong desire for personal gain."

"Desire in the directed-attention sense" seems, then, to fit well with a way that the term 'desire' is frequently used. It also captures the familiar idea that desires are unreflective elements in our practical thinking—that they "assail us" unbidden and that they can conflict with our considered judgment of what we have reason to do. A person who has a desire in the sense I am describing has a tendency to think of certain considerations and a tendency to see them as reasons for acting in a certain way. Tendencies of both these kinds figure importantly in what it is to be a rational creature. Being such a creature involves not only the capacity to make certain judgments and to be consistent about them, but also the ability to see certain considerations as reasons and to think of and see as reasons those things one has previously judged to be such. Nonetheless, neither of these tendencies is wholly under the control of a normal person. One can have a strong and recurrent tendency to see something as a reason for acting (under one's present circumstances) even though one's firm considered opinion is that it is not (under the circumstances) such a reason. This is clear not only in cases in which a person *acts* irrationally, but also in many other cases. Even if, for example, I have convinced myself that I should not be influenced by the approval or disapproval of a certain group, I may find myself wondering anxiously what they would think of something I am considering doing. When these thoughts occur, I may dismiss them immediately. Nonetheless, insofar as they involve (perhaps only momentarily) seeing something as a reason that I judge not to be one, they are instances of irrationality—a form of irrationality to which we are all subject from time to time. Even when desire in the directed-attention sense runs contrary to our reason (that is to say, our judgment) in this way, however, it remains true that the motivational force of these states lies in a tendency to see some consideration as a *reason.*[23] Akratic actions (and irrational thoughts) are cases in which a person's rational capacities have malfunctioned, not cases in which these capacities are overmastered by something else, called desire.

To sum up, I have argued in this section that we should not take "desires" to be a special source of motivation, independent of our seeing things as reasons. It is trivially true that whenever a person is moved to act he or she has an "urge" to act in that way. But the idea of such an urge fails to correspond to the ordinary notion of desire. "Desire in the directed-attention sense" comes much closer to capturing the commonsense notion of desire, but this notion doubly fails to capture a unique or independent source of motivation. First, it is not the case that whenever a person is moved to act he or she has a desire in this sense: we often do things that we "have no desire to do" in the ordinary sense, and "desire in the directed-attention sense" tracks the ordinary notion in this respect. Second, when a person *does* have a desire in the directed-attention sense and acts accordingly, what supplies the motive for this action is the agent's perception of some consideration as a reason, not some additional element of "desire." Desire in the directed-attention sense characterizes an important form of variability in the motivational efficacy of reasons, but it does this by describing one way in which the thought of something as a reason can present itself rather than by identifying a motivating factor that is independent of such a thought.

9. Reasons and Desires: Justification

Let me turn now from the supposed role of desires in motivation to their supposed role as sources of justification. Here I will be concerned with the thesis that reasons for action can or must derive their justificatory force from the agent's desires. I will treat this as a substantive claim about the reasons we have (leaving aside, for the moment, skepticism about reasons, and questions about their motivational power or epistemological status). Accordingly, my arguments will appeal to our substantive intuitions about what reasons we have and why.

It can seem intuitively obvious that many of the reasons people have depend on their desires, and that different people have different reasons for action because their desires are different. Someone who wants to go to Chicago has reason to buy a ticket. Someone who wants to become a famous author has reason to study literature and to set aside time to write every day. Someone who has a desire that his children be fluent in Italian has reason to hire a tutor or to speak Italian at home. So it is commonly held, as the standard case of having a reason for action, that a person has a reason to do X if so acting would promote the fulfillment of some desire that he or she has. ("Fulfillment" is here understood in what might be called the logical sense, in which a desire that P is fulfilled if it is the case that P; a psychological state of feeling pleased or "fulfilled" at this outcome need not be involved.)

It is widely held, I think, that many, if not most, reasons for action are based on desires in the way described by this standard case. The main controversy has been over the claim that *all* reasons are based on desires in this way, in particular over whether moral and prudential reasons are so based. To say that people have reasons not to mistreat others, or reasons to provide for their own future interests, only if doing so promotes the fulfillment of their present desires has seemed to many people to make the requirements of morality and prudence "escapable" in a way that they clearly are not. This way of putting the matter suggests that resistance to the idea that all reasons depend on desires arises from a wish to tell others what they must do and a concern that they should not so easily escape our criticism.

I will have more to say later about the force of moral reasons and about our attitudes toward people who disagree with us about what reasons they have. At the moment, however, what I want to emphasize is that, quite apart from any desire to criticize others or to influence them, reflection on the nature of our *own* reasons should lead us to resist the substantive claim that all reasons for action are based on desires.

With respect to some of our reasons, acceptance of this dependence poses no problem. It is easy to accept the claim that my reasons for eating coffee ice cream and for going to the seashore rather than to the mountains depend on the fact that these things appeal to me. And this is true not only of reasons that are trivial or have to do with "matters of taste." My reasons to help and support my friends and loved ones, for example, depend on the fact that they *are* my friends and loved ones, hence on my affection for them. But this dependence on my feelings does not render those reasons trivial; far from it.[24] The acceptability of subjective conditions in these cases is easy to explain. A large part of the point of eating ice cream or taking a vacation is doing something that I will enjoy, so one's "subjective reactions" are obviously of prime significance to the reasons one has for doing these things one way rather than another. And since affection lies at the core of relationships of love and friendship, there is nothing deflationary about the observation that these relationships depend in part on "how we feel" about the people in question (although it would be odd to say that the reasons these relationships involve depend on our "desires").

But things are different with respect to many other reasons. If I take myself to have reason to do something because it is worthwhile—to work to alleviate some people's suffering, for example, or to prevent the destruction of some great building—this reason does not seem to depend on my seeing it as a reason. Rather, I think that I would be mistaken not to see that it is worthwhile or excellent, and mistaken not to care about such things. The importance of these aims is not tied to my own enjoyment or my own affections in a way that is like either of the two cases just described.[25] Consequently, the claim that the reasons they give me derive solely from my desires, or from what I care about, seems deflationary in a way that it is not in those cases.

Reflections of this sort move many to insist that not all reasons for action depend on desires. In this section, however, I will defend the stronger claim that desires almost never provide reasons for action in the way described by the standard desire model. According to this familiar model, desires are not conclusions of practical reasoning but starting points for it. They are states which simply occur or not, and when they do occur they provide the agent with reason to do what will promote their fulfillment. I will argue first, drawing on my argument in the preceding section, that none of the candidates for the role of desire has these properties. I will then examine a variety of cases in which our reasons have subjective conditions and will show how these conditions differ in important ways from the model suggested by the terms 'desire' and 'desire fulfillment'.

I have already mentioned Warren Quinn's argument that a desire, understood simply as a functional state of being disposed to act in a certain way, lacks the power to rationalize action. From the example of the person with a strange functional state disposing him to turn on radios Quinn does not conclude that desires never provide reasons for action, but rather "that the subjectivist's account of desire is impoverished, leaving out precisely that element of desire that does the rationalizing."[26] This missing element, in his view, is the element of evaluation: the judgment that there is something good—pleasant, advantageous, or otherwise worthwhile—about performing the action. But even if we shift our attention to desires that have this kind of evaluative content we find, I believe, that they have surprisingly little force as sources of reasons.

Suppose that, as sometimes happens, I am beset by a desire to have a new computer. What does this involve? For one thing, I find myself looking eagerly at the computer advertisements in each Tuesday's *New York Times*. I keep thinking about various new models and taking their features to count in favor of having them. This is what I called above a desire in the directed-attention sense. It has clear normative content, since it involves a tendency to judge that I have reason to buy a new computer. But does my being in this state make it the case that I *have* a reason to buy a new computer (because doing this would satisfy my desire)? It seems to me clear that it does not. Such a state can occur (indeed, it often does) even when my considered judgment is that I in fact have no reason to buy a new machine, since I believe (correctly, let us suppose) that the features of the newer models would be of no real benefit to me. In such a case the fact that I have this desire gives me no reason to buy a new computer (aside, perhaps, from the indirect one that it would put an end, for a time, to my being nagged by the desire and wasting time reading computer advertisements). It is not just that the reason provided by the desire is outweighed by other considerations. I would not say, "Well, I do have *some* reason to buy the computer, since it would satisfy my desire, but on balance it is not worth it." The desire, even if it persists, provides no reason at all (except possibly the indirect one just mentioned).

Now suppose that I endorse the judgment to which the desire involves a tendency, and take myself to have good reason to buy a new machine. Even in this case, the reason that I have for buying a computer is not that it will satisfy my desire, but rather that I will enjoy having it, or that it will help me with my work, impress my friends and colleagues, or bring some other supposed benefit.[27] This conclusion may readily be accepted. It is true quite generally that my reason for doing something is almost never "that it will satisfy my desire." But it might still be argued that I have the reasons I do because I have certain desires.[28] It is, after all, very plausible to say that different people have different reasons for action because they have different desires. So we need to examine some of the cases in which this appears to be true.

I remarked above that we have no difficulty in accepting the claim that my reasons for eating coffee ice cream have subjective conditions. It seems natural to say that when I have a desire for coffee ice cream this can make it the case that I have a reason to eat some, and that others who lack that desire therefore lack this reason as well. What is going on in this case? First and most obviously, there is the fact that I enjoy eating coffee ice cream because I like the taste and the cool smooth feeling in my mouth. But this (like the relief of my thirst in the example considered in the previous section) is a matter of future enjoyment, not present desire. Moreover, if I like coffee ice cream then it is true of me almost all the time (except, perhaps, when I am sick or too full) that I would enjoy eating it, and I know that this is true. Perhaps this means that I always, or almost always, have a reason to eat coffee ice cream. But to say that I have a reason to eat some because I desire it seems to add something more specific that is true of me only when I have that desire.

What does it add? One possibility is the element of desire in the directed-attention sense. Sometimes the pleasure of eating coffee ice cream keeps coming to mind, presenting itself as a reason for getting some now, whether or not my judgment, all things considered, is that this would be a good thing. Does the fact that I am in such a state provide me with a reason? It might do so indirectly by being evidence for the conclusion that ice cream would be particularly enjoyable right now or in the near future. Often we enjoy things more at those times when they are particularly appealing for us than we do at other times when it takes an effort of will to attend to them. This seems to be true of sex as well as of reading philosophy. But it is also sometimes true that we *would* enjoy something even though we would have to drag ourselves to do it, and when this is so, we have, in advance, just as much reason to make the effort as we do when we have a desire in the directed-attention sense to engage in this activity. (Exercise is the obvious example, although for many of us "enjoy" may not be just the right word in this case.) In all these cases, however, the reasons are provided by some future enjoyment. Present desire in the directed-attention sense may be an indicator of this enjoyment, but the presence of this state does not, in itself, provide an additional reason for action in the way in which desires are supposed to provide reason to bring about their fulfillment.

A third possibility is that when we say that someone has a reason to look for coffee ice cream because he has a desire for some, what we mean is not just that he enjoys eating that flavor of ice cream, or that he presently finds himself thinking of it and seeing the prospective pleasure it offers as a reason, but that he thinks this pleasure actually is a good reason for acting now or in the near future. I think that this is often what we do mean when we say that a person has a reason to act because he or she wants something that that action would produce. When we say, for example, that a person has a reason to call the travel agent because she wants to go to Chicago, we don't mean merely that she would enjoy Chicago, or that she thinks longingly of it and finds the thought of going there tempting, but rather that she takes herself to have good reason to make the trip.[29] Here we have identified a state whose occurrence can affect the reasons an agent has, but it is misleading to call it "desire." To begin with, such states are not, as desires are supposed to be, original sources of reasons. Rather, they are instances of an agent's identifying some other considerations as reasons, and they derive their reason-giving force from a combination of these reasons and the agent's decision to take them as grounds for action.

Comparison with Michael Bratman's account of intentions may be helpful here. Bratman takes an intention to be a (possibly incomplete) plan. He argues that an agent who has adopted an intention subsequently has reason to do what will carry that intention out unless he or she has reason then to reconsider it.[30] One might ask here why having an intention can give rise to reasons when having a desire (in any of the senses I have previously canvassed) cannot. Part of the answer is that the role claimed for intention is more modest: it is not being claimed that intentions are independent sources of reasons. Rather, even when an intention does not arise from a conscious decision, its reason-giving force depends on there being something to be said for acting in the way in question. This dependence is indicated in the fact that, as Bratman's "unless . . ." clause indicates, when one's assessment of these reasons is in doubt, one has reason to rethink that intention rather than to do what will implement it. The fact that the agent has adopted this particular intention does, however, make a difference to the agent's reasons. It may be that there are many different plans of action which would be worth adopting at the present time (these could be different ways of pursuing the same goal, or ways of pursuing different ends for which a good case could be made). One function of practical reasoning is to make selections between such alternatives, and these selections, once made, affect an agent's reasons. When I have adopted a given plan, I have reason to do what will carry out that plan rather than what would have been involved in implementing some alternative scheme, but these reasons depend on the considerations counting in favor of that plan as well as on my having adopted it.

When we say that someone "wants" or "has a desire" to go to Chicago or to eat some coffee ice cream, one thing that we might mean is that the person has actually formed an intention to do one of these things and therefore has reason to do what would carry it out. But the claim might also be something weaker. In practical reasoning, we need not only to select among possible plans of action but also to select among considerations to be taken into account in deciding what to do. Just as I cannot implement all the feasible and defensible plans of action at one time, so I cannot take into account, in deciding what to do in a given interval, all the considerations that might provide good reasons for acting. I have to select and schedule. So it might be that a person who "has a desire for coffee ice cream" in the third of the senses I distinguished, has not formed an intention to get some ice cream but has taken the desirability of having ice cream as one of the considerations to be taken into account in deciding what to do in the near future. It is, so to speak, "on her deliberative agenda," whether or not she ultimately forms an intention to act on it or not. Like having an intention, taking a consideration as relevant in this way affects the reasons one subsequently has, even though it is not an original source of reasons in the way that "desires" are often taken to be. Following Bratman, we might say that if a person has selected certain considerations, and not others, to be relevant to deciding what to do in a given interval, then he or she subsequently has reason to treat these considerations (and not the others) as reasons (in the absence of reason to rethink this initial selection).

It might be objected that this discussion has described our practical thinking as much more self-conscious and reflective than it in fact is. But the attitudes I have been discussing need not involve conscious judgment. One can have an intention without having gone through a conscious process of assessing the reasons for following this course of action and judging them to be sufficient. Similarly, when we have a desire for something in the directed-attention sense (when it occurs to us spontaneously as desirable) we often take that consideration to be relevant to our future decisions without having consciously decided to give it that status. The point of the preceding discussion was that whether or not the question is consciously addressed, one's "taking" a consideration to be relevant is what has the reason-shaping consequences I described. Like the formation of an intention, such a "taking" is a move within practical thinking rather than, as desires are commonly supposed to be, a state which simply occurs and is then a "given" for subsequent deliberation. (This is shown by the fact that it continues to affect the reasons one has only in the absence of grounds for reconsideration.)

Our examination of the desire for coffee ice cream has identified three elements which might serve as reasons: enjoying something or finding it pleasant, having a desire for it in the directed-attention sense, and having given it the status of a consideration to be taken into account in future deliberation (or having the intention to pursue it). These are all factors that might differentiate a person who has a desire for coffee ice cream from someone who does not, but none of them provides a reason in the particular way that desires are often thought to do.

There is, however, a class of cases in which the fact that I "feel like" doing a certain thing (have a desire to do it in the directed-attention sense) may seem to provide me with a reason. For example, when I am walking from home to my office, I often choose one route rather than another "just because I feel like it"; that is to say, I choose it just because it is the alternative that presents itself as attractive at the time. This may be because I take this direction of my attention as a sign that I will enjoy that route more or that it has any other specific benefits. But it is possible that, considerations of enjoyment aside, I simply let the matter be decided by what happens to appeal to me at the time. One might say that in such a case I act for no reason. But even if in some such cases the fact that I "felt like" doing something is a reason in the standard normative sense, these are special, rather trivial cases, not central examples that provide the pattern on which all other cases of doing something for a reason should be modeled.

When we say that different people have different reasons because they are "interested in different things," I believe that we generally mean either that they find different activities enjoyable or exciting, or that they have "taken up" different activities, that is to say, have formed plans that make different pursuits part of their lives. But differences in what one is drawn to (that is to say, differences in desire in the directed-attention sense) can make a difference to what one has reason to take up, in a way that goes beyond any that I have so far mentioned.

This further role for desire in the directed-attention sense is illustrated by Bernard Williams' well-known example of Owen Wingrave.[31] In the story of that name by Henry James, Owen comes from a family with a strong military tradition, one in which both family tradition and military life are highly valued. He himself is being prepared for a military career, following after all his male forebears (mostly dead). Owen finds that he is, in Williams' words, "left cold" by military life, but his relatives insist that he nonetheless has reason to take up a career in the army because of the inherent value in this calling and because family tradition requires it. Williams cites this example in support of his version of the view that reasons for action depend on desires: Owen has no reason to join the army because doing so would not promote the fulfillment of any element in his "subjective motivational set." His family's protestations to the contrary amount to mere browbeating.

Now we might agree that Owen has no reason to join the army because we ourselves see no value in such a life and so think his relatives are substantively mistaken. But we should set this reason aside and suppose we agree with Owen's family that a military career is worthwhile, or else we should substitute some other worthwhile calling, such as science or music, for which we assume that Owen has talent, but which "leaves him cold." Even in such a case, I think we should agree that Owen does not have reason to take up a career he hates, but not on the grounds that Williams suggests. There are, I think, many worthwhile pursuits to which one might devote one's life. At least under favorable conditions, however, one has good reason to choose *as a career* only one of those to which one is drawn—that is to say, which one has a desire in the directed-attention sense to pursue. This is not because in such a case one's ground-level reason will be to satisfy this desire; one's most important reason will, rather, be that it is worthwhile, or exciting, or honorable, or whatever. Nonetheless, being drawn to a pursuit is (at least under favorable conditions) a condition for having a good reason to undertake it as a career. For one thing, if one takes up a career which "leaves one cold," then one is unlikely to succeed in it. For another, it's not a good thing if every morning, in order to get yourself to go to work, you have to rehearse (or have someone else urge on you) all the reasons why it is worthwhile or honorable or dashing to be a military man, or a philosophy professor, or whatever it may be.

So, while it would be a mistake to conclude from the case of Owen Wingrave that all reasons for action are a matter of what will "satisfy," in a suitably broad sense, some elements in one's subjective motivational set, this case does indicate another way in which the reasons we have can depend on subjective conditions (a type of dependence that is peculiar to choosing a career and other similar choices).

I have argued in this section that when we consider the various states that might be identified as desires we find none that can play the general role in justification commonly assigned to desires—that of states which are independent of our practical reasoning and which, when they occur, provide reason for doing what will promote their fulfillment. Many of our reasons do have subjective conditions, but these turn out, on closer inspection, to be rather misleadingly described by the terminology of desire and desire fulfillment. In the next section I will offer a different sort of reason for resisting the terminology of desires, one based not on the picture it offers of our individual reasons, but on what it suggests about the way in which these reasons interact in our practical thinking. This will lead to conclusions about the structure of practical reasoning that will be important for the discussion of moral thinking in Part II.

10. Reasons and Desires: Structure

A person who takes some consideration to be a reason for going to New York may thereby have a desire to go to New York in the broad sense of 'desire' that is common in philosophical usage. To have a desire for something in this sense is just to have some kind of pro-attitude toward it; to take there to be a reason for something is just to see some consideration as counting in favor of it. So it may seem that the distinction between having a desire, understood in this broad sense, and taking something to be a reason is merely terminological.[32] But even when the notion of desire is broadened in this way, its link with the ordinary use of the term invites a distorted picture of the structure of our practical thinking. In this section I will examine some of the differences between the structure of practical reasoning that is suggested by the desire model and that which is allowed when reasons are taken as basic. These differences are important for the chapters that follow, since it will turn out that the structure of our thinking about right and wrong, and about other values, is more adequately represented in terms of reasons rather than in terms of desires.

A desire is naturally understood as having a two-part structure: it has an object and a weight. It is a desire *for* something, typically taken to be some state of affairs, and it counts in favor of that thing with a certain degree of strength. On this view, when our desires conflict, rational decision is a matter of balancing the strengths of competing desires. If we take desires, along with beliefs, as the basic elements of practical thinking, then this idea of balancing competing desires will seem to be the general form of rational decision-making.

The object of a desire is some state of affairs: to have a desire is to desire that something should be the case.[33] Reasons, on the other hand, can support many judgment-sensitive attitudes. One such attitude is wanting, and the parallel between having a desire and having a reason is closest in the case of reasons for wanting things to go a certain way. But in the realm of reasons this is only one special case, as can be seen by taking note of the various ways in which reasons can conflict with or support one another.

Like desires, reasons can conflict in a practical sense when they are reasons for wanting incompatible things. Often these reasons, like desires, are *pro tanto*: that is to say, they are compelling reasons unless outweighed by other, better reasons, but they can be outweighed without losing their force or status as reasons. If I am trying to choose a restaurant for a group outing, the fact that one friend likes Indian food is a reason for choosing an Indian restaurant, while the fact that another member of the group prefers Italian counts in favor of a different choice. In the end I must choose one way or the other, but this need not involve deciding that one of these competing reasons did not count or was not really a relevant consideration.

But reasons can be related to one another in more complex ways. I may, for example, judge one consideration, C, to be a reason for taking another consideration, D, not to be relevant to my decision whether or not to pursue a certain line of action. In this case the relation between the reason-giving force of C and that of D is not merely practical conflict, as in the case of desires for incompatible states of affairs. The conflict is deeper. The reason-giving force of C not only competes with that of D; it urges that D lacks force altogether (at least in the given context). Often, our judgment that a certain consideration is a reason builds in a recognition of restrictions of this kind at the outset: D may be taken to be a reason for acting only as long as considerations like C are not present. In this case the reason-giving force of D is commonly said to be merely prima facie.

To make this more specific, consider a small-scale example. Suppose that I am going to play a game—tennis, say, or croquet. One thing that I may need to decide is whether I am going to "play to win." Reflecting on this question, I might reach any one of three answers. It might be that, given the nature of the occasion, my relations to the other participants, and their expectations and levels of skill, there is strong reason to play to win whether I feel like it or not (to do otherwise would involve letting others down or not standing up for myself). Alternatively, it might be that, given who I am playing with, I should not play to win even if that is what I would most enjoy; to do so would be inappropriate. The final possibility is that it might be all right either to play to win or not to do so—I can be guided by what I feel at the moment I would most enjoy.

Suppose that I reach this last conclusion, and that I do feel like playing to win, so I decide that is what I will do. Reaching this conclusion involves deciding which reasons will be relevant to how I play. The fact that a certain shot represents the best strategy will count as sufficient reason for making it. I need not weigh against this the possibility that if the shot succeeds then my opponent will feel crushed and disappointed. This does not mean that I cease to care about my opponent's feelings. I may still want him to be happy, hope that he is able to take pleasure in the game, and refrain from laughing at his missed shots.[34] My concern for his feelings is not eliminated or even diminished; I just judge them not to be relevant to certain decisions.

This example of a decision, based on reasons, that determines the reason-giving force of other considerations is an instance of a very common phenomenon. The same thing can be seen, for example, in the forms of decision-making appropriate to various formal and informal roles. Being a good teacher, or a good member of a search committee, or even a good guide to a person who has asked you for directions, all involve bracketing the reason-giving force of some of your own interests which might otherwise be quite relevant and legitimate reasons for acting in one way rather than another. So the reasons we have for living up to the standards associated with such roles are reasons for reordering the reason-giving force of other considerations: reasons for bracketing some of our own concerns and giving the interests of certain people or institutions a special place.

We all recognize that reasons for belief do not have the simple structure that the desire model of practical reasoning describes: they do not simply count *for* a certain belief with a certain weight, and deciding what to believe is not in general simply a matter of balancing such weights. There certainly are cases in which deciding what to believe is a matter of "weighing" evidence for and against the proposition in question, but this is so only because our other beliefs about the nature of the case identify those considerations as relevant for a belief of the kind in question. In general, a given consideration counts in favor of a certain belief only given a background of other beliefs and principles which determine its relevance. Because of these connections, accepting a reason for or against one belief affects not only that belief, but also other beliefs and the status of other reasons. This can happen in many ways. A reason for one belief counts against belief in propositions incompatible with it. It can also affect other beliefs by, for example, undermining (diminishing the reason-giving force of) evidence supporting them, or by discrediting objections to them.

My claim is that reasons for action, intention, and other attitudes exhibit a similarly complex structure. I do not mean to deny that deciding what to do is sometimes a matter of deciding which of several competing considerations one wants more or cares more about. My point is rather that when this is so in a particular case it is because a more general framework of reasons and principles determines that these considerations are the relevant ones on which to base a decision.

Much of our practical thinking is concerned with figuring out which considerations are relevant to a given decision, that is to say, with interpreting, adjusting, and modifying this more general framework of principles of reasoning.

These "principles" are what Kant called maxims, that is to say, principles specifying the adequacy or inadequacy of various considerations as reasons for one or another judgment-sensitive attitude. It is a familiar Kantian theme that morality is concerned with maxims; that is, that moral reasons are reasons for and against taking certain other reasons as sufficient grounds for action. I will have more to say about this in the chapters ahead. But for Kant, maxims are not just features of moral reasoning but central components of practical reasoning more generally, and my present point is that this seems intuitively to be correct. Morality aside, our practical thinking takes place within a framework of maxims and is concerned with adopting, interpreting, and modifying these principles as well as with deciding, within the framework they provide, whether we have sufficient reason for acting in particular ways.

We can see this in our ideas about what it is to adopt an aim or end. Adopting an aim is not simply a matter of assigning a positive value to a certain class of results, which then compete, on the basis of this value, with other reasons of all kinds. Rather, when we adopt an end we form the intention of pursuing it as something which has a certain role in our life: as a temporary pursuit or amusement, for example, or as a serious long-term hobby, or as a career or a goal within our career, or as one of the guiding commitments of our life.[35] Depending on the place in life that an aim is to be given, different reasons will be relevant to the decision whether to adopt it. Considerations that would be perfectly good reasons for taking up some activity as a temporary amusement would strike most of us as absurd grounds for a fundamental commitment (and vice versa). Similarly, depending on the place that a given aim has in one's life, it will have different kinds of reason-giving force in relation to one's other concerns. These two points are obviously related: *because* making golf one of the guiding aims of my life would involve giving it priority over most other concerns, I would need to give reasons for doing this that would make sense of its having that role.

The claim I am making here is a structural one. I am calling attention to familiar features of our practical thinking that, I argue, are naturally represented in terms of reasons and judgments but cannot be accounted for if we take practical reasoning to be a matter of balancing competing desires on the basis of their "strength."[36] This claim might be resisted on the ground that I have presented the competing-desire view in an overly simple form. In the case of "playing to win," for example, it might be argued that a person who has reason to play to win is just someone who prefers competing-hard-even-if-this-results-in-some-unhappiness-for-others to preserving-the-feelings-of-others-by-not-going-all-out. Such a person could also prefer avoiding-hurt-feelings-by-resisting-the-temptation-to-make-caustic-remarks to indulging-in-caustic-remarks-even-at-the-cost-of-hurt-feelings. The proponent of the desire model need not deal only with desires so broad as "a concern for the opponent's feelings," since a person can take quite a different view of hurt feelings resulting from fair competition and hurt feelings resulting from gratuitous insults.

Perhaps the results of the kind of reasoning I have described are the same as those that would be produced by a balance of desires with certain weights when the objects of these desires are sufficiently finely discriminated. But even if the results are the same, the process of arriving at these results is more adequately represented in terms of reasons than in terms of desires for finely discriminated results. Why, for example, should one feel differently about hurt feelings of the two kinds just distinguished? Because if friendship is to be compatible with other ends, then even friendship cannot require one *always* to avoid anything that would cause one's friend disappointment or distress. If friendship is not to be a tyrannical relationship, then we have to make such distinctions, and there are good grounds for suspending this concern in cases of "friendly competition," or when one is serving on a search committee, or in some other administrative capacity, but not for suspending it whenever one might get pleasure from making caustic comments. This claim depends, obviously, on a particular view of friendship. For some people, perhaps, exchanging what I might call caustic comments is a part of the pleasure of being friends. I am not here concerned to argue for one view of friendship over another. My point is that the process of deciding what one has reason to do in such cases is more a matter of reflecting on what constraints one's conception of friendship places on one's reasons than a matter of simply asking oneself what one desires, and how strongly.

Another way of preserving the desire model would be to appeal to the idea of second-order desires.[37] So, for example, a person who is deciding whether or not to "play to win" could be described as asking, not only how strongly he wants the pleasure of competition or the pleasure of making caustic remarks, and how strongly he wants to avoid certain kinds of hurt feelings, and so on, but also whether he wants to be the kind of person who is moved by one of these desires in certain circumstances. Taking second-order desires into account introduces a broader form of reflection that more closely resembles the kind of thinking I have described. But if second-order desires are really *desires*, then there is the question of how their second-order character, if it is just a difference in the objects of these desires, can give them the kind of authority that is involved when one reason supports the judgment that another putative reason is in fact irrelevant.[38] My desire to be a person who does not let considerations of personal interest influence his decisions as department chair conflicts in the practical sense with my desire, in this case, to do what will make my life easier. I cannot act in a way that will satisfy both of these desires at once. But they are just two desires that conflict with each other. The introduction of second-order desires therefore does not do justice to our sense that there is a deeper conflict, expressed in the judgment that the reason represented by the latter desire is not relevant.

I have tried in this section to call attention to features of our practical thinking that are better represented in terms of a framework of reasons than in terms of competing desires. I have not argued that we must deliberate in the way I have described—that rationality requires it—but only that we do commonly think in this way and that it seems appropriate to do so. If the category of "desires" in the broad sense that is commonly used in philosophical discussion includes what I have called "taking something to be a reason," then reasoning based on desires in this sense can allow for the forms of reasoning that I have described. But the term 'desire' in its ordinary meaning does not suggest these possibilities, and even seems to exclude them. To this extent, then, the broader philosophical use of 'desire' is not a harmless choice of technical terminology but a seriously misleading one.

11. Metaphysical Doubts about Reasons

One source of support for the idea that it would be preferable, if possible, to explain reasons in terms of desires, lies in metaphysical and epistemological doubts about the notion of a reason. Desires, according to this line of thought, are obvious and familiar elements of our psychology. Insofar as reasons are provided by desires there is no difficulty in explaining how we have reasons or how we can know what reasons we have. But if this is not the case, then it is a mystery what reasons could be, since they do not seem to be either elements of our psychology or part of "the furniture of the world" apart from us.

The conclusions reached in earlier sections of this chapter have already undermined this supposed contrast between reasons and desires. I have argued that the idea of a desire is not as clear and straightforward as is commonly supposed, and that any account of this notion that supports the motivational and justificatory roles that desires are supposed to have will presuppose the idea of taking something to be a reason. Nonetheless, to respond to these worries more fully I need to say something about what I take reasons to be and how we discover what reasons we have.

"What is a reason?" is a somewhat misleading question. If we concentrate on *operative* reasons, then it may seem as if the only things that can be reasons are beliefs: a hat's being day-glo pink can't be my reason for not buying it unless I believe that the hat is that color. But things look different when we consider the matter from the point of view of the person who has the reason. If I am explaining to someone why I did not buy the hat I *might* cite my belief about its color: "Why didn't I buy it? Because I could see that it was day-glo pink, that's why." If I did this I would be giving my operative reason. But when I am deciding what to do, and hence considering reasons in the "standard normative sense," what is relevant is something about the hat, not about my state of mind. That the hat is day-glo pink is a reason not to buy it; that admitting how I feel about such hats would hurt my friend's feelings is a reason to dissemble; and so on. What are here cited as reasons are not beliefs but the sort of things, picked out by 'that' clauses, that are the contents of beliefs.

In order for a consideration to be an operative reason for me, I have to believe it. In addition, I have to take it to be a reason for the attitude in question. These are separate attitudes. I can believe something without taking it to be a reason for something else, and I can see, without believing it, that it would, if it were the case, be such a reason. The question "What is a reason?" is misleading insofar as it suggests that reasons are a special ontological class. What is special about reasons is not the ontological category of things that can be reasons, but rather the status of being a reason, that is to say, of counting in favor of some judgment-sensitive attitude. It is this status that I am trying in this chapter to call attention to and point out some features of, even though I do not see how to explain it in terms of any other notion.

The things that are reasons are, as I have said, the same kinds of things that can be the contents of beliefs—propositions, one might say. Commonly, but not invariably, these are propositions about the natural world, that is to say, about the empirical world outside us or about our psychological states. That some proposition is someone's operative reason for a certain belief or action is also just a fact, a fact about that person's psychological states. But the judgment that such a proposition would, if it were true (or if a person had good grounds for believing it), be a *good* reason for some action or belief contains an element of normative force which resists identification with any proposition about the natural world.

This resistance can be seen in the systematic failure of hypothetical analyses of normative terms.[39] Perhaps it is true that X is a good reason for doing A if and only if I would take it to be one if I were aware of the relevant facts and responding to them in the right way. But if this is true it is only because the inclusion of the normative terms "relevant" and "in the right way" on the righthand side of the biconditional guarantees its truth, while also preventing the analysans from being a statement of natural facts, thus making the overall claim a trivial one.

One might try to turn this biconditional into a nontrivial truth by purging the righthand side of explicit normative content by saying, for example, that X is a reason for doing A if and only if I would regard it as a reason if I were vividly aware of all the relevant facts. Such attempts are open to two kinds of objections. First, they are not obviously true. Even though reasons are the sort of thing that we, as rational creatures, are in principle capable of apprehending, some of us are better able to assess some kinds of reasons than others are, not because of lack of information or of failure to engage in "critical reflection," but because of our particular sensitivity or lack of sensitivity to considerations of the relevant kind. For example, as Allan Gibbard observes, vivid awareness of the consequences of his taking bribes, particularly of what his life would be like if he had a great deal more money, might make a conscientious civil servant conclude that he had good reason to overcome his scruples and become corrupt.[40] But this does not show that he in fact has good reason to do so.

The second objection is that even if there were a true, nontrivial biconditional of the form "Something is a reason if and only if a person would regard it as one under conditions C," this would not provide a satisfactory reductive analysis of what it is for something to be a reason. This is because "R is a reason" expresses a substantive normative judgment, while the righthand half of such a biconditional (where C is free of question-begging phrases like "responding in the right way") remains a mere prediction of my reactions. As long as C is free of such phrases, the question "I would not regard R as a reason even under conditions C, but is it a reason nonetheless?" will have an "open feel."[41]

How, then, should we interpret a judgment that X is a reason for doing A? One possibility is to say that a person who accepts such a judgment takes a certain belief to be warranted, namely the belief that the relation "counting in favor of" holds between X and doing A. That this relation holds will then be a "non-natural" fact, that is to say, a fact that is neither merely a fact about our psychology nor an ordinary empirical fact about the world outside us. Alternatively, we could say that to take X to be a reason for doing A is to hold a special judgment-sensitive attitude (different from belief) in regard to X and A, namely the attitude of "taking X to count in favor of doing A."

Gibbard takes a version of the latter approach, holding that "When a person calls something—call it R—a reason for doing X, he expresses his acceptance of norms that say to treat R as weighing in favor of doing X."[42] It is worth noting, I think, that this analysis does not avoid reliance on the idea of being a reason, or "counting in favor of," since that very notion, in the form of "weighing in favor of," appears in the characterization of the attitude he describes. I do not consider this a fault in Gibbard's account, but it is relevant to an assessment of exactly what that account is supposed to accomplish. What we are presented with, it seems, is a choice between one kind of view that takes "counting in favor of" to be the content of a certain kind of belief, and another kind that (like Gibbard's) takes "counting in favor of" to be (part of) the content of a special attitude, different from belief.

Several considerations might be taken to support the latter alternative. First, as I mentioned in discussing the inadequacy of hypothetical analyses, accepting a judgment that X is a reason for doing A seems to involve an element of normative commitment to, or endorsement of, a normative conclusion, an element that may be thought to be missing from the acceptance of a mere judgment of fact. Accounts of the second kind seek to capture this element in the special features of the attitude of "*taking* X to count in favor of doing A." In Gibbard's case, for example, the element of endorsement is meant to be captured by the fact that a person who calls X a reason for doing A *expresses his acceptance* of norms that say to treat X as weighing in favor of A. By contrast, it may seem that any account which construed taking something to be a reason as a kind of belief would fail to account for this element of endorsement or normative force and would hence fall prey to an open-question objection of the kind that I argued is effective against hypothetical analyses.

Second, even if a belief account can overcome this problem (indeed, one might say *especially* if it can overcome this problem) such an account will construe "taking something to be a reason" as a belief in a kind of non-natural fact that many regard as metaphysically odd.[43] Another source of the appeal of special-attitude accounts, then, is that they avoid commitment to such facts.[44] A third objection is that a belief account seems to assume that there is some mechanism through which we are sensitive to these non-natural facts and are able to represent them. But, it is objected, there is no apparent mechanism of this kind. A special-attitude account therefore seems more plausible insofar as it understands "taking something to be a reason" as expressing a certain attitude rather than registering the truth of some fact outside us. These objections might be summed up by saying that a belief account cannot explain the normative force of judgments about reasons, that it involves implausible metaphysical claims, and that it can offer no plausible epistemology for such judgments.

My main concern here is not to settle the debate between belief and special-attitude interpretations of judgments about reasons. Although I favor a belief interpretation, my main conclusion will be that for most purposes, including mine in this book, the choice between them turns out to make very little difference, as long as there are standards of correctness for attitudes of the relevant sort. But the three objections to the belief account that I have just summarized are of concern to me because they may seem to count in favor of a kind of skepticism about reasons in general, which holds that judgments about reasons are not about anything real, but just expressions of certain attitudes.[45] It is therefore worthwhile to explain why these objections do not have the force that they may appear to have. Once this is recognized, the difference between the two kinds of account will also seem less significant.

First, it may help to diminish this tendency toward skepticism to emphasize that the considerations I have just been discussing apply to reasons of all kinds—to reasons for belief as well as to reasons for action. In particular, open-question arguments show that neither claims about what counts as evidence nor claims about what count as reasons for action can be plausibly understood as claims about natural facts. For example, the claim that events of type A are almost always accompanied by events of type B is a claim about the natural world, but the claim that this counts in favor of expecting an event of one kind, given that one of the other type has occurred, is not such a claim but, rather, a (conditional) normative judgment about reasons for belief. So what we are concerned with here is not a distinction between facts and values, or between theoretical and practical reason, as these dichotomies are normally understood.

Second, it is particularly clear in the case of reasons for belief, but no less true in the case of reasons for action, that statements about the reasons we have normally take the form of declarative sentences which obey normal laws of logic. If, then, we are disposed on reflection to confidently affirm judgments of these kinds we seem to need some reason not to take them as saying something which can be true and which can be the object of belief.

Third, the objection I referred to above as the problem of normative force does not provide such a reason. This objection was that accepting a judgment about reasons cannot be just coming to believe some truth about the world, since no such truth could have the kind of normative force that reaching a conclusion about reasons has. If by "a truth about the world" here one means a truth about the natural world outside us or about our own psychology, then this claim is one that I would agree with. As I have said, I believe this is established by the open-question argument. But a defender of the belief interpretation of judgments about reasons need not, and should not, claim that statements about reasons are statements about the natural world but only that they are the kind of thing that can be said to be true and can be the object of belief. This *general* claim gives rise to no problem about normative force. Normative force of the kind in question is just the force of recognizing something to be a reason (to "count in favor of" a certain attitude). If recognizing something to be a reason amounts to seeing the truth of a statement about reasons, then this recognition will have normative force of the requisite kind. So an objection to the belief interpretation of judgments about reasons cannot rely on the open-question argument as I have used it above, at least not in the absence of some reason for thinking that if taking something to be a reason were a kind of belief it would have to be a belief about the natural world.

"What other kind of belief could it be?" is the obvious next question, and the natural answer is "A belief about reasons, what else?" This will no doubt seem unsatisfactory, but why should it be? If there are judgments about reasons which are naturally construed as declarative sentences and in which we have a high degree of substantive confidence, then why not conclude that these judgments do indeed say something true about their apparent subject matter?[46]

The judgments whose interpretation I am concerned with here are judgments that some consideration X "counts in favor of" some attitude (that it is relevant to the question whether to hold that attitude) and judgments that, taking all the relevant reasons into consideration, there is good reason to adopt A (or to abandon or revise it). A person who accepts a judgment of the former kind should, and will insofar as he or she is rational, give X a certain role in further deliberations about A, and a person who accepts a judgment of the latter kind should, and will insofar as he or she is rational, accept (or abandon or modify) this attitude. But we should not tie an account of judgments about reasons too closely to these standard examples of their role in first-person deliberation. Questions about reasons can arise not only in the course of one's thinking about how to modify one's own beliefs and intentions (what Harman calls practical reasoning), but also in the form of hypothetical questions about what one would have reason to do under certain conditions or questions about what someone else, whose situation may be quite different from one's own, has reason to do. In most cases the process of thought that one goes through in considering a question about reasons is the same in these three kinds of cases, and the judgment that one arrives at seems to have the same content. This seems to be true, for example, when one is asking whether, in a certain situation, considerations of loyalty count against doing something that will benefit one's friend's enemy, or asking whether the controversy generated by a certain paper would make publishing it worthwhile. One arrives at a judgment about these questions in the same way whether the question is a live first-person issue, a hypothetical one, or one concerning a third party. But the practical upshot of the resulting judgment is different in these cases. Only in the first case does it directly lead to (by rationally requiring) the adoption of the intention in question. In the other cases its practical consequences are different. It may, for example, count in favor of approval, disapproval, or giving certain advice.

This similarity in content across the three cases inclines me to say that in all of them the judgment in question involves taking something to be true, namely that for a person in a certain situation X counts in favor of holding attitude A, or that a person in a certain situation has sufficient reason to adopt A (or to modify it). The distinctive motivational force of such judgments in cases of the first kind can then be accounted for by the fact that it is central to being a rational creature that one's attitudes are responsive to one's judgments about reasons: in particular that if one accepts a judgment of the form just mentioned and believes one's situation to be of the kind in question then one modifies one's attitudes accordingly, because one sees reason to do so.[47]

The considerations I have just been discussing seem to me to reduce the force of some objections to construing taking something to be a reason as a kind of belief. Nonetheless, it remains the case that when we arrive at a judgment about reasons it may not seem, intuitively, that what we are doing is coming to perceive a certain fact, existing independently of our judgment.[48] And it may also seem puzzling how we *could* be doing this—what faculty of perception or intuition we would be using. But we should be on guard here against being misled by a supposed analogy with beliefs about the empirical world. It is part of the distinctive content of empirical beliefs, such as my belief that there is a window in front of me now and trees outside that window, that they represent to me the way things are "outside me"—at a distance from my own body. Empirical beliefs, naively or not so naively understood, therefore seem to have metaphysical implications about the existence of objects in the world. This leads in turn to epistemological problems about how I can have knowledge of these objects, given that they are "out there" where I am not. One natural response is that my beliefs must be produced by these objects through some reliable causal process. But these problems, and this response, are peculiar to the case of empirical belief. There is no reason to hold that nothing can be called a *belief* at all unless it can be understood as about some subject matter at a distance from us which must somehow be represented to us, and which therefore raises epistemological problems to which causal interaction is a natural solution.

It might be replied that if judgments about reasons are to be understood as claims that can be true or false, and about which we can be mistaken, then they must be about some subject matter independent of us. Understood in the right way, this is quite correct; but when understood in that way, the independence in question does not raise metaphysical and epistemological problems. The example of mathematical judgments may be helpful here. My judgments about arithmetic are judgments about a subject matter independent of me in the sense that they involve claims (not about me) about which I can be mistaken. But understanding arithmetic as objective in this sense does not require accepting a form of arithmetical Platonism. It is enough that there are standards of arithmetical reasoning such that when I fail to follow them I am wrong. Arithmetical competence is a matter of mastering this form of reasoning and, in general, being able to tell when it is being done well, when badly. The thinking of a good mathematical reasoner "represents" or "tracks" the truth about arithmetic insofar as it takes into account the right considerations in the right way. This need not be construed as a matter of being in touch, through some mechanism analogous to sense perception, with mathematical objects which exist apart from me.

Similarly, in order for judgments about reasons to be taken to be about some subject matter independent of us in the sense required for it to be possible for us to be mistaken about them, what is necessary is for there to be standards for arriving at conclusions about reasons. Conclusions about reasons that can be reached only through modes of thought that are defective by these standards are mistaken. It is not necessary, in order to explain the possibility of being mistaken, to construe the relevant subject matter in a metaphysical way as existing outside us. The question of whether there are standards of the required sort is a substantive one within the subject in question—a matter of whether there are conclusions and ways of arriving at them that we have no reason to regard as defective. It need not be a metaphysical question about what exists or an epistemological one about how we are in touch with it.[49]

Once we move to this substantive ground, however, an obvious difference between the case of arithmetic and that of reasons for action becomes relevant. In arithmetic there are countless particular judgments which seem incontrovertibly correct, and there are general methods, of unassailable authority, for arriving at them. As far as reasons for action are concerned, however, although there are some judgments about what counts in favor of acting a certain way that command wide acceptance, there is also wide disagreement about reasons for action and, it seems, nothing like a general authoritative method for reaching such conclusions. In this respect, a better mathematical analogy than arithmetic would be set theory: there are ways of thinking about sets which reach determinate conclusions that command wide agreement, but the best efforts of mathematicians deploying these methods still leave important areas of disagreement, uncertainty, and perhaps even indeterminacy. Even this analogy may seem strained.[50] So there are purely substantive grounds for doubting whether there is such a thing as being mistaken about reasons.

That this is an important source of doubt about reasons would account for the fact that these doubts center on reasons for action rather than on reasons for belief, for which, it is assumed, there are clearer substantive standards. These are substantive doubts, then, not metaphysical doubts about reasons in general or epistemological worries about how we could be in touch with them. Substantive doubts about reasons for action may have moved some people to maintain that claims about reasons express pro-attitudes rather than beliefs, but the question of the substantive defensibility of claims about reasons for action in fact cuts across the question of how these claims should be interpreted. I have argued that if there are substantive standards relative to which judgments of a certain kind can be called correct or incorrect, then there may be no reason not to take them to express beliefs. But if there are such standards, then the choice between these two interpretations may no longer make much difference: how much should we care about the difference between saying that these judgments express beliefs and saying that they express other attitudes for which there are clear standards of correctness? A special-attitude account of judgments about reasons need not be deflationary. Nonetheless, I think that some people have been attracted to such views, and other people inspired to deny them, because they allow for the *possibility* of saying that claims about reasons for action are merely expressions of attitude, for which there are no standards of correctness. But the fact that they might allow for the possibility of saying this is no reason to reject such accounts if one has good grounds for holding that saying it would be a mistake.

12. How Do We Know What Reasons We Have?

Turning, then, to this substantive question, how do we decide what reasons for action we have, and what grounds does this process give us for taking judgments about reasons for action to be the kind of things that can be correct or incorrect? One way of discovering that one has a reason for doing something is finding out that it would advance some aim or purpose that one has. Indeed, this has often been taken as the standard case of thinking about reasons for action. But both because this case has generally been seen as less problematic than others, and because I believe that it is less representative of our thinking about reasons than has been supposed, I will postpone consideration of this case until after I have considered some examples of practical reasoning of other kinds. How, then, might we reach conclusions about reasons for action other than by figuring out what is required to achieve a given end? In particular, how do I reach the conclusion that a particular end is, or is not, something worth striving for?

First, there is such a thing as a consideration *seeming* to be a reason for a certain course of action. When I want some coffee ice cream, the pleasure of its cool taste seems to be a reason for getting some. When I have a desire for a new computer, the fact that the new models have a faster chip seems to be a reason for buying one. When parents reach the end of their rope in dealing with an unruly child, his insolent and defiant behavior may seem to them a reason for striking him. In some cases it seems to me that *I* have a reason to do something; in others it seems to me that someone else has a reason to do something (even though I may hope that she does not do it). In such cases the fact that something seems to me to be a reason may involve no motivation on my part, but when it seems to me that *I* have a reason to do something, this commonly (though not invariably) involves feeling moved to so act. I argued in Section 8, in effect, that such "seemings" are the central element in what is usually called desire. As I also argued there, they are not a matter of preconceptual appetite but involve at least vague appeal to some evaluative category.

Such "seemings" arise independently of our judgment, and they can, unfortunately, persist in the face of it.[51] To say that something *seems* to me to be a reason is not the same thing as to say that I think it is a prima facie reason. Seeming to be a reason is merely a matter of appearing to be one. I may decide, on reflection, that this appearance is illusory and that it is not a reason at all. We can distinguish four stages in the consideration of a reason, not all of which need occur in every case. The first is the one at which X seems to be a reason for attitude A (or seems not to be). Second, there is what might be called the first critical stage, at which I may decide, as I have just said, whether X really is a reason for A or not—for example, whether the pleasure of eating ice cream is a *pro tanto* reason for intending to get some, or whether it is no reason at all. (This is the first *critical* stage because seemings do not depend on our judgment.) Third, there is the second critical stage, at which I decide whether, taking account of X and of whatever other reasons I take to bear on the matter, there is sufficient reason for adopting A. Finally, fourth, I may come to have attitude A—for example, I form an intention to go in search of ice cream or to buy a computer. As I have said earlier in this chapter, when a rational agent decides (stage three) that there is sufficient reason to form an intention, stage four normally follows as a result.

I take it that the first stage ("seemings") is uncontroversial. For present purposes controversy centers on what I have called the critical stages, particularly the first. What grounds can I have for deciding that I was mistaken to think that something was a reason? How can I be justified in calling this a process of correction rather than merely a change in my reaction? To answer this we need to see what such a process may involve.

Suppose, for example, that you are enraged by your child's defiant and insolent behavior. This behavior seems to you a reason to strike the child. But is it a reason? What kind of reason would it be? Is violence appropriate because it creates fear or shows your power? Why is that desirable? Is it supposed to be good for the child, or simply to demonstrate something about you? If the latter, what does that imply or signify about your relations with the child? If the former, why think that the effects will be good? What alternatives are there, and what would their effects be? The process here is first to clarify what kind of reason this is supposed to be and then to see whether the initial tendency to take this as a reason stands the test of reflection. If your initial tendency (to think that the child's insolent behavior gives you reason to strike it) stands after this reexamination, then you conclude that it really is a reason; if it does not, then you conclude that it is not.

Suppose you conclude that it is not a reason. Why regard this as a correction of your initial reaction rather than just as a different reaction? The appropriateness of regarding it as a correction depends, first, on the fact that we have here two claims about what does or does not count in favor of a certain action, claims which can contradict one another, unlike mere conflicting pro- and con-attitudes, which can conflict only in a practical sense. But how does the process that you went through support you in taking the later judgment to be the one that is correct? Here are two reasons. First, the later conclusion is supported by a clearer and more detailed conception of what the reason in question might be—of exactly what it is that is supposed to count in favor of striking your child. Second, in virtue of this reflection, it is less likely to be affected by distorting factors such as your rage.

Of course the idea that rage is a distorting factor, rather than a reason, reflects a substantive judgment—part of a background of stable judgments about reasons against which this particular assessment is made. These background judgments are also reflected in the particular range of possibilities that you see the need to consider in canvassing possible reasons for striking the child. Even leaving moral prohibitions aside, not just anything can count as a reason for striking someone: the fact that you had an even number of pieces of fruit for breakfast, for example, is not by itself such a reason, while some benefit to yourself or others, or the requirements of an important value, could be such reasons.

A reason is a consideration that counts in favor of some judgment-sensitive attitude, and the content of that attitude must provide some guidance in identifying the kinds of considerations that could count in favor of it. If it does not, then the question of whether something is a reason for it will make no sense, and any answer will seem truly arbitrary.[52] Even when, as in the example just given, the categories of possible reasons are vague, they at least provide us with some direction in looking for an answer to the question of whether a particular consideration is a reason or not.

These background judgments about the kinds of things that can count in favor of certain attitudes are themselves open to question and piecemeal modification. Suppose I think, for example, that the only reasons there are to preserve natural objects, such as trees, forests, and canyons, are the reasons arising from the enjoyment and other benefits that these things bring to human beings. Many people question this judgment. To decide whether they might be right, I can ask myself whether I may be overlooking something, perhaps because I am not considering natural objects in the right way. I may get some guidance by asking what kind of reasons there might be for respecting or valuing these objects apart from the ones I already recognize. What kind of reasons do others claim to have? This may suggest the kind of factors that I should attend to in order to see whether I think there are reasons of these kinds, or it may give me grounds for concluding that I have no such reasons if, for example, the only basis for these reasons would be in a form of religious belief that I find untenable. Another method would begin by focusing on particular cases in order to see what reasons they seem to present. For example, I do admit that it would seem callous and somehow objectionable to cut down a great old tree just for the fun of trying out my new chain saw. So I may ask what kind of considerations count against doing this. Can this reaction be understood as a response to reasons of the kinds I already recognize? Is it mere sentimentality, or does it persist "in a cool hour"? Do similar reasons show up elsewhere?

As in the previous case, the process here is to try to characterize the potential reason more fully, to ask whether it seems, so characterized, to be a relevant reason for the attitude in question. In addition, one can look for other cases on which it would have a bearing if it were a good reason, to see whether it seems to be a reason in those cases, to test one's reactions in these cases for signs of unreliability, to consider the plausibility of alternative explanations of these reactions, and so on. In short, one tries to see whether this reason would be included in the most coherent and complete account of what reasons there are.[53]

Here, then, is a partial account of how we go about deciding what reasons for action we have, and of the grounds we have for thinking some judgments about these reasons to be correct while others are mistaken. It would be an understatement to say that this method lacks the precision and clarity of arithmetical reasoning, but it is nonetheless very similar to the process of belief revision we employ in other areas.[54] Suppose, for example, that I have a strong tendency to be taken in by the Gambler's Fallacy, and tend to think that if a fair coin has come up heads six times in a row this makes it very unlikely that the next toss will be heads. Thinking about the matter more carefully, however, I see that I have failed to distinguish between the probability of a fair coin's coming up heads seven times in a row and the probability of its coming up heads *this* time, given that it has been heads on all the past throws. Most of the improbability of an event of the first kind has already been absorbed, so to speak, in the improbability of something that has now already happened (namely the first six heads). Once I have seen my initial reaction as based on a mistake of this kind (my failure to notice a relevant distinction), my conclusion that my newer belief is correct is very stable—I have no tendency to go back on it even if I am still sometimes tempted by the fallacy and have to repeat the argument. (I will also, it might be added, be unmoved by the fact that others still find the fallacious inference convincing.) This stability is a general feature of corrections of the kinds I have been describing.

In addition to this stability in each of our judgments, there is a significant degree of interpersonal agreement on judgments about reasons that seem to all of us to be stable under this kind of reflection and criticism. It is easy to overlook this fact, since there is of course also much disagreement and controversy about reasons for action. But there is wide agreement on basic points such as that, for example, the fact that something is pleasant, or exciting, or required by a duty or by loyalty to a friend can count as a reason for doing it, or that the fact that something would be beneficial to one's family or would realize some artistic or intellectual excellence can make it worthwhile. Even such basic points may not be unanimously accepted, but for most people they have a very high degree of stability under criticism and reflection.

Let me now return to the case of instrumental reasons, which I set aside above. It is commonly regarded as the standard case of a reason for action that a person has a reason to do what will advance some end or aim that he or she has, or what will carry out some prior intention. I will concentrate here on intentions, which seem to me the most general case.

Following Bratman, I have said that the fact that B is a way of carrying out my prior intention A can count in favor of adopting intention B unless one has reason to reconsider A. This is not, however, a truth about reasons that we discover through the kind of inductive process I have described. It is a more obvious truth, built into the fabric of practical reasoning itself. To adopt an intention just *is* to give certain considerations a special place in one's future thinking. So to adopt an intention and then fail to give it a place in shaping one's reasons is a case of irrationality in the narrow sense I defined above.[55]

We can also see why this must be so (although this further reflection is unnecessary for an agent). We cannot do or try to do everything that is worth doing. So being selective is an essential part of practical thinking. Sometimes this selection is conscious and reflective, as when we decide, after careful consideration, to adopt one pursuit among many seemingly worthy alternatives. More commonly it happens without reflection, as when a newspaper article catches my attention and I decide to find out more about its subject (without weighing the comparative merits of all the others I might look into).[56]

Whether they arise from reflection or not, these intentions alter the reasons an agent has (if they are held to and she does not have reason to reconsider them). This is an important respect in which our reasons for action depend on us rather than being determined by any independent facts about what "counts in favor of" what.[57] But it is a mistake to see this as the basic case of having a reason for action.[58] Even though adopting an intention (or an end or aim) can alter the reasons one has, these are not basic sources of reasons. Selecting something as an end by adopting an intention to pursue it does not make that thing better or more valuable than the other worthy alternatives; it just gives it a particular role in the agent's practical reasoning. To put the same point more technically, the fact that an intention alters one's subsequent reasons only so long as one does not have reason to reconsider its adoption indicates that the normative force of this intention depends on the substantive reasons that made it worth adopting in the first place.

I have argued that we have a general method for thinking about reasons for action in the right way that is similar to the method employed in regard to beliefs of other kinds, that is stable in its results, and that supports wide interpersonal agreement on a significant range of conclusions. All of this taken together provides ample ground for saying that judgments about reasons for action are the kind of things that can be correct or incorrect, even though there are many cases in which we may continue to disagree as to which of these is the case.

The method I have described might be thought to be a coherence theory of reasons for action. This characterization would be inaccurate, but since it is likely to seem appropriate I need to explain why the well-known objections to coherence views do not apply to my own account. The first of these is the charge of conservatism. On this score it might be thought an embarrassment to my view that every move in the process of correction I have described depends on a prior framework of accepted judgments about reasons. It seems that I am endorsing a complacent reaffirmation of whatever we happen to think.

To this I would reply, first, that the method I have described need not be complacent since, as I meant to indicate in discussing the example of the value of nature, the accepted judgments with which we begin are not themselves immune from criticism and revision. Second, any way that I can imagine of criticizing these judgments and arriving at others would amount to an instance of this same general method. To be sure, we cannot establish in this way that we *must* accept the judgments about reasons that we do hold. All that can be established is that they seem, on reflection, to be correct. That, it seems to me, is enough, and as much as one could reasonably ask for.

It is often mentioned as an objection to coherence accounts of truth, or even of justified acceptance, that different sets of beliefs or different systems of reasons could be equally coherent and therefore, on a coherence account, equally valid, or at least equally worthy of acceptance.[59] The mere possibility that different people recognize different reasons does not present a problem of this kind, since people simply *have* different reasons because of differences in their social circumstances, in what they are interested in, and in their aims and ends. In order to present a potential problem, then, the reasons people recognize must conflict in more direct ways, as when one person holds that some consideration is a reason for acting in a certain way in a certain situation and the other denies this. It is conceivable that different people, because of differences in their experience and in the information available to them, might be led to conflicting conclusions of this kind even though they both reflected carefully in the manner I have described and were thus warranted in accepting the conclusions that they reached.

The possibility of such justificatory blind alleys is not ruled out on the account of reasons I have offered.[60] But this is not grounds for theoretical embarrassment. If we were to recognize that there were other people to whom we stood in the relation just described, it would not follow that we have no better ground for clinging to our own system of reasons than for shifting to theirs. This is because the ground we have for continuing to accept particular judgments is a matter of the substantive case for those judgments. This case is not fully captured by a formal property (such as consistency) which our overall system of judgments and theirs might possess to the same degree.[61] (This is one reason why the label "coherence theory" is misleading.)

If other people are warranted in taking certain considerations to be good reasons, and if we are warranted in holding that they are not good reasons (not even for people in their situation, with their interests, opportunities, and so on), then this must be because we have conflicting reactions which each of us is warranted in trusting after the most complete debugging available to us. This difference between us may be due, in turn, to the fact that different information or experience is available to our two groups, in which case we need to consider which of our positions is epistemologically superior. Does the information or experience that they have give us reason to mistrust our own reactions? If so, then some revision is called for on our part; if not, then we have reason to stick with our system of reasons.

Alternatively, it may be that there are no such differences in experience and information, and that we just have different reactions, one of us taking some consideration to be a reason that the other is blind to. The likelihood of brute differences of this kind is reduced somewhat by the fact that we rarely take something to be a reason *simpliciter* as opposed to taking it to be a reason of some kind, as, for example, when we disagree as to whether there is reason for engaging in a certain activity because it is worthwhile. As I have argued, this further categorization entails some idea of relevant and irrelevant grounds, hence some basis for appraising conflicting reactions. Where brute differences in reaction do occur, however, then we must ask what best explains them. Since rational creatures are not perfect judges of all reasons of all kinds, one possibility is that one or the other of us is missing something. We have to consider the possibility that the error is ours; but if reexamination of our own reactions gives no grounds for doubt, then we are justified in remaining true to our own judgments and regarding the others as strangely different.

It might be objected that the method I have described gives us no assurance that the judgments we accept are anything other than the products of habituation. This objection draws on the fact that we do sometimes say that a person's tendency to treat a certain distinction as very important is "merely a product of his upbringing," and we may take this as an explanation that undermines the rational significance of the reaction it explains. In such cases the word "merely" reflects a substantive judgment that there is in fact no good reason to treat this distinction as important. If, however, it is charged that our judgments about reasons for action *as a whole* are "merely" due to habituation, what conception of reasons backs up this "merely"? "Merely" as opposed to what? If the content of judgments about reasons suggested that they were supposed to reveal to us the facts about some "external" reality, then this charge might at least gain a foothold. But, as I have argued, this is not the case, and it is unclear what significance a world of reasons beyond those we can recognize could have.

13. Other People's Reasons

Different people can have different reasons for action, because of differences in their circumstances, their interests, and their intentions. People can also disagree about reasons, and I have been defending the view that people can be mistaken about their reasons for action—not just mistaken about what will promote their ends, but mistaken in having those ends to begin with. Attempts to claim this kind of objectivity for judgments about reasons are sometimes viewed with suspicion, on the ground that they are driven by a desire to claim the authority to criticize others and to tell them what to do. I therefore want to say something here about the diverse reasons we have for caring about what reasons other people have and about what reasons they take themselves to have.

What should be said first is that there is fundamentally no question of why we should be concerned with the reasons that other people have. We must be so concerned, insofar as we take ourselves to have any reasons at all, since any judgment about our own reasons entails claims about the reasons that others have or would have in certain circumstances. I have already made this point in passing in discussing our reasons for resisting the idea that all reasons have subjective conditions, but it is important enough to merit fuller discussion.

Suppose Jane looks out her window after a snowstorm and sees her neighbor shoveling his driveway. The snow is heavy. He is already panting, and he still has a long way to go. Jane sees that he could use help, and she takes this as a reason to get her shovel and go out. Even though she may not make them explicit to herself at the time, there are certain features of her neighbor's situation and her own in virtue of which she takes this consideration to be a reason. Perhaps she thinks that she has a reason to help only because she cares about her neighbor, or only because she would enjoy helping, or only because she expects to need his help in the future and wants to make it harder for him to refuse. On the other hand, she may be a strict moralist who thinks that she has a reason to provide such help whether she feels like it or not. Leaving this question open, let G be the set of factors, whatever they may be, in virtue of which Jane takes herself to have reason to help her neighbor.

Since she accepts the judgment that, given G, she has reason to help her neighbor, Jane is also committed to the view that anyone else who stands in the relation described by G to someone in need of help has reason to provide it. This is an instance of what I will call the universality of reason judgments. This is not a moral principle; Jane may be moved by moral considerations or she may not.[62] It is not even a substantive claim about the considerations that count as reasons, since the contents of G have been left entirely open. In particular, the universality of reason judgments is not something that should be a matter of controversy between those who hold, and those who deny, that all our reasons, or certain of them, have subjective conditions. Even if all reasons are based on desires, the universality of reason judgments still holds that if I have a reason to do something because it will satisfy my desire, then anyone else who has that same desire (and whose situation is like mine in other relevant respects) also has this reason.

The universality of reason judgments is a formal consequence of the fact that taking something to be a reason for acting is not a mere pro-attitude toward some action, but rather a judgment that takes certain considerations as sufficient grounds for its conclusion. Whenever we make judgments about our own reasons, we are committed to claims about the reasons that other people have, or would have under certain circumstances. We thus have wholly self-regarding reasons for having views about the correctness or incorrectness of the judgments people make about the reasons they have, since these judgments imply conclusions about the reasons *we* have. So situations can arise in which, if their judgments about their reasons for action are correct, our judgments about our own reasons must be mistaken. In order for such conflicts to be real, both parties must be making judgments about the same thing: for example, about whether certain considerations do in fact count in favor of a given attitude for a person in a certain situation. This means that they must be talking about the same attitude and that they must be employing similar sets of evaluative categories.

There are good reasons to expect people's judgments about reasons to be framed in terms that others around them not only could but do actually understand and use. Since we acquire the concepts involved in such judgments chiefly by imitating others, it is to be expected that in our process of selecting, from among the range of features and distinctions which might be noticed, those to which reason-giving significance is to be attached, we will generally settle on ones that others around us already recognize and see as important. This similarity in concepts makes disagreement possible. But it is one thing to disagree with others and something else to care about it. In some cases we have no reason to care. It is in itself of little importance to me that there are people out there who reject my reasons for believing that the Earth is round and who accept reasons that I would reject for following the teachings of various gurus. But I can also have good reasons for being concerned with the reasons that other people accept. These reasons are various, and it is worth noting some of them.

In some cases I should be concerned with other people's views about reasons because they might be correct and I might learn something from them. If some proof of Fermat's Last Theorem looks valid to me, but my mathematician friend thinks it is fallacious, then I have reason to look into the matter to find out why he thinks this. If my level-headed and sensitive friend thinks that abstract expressionist paintings are subtle and interesting (whereas, to me, they just look like collections of spots), then I have reason to try to see what it is he is noticing in order to decide whether I, too, should see it as a reason for taking this style more seriously. These reasons depend on what Gibbard calls an epistemological story about why our opinions diverge.[63] In the examples I have just described, these stories are ones in which my epistemological position is or might be inferior to that of the other person, in whom I have, at least initially, particular trust. When the reverse is true—when I regard the others as foolish and very likely to be mistaken—I may have no reason of this kind for being concerned with their judgments.

A second kind of reason for being concerned with other people's judgments about reasons is less dependent on epistemological considerations. Whether or not I regard others' judgments as possibly superior to mine, I have reason to be concerned with them if they may represent an emerging consensus that will affect me. Suppose, for example, that I am a figure skater and that other skaters seem to be attracted to a new style, more frantic and less fluid than what I have been striving for. I have reason to understand what it is that they find attractive about this way of skating, so that I will be able to keep up with them in competitions. Similarly, in philosophy, if others in my field start writing in a new way, for example by giving greater importance in their writings to facts about the social context in which various philosophical ideas arise, then I have reason to understand what they are doing and why they think that these matters are philosophically important, if only in order to be able to participate in debates and perhaps influence the development of the subject in a direction I would prefer.

Reasons of this kind need not depend, as those just given may seem to do, on a background of competition. They can also have a more directly personal character. If I am a member of an artistic or religious community, for example, the bond with the other members that comes from a recognition of the same values, and the shared life that this makes possible, may be of central importance to me. So if our opinions on crucial questions begin to diverge—if one of us comes to doubt the reasons supporting our central beliefs or if we come to differ about the reasons that those beliefs support—this affects me deeply. This is so not only because one or the other of us may be wrong but also because the continuation of our common life may be threatened. We may no longer be able to regard one another as fellow believers. This may be an extreme case, but concerns of this kind are present in some degree in all our lives. We all enjoy relations with others that are based at least partly on our appreciation of the same values, and when we come to differ in the interpretation of these values, or in the importance to be placed on them, these relations are threatened. I can no longer participate wholeheartedly in our activities if I no longer see them as important, or if I think that the rest of you are completely misguided in your ideas about how they should be pursued.

These examples, of relations which depend on a shared appreciation of other values, should be distinguished from a further class of cases in which the reasons in question concern the status that we ourselves have. Suppose that you regard yourself as a being with moral standing, defined by rights which limit how you may be treated. If you then learn that others with whom you generally associate see no reason to care about you or to give your interests any weight in their decisions unless it is to their advantage to do so, or that they regard you as having standing only insofar as you, like them, are a member of the elect group of true believers, this has a pervasive effect on your relations with them. This may make no difference to your personal safety or to the likelihood that you will be well treated by them; but even if it does not, it changes your standing and puts your relations with them on an entirely different footing. Because this difference matters, you have reason to care about the reasons others take themselves to be governed by in deciding how to treat you.

Quite apart, then, from any desire to judge others or tell them what to think and do, we have diverse grounds for caring about the reasons they take themselves to have. Grounds of all of the kinds just listed, and the differences between them, will figure in my discussions of values, morality, and relativism in the chapters ahead.

14. Conclusion

To return to the beginning: I will take the idea of a reason as primitive. I have tried in the intervening pages to explain and defend this choice by describing the role of reasons within a larger account of rationality, motivation, and justification. My aim has been to identify and allay various doubts that have led people to be wary of the idea of a reason and to think that it stands in need of explanation, perhaps in terms of the idea of desire. One source of such doubts is the belief that if a person has a reason for action, then it is irrational for him to fail to be motivated by it. This imposes a heavy burden on claims about reasons, since such charges of irrationality are often implausible and certainly difficult to sustain. Against this, I have argued that common sense and ordinary usage strongly support a narrower notion of irrationality, according to which it is not always irrational to fail to acknowledge a strong reason that one has.

A second source of doubt about reasons is the idea that there is an independent notion of desire, which is a clearer notion than that of a reason. Desires, on this view, are psychological states which are the basic motivators of actions and also have a fundamental role as starting points for justification. I have argued that the notion of a desire is not nearly as clear as is commonly supposed, and that the most plausible account of what a desire is presupposes the idea of "taking something to be a reason." When a rational person takes herself to have a reason for an action, I argued, this is motivationally sufficient to explain that action without any further appeal to desire. Desires turn out, on reflection, to have neither the special motivational force nor the special justificatory role commonly attributed to them.

The language of reasons, as opposed to mere desires, is crucial to an adequate description of the structure of our own practical reasoning and also to our relations with others, as rational creatures who recognize many of the same reasons and can recognize the value of each other. I have argued that although there is wide disagreement about the reasons we have, there is also a method for examining and criticizing our judgments about reasons that is sufficient to carry conviction in many cases. This commonsensical method does not amount to a decision procedure or even a theory, but it should be sufficient, I argued, to allay general epistemological doubts about reasons.

2

Values

1. Introduction

Chapter 1 explained and defended my decision to treat the notion of a reason as primitive. In this chapter I will use the notion of a reason, taken as the most basic and abstract element of normative thought, to provide a general characterization of a slightly more specific normative notion, the idea of value. This will provide the basis for the discussion, in the remainder of the book, of the specific forms of value involved in our ideas of right and wrong or, as I will say, of what we owe to each other.

Outside philosophy, the terms 'value' and 'values' are commonly used in a very broad sense to apply to a wide range of moral as well as to various nonmoral ideas. Questions of right and wrong, for example, are generally thought of as questions of value, and specific ideas of right and wrong such as justice, equity, and fidelity to agreements are naturally referred to as "values." But many other things are said to be valuable, or to represent values, in a sense that seems independent of considerations of right and wrong, including such things as works of nature, excellences in art and music, and intellectual or scientific accomplishments. Intermediate between these two areas of value—the narrowly moral and the ostensibly "nonmoral"—there are such values as loyalty to one's friends and devotion to family, as well as such things as industriousness and the avoidance of excessive consumption.

In discussions within professional philosophy, the terms 'value' and 'values' are used less frequently than 'good' or 'the good', although these sets of terms are often treated as if they were interchangeable, as when something called "a theory of value" is taken to be addressed to the questions "What is goodness?" and "What things are good?"[1]

Moreover, "the good" and "the right" are generally treated as prima facie distinct normative domains. "The good" deals with how we have reason to want the world to be, while "the right" has to do with what we may or must do. Some have maintained that the latter is in one way or another reducible to the former, but this is a distinctive and controversial claim (in a way that it could not be a controversial claim that notions of rightness are "reducible to" questions of value in the broad sense I described in the previous paragraph, since they obviously are such questions).

In this chapter I will argue that this emphasis on "the good" has had a distorting effect on our thinking about value in general, and in particular on our view of the relation between rightness ("what we owe to each other") and other values. Our most fundamental notion of value is broader than "the good" as this is often understood in philosophical discussion, and is not exclusively a notion of how it would be best for the world to go, or of what would be best for particular people. If this broader account is accepted, then the distinction between "what we owe to each other" and other values will appear less stark, not because there is no distinction to be drawn, or because the right is "reducible to" the good, but because many other values will be seen to have a structure similar to that which most obviously characterizes our ideas of right and wrong. I will argue that this is true for such values as excellences in art, science, and other endeavors; the value of important personal relations such as love and friendship; and the value of human life.

2. Teleology

A familiar and influential family of views about what is "good" or "valuable," which can fairly be called "teleological" views, takes the following form. The primary bearers of value are states of affairs or, over time, ways the world might go. These things can have intrinsic value, that is to say, value that is not a matter of their tendency to contribute to or make possible something else which is of value. Even if it is not generally possible to say with precision how much intrinsic value different states of affairs have, and even if, as some would claim, this question does not always have, even in principle, a precise answer, it remains true on this view that understanding intrinsic value is a matter of understanding (insofar as we can) which things have it and which have more, which less. As agents, our relation to states of affairs lies in being able to realize them, to prevent them from occurring, or to make their occurrence more or less likely. What we have reason to do, on this view (at least as far as questions of value are concerned), is to act so as to realize those states of affairs that are best—that is, have the greatest value. This teleological structure is often taken to be a formal feature of the ideas of "goodness" or "value" rather than part of some substantive view about which things are good.[2]

The idea that value has this teleological structure often goes together with a number of other ideas about value. Three of these other ideas are combined with teleology in universalistic hedonism, for example, which is the view that the value of a state of affairs is determined by the amount of pleasure that it contains. First, since on this view actions themselves have no intrinsic value, the value of an action is determined by the value of its consequences, that is to say, by the amount of pleasure it leads to. Second, according to universalistic hedonism this value is impartial, not only in the sense that everyone's pleasure is taken into account but also in the sense, important for our current discussion, that the value of a state of affairs gives every agent the same reason to promote it. Third, according to hedonism this value is additive. Any teleological conception of value involves maximization in a weak sense of holding that we have more reason to promote those states of affairs that have greater value. But hedonism involves the further idea that the value of a state of affairs is the sum of the values of its component parts.

Although these three ideas often go together, they are logically independent and are not shared by all teleological views. Many such views hold, for example, that actions themselves can have intrinsic value. On such a view, if I act in a way that gives a certain person pleasure, then the state of affairs that is realized consists, among other things, in the occurrence of this pleasure and the fact that it was brought about by that action. The value of that state of affairs then depends on the value of that pleasure and possibly also on the value, positive or negative, of the action. What distinguishes teleological views is not the elements of a state of affairs that they take to contribute to its intrinsic value (whether these include actions or only their consequences), but rather the idea that it is only states of affairs that have value. If actions have intrinsic value, therefore, it is as components of states of affairs—as things that *occur,* and that it is good (or bad) to have occur. To be (intrinsically) valuable, on such a view, is to be "to be promoted."

Second, a teleological conception of value need not be impartial. The teleological structure I have described is often taken to characterize not only "the good" impartially understood, but also the good from a particular individual's point of view (the way she has reason to want things to go). So a conception of value can have a teleological structure while being something that not all agents have the same reasons to promote. Finally, a purely teleological conception of value (whether impartial or not) need not be additive. It can hold that the value of a state of affairs is not the sum of the values of certain of its elements, but is arrived at in some more complicated way.[3]

My concern in this section is with the abstract thesis that value has a teleological structure rather than with these other features that teleological conceptions often share. But it is nonetheless important to bear these other features in mind, since the appeal of particular teleological views, and their distinctness from nonteleological alternatives, often depends upon them. Indeed, one may wonder whether, once it is recognized that a teleological conception of value can assign intrinsic value to actions as well as to their consequences, and that this value need not be impartial or additive, there is any content left to the bare idea of a teleological structure. It may seem that no significant difference remains between a teleological conception of value and a nonteleological one. I believe that there is a difference, and that the idea of value should not be understood in a purely teleological way. My reasons for thinking this can be brought out by considering a recent controversy between consequentialist and deontological views of morality.

It is not surprising that a purely teleological conception of value should be held by people who also accept a consequentialist account of morality, according to which an action is morally right just in case its performance leads to the best state of affairs. If rightness is a matter of promoting the good, then the good must be the kind of thing that is "to be promoted." But this view has wide appeal, as a thesis about *value*, even for many who reject consequentialism as an account of right and wrong. Thomas Nagel, for example, who argues vigorously against consequentialism as a moral theory, nonetheless seems drawn to a conception of value, or at least of "the good" impartially understood, that is exclusively teleological. When we consider the world from an objective, or impartial, point of view, he says, the first thing that strikes us is that certain things are not only good or bad from one or another personal point of view; they are also good or bad objectively. It is, for example, not only a bad thing for me that I am in pain and bad for you that you are; these things are also bad objectively speaking, and it is objectively a good thing that someone's pain be relieved.[4]

The fact that his example concerns pain is significant, since the idea that value and disvalue are a matter of being "to be promoted" and "to be prevented" has its greatest plausibility with respect to experiential states of this kind. But Nagel seems to feel a strong pull toward the view that this is true of value more generally. He is a firm believer in what are often called deontological reasons, which can count against doing certain things even though doing them would lead to better overall consequences. For example, he would hold that there are cases in which it would be wrong to torture someone, and in which I therefore have a very strong reason not to do it, even though torturing him would lead to better consequences, for example by preventing someone else from committing an even worse crime. But Nagel finds such reasons "formally puzzling" insofar as they are not based in the goodness or badness of the resulting states of affairs. "How," he asks, "can there be a reason not to twist someone's arm which is not equally a reason to prevent his arm from being twisted by someone else?"[5] Here the example concerns not just pain, but the wrongness of intentionally causing it. So the problem Nagel raises is a general one: how can there be a reason not to bring something about which is not grounded in the badness of its happening, and hence equally a reason to prevent it from being brought about by some other agent or by the forces of nature? Nagel believes that this question can be answered, but he takes it to present a difficult challenge.

Why should this challenge be so difficult? Samuel Scheffler has suggested one possible answer. What "lies at the heart of consequentialism," he says, is "a fundamental and familiar conception of rationality that we accept and operate within a very wide range of contexts."[6] This is what he calls "maximizing rationality." "The core of this conception of rationality," he writes, "is the idea that if one accepts the desirability of a certain goal being achieved, and if one has a choice between two options, one of which is certain to accomplish the goal better than the other, then it is, *ceteris paribus*, rational to choose the former over the latter."[7]

Scheffler thinks that this conception of rationality presents a problem for the deontologist in the following way. First, he supposes, plausibly but vaguely, that the deontologist regards prohibited actions such as torture, murder, and betrayal as "morally undesirable." (Here he is exploiting the possibility, mentioned above, that actions can have value apart from the value of their consequences.) Second, less plausibly, he interprets this as the view that it is intrinsically bad that such actions should occur, and that we should have the goal of minimizing their occurrence. But, as Nagel points out, cases can arise in which torturing a person will accomplish this goal better than not doing so. A deontologist like Nagel therefore violates the maximizing conception of rationality if he says that one nonetheless ought not to torture in such a case.

This argument has many instructive aspects, which merit close attention. First, the argument as I have presented it so far seems to rely on the assumption that the negative intrinsic value attached to morally undesirable actions is impartial—that is to say, that an action that has this disvalue is something that everyone (not just the agent of the action in question) has reason to prevent. Scheffler is quite right that the deontological idea that certain actions are wrong, and therefore should not be performed even to prevent similar actions by others, cannot be formulated plausibly in terms of the impartial disvalue of having such actions occur. If the reasons against committing a murder, for example, consisted of the impartial disvalue of the victim's death combined with the special intrinsic impartial disvalue of a murder's occurring, then these reasons would also apply to a case in which we must choose between preventing a murder or preventing an otherwise similar accidental death. But even those who believe that there is a special prohibition against intentional killing do not think that one must, for *this* reason, prevent the murder rather than the accident. The idea that the murder is a much worse thing to have happen would seem to imply that one must try to prevent it, even if one has a slightly greater chance of being able to prevent the accidental death. But this seems wrong. This might be taken to show that if we are to make sense of the idea of a deontological prohibition against killing by assigning intrinsic disvalue to acts of killing, this disvalue must not be impartial but rather what is sometimes called agent-relative disvalue. This is disvalue of a kind that gives the agent of such an action a special reason not to perform it, a reason that does not apply in the same way to others, such as, for example, those who might be in a position to prevent the action.

But why should this special agent-relative reason be taken to flow from the disvalue of the action, understood as an event? Why, that is, should we at this point remain within a teleological framework? One possible explanation would appeal to what might be called the purely teleological conception of reasons, according to which, since any rational action must aim at some result, reasons that bear on whether to perform an action must appeal to the desirability or undesirability of having that result occur, taking into account also the intrinsic value of the action itself. This sounds plausible, but understood as a general thesis about reasons it is mistaken. It is certainly true that in many cases in which we are faced with a choice between bringing about one consequence and bringing about another the right way to decide is by determining which of these outcomes is more desirable. But from the fact that this is often the case it does not follow that it is always so, or even that, when it is so, all the reasons bearing on the choice can be cast in the form of its being good or bad that events of a certain kind should occur.

As I argued in Chapter 1, Section 10, many of the reasons bearing on an action concern not the desirability of outcomes but rather the eligibility or ineligibility of various other reasons. So, in a case of the kind we are envisaging, such reasons will have played a role in determining that comparing the desirabilities of A and B (as assessed on certain grounds, such as their pleasantness) is the proper way to decide what to do under the circumstances. And as I also argued in Chapter 1, judging that a certain consideration does not count as a reason for action is not equivalent to assigning negative intrinsic value to the occurrence of actions based on this reason. Such a value can always simply be outweighed by some countervailing value, but the judgment that a consideration is irrelevant cannot.

This general point about the structure of reasons is relevant to the argument about "deontological prohibitions" and their allegedly puzzling character.[8] Consider, for example, the principle that one may not kill one person in order to save several others. Accepting this principle involves accepting a certain view of the reasons one has: that the positive value of saving these others does not justify killing a person. If this principle is correct, then one does not need to balance the value of abiding by it against the good to be achieved through its violation. Doing this would be flatly inconsistent with the principle itself, which holds that this good is not sufficient to justify the action in question. Someone who accepts this principle therefore does not need to appeal to the "negative intrinsic value" of killing in order to explain why she does not do what is necessary to save the greater number.

Of course there is also the question of whether one should accept such a principle to begin with. This is the question to which the claim that deontological prohibitions are "paradoxical" is most plausibly addressed, and it obviously needs an answer. My own view is that it is best answered by considering what principles licensing others to take our lives could be reasonably rejected. Whatever the best answer may be, however, an answer appealing to the intrinsic moral disvalue of a killing's occurring would not be plausible. The idea that there is such a moral disvalue is a reflection (I would say, a misunderstanding) of the principle itself, not something that could be appealed to in its justification.

It is noteworthy that Scheffler, although he speaks of "a fundamental and familiar conception of rationality," does not appeal to the teleological conception of reasons in the general form in which I have stated (and argued against) it. What he says is that "*if* one accepts the desirability of a certain goal being achieved, and *if* one has a choice between two options, one of which is certain to accomplish the goal better than the other, *then* it is, *ceteris paribus,* rational to choose the former over the latter" (my emphasis). By "accepting the desirability of a certain goal" Scheffler seems to mean adopting it as a goal, since he goes on to discuss the process of choosing between alternative ways of accomplishing it. The idea, then, is that adopting a goal means taking the fact that an action would advance that goal as something that counts in favor of that action, other things being equal. So *if* one has adopted a goal (and does not have reason to reconsider its adoption), *then* one has, other things being equal, reason to prefer actions that better accomplish it. Taken as an observation about one common but nonetheless distinctive element in practical thinking, this claim is quite correct. One thing that makes it correct, however, is that it does not claim that all the considerations that figure in determining the eligibility of an action have to take the form of "goals" and their "desirability." As I have said, it does not seem plausible to understand the deontologist's prohibition against killing in this way.

Another factor making Scheffler's claim plausible is the judicious inclusion of *ceteris paribus* clauses. But these may conceal more than at first appears. On a natural (but oversimplified) view, to adopt something as a goal is just to set a certain positive value on its accomplishment and to take this value as counting, other things being equal, in favor of any action that would bring it about. Looking at things in this way, it is natural to interpret the "other things being equal" clause as meaning "unless the action conflicts with the achievement of some other goal, whose value outweighs this one." I argued in Chapter 1 that this conception of a goal is mistaken. Adopting something as a goal is not just a matter of attaching a positive value to its accomplishment and counting this in favor of any action that would promote it (unless this is overridden by considerations coming from elsewhere). When we "adopt a goal" we normally give that goal a particular status in our lives and in our practical thinking, such as the status of a long-term career objective, or of a whim, or of something that we want to do sometime on a vacation. That is to say, the intentions that constitute adopting the goal specify the kinds of occasions on which it is to be pursued, the ways it is to be pursued, and so on. So the limitations indicated by the qualification that other things must be equal include conditions determined by our understanding of the goal and the way in which it is a goal for us, not just limitations imposed by other values that might "override" it. I will argue below that such conditions are a common feature in our ideas of value.

If the purely teleological conception of reasons is rejected, what other sources might there be for the idea that to be valuable is to be "to be promoted"? In the case of impartial value, one possibility is that it is essentially a moral idea (rather than one whose basis lies in a notion of rationality or in a conception of value that is independent of ideas of right and wrong). On this view it is (at least) part of "what we owe to each other" that we must promote certain states of affairs, plausibly called "the good." The "impartiality" of the good that is to be promoted reflects a moral requirement: we owe equal concern to each individual. "The good" so understood therefore includes the individual good of all individual human (or all sentient) creatures—that they not suffer or die prematurely and that their lives go well in other respects. (It could conceivably include some impersonal goods as well, such as justice, equality, or the apportionment of happiness in accord with virtue, but these things might also be understood as independent moral requirements.)

This "moral teleology" is to be contrasted with a nonmoral version of the kind discussed above, according to which impartiality is based in the idea of the good, rather than in the morality of right and wrong. An improvement in one person's well-being, it might be held, makes just as much of a contribution to the goodness of the overall state of affairs as the same improvement in the life of some other person who is similarly situated. (This is a substantive thesis about what is good.) Therefore, insofar as we are concerned with what is good generally (good "from the point of view of the universe," as Sidgwick says)[9] we have just as strong a reason to promote one person's well-being as to promote another's (these reasons being provided by the good that is involved rather than by any idea of what is "owed" morally to the individuals in question).

Nagel's remarks about the objective point of view seem to reflect the appeal of both moral and nonmoral teleology. On the one hand, as we have seen, he speaks of taking up an impartial point of view that sounds very much like Sidgwick's "point of view of the universe." But his discussion of this perspective sometimes seems to have a moral basis. He says, for example, that we have impersonal reasons to relieve other people's pain but not to promote every aim that they have. "It seems too much to allow an individual's desires to confer impersonal value on something outside himself, even if he is to some extent involved in it."[10] How should we understand the claim that this would be "too much"? On one natural reading it reflects an idea not about what is good but rather about "what we owe to each other," namely the idea that while we can be asked to recognize moral reasons to prevent and help alleviate each other's pain, it is "too much to ask" that we seek to advance every end that another person has. So understood, Nagel's impartial perspective is the perspective of, or a perspective within, the morality of right and wrong.

My concern at present is not with morality, but with value in a more general sense. I mention moral teleology here simply to distinguish it from the teleological conceptions of value, or of "the good," that are my main concern. The idea that to be good is simply to be "to be promoted" can seem an extremely natural, even inescapable one. It is plausible to think that, as Shelly Kagan suggests, the good simply is that which we have reason to promote. But although there are many cases in which this is true, I will argue in the following section that when we consider the particular things that most philosophers have cited as instances of the good, it becomes quite implausible to hold that all our thinking about value can be cast in this form.

3. Values: Some Examples

The things that philosophers have generally listed as intrinsically valuable fall into a few categories: certain states of consciousness; personal relationships; intellectual, artistic, and moral excellence; knowledge; and human life itself. In claiming that these things are valuable, these philosophers seem to mean that it is good that they occur. G. E. Moore was quite explicit about this, saying that in order to decide whether a thing is intrinsically valuable or not we should imagine a world in which only that thing existed and ask ourselves whether we would judge its existence to be good.[11] W. D. Ross was slightly less explicit, but his discussion of "What things are good?" also concentrates on the question of what makes some "states of the universe" better than others.[12] When we consider the things that are generally held to be intrinsically valuable, however, it becomes apparent that in most cases taking them to be valuable is not simply, or even primarily, a matter of thinking that certain states of the universe are better than others and are therefore to be promoted.

Consider first the case of friendship. Moore listed "the pleasures of human intercourse" as "one of the most valuable things we know or can imagine."[13] By this he meant that a world that contains two people enjoying the pleasures of reciprocated affection is made better, other things being equal, by containing this occurrence. Now it may be true that the existence of friendship and the pleasures it brings make a world better, but it strikes me as odd to suggest that this is what is central to the value of friendship. Surely we are right to value friendship (and presumably this is part of what Moore was affirming), so one way of looking for a more plausible account of the matter is to ask what this "valuing" involves.

A person who values friendship will take herself to have reasons, first and foremost, to do those things that are involved in being a good friend: to be loyal, to be concerned with her friends' interests, to try to stay in touch, to spend time with her friends, and so on. Someone who values friendship will also believe that she has reasons of a slightly different kind to cultivate new friendships and to keep the ones she already has, and will think that having friends is a good worth seeking. Consequently, a person who values friendship will also think it good for other people that they have friends, and will be moved to bring this about insofar as these people are of concern to her.[14] It seems overblown to say that what is important about friendship is that it increases the value of the state of the universe in which it occurs. But there is nothing odd about saying that it improves the quality of a life. So reasons of the last three kinds I mentioned (reasons to bring it about that one has friends, to keep the ones one has, and to help bring it about that others whom one cares about have friends) might be seen as restating Moore's thesis in a more modest form. They are at least like his thesis in having a teleological form: accepting them as reasons involves holding that it is good (in this case, good for the individuals in question) that friendship should occur and that friendship is therefore "to be promoted."

But the reasons in the first category, the ones involved in being a good friend, do not have this form. Some of them, such as reasons to be loyal to one's friends and not to betray them, are not teleological in this way: the primary reason to be loyal to one's friends is not that this is necessary in order for the friendship to continue to exist. Other reasons in this category are reasons to bring about certain states of affairs: to promote the interests of one's friends, for example, and to try to make them happy. But what is "to be promoted" here is not the occurrence of friendship but other specific ends.

Moreover, while all the reasons I have mentioned are ones that would be recognized by a person who valued friendship, it is the reasons in this first category (those involved in being a good friend) that are most central to friendship, and when conflicts occur these reasons take priority over the reasons we have to promote friendship (for ourselves or others). We would not say that it showed how much a person valued friendship if he betrayed one friend in order to make several new ones, or in order to bring it about that other people had more friends.[15]

I shifted, near the beginning of this discussion of the value of friendship, from the question of what it is for friendship to be valuable to the question of what is involved in valuing friendship. These are different questions. People value many things that are not in fact valuable. What I want to suggest, however, is that the claim that friendship is valuable is best understood as the claim that it is properly valued, that is to say, that the reasons recognized by someone who values friendship are in fact good reasons. Consider, as a contrast with friendship, "fanship": the state of being a devoted admirer of some famous person, such as a movie star, a singer, or an athlete. Some people value fanship. That is, they think that being a fan makes life better, more enjoyable, and more interesting. They may also think that it is important to be a good fan: that there is good reason, say, to see all the movies in which their favorite star appears as soon as they come out, and to defend the star when others criticize her, and that it would be a great thing to see the star in person, even from a great distance. According to the account of value I am suggesting, to hold that fanship is not valuable is just to hold that these reasons are not good reasons, or at least that a person who gave them great weight in shaping his life would be making a mistake. On the other hand, to hold that fanship, or friendship, *is* valuable is to hold that the reasons involved in valuing it are good ones and that it is therefore appropriate to give this notion an important place in shaping one's life.

If this claim is accepted, and if my claims about the reasons involved in valuing friendship are correct, then the claim that friendship is valuable is not primarily a claim that it is "to be promoted" or that a world in which it exists is for that reason a better one, although it will be true that if friendship is valuable then there are reasons to seek it for oneself and to promote it for others whom one cares about. When we consider the question of value in the way that Moore recommended, by asking what makes a world better, it is only reasons of this latter kind—reasons to have friendship occur—that we notice. These reasons are teleological and, in many cases, impartial. But when we take into account the perspective of the people who are friends, a wider range of reasons comes into view. These reasons are not in general impartial; some are not teleological at all; and among those that are, only a few are, directly or indirectly, reasons to bring it about that more friendship occurs. To claim that friendship is valuable is, on the view I am offering, to claim that all these reasons are good reasons.

I believe that much the same thing could be said about the value of other relationships commonly, and plausibly, held to be good, such as family relations. This may not be surprising, since friendship and family ties may be seen as moral values and "agent-relative" ones. But I believe that a similar structure can be seen in the reasons involved in values of other kinds such as the value of intellectual inquiry and understanding. I will discuss the case of scientific inquiry, but I think that what I will say holds as well for other forms of intellectual activity, in history, for example, or philosophy or mathematics.

The claim that science and scientific knowledge are intrinsically valuable supports a number of different conclusions about the reasons people have. One is that people who have the relevant ability and opportunity have reason to take up scientific inquiry as a career and to devote their lives to it. Second, those who take up science as a career have reason to try to be good scientists: to work hard, to choose lines of inquiry that are significant rather than those that are easiest or will get the most attention, to report their results accurately and in a way that will be helpful to other inquirers, and to treat the results of others fairly, recognizing their merits rather than simply emphasizing their weaknesses and deficiencies. Someone who failed to see strong reason to do these things could be said not to understand or not to care about the value of science, and to be in it just for the sake of money or fame or the thrill of competition.

Third, if science is valuable then those of us who are not scientists have reason to support scientific work as taxpayers or benefactors. Fourth, we have reason to study science and try to understand it. If science is valuable, then this kind of study is worthwhile, even if our understanding will always be highly imperfect. Finally, we have reason to respect science as an undertaking and to admire its achievements and those who make them.

One might try to account for all these reasons on a strictly teleological basis. Such an account could hold that the value of science lies, fundamentally, in the value of certain states of affairs: a world in which fundamental truths about nature are understood or investigated is for that reason a better world. People have reason to take up science as a career if they would be able to contribute to bringing about these valuable results. They have reason to be "good scientists" because by doing this they are likely to make a greater contribution of this kind. Others have reason to promote and support scientific work because this also promotes these valuable results. It is a little more difficult to explain, on this basis, why nonscientists have reason to study it. Perhaps this might be explained by broadening the class of valuable states to include the spread of even imperfect understanding. But it is easy to see why scientific work should be admired, namely, because it produces valuable results.

Such a view has great simplicity and evident appeal. It is much more plausible than the analogous claim that all the reasons involved in valuing friendship flow from the goodness of having friendships occur. But I do not think that such a view offers the most plausible account of the intrinsic value of science and scientific knowledge. To see this, consider first what the valuable states of affairs on which such a view would be based might be taken to be.

First, through their applications in technology, scientific achievements contribute to enlarging the range of things we can do, and to making our lives longer, safer, and more comfortable. These effects are no doubt valuable, but since they are not what people have in mind in claiming that scientific knowledge is *intrinsically* valuable, I will set them aside.

Second, engaging in scientific study and inquiry can be challenging, exciting, and absorbing, and it therefore enriches the lives of those who engage in it. But other pursuits are also challenging, exciting, and absorbing: mountain climbing and yacht racing, for example. Insofar as scientific inquiry is thought to make a greater contribution than these pursuits to the quality of the lives of those who engage in it, this is, I assume, because it is thought to be a more worthwhile way to use one's time and talents. Perhaps it is thought worthwhile because of the practical benefits I have just mentioned, but I do not believe that this is the only reason. If it is not, then the distinctive contribution that devoting one's life to scientific activity makes to the quality of that life depends on the fact that the activity is intrinsically worthwhile, rather than the value of the activity depending on its contribution to the well-being of those who engage in it.

This suggests that the distinctive intrinsic value of science must derive, on a purely teleological account, from the fact that states of affairs in which scientific knowledge has been attained (and perhaps also ones in which scientific inquiry is engaged in in the right way) are better states of affairs and therefore "to be promoted." This way of putting the matter leads to some puzzling questions. Suppose that what is intrinsically valuable is true belief about the world, particularly about its most fundamental features. There is the slight problem that at any given time much of what science holds to be true about the most fundamental features of nature is likely to be false. Perhaps, then, it is valuable because it is a step on the way to attaining true belief. Or perhaps what is valuable is not just the true belief that results from scientific inquiry, but the occurrence of that inquiry itself, at least when it is done well. This is in some ways more plausible, but we would then need an independent explanation of how the value of science gives even nonscientists reason to try to understand it, to the degree that they can.

The mere fact that there are problems about how this view should be formulated does not, of course, show that it is mistaken. In my view what is most implausible about such an account, however, is the basic idea that we should understand all the reasons we have to engage in, support, and study science by first identifying some class of ways that it would be better for the world to be, and then explaining these reasons by considering how the activities they count in favor of help to make the world be like this. There are some cases in which this order of explanation seems very plausible, as in the case of pain. A state of affairs in which I am in pain is, for that reason, a worse state of affairs for me, and this fact gives rise to reasons to do what is necessary to prevent it. But it is not always possible to identify outcomes whose independent value can plausibly be seen as a source of the reasons we have. In particular, even though the actions involved in scientific inquiry and study are each aimed at some end, the best account of our reasons for those actions may not flow *from* the value of these results *to* our concern with them.

An alternative line of explanation would begin with the idea that we have good reason to be curious about the natural world and to try to understand how it works. A person who responds to nature in this way is right to do so, and someone who fails to have this response is missing something. Since science is by far the most successful attempt at such understanding, studying it and trying to contribute to it are things we have reason to do: both are rational responses to our justified curiosity about the world. It follows that I have reason to adopt the goal of reading good books about science for laymen, and that scientists have reason to adopt the goal of coming up with new and better theories (quite apart from the usefulness of the knowledge that may be so gained). So we each correctly regard the achievement of these goals as good (even intrinsically good). But this is a conclusion from the claims about reasons I have mentioned, not their source.

Things look slightly different in this respect when we consider the matter from the point of view of a patron or benefactor, someone who gives money to support scientific research, or to educate the public about science. Such a person is properly moved by the thought that it is good that scientific research should occur and that more people should appreciate its results. The reasons that move such a person are like those that figure in the Moorean perspective I mentioned earlier, and like some reasons that could move a person to promote the friendships of others. I am not suggesting that they are not good reasons, but only that they are not as central as might be supposed to the idea of the value of science.

A similar divergence of perspectives shows up when we consider two other reasons for thinking that the pursuit of scientific knowledge is a good thing to have occur. For example, science is to be admired and promoted because it is a form of human excellence, involving highly developed intellectual skills devoted to questions that merit inquiry. But from the point of view of practitioners of science, the reason for striving and thinking in the ways that constitute this excellence is that this is the best way of inquiring into their subject, not simply that it produces instances of excellence. Science may also merit our respect and admiration as a complex cooperative endeavor, extending over time and yoking together the highly developed capacities of many individuals. Someone who failed to appreciate this human and social aspect of science, and valued it only for its results, would be missing something important. But from the point of view of a practitioner, understanding this aspect of the value of science involves seeing reasons to respect the norms of the scientific community, not just reasons to think it good that that community exists.

It might seem that there is small difference at best between this account of the value of science and a purely teleological one. If fundamental questions about the natural world are worth inquiring into, doesn't this mean that the results produced by this inquiry, if it succeeds, are good? Otherwise, why would they be worth striving for?

In one sense this is quite true: if a state of affairs is worth striving for, then it is good. But there remains an important question about the order of explanation. What I am suggesting is that if we want to understand why scientific inquiry is worth engaging in and its results worth studying, we do better to consider why the questions it addresses are important and why it offers an appropriate way of trying to answer them than to focus on any particular results that scientific investigation or the study of science might produce (by, say, imagining a world containing a great scientific discovery, or one containing someone with the very imperfect understanding of quantum mechanics that I could attain by studying it in my spare time). Such results are, I believe, worth striving for, but to see why this is so we need to look elsewhere. If we begin with the reasonableness and appropriateness of curiosity about the world, and with the merits of science as a way of responding to this curiosity, this leads next to the various more specific ways in which responses to this curiosity can be incorporated into our lives. We thus arrive at a unified explanation of the various reasons mentioned above: reasons to devote oneself to science if one has the ability and opportunity, reasons to support it as a patron, reasons for others to try to understand it to the degree that they can, and so on. These are reasons to adopt certain goals and to regard their attainment as good. But, as I suggested above in discussing Scheffler's remarks about rationality, from the fact that deciding how to pursue one's goals plays an important part in practical thinking we should not conclude that goals are where all explanations of value must begin.

4. An Abstract Account of Value

The examples of friendship and science suggest the following general picture. We value many different kinds of things, including at least the following: objects and their properties (such as beauty), persons, skills and talents, states of character, actions, accomplishments, activities and pursuits, relationships, and ideals. To value something is to take oneself to have reasons for holding certain positive attitudes toward it and for acting in certain ways in regard to it. Exactly what these reasons are, and what actions and attitudes they support, will be different in different cases. They generally include, as a common core, reasons for admiring the thing and for respecting it, although "respecting" can involve quite different things in different cases. Often, valuing something involves seeing reasons to preserve and protect it (as, for example, when I value a historic building); in other cases it involves reasons to be guided by the goals and standards that the value involves (as when I value loyalty); in some cases both may be involved (as when I value the U.S. Constitution).[16]

To claim that something is valu*able* (or that it is "of value") is to claim that others also have reason to value it, as you do. We can, quite properly, value some things more than others without claiming that they are more valuable. So, for example, it is natural to say, and would be odd to deny, that I value my children; but it would be odd for me to put this by saying that they are valuable (except in the sense that everyone is). The reason behind this oddness is the one just mentioned: claiming that something is valuable involves claiming that its attributes merit being valued generally, and valuing one's own children above others, in the sense in which we all do this, lacks this impersonal quality and this dependence on what is merited or called for by their attributes. The present discussion of value is about what it is to be valuable rather than about valuing. I have discussed the latter only because it provides a helpful stepping-stone.

It is helpful in part because it draws attention to the variety of things that can be valuable and the variety of reasons that are involved in their being valuable. Believing that something is valuable can involve believing that there is reason to promote its existence, but it does not always involve this. Commonly, as we saw in the cases of friendship and scientific knowledge, the judgment that something is valuable depends on further judgments about what things there is reason to bring about. As we saw in those cases, however, these judgments do not exhaust the relevant ideas of value, and they need not all flow from a central judgment about what it would be good to have exist or occur.

What I have sketched here is an abstract description of the structure of the idea of value, which contrasts with the familiar teleological conception of this structure. It is not a "theory" of value: neither a systematic account of which things are valuable, nor an explanation of the "source" of value. My account contains two separate elements, which are independent and should be distinguished. One is the idea, emphasized in the preceding section, that value is not a purely tele-ological notion. The other is the claim that being valuable is not a property that provides us with reasons. Rather, to call something valuable is to say that it has other properties that provide reasons for behaving in certain ways with regard to it. I am led to this "buck-pass-ing" account of value by the following reflections on Moore's open-question argument about 'good'.[17]

We judge things to be good or to be valuable because of other properties that they have. Often these are physical or psychological properties, as, for example, when we judge something to be good because it is pleasant, or judge a discovery to be valuable because it provides new understanding of how cancer cells develop. But being good or valuable cannot be identified with any such "natural" prop-erty or, more generally, with any non-normative property. This is the lesson of the open-question argument. The question "X is pleasant, but is it good?" has what Moore called an "open feel." That is to say, it seems clearly to be a real question, and Moore pointed out that the same will be true of any question of the form "X is P, but is it good?" where 'P' is a term for some natural or metaphysical property. This openness, which marks questions about value as well as about good, can be explained in the following way.

Judgments about what is good or valuable generally express practi-cal conclusions about what would, at least under the right conditions, be reasons for acting or responding in a certain way. Natural or "metaphysical" facts may provide the grounds for such practical con-clusions, as the facts that a thing is pleasant, or casts light on the causes of cancer, do in the examples I just gave. Judging that these facts obtain need not involve explicitly drawing these conclusions, however. Questions such as "This is C, but is it valuable?" (where 'C' is a term for some natural or "metaphysical" property) therefore have an open feel, because they explicitly ask whether a certain practical conclusion is to be drawn. Even if one believes that the properties that 'C' refers to provide grounds for drawing this conclusion, just saying that something has these properties does not involve drawing it. So the question feels "open" even if one believes that the answer to it is "yes."

But even if being valuable cannot be identified with having any set of natural properties, it remains true that a thing's having these properties can be grounds for concluding that it is valuable. What, then, are the relations between these natural properties, the property of being valuable, and the reasons that we have for behaving in certain ways in regard to things that are valuable? There seem to be two possibilities. The first is that when something has the right natural properties it has the further property of being valuable, and that property gives us reason to behave or react in certain ways with regard to it. Moore seems to be taking this view about goodness when he says that it is a simple, unanalyzable, non-natural property. The alternative, which I believe to be correct, is to hold that being good, or valuable, is not a property that itself provides a reason to respond to a thing in certain ways. Rather, to be good or valuable is to have other properties that constitute such reasons.[18] Since the claim that some property constitutes a reason is a normative claim, this account also takes goodness and value to be non-natural properties, namely the purely formal, higher-order properties of having some lower-order properties that provide reasons of the relevant kind. It differs from the first alternative simply in holding that it is not goodness or value itself that provides reasons but rather other properties that do so. For this reason I call it a buck-passing account.

Buck-passing accounts of goodness and of value are supported in two ways by intuitions about the reasons we have to choose, prefer, recommend, and admire things that are valuable. First, when I consider particular cases it seems that these reasons are provided by the natural properties that make a thing good or valuable. So, for example, the fact that a resort is pleasant is a reason to visit it or to recommend it to a friend, and the fact that a discovery casts light on the causes of cancer is a reason to applaud it and to support further research of that kind. These natural properties provide a complete explanation of the reasons we have for reacting in these ways to things that are good or valuable. It is not clear what further work could be done by special reason-providing properties of goodness and value, and even less clear how these properties could provide reasons.

A second source of support for a buck-passing account is the fact that many different things can be said to be good or to be valuable, and the grounds for these judgments vary widely. There does not seem to be a single, reason-providing property that is common to all these cases. The most likely candidate might be "being the object of desire." But, as I argued in Chapter 1, the fact that I desire something does not itself provide me with a reason to pursue it. Being an object of a rational or "informed" desire may be correlated with the presence of such reasons, but these reasons are provided not by this hypothetical desire, but by the considerations that would give rise to it, or make it "rational."

I therefore accept buck-passing accounts of both goodness and value. One could accept such an account while still holding a purely teleological conception of value, since nothing in the argument just given rules out the possibility that the reasons associated with something's being valuable are all reasons to promote it, or perhaps to promote states of affairs in which it figures in various ways.[19] My rejection of the latter view is based on the consideration of examples like those mentioned earlier, in which being valuable involves there being reasons to act or to respond in a wider variety of ways.

One natural objection to this very abstract account of value is that it represents an objectionable form of intuitionism, because it holds that judgments about value involve appeals to diverse intuitions about what is "fitting" or "appropriate." There are two ways of taking this objection: one methodological, the other substantive. As far as the first is concerned, it is true that my argument has proceeded by calling attention to what might be called "linguistic intuitions," that is, to the fact that much of what we say about values and what is valuable does not fit the model according to which value is a matter of being "to be promoted." Even if I am right in my claims about what we usually say, this of course does not settle the matter. We need to decide whether we have reason to go on making these claims or whether, on reflection, we think we should revise our practice, perhaps bringing it more into line with this familiar teleological model. This choice is not between "appeals to intuition" and some other form of argument. Rather, it is a matter of deciding which of our "intuitions" best stands the test of careful reflection. Here we must use the method I described in Chapter 1 as applying to any decision about what reasons we have. The charge of appealing to "intuition" does not favor one answer over the other.

It is also true, as the substantive version of the objection would charge, that if we accept a view of the kind I have described then our subsequent thinking about value may be messier (and involve more independent appeals to "intuitions" of appropriateness) than it would if we adopted some more regimented and unified account, such as one that identified value with certain specific quantities that are to be maximized. But if this is true it will be true only because we have decided, in accepting the account I describe, that these diverse questions of appropriateness are indeed relevant. It would be a mistake to ignore judgments that we in fact take to be relevant just for the sake of greater neatness in our thinking.[20]

The complexity that judgments of value have on the account I am offering is thus not, in my view, an objection to that account. Once one recognizes the variety of things that can be valuable and the variety of responses that their value calls for, it becomes highly implausible that there could be a systematic "theory of value." Understanding the value of something is not just a matter of knowing *how valuable* it is, but rather a matter of knowing how to value it—knowing what kinds of actions and attitudes are called for. It is an advantage of the present account that it calls attention to this aspect of our ideas of value, one that is easily concealed by the assumption that the primary question about the value of something is *how great* that value is.[21]

This distinction—between the question of how valuable something is, and the question of how it is to be valued—can be seen clearly in the case of the value of art and music. It might be tempting to trace the value of these pursuits to its being good that certain forms of experience or enjoyment should occur. There surely are good reasons to want these experiences to occur, and they provide good grounds for supporting museums, concerts, and public education in the arts. But these reasons do not constitute a complete account of the values in question. This can be brought out by considering the different ways in which people might disagree about these values. One kind of disagreement would be about *how valuable* this kind of experience is, and whether it is worth the effort and resources that would be needed to produce it. This is an important kind of disagreement. But another kind of disagreement one might have about musical experience is not about how valuable it is, but rather about the attitude with which one should approach it: is it to be savored or contemplated in a serious and concentrated way, or taken more lightheartedly, even casually, as something diverting and amusing?[22]

These are only two among many possible answers, and different answers will be appropriate when different music is in question. A disagreement of this kind is not just a disagreement about the mood and outlook that are necessary in order to induce the kind of experience it is valuable to have but, rather, a disagreement about the attitudes one should have toward that experience itself. It would be very natural and appropriate for one person to say of someone else with whom he or she disagrees on this question that that person "does not understand the value of this kind of music." Having recordings of Beethoven's late quartets played in the elevators, hallways, and restrooms of an office building, for example, would show a failure to understand the value of music of this kind. What I am suggesting is not that this would show a lack of respect for this music, but rather that it shows a lack of understanding of what one should expect from it, and in what way it is worth attending to. The question of what music, if any, to play in such a setting may not be a weighty one. But it illustrates a point of more general importance: that understanding the value of something often involves not merely knowing that it is valuable or how valuable it is, but also how it is to be valued.

5. The Shadow of Hedonism

If, then, many of the things commonly recognized as values fail to fit the model according to which thinking about value starts from the idea that certain states of affairs are "to be promoted," this raises the question of why teleological conceptions of value have had such wide appeal.

One hypothesis is that this conception of value arises as a corollary of hedonism but then persists after hedonism is abandoned. If a simple form of hedonism were correct as an account of value—if the only things valuable in themselves were pleasure and the absence of pain—then value would have a teleological structure.[23] On such a view, states of affairs would be the bearers of value; they would be more or less valuable depending on the amount of pleasure and pain they contained; and the reasons generated by value would all be of the same simple form: reasons to bring about the most valuable states of affairs. Hedonism is no longer widely accepted as a theory of value, but even those who reject it may retain the assumption that whatever the correct account of value may be it will have this same form.

This line of thinking certainly plays a role in discussions of consequentialism about right and wrong. It is often said that utilitarianism was a conjunction of consequentialism, the view that the morally right action is the one with the best consequences, and hedonism, the view that "best" is to be understood in terms of pleasure and the absence of pain. Hedonism, it is then said, is not a satisfactory account of value and should be rejected, but this leaves consequentialism, which should be retained since it has great plausibility considered apart from any particular account of what "the good" is.[24]

This way of looking at things strikes me as revealing but not convincing. If a simple form of hedonism were the correct account of value, then there would be a sharp distinction between actions, which have no intrinsic value, and their consequences, states of affairs, whose intrinsic value is determined by the amount of pleasure and pain that they involve. This makes consequentialism about right and wrong—the claim that the moral status of actions is determined by the amount of value they lead to—more plausible. If hedonism is rejected, however, then one natural source of support for the idea that value always has a teleological structure is lost. An abstract form of consequentialism about right and wrong—the doctrine that the morally right action is the one with the best consequences, whatever 'best' may mean—is not left standing in the way suggested above, since it is no longer so clear that "the good" (understood as summing up our conception of value) is something that inheres in states of affairs and is to be "maximized." This is not to say that consequentialism could not be reformulated on the basis of some other conception of value. The point is that its plausibility will depend on the plausibility of some substantive conception of value that, like hedonism, has a teleological form.[25]

One alternative is the idea that the value of a state of affairs is determined by the levels of well-being of the individual lives that occur in it. I will consider this idea in the next chapter. Teleology about value also draws support from the fact that even if hedonism is false as a general account of value, there are nonetheless a number of important values which seem to fit the model of "states of affairs to be promoted." Pain and death are obvious examples: it is plausible to claim that their normative significance consists simply in the fact that they are to be avoided or, in the case of death, postponed as long as possible. These values figure prominently in examples that are cited to trigger our consequentialist intuitions. ("Suppose you were faced with a choice between one action, which will lead to the painful death of one innocent person, and another, which will lead to the deaths of five . . .")

As these cases illustrate, pain and death very often provide reasons by contributing to the value or disvalue of states of affairs, which we then have reason to promote or prevent. But pleasure, pain, and death, important though they are, do not exhaust the range of values and disvalues, and, for reasons pointed out above, they are not in this respect representative of many other values. Moreover, examples of the kind just mentioned, taken in isolation, do not give us a complete picture of these values themselves. Consider the case of death. In addition to the questions of whether death is bad, and of how bad it is, there are further questions of the kinds I have mentioned above about how this disvalue is to be understood. Since death is bad just in case it would be better to live longer rather than have one's life end, the disvalue of death is just one aspect of the positive value of life. So questions about how this value is to be understood include such questions as: How should our thinking about the value of life be affected by the fact that it is finite? What attitude should we have toward this fact? fear? resignation? How should we take account of the possibility of death in deciding how to live? I do not think that satisfactory answers to these questions can all be read off from a proper assessment of how bad a thing it would be to die in various ways at various points in one's life. The reverse is more plausible: the quantitative judgments we arrive at in particular cases are best seen as flowing from, and shaped by, a set of more general attitudes of the kind I am describing. But these questions of attitude will be left out if we focus simply on the idea that death is to be avoided and on asking how bad it is to die sooner rather than later.

This illustrates a general point that I mentioned in discussing Scheffler's appeal to the maximizing conception of rationality. Paraphrasing Scheffler, if it is my goal to avoid dying, and I have a choice between two options, one of which is more certain to accomplish this goal than the other, then it is rational, *ceteris paribus,* to choose this option. But understanding the disvalue of death is in large part a matter of understanding when and in what ways I should make this my goal, and when to regard other things as "equal." This important dimension of value is left out when one focuses simply on a goal, taken as given, and on consequent reasons for achieving it.

Similar remarks apply to pain. We can ask not only "How bad is it?" but also "What kind of concern should we give to preventing it?" In the case of pain and death these questions of attitude and interpretation may seem minor in relation to the reasons we have simply to avoid them. I believe that this reaction is mistaken even in those cases, but this error is more obvious in the case of some forms of pleasure, particularly those pleasures that have a high degree of intentional content (that is, the pleasure depends on having a certain belief) and in which this content involves other people. Examples would be the pleasure of competition, the pleasure of successful cooperation, the pleasure of shared laughter, sexual pleasure, and the pleasure of being admired by someone whom you respect. These pleasures involve specific relations with other people, and specific attitudes toward them and toward our relations with them. (The pleasure of winning in a competition, for example, generally involves thinking that triumphing in this way is something worth seeking.) The judgment that an instance of one of these pleasures is "good"—that a state of affairs involving it is "to be promoted"—thus depends on prior judgments about the appropriateness of the behavior and attitudes toward others that it involves. Understanding the value of these pleasures, then, is a matter of understanding this larger evaluative framework. This may not be true of all pleasures—some, like some pains, have little if any intentional or evaluative content—but it is true of many.

It appears, then, that the values we recognize do not, in general, have a simple teleological structure. Although recognizing these values involves seeing that there are reasons to promote various states of affairs, not all the reasons they involve have this form. One might defend the idea that our thinking about value is nevertheless teleological at the most fundamental level by arguing that all the values I have mentioned—pleasures, the avoidance of pain and death, friendship, and the achievement of artistic and intellectual excellence—are of value only insofar as they contribute to individuals' well-being, and that well-being is a value that is "to be promoted." What individuals have reason to do (considering themselves alone) is to promote their own well-being, and what is important from a moral point of view is the well-being of people generally. I will consider this idea of well-being as a master value in the next chapter. Before turning to that, however, I want to consider further the question of the value of human life.

6. The Value of Human (or Rational) Life

We all agree that human life is of great value. The question is how this value should be understood. One thing that the claim that human life is valuable might be thought to entail is that it is a good thing that human, or rational, life exists—that a world is made better by containing it. Perhaps this is so, but what is central to that value is not a matter of anything's existence being good in this sense—not, for example, a matter of the world's being made better by there being more human life rather than less.

It is true that appreciating the value of human life involves seeing that we have strong reason not to destroy it and reason to protect it when we can. Given that we have reason to do these things—to aim at preserving human life and at not destroying it—and given that we believe that others have these reasons as well, we also have reason to think it a bad thing when we or others fail in these aims. But this thought is a derivative one, which follows from the reasons we have to preserve life and not to destroy it. Those reasons themselves do not flow from the thought that it is a good thing for there to be more human life rather than less. This is shown by the fact that while we have strong reasons to protect human life and not to destroy it, we do not have the very same reasons to create more human life when we can. Insofar as we have reasons to create new life, these are different from, and weaker than, our reasons not to destroy it. But these reasons would be the same if they all flowed from the fact that the existence of a human life is a good thing.

Appreciating the value of human life is primarily a matter of seeing human lives as something to be respected, where this involves seeing reasons not to destroy them, reasons to protect them, and reasons to want them to go well. Many of the most powerful of these reasons, however, are matters of respect and concern for the person whose life it is rather than of respect for human life, or for this instance of human life, in a more abstract sense. The difference between these two forms of respect comes to the fore in cases of euthanasia and suicide.[26]

Suppose a person is in an irreversible coma. Would it show a lack of the respect called for by the value of human life to end this life by withholding food and other life supports, or to fail to protect it by providing protection against disease? Would a person who faces a life of endless unremitting and incapacitating pain show a lack of respect for his or her own life by seeking to end it? These questions are controversial, but I believe that the answer in both cases is "No." This suggests that while appreciating the value of human life involves seeing that there are strong reasons for protecting life and for not destroying it, these reasons are restricted by the qualification "as long as the person whose life it is has reason to go on living or wants to live."

Just as murder shows a lack of respect for human life, there can be cases in which suicide does so as well. We might say, of a person who commits suicide out of a cynical conviction that nothing is worth doing, or out of disappointment at being rejected by a lover, that he or she showed a lack of understanding of the value of life and allowed it to be wasted. One could say the same thing of a person who stayed alive but spent his life in utter idleness or mired in cynical nihilism. What such people have in common with the criticizable suicides just mentioned is a failure to see the reasons they have to go on living, reasons provided, for example, by their possible accomplishments, by the good they might do for others, and by the pleasures they could attain. This leads toward the idea that, at least from the point of view of the person whose life it is, the value of life may be identified with the reasons one has for living it. This would be in line with the conclusion reached earlier, that we have reason to protect a life only insofar as the person whose life it is has reason to go on living it or wants to do so. We might say, then, that recognizing the value of human life is a matter of respecting each human being as a locus of reasons, that is to say, recognizing the force of their reasons for wanting to live and wanting their lives to go better.

This view is still unsatisfactory for at least two reasons. The first is that, as stated, it is open to an "ideal observer" interpretation, which takes appreciating the value of human life to be a matter of recognizing the force of all the reasons that various human beings have. (This is like what Nagel calls the objective point of view.) Unless more is said, this is impossibly unwieldy, since we cannot respond to or even contemplate all these reasons at once. It is not adequate simply to say that we are entirely free to choose which of these reasons to respond to (in the way that we are free to choose which, if any, of the various worthwhile forms of excellence we want to give a role in our lives). An adequate account of the value of human life needs to say more about the claim that these reasons have on us.[27]

The second objection points us in the direction of a solution to this problem. While the view just described recognizes what is distinctive about human or, more generally, rational life by characterizing us as creatures who have reasons, it does not exploit the full depth of this characterization. What it mentions is that we are creatures who have reason to want certain things to happen. This presupposes, but does not mention, that we are creatures who have the capacity to assess reasons and justifications. It also does not mention that we have the capacity to select among the various ways there is reason to want a life to go, and therefore to govern and live that life in an active sense.

Appreciating the value of human life must involve recognizing and respecting these distinctive capacities.

Taken together, these two objections suggest the following view. We cannot respond to all the reasons that every human creature has for wanting his or her life to go well; so we must select among these reasons; and we should do this in a way that recognizes the capacity of human beings, as rational creatures, to assess reasons and to govern their lives according to this assessment. In my view the best response to these two considerations is this: respecting the value of human (rational) life requires us to treat rational creatures only in ways that would be allowed by principles that they could not reasonably reject insofar as they, too, were seeking principles of mutual governance which other rational creatures could not reasonably reject. This responds to the problem of selecting among reasons in a way that recognizes our distinctive capacities as reason-assessing, self-governing creatures.[28]

I do not claim that this is the only possible response to the problem of understanding the requirements of valuing human life, much less that I have offered a strict argument for it. This idea does, however, seem to me the best and most plausible response to the considerations I listed. In the remainder of this book I will argue for this same idea as the best understanding of our ideas of right and wrong, or of "what we owe to each other." Taken together, these two arguments provide a way of reconciling the general perspective of value with that of morality in the narrow sense.

As I said at the beginning of this chapter, there is often thought to be a sharp tension between these realms—between what is sometimes called "deontological morality" on the one hand and our ideas of value on the other. What I have tried to show here is that this tension is exaggerated. Being valuable is not always simply a matter of being "to be promoted." Most of the things properly recognized as values have a more complex structure. So rights and duties should not be seen as odd because they do not take this simple form. Moreover, one plausible understanding (to my mind the most plausible) of one paramount value, the value of human life, leads directly to the core of the morality of right and wrong. Looking back, it seems to me that this is what one should expect: the idea of valuing human life and the idea of respecting one's duties and other people's rights ought to be closely related, if not the very same thing. One way for this to be true is the one described by consequentialism, according to which ideas of right, wrong, and obligation are made subservient to a purely teleological conception of the good. As I have just said, I believe that there is another way to achieve this reconciliation, one that gives a more fundamental role to considerations of right and wrong. I will begin developing that side of my argument in Part II, after considering the idea of well-being in more detail.

3

Well-Being

1. Introduction

The account of values offered in the previous chapter was pluralistic and not, at base, teleological. I argued that there are many independent values and denied that to be valuable is always to be "to be promoted." Against these claims, both the unity of value and its teleological structure might be defended by arguing that all other things are of value only insofar as they contribute to individual well-being and that this value is teleological in form: it is something that is "to be promoted." In the present chapter I will argue that this claim is mistaken. Well-being is not a "master value" in this sense. In this regard, the present chapter looks back to the preceding one and attempts to complete its argument. But it also looks forward to the chapters to come insofar as it seeks to characterize and assess the importance of the notion of well-being, which has generally been taken to be of particular importance for moral argument.

It is commonly supposed that there is a single notion of individual well-being that plays the following three roles. First, it serves as an important basis for the decisions of a single rational individual, at least for those decisions in which he or she alone is concerned (that is to say, in which moral obligations and concerns for others can be left aside). Second, it is what a concerned benefactor, such as a friend or parent, has reason to promote. Third, it is the basis on which an individual's interests are taken into account in moral argument. This last claim is most plausible when the morality in question is utilitarian, since on a utilitarian account the moral point of view is just the point of view of a benefactor who is impartially concerned with everyone, and hence, if the second claim is correct, with the well-being of everyone. But it is commonly said that any moral theory, even a nonutilitarian one, must rely on a notion of individual well-being insofar as it acknowledges a general duty of benevolence and particular duties to care for others (such as the duties of parents toward their children), and insofar as it holds that moral principles are to be justified, at least in part, by the impact they have on individuals' lives.

Well-being is supposed to play all three of the roles I have just listed, but the first of these roles is generally held to be primary: well-being is important in the thinking of a benefactor and in moral argument because of its importance for the individual whose well-being it is. In particular, although the notion of well-being is important *for* morality, it is not itself a moral notion. It represents what an individual has reason to want for him- or herself, leaving aside concern for others and any moral restraints or obligations. Well-being is thus an input into moral thinking that is not already shaped by moral assumptions.

Well-being is also commonly supposed to be a notion that admits of quantitative comparisons of at least some of the following kinds: comparisons of the levels of well-being enjoyed by different individuals under various circumstances, comparisons of the increments in a single individual's well-being that would result from various changes, and perhaps also comparisons of the amounts of well-being represented by different lives, considered as a whole. It is taken to be an important task (important both for moral theory and for theories of "rationality" or "prudence") to come up with a theory of well-being: a systematic account of "what makes someone's life go better" that clarifies the boundary of this concept (the line between those things that contribute to a person's well-being and those that are desirable on other grounds) and perhaps provides a clearer basis for quantitative comparisons of the kinds just mentioned.

I will argue in this chapter that many of these suppositions are mistaken. To put the point briefly: it is a mistake to think that there is a single notion of well-being that plays all the roles I have mentioned and that we need a theory of well-being to clarify this concept. We do have a rough intuitive idea of individual well-being, and we can make rough comparative judgments about what makes a life go better and worse from the point of view of the person who lives it. But this concept of well-being has surprisingly little role to play in the thinking of the rational individual whose life is in question. It sounds absurd to say that individuals have no reason to be concerned with their own well-being, because this seems to imply that they have no reason to be concerned with those things that make their lives better. Clearly they do have reason to be concerned with these things. But in regard to their own lives they have little need to use the concept of well-being itself, either in giving justifications or in drawing distinctions. In particular, individuals have no need for a theory that would clarify the boundaries of their own well-being and provide a basis for sharper quantitative comparisons.

From a third-person point of view, such as that of a parent or benefactor, a notion of well-being has greater significance. In moral thinking, also, we may need to appeal to various conceptions of well-being and to make comparisons of how well-off people would be under various conditions, as measured by these conceptions. But what are employed in moral argument are generally not notions of well-being that individuals would use to evaluate their own lives but, rather, various moral conceptions of how well-off a person is—that is to say, conceptions that are shaped by one or another idea of what we owe to and can claim from one another. This is most obvious in political philosophy in the various standards that have been proposed as measures of distributive shares for purposes of assessing claims of justice, such as Rawls's primary social goods (income and wealth, powers and liberties, and the social bases of self-respect) and Sen's capability sets (which include the "functionings" such as good health, ability to take part in social life, and so on of which an individual is capable).[1] From an individual's own perspective, these criteria offer very incomplete measures of how well his or her life is going. One life might be much better than another from an individual's point of view—happier, more successful, and so on—even though the two lives were the same as measured by Rawls's or Sen's criteria. This divergence is due to the fact that these criteria are supposed to measure only those aspects of a life that, according to the theories in question, it is the responsibility of basic social institutions to provide for. I believe that the conceptions of well-being that figure in moral thinking more generally can be expected to diverge in similar ways from the conceptions that individuals might use in assessing their own lives. Whether they diverge or not, however, these conceptions of well-being will be moral conceptions, that is to say, they derive their significance, and to a certain extent their distinctive shape, from their role in the moral structures in which they figure.

My argument will proceed as follows. In the next two sections I will identify the intuitive question of well-being that I am discussing and identify some of the fixed points that any plausible theory of well-being in this sense would have to preserve. I will then argue that the concept of one's own well-being in the sense thus characterized has little role to play in the thinking of a rational individual, and that in thinking about his or her own life an individual has no need for a theory of well-being that would, for example, clarify the boundaries of this concept. After defending this claim I will return to the question of the significance of well-being from third-person and moral perspectives.

2. Questions of Well-Being

The notion of well-being that I am concerned with here is, though somewhat vague, nonetheless intuitively familiar and widely discussed. It is, for example, the subject of James Griffin's book *Well-Being* and of Derek Parfit's well-known discussion of "What Makes Someone's Life Go Best?"[2] Both of these discussions take up the question of well-being partly because of its significance for morality, but both treat it as a question that, first and foremost, can be asked by, and is important to, the person whose life it is. Even when we focus on assessments of a life from this perspective—the point of view of the person whose life it is—there are a number of different questions that can be asked. To identify the question of well-being with which I am concerned it will be helpful to begin by distinguishing it from four other ideas of "the quality of a life" with which it might be confused.

On one natural interpretation, the quality of life can mean the quality of the conditions under which life is lived, including such things as protection against illness and danger, access to nutrition, the availability of education, and other opportunities and resources. Quality of life in this sense, which might be called "material and social conditions," seems to be what we have in mind, for example, when we say that the quality of life in Japan or Sweden is higher than in Somalia. Although there may be disagreements about what they include, the idea of material and social conditions is a relatively clear one, and it captures one important aspect of a life, viewed from the point of view of the person who lives it. But well-being, viewed from that point of view, includes more than this: one person can have a much better life than another—much happier and more successful, for example—even though their lives are lived under equally good or bad material and social conditions.

The phrase "from the point of view of the person who lives it" calls to mind a second aspect of a life, namely its experiential quality, or "what it would be like to live it." Like material welfare, experiential quality is a relatively clear notion, and an important one. We all care about the experiential quality of our lives, and have reason to do so. It has sometimes been claimed that the quality of a life in the sense I am concerned with—the level of well-being it represents—is completely determined by its experiential quality.[3] This is a substantive claim, one which can sensibly be denied. It makes sense to say that the life of a person who is contented and happy only because he is systematically deceived about what his life is really like is for that reason a worse life, for him, than a life would be that was similarly happy where this happiness was based on true beliefs. To take the standard example, it makes sense to say that the life of a person who is happy only because he does not know that the people whom he regards as devoted friends are in fact artful deceivers is worse, for the person who lives it, than a similar life in which the person is made happy by true friends. I myself believe that this claim not only makes sense but is in fact true. Even if I am mistaken, however, and experiential quality is the complete and correct answer to the question of well-being, this is not true by definition. So the question of well-being and the question of experiential quality are not the same question.

A third interpretation of the quality of a life is the degree to which it is particularly admirable and worthy of respect—what I will call its worthiness or value. Value in this sense is, again, clearly distinct from well-being. The life of a person who sacrifices his own well-being for the sake of others may be, for that reason, a particularly valuable one, and in order for this to be true there must be a sacrifice involved.

The question of whether a person should prefer such a life of sacrifice over the available alternatives would be an example of what I will call the question of choiceworthiness. Each of the first three notions I have considered—material welfare, experiential quality, and worthiness or value—is a factor that may bear on the choiceworthiness of a life. So also is well-being in the sense I am discussing. We might say, for example, that there is reason to choose a certain life because of its great value, even though it involves a low level of well-being, or that the value of a life did not in fact make it worth choosing given the sacrifice in well-being that it would involve.[4] So choiceworthiness is a different notion from any of the other four taken alone.

The intuitive notion of well-being that I am concerned with, then, is an idea of the quality of a life for the person who lives it that is broader than material and social conditions, at least potentially broader than experiential quality, different from worthiness or value, and narrower than choiceworthiness all things considered. Having roughly identified the question of well-being and distinguished it from some others, I want now to consider how this question might be answered.

3. Accounts of Well-Being

Answers to the question "What makes someone's life go better?" are commonly divided into three types: experiential theories, desire theories, and "objective list," or, as I will call them, "substantive good" theories.[5] Experiential theories hold that the quality of a life for the person who lives it is determined completely by what I called above its experiential quality. Desire theories hold that the quality of a person's life is a matter of the extent to which that person's desires are satisfied. The hallmark of such views, as I will understand them, is that there is no standard apart from a person's desires for assessing the quality of his or her life. Substantive-good theories are just those that deny this claim, and hold that there are standards for assessing the quality of a life that are not entirely dependent on the desires of the person whose life it is. On this way of looking at things, experiential theories count as one kind of substantive-good theory, since they deny that the fulfillment of desires for things other than states of consciousness can make a life better.[6]

Experiential theories provide a clear boundary for the concept of well-being: something contributes to well-being if, but only if, it affects the quality of one's experience. This clarity can be seen as a theoretical advantage; the problem, however, is that these boundaries are implausibly narrow. The difference between true and false friends, which I have already mentioned, is only one obvious example of the ways in which the quality of a life, for the person who lives it, depends on factors that go beyond its experiential quality.

Desire theories can accommodate these factors, since they hold that a person's life can be made better or worse not only by changes in the experience of living that life but also by changes in the world that affect the degree to which the world is the way that person desires it to be. But these theories are also open to serious objection. The most general view of this kind—it might be called the unrestricted actual-desire theory—holds that a person's well-being is measured by the degree to which all the person's actual desires are satisfied. Since one can have a desire about almost anything, this makes an implausibly broad range of considerations count as determinants of a person's well-being. Someone might have a desire about the chemical composition of some star, about whether blue was Napoleon's favorite color, or about whether Julius Caesar was an honest man. But it would be odd to suggest that the well-being of a person who has such desires is affected by these facts themselves (as opposed to the pleasure he or she derives from having certain beliefs about them). The fact that some distant star is made up of the elements I would like it to be does not seem to make my life better (assuming that I am not an astronomer whose life work has been devoted to a theory that would be confirmed or refuted by this fact).

A second problem concerns the relation between desires and reasons for action. One thing that presumably makes desire theories of well-being plausible is the idea that if a person has a desire for something, then (other things being equal) he or she has reason to do what will promote that thing. But if what I have argued in Chapter 1 is correct, then having a desire for something hardly ever provides a person with a reason to promote it. If this is correct, then it presents a problem for desire-based accounts of well-being, since it would be odd to claim that the factors that make something contribute to one's well-being do not provide reasons for pursuing it.

These objections can be partially met by shifting to what is commonly called an "informed desire" theory. On this view, the quality of a life for the person who lives it is determined by the degree to which that person's *informed* desires are satisfied, where informed desires are ones that are based on a full understanding of the nature of their objects and do not depend on any errors of reasoning.[7] This constraint narrows the range of factors that contribute to a person's well-being. (Presumably not many of us would have informed desires about what Napoleon's favorite color was.) It also supplies a link between what contributes to our well-being and what we have reason to promote, since a person who has an informed desire for something is likely to have a reason for wanting to bring that thing about.

But neither of these responses meets the objection in question. First, the idea of an informed desire is often understood as a purely hypothetical notion—what the person would desire under certain conditions—and is often used as a way of avoiding appeal to the normative idea of what a person has reason to desire. When "informed desire" is understood in this way, a notion of well-being based on it will lack a sufficiently close connection with what a person has reason to want and to do. It may be *likely* that a person has reason to want those things for which he or she would have an informed desire, but this is by no means certain.[8]

Even if we overlook this problem, however, and identify "informed desire" with "rational desire," there remains the problem that the objects of a person's informed desires are likely to include many things that are not related to the quality of the desirer's own life, intuitively understood. Suppose, for example, that I very much admire a certain person, and therefore desire that her struggle and sacrifice will be crowned with success and happiness. This may be a rational desire as well as an informed one; it might, quite properly, be strengthened by fuller knowledge of the person's life and character. Even if this is so, however, if I have no connection with her beyond my admiration and this desire, then the quality of my life is not affected one way or the other by her fate.[9]

The shift to informed desires also represents an important change in the role of desires as determinants of well-being. If a full appreciation of the ways in which my life would be changed if I could speak French well would lead me to have a strong desire to master that language, then it is likely both that I have reason to do this, and that doing it would contribute to my well-being. But what role does the desire that I would have play in making these things true? What makes it the case that I have reason to learn French is the enjoyment and other benefits I would gain from being able to speak it, not the desire that full awareness of these benefits would generate. Informed desires may correspond to reasons, and the things that fulfill them may contribute to our well-being, insofar as these desires are responses to considerations that make their objects desirable. But an account of well-being based on these facts is quite different from one based on the idea that what advances a person's well-being is the fulfillment of his or her desires.

Despite these objections, the idea that desire fulfillment is the basis of well-being has had wide appeal. Why should this be so? As I remarked in Chapter 1, the term 'desire' can be understood to refer to a number of different things, and it seems likely that those who have offered desire-based accounts of well-being may have been understanding 'desire' in such a way that these objections do not arise or are less troubling. It will be instructive to consider two of these possible interpretations.

On one interpretation, "desires" are understood as "preferences" in the sense that figures in formal theories of individual and social choice. A central claim of these theories is that the preferences of a rational individual will satisfy certain axioms and can therefore be represented by a utility function $u(x)$, such that for any states x and y, $u(x) > u(y)$ if and only if the individual prefers x to y. It might seem that a person's level of utility, as defined by such a function, should be taken as a measure of well-being in the sense we are now concerned with, and that this would amount to a desire-based theory of well-being. So it is worth asking whether such theories are subject to the objections I have just considered.

The short answer is that these objections do apply insofar as the theories in question are taken to be, or involve, theories of well-being, but that this is not how those theories are most plausibly understood. Formal theories of individual choice, such as those specified by the Savage or the von Neumann–Morgenstern axioms, are, as that name implies, most plausibly understood as accounts of what it is most rational for an individual to choose. In theories of this kind, preferences are taken as expressing an individual's conclusions about the relative desirability of various outcomes or policies, and claims are then made about what an individual has most reason to do, given these preferences. This need not involve the claim that preferences are the most fundamental starting points for individual deliberation, so it need not be an objection to such a theory to point out that from an individual's own point of view his or her preferences are not basic sources of reasons. My preference for A over B may be a reason for having certain preferences regarding probability mixtures of A, B, and other outcomes, but that preference is not what makes A more desirable than B from my point of view; what does that is, presumably, certain features of A and B. The failure of preferences to be basic sources of reasons thus need be no embarrassment to formal theories of rational choice. Nor is the wide range of possible objects of preferences a problem for such theories. They are offered not as accounts of well-being (of "what makes a person's life go better") but rather of what a person has reason to do or to choose all things considered, and the grounds on which these choices are to be assessed are explicitly intended to include preferences for things other than the person's own well-being.[10]

Formal theories of *social* choice are themselves subject to various interpretations.[11] On one common interpretation, however, they concern the way in which social choices should be based on individual preferences. So understood, they begin with a set (the "domain") of alternatives among which "society" is to choose. The basic assumption of such theories is the plausible ethical one that since these are the decisions of a society they should be based on the preferences of the members of that society, and the question that these theories address is how, more exactly, they should be so "based." It is central to the ethical idea behind such theories that for purposes of social decision-making individual preferences should be treated as sovereign (and that it would be "paternalistic" to second-guess them). This is quite compatible with the fact that, from the points of view of the individuals themselves, these same preferences are not the starting points of practical deliberation but depend on other considerations, in the way pointed out above.

Nor is the broad range of possible objects of these preferences (the fact that they may be preferences for things that lie beyond the bounds of the individuals' own lives) a problem for theories of social choice as I am now interpreting them. The domain includes all those things that society has to decide about, and this will naturally include things outside the life of any single member. There may, of course, be controversy about which alternatives should be included in the domain of social choices over which all the members of the society should have a say (should this domain include what members of the society do in private, for example?).[12] And there are also questions about which preferences are entitled to be taken into account (should preferences based simply on hatred for other groups be counted?).[13] These are moral questions, and the answers to them reflect judgments about justice and political rights, not simply about the scope of individual well-being. It follows that the individual utility functions which figure in social choice theory, even though they are based on individual preferences, are shaped by the larger moral and political theory of which they are a part. They do not reflect merely a conception of what would make the individuals' lives go better or even simply of what is good from the point of view of these individuals. Insofar as these functions express anything that could be called a conception of well-being at all, it is what I called above a moral conception, rather than a personal one.

Formal theories of social choice can, of course, be understood in a different way: as accounts of how what is good from the point of view of society must be related to what is good from the point of view of the individuals who make it up. Standard terminology can pull one toward this interpretation. Kenneth Arrow, for example, after presenting the problem of social choice in much the way I have above, goes on to call a function which determines a single social ordering of the domain given any collection of individual orderings a "social welfare function."[14] This sounds like a measure of how "well-off" the society is, and thus invites one to regard individual utility functions in turn as measures of individual well-being, the idea being that the welfare of a society must be made up of the welfare (that is, the well-being) of its members. But once individual utility is regarded in this way, the theory is open to objections of the kind raised above to desire-based accounts of well-being—for example to doubts as to whether a person's well-being is increased by the fulfillment of any preference, regardless of what its object may be.

I conclude, therefore, that the preference-based conceptions of utility that are used in formal theories of individual and social choice avoid the objections to desire-based accounts of well-being that I mentioned above just insofar as they do not involve conceptions of well-being in the relevant sense. Insofar as desire-based theories of well-being are modeled on the preference-based accounts of individual utility that flourish in social choice theory, or are taken to derive support from such theories, this involves mixing up two quite different things: personal conceptions of well-being and explicitly moral ones.

Let me turn, then, to another possible source of support for desire-based accounts of well-being. As I observed in Chapter 1, one of the things that can be meant by saying that a person has a desire for something in the broad sense in which that term is often used is that achieving or getting that thing is one of that person's aims. Moreover, it is also true that success in one's aims, at least insofar as these are rational, is one of the things that contribute to the quality of a life, viewed from a purely personal perspective.[15] It seems likely, therefore, that some of the appeal of informed-desire accounts of well-being comes from the undoubted appeal of this related idea. I will argue that at least the following is true: the idea that success in one's rational aims contributes to one's well-being can account for a number of the intuitions that have seemed to support informed-desire theories while avoiding most of these theories' implausible implications.

Both the idea of informed desires and the related idea of rational aims are open to broader and narrower interpretations. On the one hand, they can be understood to include those aims or desires that a person would have good reason to have. On the other hand, by a person's rational aims we might mean aims that he or she actually has, insofar as these are rational (that is to say, insofar as the nature of these aims does not provide good reason to revise or abandon them). I will refer to these as, respectively, the broad interpretation of rational aims and the narrow interpretation. My focus in what follows will be on the narrow interpretation.

I mentioned above, as a problem for an informed-desire theory of well-being, that on such a view the value of desire fulfillment seems in the end to play no real role in explaining why some things contribute to a person's well-being. It may be true that something contributes to one's well-being only if one has reason to desire it. But even when this is so, what makes this thing good will not be the fact that it would satisfy that hypothetical desire but rather those considerations, whatever they may be, that provide reasons for desiring it. The fact of desire itself seems to play no role.

By contrast, the narrow interpretation of the idea of a rational aim preserves a real role for the analogue of desire—that is to say, for the fact that a person actually has a certain aim—while also preserving the "critical" element that motivates the shift to informed desires. The requirement that an aim be rational incorporates this critical element by allowing for the possibility of substantive criticism of aims. This requirement also accommodates the fact that from an individual's own point of view what makes an aim worth adopting and pursuing is, first and foremost, not merely its being chosen or desired but the considerations that (in his or her view) make it worthwhile or valuable. (Given this fact, an aim that is open to rational criticism is defective from the point of view of the person who has it, not merely from that of a critical third party.) But one cannot respond to every value or pursue every end that is worthwhile, and a central part of life for a rational creature lies in selecting those things that it will pursue. It thus makes a difference whether an aim has been adopted, and this is the rationale behind the narrow interpretation of "rational aim": if something is one of a person's aims, then (provided it is rational) success in achieving it becomes one of the things that make that person's life better.

The term 'aim' invites an interpretation that is both voluntaristic and teleological: an aim is something one "adopts," and having an aim is a matter of intending to bring about a certain result. For present purposes, however, 'aim' needs to be understood in a way that is broader than its normal meaning in both of these respects. If I have the aim of being a good son, then succeeding in this contributes to my well-being even though there was no moment at which I "adopted" this aim or consciously formed this intention. Moreover, the forms of success that contribute to well-being include living up to one's values, and as I argued above this is generally not simply a matter of achieving certain results. If, for example, I am committed to being an upright and honorable person, living up to this ideal is a matter not merely of promoting certain results, but rather of responding properly to the various reasons that these ideals involve.

The idea that well-being depends, at least in part, on success in one's rational aims yields an account of well-being that has the "flexibility" which has been held to be an advantage of informed-desire views. James Griffin, for example, finds objective accounts of well-being unsatisfactory because they seem to prescribe the same list of goods for everyone, and he argues that an informed-desire account is to be preferred for this reason.[16] As Griffin recognizes, any plausible substantive-good theory will allow for the fact that different people have different needs, and any theory that recognizes pleasure as a good will take account of the fact that different activities and experiences will bring pleasure to different people. But, by incorporating the idea of success in one's rational aims, a substantive-good account can provide a further degree of flexibility, which may be what Griffin has in mind. Since different people can have different rational aims, an account that makes success in one's rational aims one determinant of well-being will allow for a further degree of variability without incorporating the full-blown subjectivity that makes desire theories implausible.

The shift from "informed desires" to "rational aims" also provides a basis for plausible responses to several other objections to desire theories that I mentioned above. The first of these is the fact that the range of a person's possible desires—even of informed desires—is much wider than his or her well-being, intuitively understood. This ceases to be a problem when we shift from informed desires to rational aims. I mentioned above that the fulfillment of a person's desire that a distant star should have a certain chemical composition would not, normally, contribute to that person's well-being, but that things might be different if the person were an astronomer who had devoted his or her life to the development of a theory that would be confirmed or refuted by this evidence. The need for this qualification illustrates the fact that, although one can have a rational desire for something that is quite unrelated to one's life, when something becomes one of a person's rational aims it thereby becomes something that affects how his or her life goes. This example also illustrates the fact that a rational aim of the kind whose fulfillment significantly affects a person's well-being is not an episodic state, as a desire may be thought to be. If I have merely decided (with good reason) that I intend to do a certain thing someday, but have not done anything more about it, then the fulfillment of this aim does little or nothing to make my life better in the way we are presently discussing. The aims whose fulfillment makes a significant contribution to a person's well-being are ones that that person has actually acted upon and, typically, given a role in shaping his or her other activities and plans. The fulfillment of that aim then makes a difference to the person's life by making these plans and activities successful ones.[17]

A second problem for desire theories concerns the way in which the fulfillment of various desires contributes to well-being. One idea would be a "summative" conception according to which a person's overall well-being is measured by the sum of his or her desires that are fulfilled, that is to say, by the number of desires that are fulfilled, perhaps weighted by their intensity and by the length of time they are held. But it does not seem that a person's well-being is in fact always increased by increasing the number of desires or even aims that he or she fulfills. If this were so then everyone would be advised to adopt as many desires or aims as possible as long as these could be satisfied. This seems absurd.[18] When we shift to rational aims, however, the absurdity of this conclusion points directly to a natural way of avoiding it. The fulfillment of an aim contributes to one's well-being only if that aim is one that it is rational to have. But the fact that adopting a certain aim, which could easily be satisfied, would be a way of producing a state of "having fulfilled an aim" is not, in general, a good reason for adopting that aim.[19] So if that is one's only reason for having an aim, fulfilling it does not contribute to one's well-being.

But even if the fulfillment of any aim that is rational contributes to a person's well-being to some degree, it does not seem that the component of well-being that depends on rational aims is measured simply by the number of such aims that are fulfilled. Some aims contribute more than others to the quality of a life. One thing that makes a difference is the degree to which these aims are worth pursuing: success in some important undertaking contributes more to the quality of a life than success in a relatively trivial one. Another, related difference is the role that an aim has in the person's life. Many rational aims are quite specific and limited, such as the aim of solving a certain puzzle, or getting to the top of a mountain, or helping a friend out of some difficulty. Other aims take the form of what Joseph Raz has called "comprehensive goals"—plans or intentions that shape a large part of one's life.[20] Success in these more comprehensive goals has a larger effect on a person's life than success in more limited aims, and consequently, as I noted in passing in discussing the previous objection, makes a greater contribution to well-being. Moreover, our more limited aims often depend on, are shaped by, and derive added significance for our well-being from, these comprehensive aims.

As Raz has emphasized, our goals have a "hierarchical" character.[21] Comprehensive goals, such as the goal of succeeding in a certain profession, or being a good parent, are of necessity quite abstract. They need to be filled in by successively more specific plans and goals. For example, someone who wants to be a successful physicist has reason to get the necessary kinds of training. This involves attending the right schools and universities, taking the right courses, reading certain books and articles, going to class and to the laboratory, finding the right instruments for an experiment, and even more specific goals and actions.

The idea of "comprehensiveness" that is intended here is a comparative notion. I am not suggesting that everyone has or should have a single comprehensive goal, or "plan of life." Perhaps few people have such goals. But most people do have (relatively) comprehensive goals of a more modest sort, defined by careers, friendships, marriages and family relations, and political and religious commitments. Many of the specific goals that we set out to achieve in action are goals that we have reason to pursue at least partly because of their relation to more abstract goals of this kind, and succeeding in these more specific goals, or failing to do so, has special significance for the quality of our lives in virtue of this relation. This brings out one of the things that is wrong with a purely "summative" view. Succeeding in many of our goals contributes to our well-being not just by being a little unit of "success" in something worthwhile but also by contributing to the larger goals which give us special reason to pursue them.

More comprehensive goals can have two kinds of "priority." First, they have priority over the more specific goals that they give us reason to pursue because they provide the reasons that make those subsidiary goals rational. Second, they can have, and can confer on the subsidiary goals they support, priority over unrelated goals: we can have reason to attach more importance to aims that are required by some comprehensive goal (a career, a friendship, or some other commitment) than to other aims that might, in themselves, be equally worth pursuing. These forms of priority would be puzzling if they were thought to flow merely from the more comprehensive character of the goals in question. Why should comprehensiveness entail importance? The answer is that to hold something as a comprehensive goal just is to hold it as a goal that has priority of the two kinds described above. So this priority is justified by the reasons that support adopting something *as* a comprehensive goal in the first place and that continue to give one reason not to reconsider that decision.[22]

I conclude that the idea that well-being is advanced by success in one's rational aims can explain the intuitions that seem to support informed-desire accounts of well-being, and can do so in a much more convincing way than informed-desire accounts themselves. This makes it plausible to suppose that much of the appeal of informed-desire accounts of well-being derives from a failure to distinguish between informed desires and rational aims. Whether this is so or not, any plausible account of what makes a life go better from the point of view of the person who lives it must recognize success in one's rational aims as one component of well-being.

Success in one's rational aims is not, however, a complete account of well-being. Pleasure, the avoidance of pain and suffering, and other forms of what Sidgwick called "desirable consciousness" can contribute to one's well-being whether or not one has "aimed" at them. In addition, the idea of success in one's rational aims does not even capture all the nonexperiential factors that make a life better even if most, or perhaps even all, of these factors depend on one's aims.

To see this, consider again the example of friendship. A person cannot get the intrinsic benefits of friendship without being him- or herself a friend, which involves valuing friendship, that is to say, having being a good friend as one of one's aims in the broad sense of 'aim' that I have been using. A misanthrope, who cares nothing for friends but to whom others are nonetheless devoted, may get some of the instrumental benefits of friendship, such as the help that friends provide, but not those benefits that involve standing in a certain special relation to others, since he does not stand in that relation to anyone. It is debatable whether the life of such a person would be better if these people genuinely cared about him than it would be if they treated him in exactly the same way out of other motives. Even if this does make a difference, however, it does not make as important a difference as it would in the case of a person who himself cared about friendship and regarded these people as friends. But even though the greater difference that the genuineness of friends makes in the latter case depends on the person's having a certain aim, this contribution to well-being is not plausibly accounted for simply by the idea of success in one of one's rational aims. The point is a general one: a life is made better by succeeding in one's projects and living up to the values one holds, provided these are worthwhile; but if these aims *are* worthwhile then succeeding in them will also make one's life better in other ways. This is true of friendship because standing in this relation to others is itself a good (albeit one that depends on one's having certain aims), and I believe that the same can be said of, for example, the achievement of various forms of excellence.

It is an interesting question whether there are factors that contribute to well-being but are neither experiential nor dependent on a person's aims in the broad way just described. It might be argued that there are not. In order for something to affect a person's well-being, the argument might run, it must affect how things go *for that person*. Both experiential goods and factors involved with that person's aims satisfy this condition, but it is difficult to see how anything else could do so.[23] Physical health might be cited as a possible example, but it is not clear that it is one. Would a person's well-being in the sense we have been discussing (that is to say, the quality of her life) be diminished by the pathological functioning of some internal organ, even though this did not affect either the quality of her experience or the achievement of goods connected with her aims? If, for example, she died in an accident before this condition became apparent, it would be true that while she was alive her health was less good than she thought, but not clear that her life was therefore worse than it would have been had she been entirely healthy up to the end.

Leaving this question open, I conclude that any plausible theory of well-being would have to recognize at least the following fixed points. First, certain experiential states (such as various forms of satisfaction and enjoyment) contribute to well-being, but well-being is not determined solely by the quality of experience. Second, well-being depends to a large extent on a person's degree of success in achieving his or her main ends in life, provided that these are worth pursuing. This component of well-being reflects the fact that the life of a rational creature is something that is to be *lived* in an active sense—that is to say, shaped by his or her choices and reactions—and that well-being is therefore in large part a matter of how well this is done—of how well the ends are selected and how successfully they are pursued. Third, many goods that contribute to a person's well-being depend on the person's aims but go beyond the good of success in achieving those aims. These include such things as friendship, other valuable personal relations, and the achievement of various forms of excellence, such as in art or science.

These intuitive fixed points provide the basis for rough judgments of comparative well-being: a person's well-being is certainly increased if her life is improved in one of the respects just mentioned while the others are held constant. But this list of fixed points does not amount to a *theory* of well-being. Such a theory would go beyond this list by doing such things as the following. It might provide a more unified account of what well-being is, on the basis of which one could see why the diverse things I have listed as contributing to well-being in fact do so. It might also provide a clearer account of the boundary of the concept—the line between contributions to one's well-being and things one has reason to pursue for other reasons. Finally, such a theory might provide a standard for making more exact comparisons of well-being—for deciding when, on balance, a person's well-being has been increased or decreased and by how much.

I doubt that we are likely to find a theory of well-being of this kind. It does not seem likely, for example, that we will find a general theory telling us how much weight to assign to the different elements of well-being I have listed: how much to enjoyment, how much to success in one's aims, and so on. I doubt that these questions have answers at this level of abstraction. Plausible answers would depend on the particular goals that a person has and on the circumstances in which he or she was placed. Perhaps a theory might tell us which goals to adopt, or at least which ones not to adopt. It does seem that there are answers to such questions, but I do not think that they are likely to be delivered by anything that could be called a general theory. Even if there were such a theory, moreover, it would need to be not just a theory of well-being, but a more general account of what is valuable and worthwhile.

One thing that philosophical reflection can do is to tell us more about particular goals: what is good or bad about them, how they are related to each other, and how their value is to be understood in the sense I described in the previous chapter. There is certainly much to be learned in this way even if it does not, for the reasons just stated, amount to a theory, or to a theory of well-being. Conclusions of this kind can be useful to us in deciding how to live our lives. But from a first-person point of view it does not matter very much whether a more general and ambitious theory of well-being is possible or not, since we do not need answers to many of the questions that it would answer. This is true in part because, as I will argue in the next section, the concept of well-being in general and its boundaries in particular are less important from the point of view of the person whose life is in question than is often supposed.

4. The Importance of Well-Being: First-Person Perspectives

There are two related ways in which the importance of the concept of well-being in a given mode of thinking might be shown. First, it might be shown in the role that concept plays in explaining and helping us to understand the importance of the particular things that contribute to well-being. Second, it might be shown in the significance of the boundary of that concept—the difference it makes whether something is or is not a contribution to well-being. I will argue that insofar as the concept of well-being has importance of either of these two kinds it does so mainly from a third-person point of view, such as that of a benefactor or from the point of view of moral theory. From the point of view of the person whose well-being it is the concept of well-being does not appear to be significant in either of these two ways.

There are at least two levels of practical thinking at which the idea of one's own well-being might be significant. It might be significant in everyday decisions about what to do or what particular goals to aim at, or it might play a role in larger-scale decisions about how one's life is to go, such as what career to pursue or whether or not to be a parent. Taking the former case first, it is certainly true that we have reason, in everyday decisions about what to do, to aim at things that contribute directly to our well-being, intuitively understood. We have reason to seek enjoyment, for example, to avoid illness and injury, and to do what will promote success in achieving our aims. But the idea of well-being plays little if any role in explaining why we have reason to value these things. If you ask me why I listen to music, I may reply that I do so because I enjoy it. If you asked why that is a reason, the reply "A life that includes enjoyment is a better life" would not be *false,* but it would be rather strange. Similarly, it would be odd to explain why I strive to succeed in philosophy by saying that my life will be a better life if I am successful in my main aims, insofar as they are rational. Again, this is true, but does not provide the right kind of reason. It would make more sense to say that I work hard at philosophy because I believe it is worthwhile, or because I enjoy it, or even because I long for the thrill of success. But these things in turn are not desirable because they make my life better. Enjoyments, success in one's main aims, and substantive goods such as friendship all contribute to well-being, but the idea of well-being plays little role in explaining why they are good. This might be put by saying that well-being is what is sometimes called an "inclusive good"—one that is made up of other things that are good in their own right, not made good by their contributions to it.

But even if well-being has little role to play in explaining why the things that contribute to it are good, it might still constitute a significant category of goods. One way in which this might be true would be if losses in well-being of one kind could be fully made up for by other gains in well-being, but not by considerations of other kinds. Even if other considerations constitute good reason for accepting a loss in well-being, this loss remains a loss, but (the suggestion runs) when we give up one element of well-being for another (such as when we give up a pleasure now for the sake of an equal or greater pleasure later) there is no real loss. This might be put by saying that well-being constitutes a distinct "sphere of compensation."

This idea is appealing, but mistaken. We do speak of making a sacrifice when, for example, we give up comfort and leisure for the sake of a family member or a friend, or for the good of some group, team, or institution of which we are a member. But it also feels like a sacrifice when we give up present comfort and leisure for the sake of our own longer life or future health. The fact that in the latter case we will be "paid back" in the same coin, our own well-being, does not make this case feel less like a sacrifice than the other at the time that it is made. The term 'sacrifice' is appropriate in both cases because we give up something of present, palpable appeal for the sake of some other, possibly more distant concern. This is often difficult to do, and the difficulty is not erased in the latter case by the fact that this concern is for our own future welfare. One might reply that it *should* be erased, and would be if we were fully rational. But why should this be so in one case but not the other? In both cases we are giving up something that we have reason to want for the sake of some other consideration that we judge to be more important. The idea that in one case there is no real sacrifice because we are paid back in kind is belied by the experience of making such choices as well as by an examination of the reasons supporting the alternatives when considered alone. If present and future experiential goods were desirable only because of the contribution they make to some separate good—my overall well-being (or the experiential quality of my life)—then giving up present comfort and leisure for the sake of greater comfort later would be no sacrifice at all. As I have argued above, however, this does not seem to be the case: well-being is more plausibly seen as an inclusive good.

In arguing against the idea that well-being is a distinct sphere of compensation I have been arguing, in effect, that the notion of net overall well-being—a notion that brings together and balances against one another all the disparate things they contribute to the quality of a life—is not one that the person whose well-being is in question often has occasion to use and be guided by. We often do ask, quite properly, when deciding on a course of action, whether the benefits it would bring us are worth its costs: whether, for example, the inconvenience and discomfort of regular oral hygiene now is worth putting up with to avoid the risk of other, perhaps greater discomfort later on. This is a comparative judgment about factors that contribute to our well-being, but in order to make it we do not need an overall notion of well-being of the kind just mentioned. In other cases, when we need to decide whether we should make some sacrifice in order to achieve a goal, we are comparing more disparate factors. We must decide whether, given the importance of the goal, it is worth making the effort, suffering the inconvenience, or putting up with the other costs that are involved. But this judgment is unlikely to be, or to involve, an assessment of our overall well-being. In order to estimate the net effects on our well-being in such a case we would need to determine the contribution that achieving this goal would make to our well-being, separating this from the other reasons for pursuing it and balancing it against the costs in well-being that this pursuit would involve. It does not seem, however, that we have need to make this kind of calculation.

Consider, for example, the reasons which move us to promote the interests of our families and of groups or institutions with which we have other special relations. These reasons are often seen as having an ambiguous status. Viewed in relation to our own comfort and leisure, they seem "altruistic," but from the point of view of what is sometimes called "impersonal morality" the reasons one has to promote the interests of one's family, one's group, or one's team or institution appear to be self-regarding. This ambiguity is also apparent from a first-person point of view: on the one hand, we would not want to think that we promote the interests of our friends, families, and institutions for "selfish" reasons, but, on the other hand, we would not be good friends or family members or loyal members of our institutions if we did not feel a loss to them as a loss to us. From a first-person point of view, however, we have no reason to resolve this ambiguity by deciding where the limits of our well-being should be drawn. It is of course important to us—important in our moral self-assessment—that our concern for our friends and family is not grounded entirely in benefits they bring to us. But, given that we care greatly about our family or friends, we have no need to determine the degree to which we benefit from benefiting them.

From an individual's own point of view, the boundaries of well-being are blurred, because many of the things that contribute to it are valued primarily for other reasons. This point is not limited to cases such as concern for friends and family. As I argued above, success in one's main rational aims is an important component of well-being. But we generally pursue these aims for reasons other than the contribution that this success will make to our well-being, and from a first-person point of view there is little reason to try to estimate this contribution.

It might be objected that I have obscured the distinctive role of an agent's own well-being in his or her practical reasoning by considering only the contrast (or lack of it) between considerations of well-being and other ends that a person in fact cares about, with good reason. What is distinctive about well-being and the goods that make it up, it may be claimed, is that in contrast to other aims, which a person can adopt or not without rational defect, one's own well-being marks out a category of considerations that it is irrational not to care about.

This objection relies on a misuse of the charge of "irrationality" of the kind discussed in Chapter 1. As I pointed out there, there certainly are cases in which our failure to give weight to considerations of well-being is irrational. These are cases in which, for example, we judge that these considerations are good reasons for acting a certain way but then fail to act accordingly. But there is nothing in these cases that has to do particularly with well-being. They are merely instances of the general truth that it is irrational to fail to give a consideration the weight that one judges it should have. In other cases, we may fail to give weight to the fact that something would promote our well-being because we fail to see that it provides us with a reason, or because we judge that it does not. If this is a mistake, then it leaves us open to rational criticism. But it does not make us irrational, except in the (overly) broad sense in which a person is irrational whenever he or she fails to see that some consideration clearly provides her with a strong reason. Here again, there is no special connection between well-being and rationality.

In the argument of this section so far, I have been considering the role of well-being in everyday decisions about what to do. I have claimed that while the particular things that contribute to one's well-being—things such as enjoyments, health, and success in one's central aims—are important sources of reasons in our everyday decisions about what to do, the concept of well-being itself, the boundaries of this concept, and estimates of the net effect that particular decisions would have on our overall well-being do not have a very significant role to play. In retrospect, this may not seem surprising. It would be odd to make our everyday choices as "artists of life," choosing each action with an eye to producing the best life just as an artist might select dots of paint with the aim of improving the value of the whole canvas. But this may be odd only because the effect that one of these choices has on our overall well-being is usually so small. We might expect the role of the idea of well-being to become more important when we shift from everyday decisions about particular actions to longer-range choices about what career to follow, where to live, or whether to have a family. Surely, it might be thought, when we are adopting our most comprehensive goals what we should be looking for are those that will make for the best life. If this is so, then well-being will also play a crucial, though less obvious, role in everyday decisions. Even if we do not aim at our own well-being in many of these ordinary choices, they will nonetheless be "controlled by" more comprehensive plans which, ultimately, are appraised on the grounds of the quality of the life they offer "from the point of view of the person who lives it."

A maximally comprehensive goal, if one had such a thing, would be a conception of "how to live," but it would be misleading to call such a goal a conception of well-being. Viewed from the point of view of the person whose goal it is, a comprehensive goal is not simply a conception of well-being, since the reasons that it provides derive from the aims and values that it includes, and as we have seen these will generally include reasons that are not grounded in the well-being of the person in question. From the point of view of someone deciding which comprehensive goal to adopt, it may be true that such a goal should be selected with the aim of finding the plan that will make for "the best life." But what this term means here is the most *choiceworthy* life. As I argued above, the question of choiceworthiness is not the same as the question of well-being, since it makes sense to say that a person had good reason to choose a certain plan of life even though it involved a lower level of well-being—was worse from the point of view of the person who lived it—than some available alternative. This life might be more choiceworthy because of its greater value, for example, or because it offered the only way of fulfilling an obligation to care for a relative.

Even if the question to be asked in choosing a plan of life is the question of choiceworthiness rather than the question of well-being, however, this still leaves open the possibility that one's well-being may play a particularly important role in answering this question. The fact that a person could have reason to adopt one plan of life despite the fact that it offered a lower level of well-being than some alternative may show that choiceworthiness and well-being are not the same thing. But the fact that it could make sense to make the opposite choice—for example, to reject a life of devotion to some project because of the sacrifices in well-being that it would involve—seems to show that well-being is at least one important factor in such choices.

Many of the things that contribute to one's well-being, such as health, enjoyments, and freedom from pain and distress, are certainly important factors in such a choice. The idea of overall well-being may also play a role, but this is less clear, in part because the notion of well-being that can be appealed to in this context is unavoidably abstract and indeterminate.[24] Success in one's main aims is, as we have seen, an important element in well-being. But the stage we are now considering is one at which these aims are being chosen, so it is not yet known what will promote our well-being by contributing to our success in achieving them. Well-being becomes much more determinate only once our central aims are chosen.

In deciding what aims to adopt, we may of course give some weight to the consideration that since success in our aims makes for a better life this provides some reason to choose aims that we can achieve, and to prefer a life in which we can achieve the aims we choose. But although this is *a* consideration it does not seem to be a very significant one. In many cases we have independent reasons not to adopt aims that are utterly futile, since pursuing them will make no contribution to the values that make them worthwhile. In addition, the bare idea of "accomplishment"—success in one's rational aims whatever these may be—is a very abstract goal, and has less weight than the value of particular goals that we may adopt. When, for example, Tolstoy's character Ivan Ilych surveys his life and finds it wanting, what he regrets is not the lack of accomplishment in this abstract sense. His distress has force because it is more concrete: what bothers him is the fact that he has devoted his life to things that now strike him as unimportant, and neglected others that would have been worthwhile.[25]

Aside from the two practical standpoints I have considered—the one we adopt when making everyday choices and the one we adopt when making decisions about larger-scale life plans—there is also the point of view we adopt when we step back from a life and ask, without either of these practical ends in view, how good a life it is. The idea of well-being may have a greater role in this kind of evaluation. This is suggested by the fact that when we take up this point of view we are likely to consider features of a life considered as a whole, not merely the value of particular elements within it. From this point of view, for example, we might say that a life is better if it is "well balanced" and involves responses to and achievement of a variety of goods, or that a life that begins badly but ends in success and happiness is a better life than one that contains the same particular goods differently arranged, so that it begins well but ends badly.[26] Of course, most lives that begin well but end badly differ in experiential quality from lives that are otherwise similar but have the opposite trajectory, and one advantage of a well-balanced life may also be that exclusive concentration on a few goals yields diminishing returns both in enjoyment and in what is accomplished. The claims I have in mind, however, hold that even apart from these more concrete differences, a well-balanced life, or a life with an upward trajectory, is a better life for the person who lives it. These claims, and the evaluative standpoint from which they are made, are quite intelligible. Perhaps the claims are even correct. But they do not strike me as very important. Well-being in this refined sense is not the central notion by which our lives should be guided.

I conclude, therefore, that the concept of one's overall well-being does not play as important a role as it is generally thought to do in the practical thinking of a rational individual. Succeeding in one's main aims, insofar as these are rational, must be a component in any plausible notion of well-being. But this idea serves as an evaluative Trojan horse, bringing within the notion of well-being values that are not grounded in it. From an individual's own perspective, which takes his or her main goals as given, what matter are these goals and other particular values, not the idea of well-being that they make up. From a more abstract perspective, taking these goals as not yet determined, we can say that a life goes better if the person is more successful in achieving his or her main rational goals (whatever these may turn out to be), but the conception of well-being that can be formulated at this level is too indeterminate, and too abstract, to be of great weight.

Concentrating on well-being, and hence on the contribution that success in one's rational goals makes to the quality of one's life, has two effects which are distortions from the person's own point of view. Since well-being is a state, which is to be "brought about," one effect of concentrating on well-being is to represent all values in terms of reasons to bring about certain results. But this is not how things seem from the point of view of a person whose rational aims include commitments to values that are not teleological. An individual who rationally holds these values has reason to deliberate and to act as they require. As I argued in Chapter 2, this is not the same thing as seeking to maximize the degree to which one's actions, over one's whole life, are in conformity with these values.

Concentrating on well-being also has the effect of transforming all a person's aims into what appear to be self-interested ones. This point might be put by noting that there are two ways in which the idea of "the good for p," where p is some individual, might be understood. In the first, broader sense, "the good for p" includes all those things that p has reason to aim at and to value—"the good," from p's point of view.[27] But "the good for p" can also be understood in a narrower sense in which it includes things just insofar as they are *good for p*, that is to say, insofar as they benefit p by making his or her life better. The idea of well-being has a similar dual character. On the one hand, when we say that something contributes to a person's well-being it sounds as if we are saying that it benefits him or her. But from an individual's own point of view many of the things that contribute to his or her well-being are valued for quite other reasons.[28] From this point of view the idea of one's own well-being is transparent. When we focus on it, it largely disappears, leaving only the values that make it up.[29]

5. The Importance of Well-Being: Third-Person Perspectives

These effects of concentrating on well-being cease to be distortions when we shift from a first-person point of view to the perspective of a benefactor, such as a friend or parent. A benefactor has reason to do what will benefit his or her intended beneficiary and to do it because that person will benefit.[30] So the analogue of what was, from the first-person point of view, a distorting self-centeredness is not a problem from this perspective. Nor is there a problem of transparency: our benefactors' reasons do not generally take the same form as our own, even though they arise from reasons that we have. Consider three classes of such reasons.

In the first class of cases, I have reason to do certain things because I will benefit from them: I have reason to do what will bring me pleasure, for example, what will relieve my pain, what will extend my life, and what will ensure my comfort in the future. In the second class of cases I also have reason to do certain things because of their relation to me: I have reason to promote the safety and security of *my* parents and children, for example, to do what will benefit *my* friends, and what will make *my* department and university flourish. But in these cases my reasons are not (or need not be) grounded in imagined benefits to myself. In the third class of cases my choice of certain aims may not depend on any relation to me at all. I may, for example, work to prevent Venice from collapsing, or to save the rain forest. Insofar as these are my aims, however, succeeding in them makes my life better. So, taking these three classes together, from my point of view the range of things I have reason to promote, whether or not it is broader than the class of things that will benefit me, is at least broader than the class of things I have reason to promote because they will benefit me.

From my benefactor's point of view, however, benefiting me has special significance. In the first of the three classes just listed, the reason my benefactor has to promote things (my pleasure, my health, and so on) is the same as my own. My benefactor may also have reason to promote the things listed in my second class (the health and comfort of my family, the flourishing of my city) because of their connection with me, but in these cases the benefactor's reasons differ from mine. If my benefactor saves my child or my parents, or restores some buildings in my city, and does this *qua* benefactor, that is to say, *for me,* he is doing it because he sees this as benefiting me in some way, or at least because *I* want it. In my own case, by contrast, I would hope not to be moved by such reasons: I see myself as acting for the sake of others. Finally, in the third class of cases, although a wealthy benefactor who saved Venice might say that he did it for me, meaning just that he did it because he knew I wanted Venice to survive, this seems odd (as well as unlikely). It is odd partly because this reason is so clearly distinct from the reasons why Venice is worth saving, which have nothing to do with me. It makes more sense to think of my benefactor as contributing to *my campaign* to save Venice, in order that that campaign should succeed. Here the connection with me is more plausible although, again, it is a connection that I hope is not crucial to my own motivation.

These examples illustrate two points. The first is the divergence between the first-person and third-person outlooks. The second is that it is not clear how important the boundaries of well-being are, even from a benefactor's point of view. I have been speaking so far of "a benefactor," understood as someone who has reason to do what benefits me (that is to say, contributes to my well-being), and I have spoken as if friends, parents, and spouses are all benefactors in this sense. But this way of putting things is too schematic. It is not always clear that someone who stands in one of these relations to us therefore has reason to do what will "make our life go better," as opposed to reason to help us to do what we have reason to want to do, whether or not this will conduce to our well-being. Suppose, for example, that I have good reason to pursue a career as an artist, or as a labor organizer, even though this may lead to a lower level of well-being for me overall because of the difficulty and discomfort that this life involves. Suppose also that I cannot do this without help from some friends or family members. Do they have reason to help me even though they are not thereby promoting my well-being? It seems to me that they may.[31] But the answer may depend on the nature of the relation that the person stands in to me—whether it is a friend, a lover, a parent, or some other family member. Just clarifying the notion of well-being will not settle the matter.

Both of these points—the lack of transparency and the fact that while well-being may be significant it does not provide a uniquely important definition of the concern that others should have for us—are apparent also from a moral perspective, to which I will now turn.

6. The Importance of Well-Being: Moral Perspectives

As I remarked at the beginning of this chapter, it is commonly sup-posed that there is a single notion of individual well-being that (1) serves as a basis for the decisions of a single rational individual, at least as far as he or she alone is concerned (that is to say, leaving aside moral obligations and concerns for others); (2) is what a concerned benefac-tor, such as a friend or parent, has reason to promote; and (3) is the basis on which an individual's interests are taken into account in moral argument. This notion of well-being is assumed to admit of at least rough quantitative comparisons of levels and increments, and to be independent of morality.

If what I have argued so far is correct, however, then at least the first part of this common assumption is mistaken. The particular goods that make up well-being are important from the point of view of the individual whose well-being it is, and we can make and need to make at least rough quantitative comparisons within these dimensions of well-being (comparisons of levels of comfort and enjoyment, for ex-ample). But the boundary between one's own well-being and other aims is unclear, and we have no need to clarify it. It does not matter that quantitative comparisons of levels or increments of our own overall well-being are difficult to make. We rightly view the world through a framework of reasons, largely shaped by the aims and values that we have adopted, and we rightly make particular decisions by determining what these reasons support on balance, not by comparing net changes in our overall balance of well-being. Among these reasons are those provided by ideas of right and wrong, justice, and other moral values. These values constitute some of an individual's most important "aims" in the sense I have been discussing, and as I will argue in the next chapter they also play an important role in shaping a person's other goals, including the most comprehensive ones. It fol-lows that an individual has little use for a notion of well-being that abstracts from moral considerations.

In light of this, it is reasonable to ask why it should have been thought that there was a notion of well-being of the kind just de-scribed, one that plays a central role both in individual decisions and in moral argument. One explanation is that this is another instance of "the shadow of hedonism." If what an individual had reason to do (considering only him- or herself) was simply to promote his or her own pleasure, and if what morality required of us was simply to give positive weight to promoting the net pleasure of others, then something close to the picture described above would be correct. There would be a single notion of well-being (in this case pleasure) that played the role described in both individual and moral thinking and in the thinking of a concerned benefactor. This notion would be defined independently of any moral ideas about what an individual was entitled to or what he or she was obligated to do, and it would admit of quantitative comparisons. One possibility, then, is that the idea that there is a notion of well-being with these properties results from supposing that although hedonism is false there must be some other notion that plays this same role.

The idea that there must be such a notion might also arise from what are taken to be the needs of moral theory. A theory of the morality of right and wrong might rely on a notion of well-being in three ways. First, this notion might figure in the content of moral requirements. For example, we may be morally required, at least in certain circumstances, to promote the well-being of others, giving preference to those whose well-being we can improve the most, or to those whose level of well-being is the lowest, or both. Second, well-being might play a role in the justification of moral principles even when it does not figure in their content. A principle requiring us to respect a certain right, for example, or to refrain from treating any individual in specified ways, might be justified on the ground that its observance would promote individual well-being. On the view I will argue for in this book, for example, principles are assessed by asking whether they could or could not be reasonably rejected. So some basis is needed for assessing the force of various possible grounds for rejecting principles, and it might be thought that a notion of well-being is needed to provide this basis: that, for example, the strength of a person's objection to a principle is properly measured by the cost that that principle would have for that person's well-being, or by the level of well-being to which he or she would be reduced if it were accepted. Third, insofar as a moral theory needs to provide some justification for morality as a whole—some answer to the question "Why be moral?"—it might seem, again, that this is best supplied by showing how morality contributes to each person's well-being.

The first and second of these tasks require a notion of well-being that admits of quantitative comparisons. The second and third appear to require a notion that is important to individuals and independent of morality itself. It would seem to be circular to justify moral principles on grounds that already presupposed what people were entitled to, and it would seem that an interesting answer to the question "Why be moral?" must proceed by linking morality to something that individuals can be assumed to care about without supposing that they are already concerned with morality itself. Putting these points together, we seem to reach the conclusion that moral theory requires a notion of well-being with the properties listed above, and that it is therefore an important task for moral theory to come up with a systematic account of well-being that meets these requirements.

This line of thinking may be in part responsible for the widespread belief that there is a notion of well-being of the kind I have described, and it would explain the emphasis generally given to theories of well-being in moral philosophy. As a substantive matter, however, I do not believe that these claims about the importance of well-being for moral theory are sound. My reasons for thinking this will be spelled out more fully in the chapters to come. Anticipating that discussion somewhat, let me say a few words here about each of the ways in which a theory of right and wrong might be thought to rely upon a notion of well-being: in the content of moral principles, in the justification offered for these principles, and in the justification of morality as a whole.

First, as to content, there certainly are some moral principles whose content involves overall assessments of how well-off various individuals are. The clearest examples are principles for assessing the justice of social institutions and policies. Applying these principles often requires us to make comparative judgments of how well-off different people are, or would be under alternative policies, and perhaps also judgments about the relative magnitude of these changes. Moreover, the notions of better and worse off that are employed here are not transparent in the way noted above: the fact that a certain change in someone's situation would make that person better off in the relevant sense gives that change moral significance, and it is therefore important to draw clearly the boundary between those changes that do and those that do not have significance of this kind. This is therefore a place where something like a theory of well-being seems to be needed, and it is noteworthy that most of the systematic accounts that have been offered of how well-off a person is have in fact been developed to serve the needs of such principles.

These accounts do not, however, generally coincide with the intuitive notion of individual well-being. They are either broader than this notion, as are the utility functions underlying social choice theories as

I interpreted them above, or else narrower, as are such notions as Rawls's primary social goods or Sen's capability sets. All these notions are shaped by moral ideas arising from the particular moral questions that they are supposed to answer: in the case of social choice theory by a conception of citizens' right to have their preferences taken into account in shaping social decisions, and in the case of Rawls's and Sen's accounts by ideas about the line between those aspects of individuals' situations that are the responsibility of social institutions and those that are properly left to individuals themselves.

There may, of course, be other moral principles whose content is specified in terms of something closer to the intuitive idea of well-being. For example, there might be a principle of benevolence requiring us to promote the well-being of others insofar as we can do so without great sacrifice. A theory of well-being might then be needed in order to interpret this duty. But it does not seem to me, intuitively, that the duty of benevolence that we owe to others in general in fact takes this form—that is to say, a form that requires us to clarify the boundaries of well-being and to make overall assessments of the quality of various lives. Parents certainly have reason to want their children's lives to go as well as possible, taking into account all the various elements of well-being, and they may be open to moral criticism when they fail to promote this. But the concern we owe to others in general is more limited. We are certainly required to avoid harming or interfering with others, and to benefit them in specific ways, such as by relieving their pain and distress, at least when we can do so without great sacrifice. But these duties do not, it seems to me, derive from a more general duty to promote their well-being, and we therefore do not need a theory of well-being in order to figure out what our duties to aid others require of us. I may, of course, be mistaken about this. There may be a more general duty of this kind, but if there is such a duty, its content, like that of the principles of justice referred to above, will be shaped by moral considerations, not simply read off from a notion derived from the realm of individual rationality, where, as I have argued above, the idea of overall well-being in any event plays little role.

Even if the idea of individual well-being does not figure explicitly in the content of moral principles or principles of justice, however, it might be suggested that this notion plays a role at the deeper level at which these principles are justified. So, for example, in arriving at standards for the justice of distributions we might start from the idea of individual well-being as the most basic ground for assessing a person's situation, and then ask which, of the various things that promote well-being, are properly the responsibility of social institutions and which are the responsibility of individuals themselves. If the justification of moral principles generally followed this pattern, then it would be important to clarify the notion of well-being in order to have a clearer idea which principles are justified.

It is true that when we are assessing the justifiability of moral principles we must appeal to things that individuals have reason to want, and that many of these are things that contribute to well-being intuitively understood. As I will argue in Chapter 5, however, not all the reasons that individuals have for rejecting principles are of this form, so we cannot delimit the range of considerations that figure in justification by defining the boundaries of well-being.

Moreover, the well-being of any given individual is quite indeterminate until we know what his or her main aims are. This means that at the level of argument at which we are choosing principles or policies to apply to individuals in general, well-being is not yet well defined. All we have to work with is an abstract notion of well-being which includes various place holders, such as "success in one's main rational aims, whatever these may be." There are two ways of responding to this indeterminacy. On the one hand, one might argue that, although we cannot say, in advance, what will promote the well-being of the particular individuals who will be affected by a principle, we do know that individuals have reason to value well-being abstractly described, and the principles they have reason to accept will therefore be ones that include this notion in their content—such as principles which tell us to promote the well-being of particular individuals with whom we interact, whose well-being is determinate and can be known. Alternatively, justification can appeal to more specific forms of opportunity, assistance, and forbearance that we all have reason to want, rather than to the idea of well-being abstractly conceived. This leads to a moral analogue of Rawls's primary social goods or Sen's capability sets.

Another consequence of the fact that what advances a person's well-being depends on what aims he or she has adopted is that the content of well-being itself depends on decisions that are plausibly seen as the responsibility of the individual in question. So questions of responsibility cannot be deferred to the stage at which well-being is well defined and we are asking only what will promote it. In particular, deciding between the two strategies of justification just described—between appealing to an abstract idea of well-being and appealing to concrete factors that contribute to it—involves a substantive moral choice. It follows that, to the degree that the concept of well-being plays a role in the justification of moral principles, it does not serve as a starting point for justification that is itself without moral presuppositions. This may seem to pose a problem for moral theory, but I will argue in Chapter 5 that it does not. While a justification for a moral principle would be circular if it presupposed that principle itself, it is unnecessary and, I believe, unrealistic, to demand that such justifications be free of all moral content.

Let me turn, finally, to the possible role of well-being in answering the question "Why be moral?" When a conception of well-being figures in the content of a moral principle, its boundaries mark an important moral distinction: it is thus not transparent in the way that it becomes from a first-person point of view. The perspective of a person who is applying such a principle is in this respect like that of a benefactor, as I described it above. But the question "Why be moral?" is asked from a first-person point of view. That is to say, we are asking what reasons an individual has to take moral requirements seriously. An answer must therefore be framed in terms of reasons as they appear to the agent whose reasons they are. From this point of view, I have argued, the concept of well-being is largely transparent: the things that make it up are important but its boundaries are not. The absence of a clear boundary here would be a problem for moral theory if an explanation of our reasons for caring about right and wrong had to involve showing how this concern serves ends that can be certified as nonmoral. But an account of the motivational basis of right and wrong need not take this form. It is enough to characterize our ideas of right and wrong themselves in a way that makes clear why they are worth caring about and how it can make sense, given the other things we have reason to value, to give them the importance that they claim. I will offer such an account in the next chapter.

7. Conclusion: Well-Being Not a Master Value

I have tried in this chapter to characterize the intuitive idea of well-being—of what makes someone's life go better—and to identify the fixed points that any plausible account of this notion would have to include. It would be absurd to deny that well-being is important—that it matters how well our lives go. But I have argued that the concept of well-being has less importance, or at least a different kind of importance, than is commonly supposed.

From a first-person point of view, the things that contribute to (one's own) well-being are obviously important, but the concept of well-being plays little role in explaining why they are important, and the boundaries of this concept are not very significant. Well-being has its greatest significance from a third-person point of view, such as that of a benefactor, and, at least arguably, in our thinking about right and wrong. From both of these perspectives it remains true that the importance of the things that contribute to a person's well-being are important because of their importance to that person. But the importance of well-being as a *category,* and the shape and importance of particular conceptions of well-being, derive from the distinctive features of those perspectives: from the distinctive concerns of a (certain kind of) benefactor, and from the special requirements of moral argument.

Let me return, finally, to the idea that well-being is a "master value": that other things are valuable only insofar as they contribute to individual well-being. There is an element of truth in this idea, but put in this way it invites misunderstanding. The misunderstanding would be to take well-being to be a good separate from other values, which are made valuable in turn by the degree to which they promote it. As we have seen, well-being is not a separate good in this sense. It is best understood as an "inclusive" good, and among the things that make a life more successful, and hence better for the person who lives it, is the successful pursuit of worthwhile goals. Although successful pursuit of all these goals contributes to the agent's well-being, this contribution is not always what makes them worthwhile. In some cases, what makes an activity worthwhile is its contribution to the well-being of others, so in these cases well-being in general (one's own and that of others) is what is fundamental. But not all values are of this kind. Consider two classes of examples.

The first are various moral values. Treating others fairly may make my life, and theirs, go better, but this is not my reason for believing it to be worthwhile. Rather, it is worthwhile because it is required by the more general value of treating others in ways that could be justified to them. Living up to the requirements of this more general value may also make our lives better, by making it possible for us to live in greater harmony with one another. But, again, this possible contribution to our well-being is not the only thing, or the most basic thing, that gives us reason to be concerned with what we owe to each other. One more basic reason is the fact that this is part of what is required by our value as rational creatures.

The second class of examples are the values of various forms of excellence. If I devote my life, or a part of it, to research in pure mathematics or to mastering the rudiments of theoretical physics, these activities contribute to making my life better. But what makes these pursuits worthwhile is not that contribution (or the possible contribution that their applications might make to the well-being of others) but rather the fact that they constitute serious attempts to understand deep and important questions.

The element of truth in the idea that other things are valuable only insofar as they contribute to individual well-being might be put as follows. First, a reason to value something is a reason *for us* to value it, that is to say, a reason to adopt certain attitudes toward it and to allow the idea of respect for, and perhaps pursuit of, that value to shape our lives in certain ways. Second, if we have reason to value something and do value it, then responding in the ways just described will count among our rational aims in the broad sense defined above, and our lives will be more successful, hence better, if we do this.[32] Perhaps there are some things that are of value—the grandeur of the universe might be an example—which no one is ever in a position to respond to in any way except passively, by being in awe of it, say. In such a case it might stretch the idea of success in one's aims, and the idea of well-being, too, far to say that responding in this way made one's life better. If there are such values, however, they are rare, and it remains true that most things are of value only if they figure in the well-being of at least some individuals.

But even if there are no such values and it is therefore true that nothing is of value unless it contributes to (or forms a part of) individual well-being, this still would not be true in the way that would be required to make well-being a "master value" in the sense described above: not all values would be reducible to the value of well-being.[33] So the values that properly guide us remain plural, and are not exclusively teleological.

PART II

RIGHT AND WRONG

4

Wrongness and Reasons

1. Moral Motivation

A satisfactory moral theory needs to explain the reason-giving and motivating force of judgments of right and wrong. This is commonly referred to as the problem of explaining moral motivation. I will continue to use this familiar label, but I want to stress at the outset that it is misleading in two important respects. First, it suggests that the problem in question is one of understanding how people are motivated rather than of understanding the reasons they have. As explained in Chapter 1, I hold that the question of reasons is primary and that once the relevant reasons are understood there is no separate problem of motivation. Second, the term "moral motivation" suggests a problem about motivation, or reasons, for *action:* a problem of understanding a special form of motivation, or a special kind of reason, that is triggered when one decides that it would be wrong not to do something, and can move one, even in the face of strong countervailing considerations, to do it. As I will argue below, this formulation seems to me to be overly narrow. But, taking the problem in this form for the moment, I want to examine some of the questions it raises and some of the problems involved in answering them.

The task of explaining how the fact that an action would be wrong provides a reason not to do it can be seen, first, as a task of self-understanding: we want to understand the reasons we are responding to when we are moved by moral considerations. But there seems to be more at stake than mere interpretation of the reasons we take ourselves to have. Even from the point of view of those of us who already care about right and wrong, a mere portrait of what it is we care about may seem to give us less than what we want: what we want to know is not merely what we care about when we care about right and wrong but why this is something we must care about. This concern is magnified when we turn to consider others: it seems that an adequate account of the morality of right and wrong should explain not merely what those who care about it are moved by but also why its importance is something that everyone has strong reason to recognize.

This might be put by saying that what the question "Why be moral?" calls for is not mere self-understanding but justification: an account of why we and others have compelling reason to be moral. But 'justification' is a misleading term for what is needed here. It is misleading to say that what those of us who already care about right and wrong are looking for in our own case is a justification, because this suggests that we think we should abandon our concern with right and wrong unless some additional ground for it can be provided. It is also misleading to say that we are looking for a way of justifying the morality of right and wrong to someone who does not care about it—an "amoralist"—because this suggests that what we are looking for is an argument that begins from something to which such a person must be already committed and shows that anyone who accepts this starting point must recognize the authority of the morality of right and wrong. I myself doubt whether such a justification can always be provided. What we can provide, and what seems to me sufficient to answer our reasonable concerns, is a fuller explanation of the reasons for action that moral conclusions supply. In giving this explanation, however, we must address the problem of the moral "must"—the seeming necessity of moral demands—in two slightly different forms.

The fact that an action would be wrong constitutes sufficient reason not to do it (almost?) no matter what other considerations there might be in its favor. If there are circumstances in which an agent could have sufficient reason to do something that he or she knew to be wrong, these are at best very rare. But if right and wrong always or even almost always take precedence over other values, this is something that requires explanation. How can it make sense, if we recognize values other than right and wrong and take them seriously, to claim that reasons of this one kind have priority over all the rest? I will refer to this as the problem of the *priority* of right and wrong over other values.

This is the first way in which moral reasons seem to have a special force that needs to be explained. The second concerns our attitude toward people who are not moved by considerations of right and wrong. Failure to see the reason-giving force of such considerations strikes us as a particularly serious fault. This failure is not, in my view, a case of irrationality. (It could be called this only in the overextended sense in which it is irrational to fail to respond to any strong reason.) Nonetheless, failing to be moved by the fact that an action would be wrong seems quite different from merely being deaf to the appeal of reasons of some other kind, such as failing to see the value of art or literature, say, or the value of great works of nature. It strikes us as a more serious and important kind of fault. This is not just a difference in *moral* importance. It is no doubt trivially true that moral failings are more serious, from a moral point of view, than nonmoral failings. But it also seems true, in a more general sense which requires explanation, that there is a difference between a lack of concern with considerations of right and wrong and a failure to respond to reasons of other kinds, and that the former is a more serious failing in this more general sense, one with particularly grave implications. I will refer to the problem of explaining this difference as the problem of explaining the special *importance* of considerations of right and wrong.

The problem of priority is a problem of explaining how considerations of right and wrong can play a certain role in the thinking of an agent. The problem of importance concerns the significance, for a third party, of the fact that an agent does or does not give moral considerations this role. Taken together, these two problems capture much of the concern that I mentioned above in discussing the idea of the moral "must." I do not believe that an adequate answer to either of them needs to take the form of a justification of morality, but they are two related features of our notions of right and wrong that any adequate account of moral motivation must explain.

2. Formal and Substantive Accounts of Moral Motivation

Attempts to explain how the fact that an action is wrong provides a reason not to do it face a difficult dilemma. Understood in one way, the answer is obvious: the reason not to do the action is just that it is wrong. But this is surely not the kind of answer that is wanted: it simply takes the reason-giving force of moral considerations for granted. Suppose, on the other hand, that we were to appeal to some clearly nonmoral reason, such as that people have reason to be morally good because, taking into account the effort that deception requires, the likelihood of being found out, and the costs of social ostracism, it is in their self-interest to be moral. This account might supply a reason for doing the right thing, but it would not be the kind of reason that we suppose a moral person first and foremost to be moved by. I will refer to this as Prichard's dilemma.[1] So a satisfactory answer to our question must not, on the one hand, merely say that the fact that an action is wrong is a reason not to do it; but it must, on the other hand, provide an account of the reason not to do it that we can see to be intimately connected with what it is to be wrong. Answers can thus be arrayed along one dimension according to their evident moral content, ranging from those that appeal to what seem most obviously to be moral considerations (thus running the risk of triviality) to those having the least connection with moral notions (thus running the risk of seeming to offer implausibly external incentives for being moral).

Explanations of the importance of morality and its reason-giving force can also be compared along another dimension, according to their degree of formality or, on the other hand, of substantive content. The strategy of formal explanations is to appeal to considerations that are as far as possible independent of the appeal of any particular ends. Kant's theory is a leading example insofar as he undertakes to show that anyone who regards him- or herself as a rational agent is committed to recognizing the authority of the Categorical Imperative. Habermas also appears to follow a formal strategy insofar as he argues that valid moral principles can be derived in argument following rules that must be presupposed by anyone who undertakes to engage in argument at all.[2]

The alternative strategy is to explain the reason-giving force of moral judgments by characterizing more fully, in substantive terms, the particular form of value that we respond to in acting rightly and violate by doing what is wrong. The aim is to make clearer what this particular form of value is and to make its appeal more apparent. Alasdair MacIntyre has observed, for example, that the Christian version of Aristotelian morality gave morality a twofold point and purpose: to say what will lead to the attainment of man's true end, and what is required by God's law.[3] These amount, in the terms I am using here, to two substantive accounts of the reason-giving force of morality. MacIntyre contrasts them with what he calls the Enlightenment project of grounding moral requirements in a conception of reason that dispenses both with the idea of divine authority and with that of a distinctive human telos. Insofar as it appeals only to a conception of rationality rather than to any specific good, this is an example of what

I am calling a formal strategy. (I leave aside the question of whether this was the "Enlightenment project" and whether it is, as MacIntyre argues, unrealizable.)

Formal accounts have been attractive because it has seemed that the force and inescapability of the moral "must" would be well explained by showing that moral requirements are also requirements of rationality, and not dependent on the appeal of any particular good. But although showing this might provide the secure basis that some have sought for the demand that everyone must care about morality, it does not give a very satisfactory description of what is wrong with a person who fails to do so. The special force of moral requirements seems quite different from that of, say, principles of logic, even if both are, in some sense, "inescapable." And the fault involved in failing to be moved by moral requirements does not seem to be a form of incoherence.

For these reasons, looking for a substantive account seems to me a more promising strategy. The main difficulty for such accounts is that it is not clear that they can give sufficiently strong answers to the questions of importance and priority. Once we identify one particular substantive value as the source of moral reasons it may be difficult to explain why that value should take precedence over all others, and why it is a value that, more than any other, everyone must recognize. This difficulty has not seemed insuperable, however, and in fact the accounts of morality that have drawn the widest support have generally been substantive ones. The ideas of God's will and the human telos, for example, seemed to many to provide successful accounts of morality because they seemed to have the necessary priority and importance. (And there are of course many who think that if these beliefs are lost then no adequate basis for morality can be found.)

In our own time, the leading substantive account of moral motivation has been that offered by utilitarianism. In fact it seems to me that a large part of the appeal of utilitarianism lies in the fact that it identifies, in the idea of "the greatest happiness," a substantive value which seems at the same time to be clearly connected to the content of morality and, when looked at from outside morality, to be something which is of obvious importance and value, capable of explaining the great importance that morality claims for itself.

Utilitarians' objections to nonutilitarian accounts of morality, such as Bentham's famous animadversions against rights, may seem to involve a claim to metaphysical superiority. Utilitarianism, it is claimed, bases morality on something undoubtedly real—human welfare. Rights and duties, on the other hand, seem to be mere ideas, without any foundation in reality. But the basic issue here is less a matter of metaphysical reality than one of reason-giving force. The familiar charge of "rule worship," for example, derives its force from the presupposition that human welfare is something important and worth caring about and that rules (considered apart from any utilitarian foundation) are, by comparison, arbitrary.[4] The plausibility of this presupposition makes the answering charge of "welfare worship" seem weak (even though there is, I believe, quite a lot to be said for it).

One problem with the utilitarian account is that the idea of the greatest happiness, despite its general moral significance, does not seem to be sufficiently closely linked to our ideas of right and wrong. Many acts are wrong even though they have little or no effect on people's happiness, and the fact that an action would promote aggregate happiness does not guarantee that it is right. Moreover, even where happiness, or at least individual well-being, is clearly at stake, its appeal alone does not seem to account for the motivation we feel to do what is right and to avoid what is wrong. When, for example, I first read Peter Singer's famous article on famine and felt the condemning force of his arguments, what I was moved by was not just the sense of how bad it was that people were starving in Bangladesh.[5] What I felt, overwhelmingly, was the quite different sense that it was *wrong* for me not to aid them, given how easily I could do so. It is the particular reason-giving force of this idea of moral wrongness that we need to account for.

Mill's view offers a way of responding to this problem. While he appeals to "the greatest happiness of the greatest number" to explain the importance of morality, he offers a separate account of how people are moved to act in the ways it requires and a separate account of the idea of moral wrongness.[6] In chapter 5 of *Utilitarianism* Mill distinguishes between classifying actions as expedient or inexpedient (that is to say, as conducing or not conducing to the general happiness) and classifying them as right or wrong. "We do not call anything wrong," he says, "unless we mean to imply that a person ought to be punished in some way for doing it; if not by law, by the opinion of his fellow creatures; if not by opinion, by the reproaches of his own conscience."[7] Mill seems to intend this as an account which captures most of what we ordinarily mean by right and wrong and interprets these notions as ones that he regards as normatively important (at least if the words 'ought to be punished' are understood in the light of the utilitarian formula, as meaning "the greatest happiness would be produced if they were to be punished").

There is clearly something right about this account. Even on a nonutilitarian view, the idea that an action is of a kind that there is reason to have discouraged is surely not unrelated to the idea of its being wrong. The challenge is to formulate this relation correctly and to spell out how believing an act to be wrong is connected to seeing a reason not to perform it. The fact that it would be a good thing if people were discouraged from such actions by threat of legal punishment and social disapproval, or by an ingrained tendency to feel disapproval toward themselves, could provide a reason to acquire such a tendency, but that does not amount to a reason not to so act. What we need to do, then, is to explain more clearly how the idea that an act is wrong flows from the idea that there is an objection of a certain kind to people's being allowed to perform such actions, and we need to do this in a way that makes clear how an act's being wrong in the sense described can provide a reason not to do it.

3. A Contractualist Account of Motivation

Contractualism offers such an account. It holds that an act is wrong if its performance under the circumstances would be disallowed by any set of principles for the general regulation of behavior that no one could reasonably reject as a basis for informed, unforced general agreement.[8] I will defer discussion of the normative content of this account until later chapters. It should at least be clear, however, that it overlaps to a significant degree with Mill's definition of wrongness while not coinciding with it exactly. If we all have good reason to want acts of a certain kind not to be performed, then it is likely that any principles allowing such acts could be reasonably rejected, hence that they will be wrong. But it does not follow that this will be so in every case in which a greater balance of happiness would result from such acts' being punished.

According to contractualism, thinking about right and wrong is in one respect like thinking about the civil and criminal law: it involves thinking about how there is reason to want people in general to go about deciding what to do. But thinking about right and wrong differs from thinking about law in a number of crucial ways. One of these is that the reasons that guide us in thinking about what the law should be are commonly very different from the "sanction" that moves us to obey it (whether this is fear of punishment or a sense of obligation). In the case of the morality of right and wrong, however, these two kinds of reasons flow from the same more general reason: the reason we have to live with others on terms that they could not reasonably reject insofar as they also are motivated by this ideal. Because we have this reason we have reason to attend to the question of which actions are right and which wrong, that is, to try to determine what would be allowed by principles that others could not reasonably reject, and we also have reason to govern our practical thought and our conduct in the ways that these principles require.

This account of moral motivation has much in common with another idea mentioned by Mill. In the chapter of *Utilitarianism* devoted to moral motivation Mill does not appeal directly to the substantive value of "the greatest happiness of the greatest number," but invokes instead what he calls "the social feelings of mankind; the desire to be in unity with our fellow creatures."[9] The ideal to which contractualism appeals—that of being able to justify your actions to others on grounds that they could not reasonably reject—is very similar to Mill's idea of "unity." One important difference, however, is that Mill takes himself to be describing a sentiment—a natural feature of human psychology—which explains how the motivation to act in accordance with utilitarianism could arise on some basis other than social conditioning. By contrast, on the account I am offering there is no need to appeal to a special psychological element to explain how a person could be moved to avoid an action by the thought that any principle allowing it would be one that others could reasonably reject. This is adequately explained by the fact that people have reason to want to act in ways that could be justified to others, together with the fact that when a rational person recognizes something as a reason we do not need a further explanation of how he or she could be moved to act on it.

The reason which contractualism emphasizes, the reason we have to want to be able to justify our actions to others on grounds that they (if similarly motivated) could not reasonably reject, must be distinguished from the reasons we often have for wanting to be able to justify our actions to others on grounds that they actually do or will accept. It would be pleasant to live in actual harmony with others and to have them approve of the way we behave toward them, and it is unpleasant to be in conflict with those around us and to suffer their disapproval. But the appeal of actual agreement cannot be the motivational basis of morality, since there are obviously cases in which acting morally requires one to resist the prevailing consensus about what is and is not justified. If, for example, the people who are the victims of one's action are fully convinced that their interests are much less important than those of others, they may be quite happy with, and even grateful for, much less than is their due. But it does not follow from the fact that they (and others) accept your action as justified that that action is morally correct.

Actual agreement with those around us is not only something that is often personally desirable; it is sometimes morally significant as well. There are many cases in which morality directs us to seek consensus or to secure the permission of others before acting. But where actual agreement is morally significant this reflects a particular substantive judgment within morality, and the significance of this kind of agreement should be clearly distinguished from the ideal of hypothetical agreement which contractualism takes to be the basis of our thinking about right and wrong.

Why accept this account of moral motivation? I accept it, first, because it seems to me to be phenomenologically accurate. When I reflect on the reason that the wrongness of an action seems to supply not to do it, the best description of this reason I can come up with has to do with the relation to others that such acts would put me in: the sense that others could reasonably object to what I do (whether or not they would actually do so). Second, as I will argue more fully below, this account seems to offer the right kind of response to Prichard's dilemma, by describing an ideal of relations with others which is clearly connected with the content of morality and, at the same time, has strong appeal when viewed apart from moral requirements.

Third, the ideal of justifiability to others plays a large enough role in our practical reasoning to enable it to account for the complexities of "moral motivation." As I mentioned at the beginning of this chapter, moral motivation is often discussed as if it were solely a matter of motivation to act—a source of motivation that is triggered by the conclusion that acting in a certain way would be morally wrong and then weighs against competing motives (like the sanction that is attached to violating the law). This "sanction model" is false to the facts of moral experience. "Being moral" in the sense described by the morality of right and wrong involves not just being moved to avoid certain actions "because they would be wrong," but also being moved by more concrete considerations such as "she's counting on me" or "he needs my help" or "doing that would put them in danger." A morally good person is sometimes moved by "the sense of duty" but more often will be moved directly by these more concrete considerations, without the need to think that "it would be wrong" to do otherwise. The latter thought is more likely to come to the fore as a motivating consideration in cases in which we have failed to do what we ought or are feeling tempted to do so.

The contractualist account can explain these facts about moral motivation, because the source of motivation that it identifies—the ideal of justifiability to others—does not figure merely as a "sanction" that is triggered when we have concluded that an action would be wrong. It also provides a higher-order reason to shape our process of practical thinking in the ways that are necessary to make it one that others could reasonably be asked to license us to use. Three features of this "shaping" deserve mention here: it can be seen in both positive and negative aspects, and its function is a dynamic one.

First, positively, since others could reasonably refuse to license us to decide what to do in a way that gave concrete factors such as those listed above no weight, the aim of justifiability to others gives us reason to recognize these considerations as ones that are generally relevant, and are in some circumstances compelling reasons to act.

Second, negatively, "being moral" involves seeing certain considerations as providing no justification for action in some situations even though they involve elements which, in other contexts, would be relevant. The fact that it would be slightly inconvenient for me to keep a promise should be excluded as a reason for not doing so. Even if I am in great need of money to complete my life project, this gives me no reason to hasten the death of my rich uncle or even to hope that, flourishing and happy at seventy-three, he will soon be felled by a heart attack. Against this, it might be claimed that I do have such reasons and that what happens in these cases is that I conclude that an action (breaking the promise or hiding my uncle's medicine) would be wrong and that the normative consequences of this conclusion then outweigh the very real reasons I have to do it. But this does not seem to me, intuitively, to be correct. It does not seem true even of most of us, let alone of a person who was fully moved by moral reasons, that the moral motivation not to act wrongly has to hold in check, by outweighing, all these opposing considerations. It is, phenomenologically, much more plausible to suppose that, certainly for the fully moral person and even for most of us much of the time, these considerations are excluded from consideration well before the stage at which we decide what to do. Being moral involves seeing reason to exclude some considerations from the realm of relevant reasons (under certain conditions) just as it involves reasons for including others.[10] The contractualist account can explain this fact, since these considerations are ones that others could reasonably refuse to license us to count as reasons.

Contractualism can also explain why the motive of "not acting wrongly" plays a more prominent role in cases in which we act badly or are tempted to do so. The reason that contractualism sees as basic to moral motivation applies in the first instance to our overall practice of practical reasoning—it is a reason to govern ourselves in a way that others could not reasonably refuse to license. The reason we have to avoid a course of action that we believe to be wrong is one of the many more specific reasons that flow from this, since an action is wrong just in case it would not be allowed by any system of governance that meets this standard. When one has reached the conclusion that a course of action would be wrong but is tempted to pursue it nonetheless, the considerations that one finds tempting are ones that have been excluded or overridden at an earlier stage—that is, they have been ruled out as reasons insofar as one is going to govern oneself in a way that others could not reasonably reject. What one is asking in such a case is therefore how much one should care about living up to this ideal, and this question thus presents itself in the form: How much weight should I give to the fact that doing this would be wrong? Cases of this kind are all too familiar. What I am suggesting, however, is that their familiarity (and drama) should not distract us from the existence of many other cases that do not take this form because our acceptance of the aim of justifiability to others has led us to set these potentially competing reasons aside conclusively at an earlier stage in our deliberation, or even to exclude them from consideration altogether, so that they do not even occur to us as potential reasons which then need to be ruled out.

Third, and finally, the "shaping" role of the aim of justifiability to others is a dynamic one. There is no fixed list of "morally relevant considerations" or of reasons that are "morally excluded." The aim of justifiability to others moves us to work out a system of justification that meets its demands, and this leads to a continuing process of revising and refining our conception of the reasons that are relevant and those that are morally excluded in certain contexts. I will describe this process more fully in the chapters ahead, but what I will describe is a continuing process, not a fixed list of results.[11]

To summarize, I have so far claimed that contractualism offers an account that accurately describes moral motivation as many of us experience it, and that it can account for the diversity of moral reasons and for the diverse roles that moral motivation plays in our practical thought. I have also claimed, but not yet shown, that it provides a plausible response to Prichard's dilemma. I will return to this claim in the following sections, where I will argue that contractualism can also explain the special importance of the morality of right and wrong and its priority over other values.

4. Importance

In our assessments of ourselves and others, being "left cold" by morality counts as a more important fault than merely failing to see the force of reasons of some other kind. The task of this section is to show how contractualism can explain this importance. Let me begin by considering some of the things that we might say about amoralists, who can understand the difference between right and wrong but do not see, and perhaps even deny, that it is anything they have reason to care about. First, unless their situation differs from ours in ways that are morally relevant, we must say that the moral reasons that apply to us apply to these people as well. This much is required by what I called, in Chapter 1, the universality of reason judgments. Looked at in this way, their case is quite different from that of people who "have different tastes," such as those who do not enjoy skiing or do not like the taste of bananas. In these cases, the main point of the activities in question is a certain kind of enjoyment; so people who do not get this enjoyment from the activities lack reasons to engage in them. But morality is not aimed at enjoyment, so the reasons to give it a place in one's life are not conditional in this way.

Failure to care about right and wrong does not make a person irrational in the sense in which I am using that word, but a person who is left cold by moral considerations does fail to appreciate reasons that apply to him or her. Just saying this, however, does not seem to capture the seriousness of such a failure. There are many other cases of people who fail to see the force of certain reasons, such as people who fail to see the value of science or of historical understanding, and people who think that the Grand Canyon is just a big ditch that might as well be filled in if that proves to be economically advantageous. All these people can be said to be "missing something" in at least two senses: there is a category of reasons, a form of value, that they are failing to appreciate; and their lives are poorer because of this lack. But it would understate our reaction to an amoralist to say only that he or she is "missing something" in these senses.

So we need a further explanation. I should emphasize that what I am trying to explain here is not the special stringency of moral considerations—some special rational force—that moral reasons have over the agents to whom they apply, but rather the special significance *for us* of someone's failing to be moved by these reasons.[12] To understand this significance it will be helpful to return to a point made at the end of Chapter 1, that the reasons that a person recognizes are important to us because they affect the range of relations we can have with that person. In many cases these effects are quite local. If someone does not see the point of music, or of chess, or does not appreciate the grandeur of nature, then one cannot discuss these things with him or enjoy them together. "Blind spots" such as these may stand in the way of certain relations with a person, but they leave much of life untouched. A person who cannot share our enthusiasm for one or another valuable pursuit can still be a good neighbor, co-worker, or even friend. The effects of a failure to be moved by considerations of right and wrong are not, however, confined in this way. This failure makes a more fundamental difference because what is in question is not a shared appreciation of some external value but rather the person's attitude toward us—specifically, a failure to see why the justifiability of his or her actions to us should be of any importance.[13] Moreover, this attitude includes not only us but everyone else as well, since the amoralist does not think that anyone is owed the consideration that morality describes just in virtue of being a person.

People with a consuming interest in one activity often feel that a large gulf separates them from those who cannot see the point or value of that pursuit. The gulf that some religious people feel separates them from unbelievers may be an extreme case of this. But even this feeling of distance has the personal character I have just mentioned only if the believer feels that denying his religion involves denying his standing as a person and that of others as well. Conceivably, some believers may see things this way. What I am suggesting is that almost all of us have reason to see the gulf separating us from an "amoralist" as having this character, and that this accounts for the special importance we attach to seeing the force of moral considerations.[14]

5. Priority

Let me turn now to what I called above the problem of priority. This is the question of how the morality of right and wrong is related to our other values and how it could make sense to give it priority over them. As I pointed out in Chapters 1 and 2, values can conflict in a practical sense when they give rise to incompatible demands to action, but even when no act is in view they can conflict in a deeper sense when one value involves giving certain considerations a status as reasons that another value rules out. Since morality involves very general require-ments governing the reasons we can accept, it can conflict with many other values in this second, deeper way.

This deeper form of conflict is illustrated by an objection that Ber-nard Williams has raised against both utilitarian and Kantian concep-tions of morality. Williams considers the suggestion that, in a situation in which one could save only one of two people, it would be contrary to the impartial regard for every person that these forms of morality require to save one of them because of some special tie, for example because that person was your friend or your spouse.[15] This is not merely a case of practical conflict. The suggestion is that a morality that required this kind of impartiality (that declared love or friendship to be an impermissible reason for saving one person rather than the other) would rule out love and friendship altogether, since it is essen-tial to these relations that one would have reason to give preference to a friend or loved one in such a situation.

The natural first response to this objection is to argue that morality does not in fact demand the kind of impartiality that is here sug-gested.[16] Along this line, I will argue in Chapter 5 that principles could reasonably be rejected on the ground that they left no room for valuing other things that are important in our lives. But this response needs to be supplemented by another. Williams sometimes appears to suggest that the demands of love and friendship have already been unaccept-ably curtailed if one even needs to give an argument to the effect that it is permissible, in situations of this kind, to give preference to a friend or spouse. A person who would think in this way would have, he says, "one thought too many," which would get in the way of wholehearted devotion.[17] Williams himself qualifies this point; he recognizes that the demands of friendship cannot have unconditional priority. This leaves us with two questions: what kind of priority does friendship demand, and to what extent are its demands themselves limited by some recognition of the demands of morality?

Generalizing from this example, we can address the problem of priority in two ways: first, by arguing that morality does in fact leave room for other values; and, second, by arguing that these values themselves, properly understood, give way to morality's demands when conflicts arise. I will take up the first of these points, which has to do with the content of morality, in Chapter 5. Here I will concentrate on the latter, since there is something to be learned about the nature of moral motivation by seeing how moral reasons are related to values of other kinds.

I will begin with a discussion of friendship. This discussion has a dual purpose. First, as we have seen, friendship is a prime example of a personal value that may conflict with the demands of the "impersonal" morality of right and wrong, so this discussion can illustrate a general strategy for responding to the problem of priority. But friendship is also a value that makes demands on us and can thus be seen as raising problems analogous to those of morality. Instead of asking "Why be moral?" we might ask "Why be loyal to one's friends when this requires sacrificing other goods?" Considering the answer to this question will help to cast light on the general problem of moral motivation.

It may seem that in answering the question "Why be loyal?" we face an analogue of Prichard's dilemma. The answer, "Because friendship requires it," seems to be no response at all to the question that is being asked. But if, on the other hand, we cite some value other than friendship—if, for example, we appeal to the benefits of having friends—then this seems the wrong kind of response. A person who was "loyal" for that kind of reason would not be a good friend at all.

The right response to this dilemma is, first, to characterize the relationship that friendship involves in a way that makes clear why it is something desirable and admirable in itself. Given such a characterization, we can then see how, on the one hand, being a friend will also bring other benefits (such as enjoyable companionship, help, and support) and why, on the other, being a friend involves seeing "because loyalty requires it" as a sufficient reason for doing something even though it involves a sacrifice of other goods. By bringing these two elements together as aspects of a single value, such an account enables us to see that the analogue of Prichard's "dilemma" is not really a dilemma at all. It merely appears to be one because it presents two essential aspects of friendship as if they were competing answers to the same question. A person who was loyal to a friend simply to have the benefits of friendship would not be a true friend. A true friend has to see loyalty as in itself sufficient reason to bear a burden. On the other hand, a person who did not regard friendship as a good to him, did not enjoy it and see it as an important ingredient in a good life, would not be a real friend either, but only following a strangely cold imperative. Being a friend involves both feeling friendship's demands and enjoying its benefits.

Of course friendship also leaves one open to certain pains—to feelings of loss and betrayal if one's friend is false or disloyal and to feelings of guilt if one is disloyal oneself. This is genuine guilt—self-reproach—not just regret that one has lost the value of friendship, since one can properly feel it whether or not the friendship is destroyed as a result of one's action.

There are obvious similarities between the case of friendship as I have described it and that of the morality of right and wrong, and my strategy in responding to the problem of moral motivation is analogous to the response I have just sketched to Prichard's dilemma in the case of friendship. The contractualist ideal of acting in accord with principles that others (similarly motivated) could not reasonably reject is meant to characterize the relation with others the value and appeal of which underlies our reasons to do what morality requires. This relation, much less personal than friendship, might be called a relation of mutual recognition. Standing in this relation to others is appealing in itself—worth seeking for its own sake. A moral person will refrain from lying to others, cheating, harming, or exploiting them, "because these things are wrong." But for such a person these requirements are not just formal imperatives; they are aspects of the positive value of a way of living with others.

Duty is most familiar in its negative form, in the feeling of unwelcome constraint and the experience of moral guilt. According to the account I am offering, the pain of guilt involves, at base, a feeling of estrangement, of having violated the requirements of a valuable relation with others. So understood, this familiar negative aspect of morality corresponds to a positive "pull": the positive value of living with others on terms that they could not reasonably reject.

I believe that this is a powerful source of motivation. It is more general than the special case of moral guilt since it applies also in cases in which personal conduct is not the only, or the main, issue; and it can work for ill as well as for good. I believe that its motivational influences can be seen at work in the transformation of the moral and political atmosphere of the United States in the late 1960s and early 1970s. In the 1950s many Americans believed, naively, that their institutions were uniquely justifiable; that America was free of class barriers, and that it was a society in which benefits were fairly earned. They therefore felt that they could enjoy these benefits in the comforting confidence that the institutions through which they had acquired them, though not perfect, were closer than any others to being ones that no one could reasonably object to. The combined blows of the civil rights movement and the movement that arose in reaction to the war in Vietnam shattered these illusions beyond repair. Different people reacted to this in different ways, some by protesting against the war and working for civil rights, others by vehemently denying that the charges of injustice at home and criminality abroad had any foundation. What these reactions had in common was a deep sense of shock and loss; both testify, I believe, to the value people set on the belief that their lives and institutions are justifiable to others. Of course one could say that what people care about (and were concerned about in this case) is that their institutions be just and their lives not be morally corrupt. What I am adding to this (and what I believe the phenomenology of the particular historical case bears out) is the claim that what is particularly moving about charges of injustice and immorality is their implication for our relations with others, our sense of justifiability to or estrangement from them. Unlike friendship, morality is commonly seen as a form of constraint, not as a source of joy or pleasure in our lives. I am suggesting, however, that when we look carefully at the sense of loss occasioned by charges of injustice and immorality we see it as reflecting our awareness of the importance for us of being "in unity with our fellow creatures."

The sense of loss that I am describing here is not merely a matter of feeling guilty or distressed at the thought that one's life and institutions do not measure up to one's moral goals. It also involves the loss of other goods: one cannot take the same pleasure in one's cooperative relations with others as members of the same firm or university, say, if one comes to believe that they are being asked to participate on terms they could reasonably reject, and the meaning of one's own successes and accomplishments is undermined by the thought that they were attained on terms that were basically unfair.[18] This bears on the problem of priority because it indicates how other goods, which may be thought to conflict with the demands of right and wrong, also depend on the value which underlies these demands.

As my historical example illustrates, the motivation I am describing does not always move us in a morally admirable direction. If there are people who might charge us with injustice, citing a principle that we could live up to only at some cost, we can respond to this situation in several different ways. One is to accept the principle and the charges and to try to make amends. A second is to deny the validity of the principle. A third is to accept the principle but to try to avoid recognizing that there are people whose claims against us it would legitimate. If we are moved wholeheartedly by the value of justifiability to others then we cannot take the second route unless we judge, after due consideration, that the principle in question is one that can reasonably be rejected, and we cannot take the third route unless we think that the charges in question are without merit. But acceptance is often less than wholehearted, and just because people do set a high value on the idea that their lives and institutions are justifiable to others they may be strongly tempted to "avert their eyes" from the merits of the charges against them. Sometimes this involves "walling off" (trying not to think about) the people whose fate raises these charges.[19]

For most of us, this is something that can be done only with unease. A person who could manage it without unease—who could simply ignore the fate of others without having to "wall them off"—would be the kind of amoralist I mentioned above. It might seem that such a person could be immune to the claims of strangers while still enjoying friendship and the goods of other relations with specific individuals. Such a person might have strong ties of affection which would be much like friendship, but would they be the same? I do not think that they would, for the following reason.

Friendship, at least as I understand it, involves recognizing the friend as a separate person with moral standing—as someone to whom justification is owed in his or her own right, not merely in virtue of being a friend. A person who saw only friends as having this status would therefore not have friends in the sense I am describing: their moral standing would be too dependent on the contingent fact of his affection. There would, for example, be something unnerving about a "friend" who would steal a kidney for you if you needed one. This is not just because you would feel guilty toward the person whose kidney was stolen, but because of what it implies about the "friend's" view of your right to your own body parts: he wouldn't steal them, but that is only because he happens to like you.

As is well known, it is crucial to friendship that we are moved to do things for a friend by the special affection and regard that we hold for him or her as a friend, not simply by consideration of a kind that we owe to everyone. But what the kidney example brings out is that friendship also requires us to recognize our friends as having moral standing as persons, independent of our friendship, which also places limits on our behavior.

I am not arguing here that one must accept the form of morality that I am describing in order to be capable of "real friendship." My aim here is not to force an "amoralist" or anyone else to accept this conception of morality, but rather to answer a certain objection to that conception, namely that it does not leave sufficient room for special relationships, such as friendship, that we have reason to value. In order to reply to this objection, it is enough to show that there is a form of friendship that is worth valuing, and in fact seems to capture what we normally mean by friendship, that does not clash with the requirements of morality in the way that the objection suggests. If, as I have just maintained, the conception of friendship that we understand and have reason to value involves recognizing the moral claims of friends *qua* persons, hence the moral claims of nonfriends as well, then no sacrifice of friendship is involved when I refuse to violate the rights of strangers in order to help my friend. Compatibility with the demands of interpersonal morality is built into the value of friendship itself. I have argued, in addition, that this is not a watered-down version of friendship in which the claims of friends have been scaled back simply to meet the demands of strangers. Rather, it is a conception that has particular advantages from the point of view of friends themselves. In order to defend these claims, I need not deny that there are other conceptions of friendship—such as that illustrated by Achilles and Patroclus in Homer's *Iliad,* perhaps—which do not have the character just described. But the claim that it would clash with the demands of this ideal of friendship is a much less forceful objection to morality as I describe it than the charges, to which I have responded, that it is incompatible with friendship as we understand it, or with the conceptions of friendship that we have most reason to value.

I believe that what I have argued here in the case of friendship is true as well of other personal relations whose demands may seem to conflict with morality, such as family ties and relations with other members of a team or cooperative enterprise. If this is correct, then the degree to which there is a conflict between the morality of right and wrong and the goods of personal relations depends greatly on the society in which one lives.[20] If no one in my society understands friendship as having the moral content I have just described, then a relationship with others on this footing is not available to me. If everyone in my society sees the world as divided between "them," the outsiders to whom nothing is owed, and "us," who are bound by relations of blood, affection, and patronage, then I really am faced with a choice between actual ties with my fellow citizens—strong and warm, perhaps, if also fierce—and the requirements of morality, grounded in an ideal of relations with others that must remain purely ideal. I have tried to argue that we are not in fact faced with this choice, but it must be conceded that others could be.

A complete response to the problem of priority would involve extending this account of friendship to cover all the other values that might conflict with the demands of the morality of right and wrong. I obviously cannot give such a complete account here. All I can do is to indicate briefly how the extension would go. In all these cases, just as in that of friendship, there is a three-part strategy. The first is to argue that insofar as these are things that people have reason to pursue and to value, these reasons will be among those that can make it reasonable to reject some principles. Therefore there will be pressure within the morality of right and wrong to make room for these values. But there will of course be limits, and the second part of the strategy (which divides into two subparts) is to argue that when these limits are reached we have good reason to give priority to the demands of right and wrong. This can be done in part by appealing to the great importance of justifiability to others and to the particular interests that moral principles protect, and in part by arguing that the other values, properly understood, have a built-in sensitivity to the demands of right and wrong. An argument of this last form was particularly important in the case of friendship, and I believe that the same would be true for other values in which relations with other people are the central concern, such as the values of family life and those of loyalty to various groups.

A more mixed argument is likely to be relevant with regard to the value of pursuits and excellences such as scientific and artistic accomplishment. On the one hand, since the values involved in these cases are forms of collective human activity, these values, like that of friendship, will be sensitive to the requirements of justifiability to others. Consider, for example, a scientist who, convinced of the promise of his own line of research, thought that the value of scientific progress justified him in deceiving his competitors and co-workers about certain experimental results, in order to dampen criticism and keep grant money coming for his crucial research. This person would not only be violating moral requirements but also failing to understand properly the value of his own enterprise. Science is a collective undertaking by a community of inquirers over time, and as such it depends on truthfulness in reporting what one has done in one's experiments and what results were obtained. Someone who fails to see this fails to understand an important aspect of the value of science itself—fails to see what respecting that value involves.

This response covers only certain cases of conflict between duties to others and the value of pursuits or excellences. Consider instead the case of a person who wants to carry out some valued project (a scientific experiment or an artistic project) despite the fact that it presents a serious threat to public health and safety. To respond to this kind of challenge we need to follow the second part of the strategy I outlined and make a direct claim of priority for moral requirements over the reasons provided by the value in question. It may be helpful here to recall that, as I argued in Chapter 2, the value of such pursuits and accomplishments is not well understood simply in terms of some class of results that make the world better by their occurrence. Rather, to think of art or science as valuable is to think that there are good reasons for taking them seriously and incorporating the pursuit, study, and appreciation of them into our lives in certain ways. The question then is, in what ways? More specifically, does a proper understanding of their value involve recognizing reasons for pursuing them that demand priority over what we owe to other people? It seems to me clear, although I will not argue the point in detail, that it does not, and that the claim that it does involves an exaggerated and distorted view of these values.

A challenge of this second kind may seem to have particular force in the case of the value of natural objects such as forests, species, and oceans. This is because it is most tempting in these cases to think of the value in question in consequentialist terms: that is, to think of this value as consisting in the fact that it is good—that it makes the world better—that such things exist and be unspoiled. But in this case too, this view is mistaken. Understanding the value of nature involves seeing the reasons we have to appreciate and respect it. Respect for the value of natural objects demands that we not destroy them without good reason, but this strongest demand does not seem likely to yield a direct conflict with what we owe to other people. Respect for the value of natural objects also gives us reason to try to prevent others from destroying them without good reason, by refusing to cooperate in this and by trying to persuade others of their value. But a refusal to take actions that violate the rights of other people in order to prevent them from destroying natural objects does not, in my view, show a lack of respect for the value of those objects on our part.

6. Some Objections

Even under favorable circumstances the relation with others on which the form of moral motivation that I am describing is founded may seem implausibly ideal. The motivational basis of friendship makes sense because friends play a real and important role in one's life. But morality, as I am describing it, requires us to be moved by (indeed to give priority to) the thought of our relation to a large number of people, most of whom we will never have any contact with at all. This may seem bizarre. But if the alternative is to say that people count for nothing if I will never come in contact with them, then surely this is bizarre as well. Surely I have good reason not to throw debris out of my plane as I fly over places where I will never land, and reason to take care about sending hazardous waste to places I will never visit or hear from. It matters that there are, or will be, people out there with lives that will be affected by what I do.

Still, someone might agree that what happens to these people matters morally, yet question whether our concern about them is at base a concern about the justifiability of our actions to them. Why isn't it more plausible to say simply that their lives have value and that what a moral person is moved by is the recognition of that value? Why bring in justification?[21]

In assessing this challenge it is important to bear in mind that what I am claiming to be central to moral motivation is not the activity of actual justification to others (which does make sense only in relation to individuals with whom we are in contact and communication) but rather the ideal of acting in a way that is justif*able* to them, on grounds they could not reasonably reject. Even with this qualification in mind, however, justifiability may still seem at best secondary. What is primary, it might be said, is the value of people's lives, or the moral legitimacy of their claims. It is these that determine whether an action is justifiable. To say that a moral person cares about the justifiability of his or her actions to others is at best a roundabout way of saying that such a person is concerned to act in a way that is responsive to the value of others' lives and to their valid moral claims. This amounts, perhaps, to a concern that one's actions should be morally justifiable, but the idea of justification *to others* seems to play no real role.

But what is meant here by the "value of human life" or by "valid moral claims"? When we speak of recognizing the value of some object, such as the Grand Canyon, or Picasso's *Guernica,* or the great whales, what we seem to have in mind is that there is reason to preserve and protect these things, and that there is reason to try to experience them in the right ways, so that we will understand and feel the force of the properties that make them valuable. Recognizing the value of human life is also, in part, a matter of seeing that it is a bad thing, a reason for sadness and regret, when people are killed or when their lives go badly in other respects. As I argued in Chapter 2, however, respecting the value of human life is in another way very different from respecting the value of objects and other creatures. Human beings are capable of assessing reasons and justifications, and proper respect for their distinctive value involves treating them only in ways that they could, by proper exercise of this capacity, recognize as justifiable. This is why it made sense, in formulating this objection, to speak of "respecting their valid moral claims."

Now someone might accept the idea that respecting the distinctive value of human beings is a matter of treating them in accord with their valid moral claims, but then add that the validity of an individual's moral claim to be treated in a certain way, and the reason-giving force that that claim has if it is valid, are independent of and prior to the ideas of justification and justifiability. There are two claims here, representing two different challenges to contractualism. The stronger claim is that not only the content of the morality of right and wrong but also its reason-giving force are independent of and prior to the idea of justifiability to others. The weaker challenge accepts the idea that justifiability to others is an important component in moral motivation but claims that there is a standard of rightness that is prior to this notion of justifiability, and that an action is justifiable in the relevant sense just in case it is right.

The stronger claim could be defended negatively by arguing that the contractualist idea of justifiability simply does not seem, intuitively, to describe the reasons that considerations of right and wrong entail. I have done my best in this chapter to rebut this negative attack. A positive defense of the stronger challenge would consist in offering some alternative account of the motivational power of considerations of right and wrong. I cannot respond to these defenses fully without considering every alternative that might be offered. Put in the broadest terms, my view is that insofar as other accounts of the reason-giving force of right and wrong avoid the "triviality" horn of Prichard's dilemma they seem to me to fail the intuitive test posed by the negative defense just mentioned: they lack a tight enough intuitive connection with our ideas of right and wrong.[22]

The weaker challenge to contractualism accepts the idea that justifiability to others has motivational force, but denies that this idea can be given content without appealing to some independent standard of right and wrong. Against this, a defense of contractualism has to argue that the idea of justifiability to others can be seen to play an important role in shaping our thinking about right and wrong, and that particular moral arguments seem to establish that an action is wrong just when, and just because, they show that so acting could not be justified to others on grounds they could not reasonably reject. This is what I will argue in the following chapters.

It may be helpful here to consider another form of the charge that contractualist morality is excessively "ideal." This is what might be called the problem of moral overload: how can we possibly be asked to take into account the reasons that every human being (or even everyone affected by our action) would have for rejecting a principle? This is a recipe for moral gridlock, since every principle is one that someone has a reason to object to.

Kant himself raised this objection against the Golden Rule. In a footnote in his *Groundwork for the Metaphysics of Morals* he points out that the requirement that we not do unto others what we would not want done to us is, among other things, unacceptably restrictive, "for on this ground the criminal could argue against the judge who sentences him, and so on."[23] Kant's reply, I take it, is that to answer the question of right and wrong what we must ask is not "What would I want if I were in another's shoes?" or even "What would be advantageous from each person's point of view?" but rather "What general principles of action could we all will?" At this point the idea of justifiability to others and the idea of respecting their value cease to be distinct. As Kant said, the formula "Act only on a maxim that you can will to be a universal law" and the formula "Act in such a way that your maxim treats humanity (whether in your own person or that of another) as an end in itself, not merely as a means" come to the same thing. To avoid gridlock we must move away from the idea that each person's life or each person's happiness "matters" to the question of an acceptable system of general principles of action. Acceptable principles could not require us, in deciding what to do, to consider how every actual individual would feel about it. And in deciding which systems of principles are "acceptable," we cannot envisage the reactions of every actual person. We can consider only representative cases, and take into account only those objections that a person could raise while recognizing the force of similar objections by others.[24] The principles that meet this test may still be very demanding, and they go as far in recognizing the claims of each as is compatible with similar recognition of the claims of all. This is what the idea of justifiability to others, on terms that no one similarly motivated could reasonably reject, is meant to capture.

7. Fragmentation of the Moral

Within contemporary moral philosophy, the term 'morality' is commonly used to refer to a particular normative domain including primarily such duties to others as duties not to kill, harm, or deceive, and duties to keep one's promises. I believe that the contractualist view I am presenting offers a good account both of the content of "morality" so understood and of its motivational basis.

But the term 'morality' is commonly used in a broader sense. At least in many quarters, for example, the proper form of sexual conduct is seen as a central moral question. Some believe that masturbation and sodomy between consenting adults are prime examples of moral wrongs, and others at least think that the propriety of such practices is a serious moral question. On the view I have been presenting, by contrast, while some actions involving sex are morally wrong—actions such as rape, other forms of coerced sex, and the irresponsible begetting of children—these wrongs can be seen as violations of general moral principles against coercion and the infliction of harm. The idea that there are specific moral prohibitions against certain forms of sexual conduct—against masturbation, for example, or against sexual relations between two men or between two women—has no plausibility whatever when the term 'moral' is understood to refer to "what we owe to each other."

Moreover, even many who would agree that the forms of sexual conduct just mentioned are not morally wrong nonetheless use the term 'morality' to cover much more than is included in the account presented here. Many would say, for example, that someone can be open to moral criticism for failing to have special concern for the interests of his friends or his children. One can, of course, argue that these obligations can be accounted for within the contractualist framework when the special features of our relations with these people are taken into account. Obligations to our friends, for example, might be explained by arguing that in treating people as friends we invite them to form expectations about our concern for them and that it is wrong to disappoint such expectations, and obligations to one's children might be explained by the fact that they are particularly dependent on us for support and protection. No doubt there are obligations of both these kinds, but they do not seem to cover all that we expect of friends and parents. Moreover, even if they did, they do not have the right kind of motivational basis: we expect a good friend or parent to be moved by special concern, not just by a general sense of obligation. A friend or parent who was moved only by the considerations I have just described would be deficient in this respect, and many would describe this as a moral deficiency.

Many also believe that they can be properly subject to moral criticism for not striving to meet high standards in their profession or for not developing their talents, even when failing to do these things does not violate any duty to others. And at least some people hold that the wanton destruction of works of nature, such as cutting down a great old redwood tree "just for fun," is morally wrong in a sense that does not depend on any claim that it deprives other human beings of resources or opportunities for enjoyment.

These examples are rather varied, and they may call for a number of different responses. But taken together they offer considerable support for the conclusion that the contractualist view I am presenting does not account either for the content or the motivational basis of all that the term 'morality', as it is used by many if not most people, is commonly taken to cover.[25] There are several possible responses to this divergence.

The first would be to hold that this wider use of 'moral' and 'morality' is mistaken. On this view, contractualism gives a complete account of the set of requirements with the distinctive kind of authority that the term 'morality' entails. The wider range of duties and obligations just described may include some that deserve to be taken seriously, but they are not properly called moral.

A second response would be to conclude that this divergence shows that contractualism is mistaken. On this view, any adequate account even of that part of morality that I am calling "what we owe to each other" must show it to be continuous with morality in the wider sense described above (at least with those parts of it that merit our respect). All these requirements should be shown to have the same subject matter and the same kind of authority.

A third response would be to conclude that most of us commonly use the terms 'moral' and 'morality' to refer to a diverse set of values, and that while contractualism characterizes a central part of the territory called morality, it does not include everything to which that term is properly applied. This conclusion seems to me to be correct. It seems correct because, on reflection, it is apparent that the values at stake in the examples listed above draw on sources of motivation that are distinct from the one that underlies the requirements of morality in the narrow sense, or "what we owe to each other." These values are related to this central moral idea in important ways, but they are not reducible to it.[26]

Consider first the cases of friendship and family relations. A person who took pleasure in the company of others, and in shared activities with them, who never treated others unfairly or took advantage of them, might nonetheless not be a friend to anyone, because he did not see what was good about closer relations with them—relations that would involve mutual concern for one another's welfare and a mutual willingness to make sacrifices for the other's sake. These commitments might strike the person merely as encumbrances. Similarly, a man who took good care of his children, because he recognized that he was responsible for their existence and that no one else would look after them if he did not, might still lack the motivation that a good father would have. Such a person, as I have described him, is certainly lacking in affect, but this is not the whole problem. Affect is not a separable psychological element that might be added to the bare moral obligations I have described in order to produce an admirable parent. The lack of affect is a sign of the fact that the person I have described fails to see the good of being a parent—fails to see having children and caring for them as a way in which it is desirable to live. Without this evaluative element, mere affect would be meaningless. (The analogous case would be a "friend" who had "warm feelings" toward his associates but regarded obligations to them as merely burdensome.)

The values of friendship and parenthood are not independent of the narrower morality of "what we owe to each other." As I argued in Section 5 for the case of friendship, they are both shaped by it and shape it in turn. They are shaped by it insofar as they are relations with others who must be recognized as persons with moral standing that is independent of this relationship; they shape it because they represent important forms of human good which any set of principles that no one could reasonably reject must make room for. But being a good friend or parent involves understanding and responding to values that go beyond this central form of morality.

I believe that this is also the best way to understand the other examples of morality in the broader sense that I mentioned above. I suggested there, for example, that a person who failed to strive for high standards in her work, or failed to develop talents that she has, might be open to moral criticism on grounds other than that she failed to fulfill her obligations to others. The most plausible form for such criticism to take is a charge that she fails to understand why achieving high standards, or developing her talents, is valuable or fails to be moved by this value if she does see it. (Analogous criticism might be leveled at a person for putting *too much* weight on these aims, or for emphasizing them in the wrong way. Such a person could also be said to misunderstand the values in question.) Since developing one's talents and striving for excellence in one's work generally involve working with other people, these values are not independent of what we owe to each other. They bear the dual relation to this part of morality that we saw in the case of friendship and family relations but, like those values, are not reducible to or derivable from this core of general obligations.

These examples provide a fruitful model for understanding the ways in which sex raises moral issues. Sexual morality gets a bad name from being identified with a list of prohibitions, such as those concerning masturbation, sodomy, and other "deviant" sexual practices. But it would be a mistake to conclude, from the implausibility of these prohibitions, that sex lies outside morality in a sense that implies that sexual attitudes and practices are immune to serious criticism as long as they do not involve the violation of generic moral prohibitions against coercion, deception, and so on. The idea that masturbation is morally forbidden is ridiculous, but a preoccupation with masturbation could reflect a failure to understand the importance and value of sex and sexual pleasure (by giving it too much importance, for example, or by misconceiving what is desirable about it). In reply, it might be said that masturbation generally involves fantasizing about other people, and that when it is morally objectionable this is because the attitudes it involves are incompatible with what we owe to others. This may be true in some cases, but it does not avoid the basic point, that in order to explain why these attitudes are objectionable we need to understand the special importance and significance of sexual relations. (Similarly, in order to understand why rape is an especially serious wrong, worse than mugging, we need to understand the special reasons people have for valuing sexual intimacy and sexual relations and for wanting to have control over them.) This illustrates the dual relation we saw above between the core morality of what we owe to others and other values. Since most sex, like work and friendship, involves other people, its value cannot be understood apart from our duties to them. But these duties in turn are shaped by the special reasons we have to value specific goods, of which sexual relations are one example, and not every failure to understand these goods is simply a mistake about what we owe to others.

Shifting from the question of what forms of sex are morally permitted to the question of how the value of sex should be understood broadens the domain of "sexual morality." It allows, for example, for the fact that the importance given to sex and sexual attractiveness in much contemporary advertising and popular culture involves a serious misvaluation of sex, while the relations between many same-sex couples do not. Speaking of "the value of sexual relations" in the way I have been doing should not be taken to imply that there is "one correct way" in which sex should be understood. There may in fact be many different ways of understanding the value of sex that are defensible and worthy of respect. Even if there are not, there are surely many different forms of sexual practice that are compatible with this value.

The question of the value of sex seems to me to be unfortunately neglected, perhaps because discussion has been divided between those who believe that sex is central to morality but identify "sexual morality" with the conventional set of prohibitions against "deviant" acts, and those who, in reaction to this position, maintain that sex is "not a moral issue." In this context, although the Catholic doctrine that all forms of sexual relations that are not "essentially procreative" are morally forbidden strikes me as mistaken, it at least can be seen as having the merit of starting from the right question, of how sexual relations should be understood and properly valued. More attention to alternative answers would be a good thing.

The values I have been discussing are all matters about which we have good reason to want to be in (actual) agreement, or something close to it, with people around us. We cannot have friendships unless there are others who share our idea of what friendship involves; striving for excellence in a field is much less meaningful without some community of others who see the point of our striving; and so on for other cases. The same thing is true in the case of what we owe to each other: we have good reason to want to live with others who share our notions of justifiability. But in this case an idea of (hypothetical) agreement plays a further and deeper role. The ideal of justifiability to others is what gives rise to the categories of moral argument in this narrower sense, shapes them, and gives them their importance. Nothing like this is true in the other cases. Agreement about these values is desirable and a measure of it even essential, and they are to a degree shaped by the requirements of justifiability to others. Nonetheless, these values do not arise simply out of a quest for terms of justification but rather out of a shared sense that certain things are worthwhile.[27]

Given this difference and others I have noted, it may be asked why I do not draw the first conclusion listed above, that the term 'morality' should be restricted to this narrower domain. I have not drawn this conclusion for several reasons. First, what seems to me most important is to recognize the distinctness of the various values I have discussed and their complex relation to what we owe to each other. Once the nature and motivational basis of these values is recognized, it does not matter greatly how broadly or narrowly the label 'moral' is applied. Second, even if these values go beyond what we owe to each other (as is shown by the fact that one cannot arrive at an understanding of them just by thinking about what principles others could not reasonably reject), they are, as I have tried to show, related to this part of morality in complex ways. There is therefore no point in exaggerating the difference by calling one "moral" and the others "nonmoral."

Finally, however "morality" in the broad sense should be understood, it is a fact that many, perhaps most, people use this term to cover more than just what we owe to each other. Demanding that the term be restricted to this narrow domain would therefore be seen by many as denying the importance of the values that would thereby be excluded from the domain of morality, and resisted on that account. This seems to me a battle that is best avoided. As I have already said, what is important is to understand the nature of these diverse values and the relations between them.[28] The advantages of recognizing diverse but related forms of value as all entitled to the name of morality is illustrated by the question that I will discuss in the next section: How wide is the range of creatures whose treatment by us falls within the part of morality that contractualism describes?

8. The Scope of Morality

Before turning to the task of describing this idea of reasonable rejection in more detail I want to say something about the scope of the part of morality that I am calling "what we owe to each other." What is the range of creatures to whom these duties are owed, and who thus can be wronged in the sense I have been describing? This question is appropriately addressed here because an answer to it depends on the point and reason-giving force of moral requirements. The class of creatures who can be wronged in this sense is the class of creatures to whom we can stand in the relation that underlies the form of moral motivation I have been describing in this chapter.

Any account of the scope of morality, or of some important part of it, is bound to be controversial, but a philosophical account of our ideas of moral right and wrong should at least provide some basis for understanding what this disagreement is about, and why some answers seem plausible while others are definitely ruled out. It is often thought that contractualism provides no plausible basis for addressing this question. Either it provides no basis at all, since a contractualist theory must begin with some set of contracting parties as its starting point; or it suggests an answer which is obviously too restrictive, since a contract requires parties who are able to make and keep agreements and who are each able to offer the others some benefit in return for their cooperation.

Neither of these objections applies to the version of contractualism that I am presenting. To answer them briefly: contractualism as I understand it locates the source of the reason-giving force of judgments of right and wrong in the importance of standing in a certain relation to others. Morality will thus include all those with respect to whom one has strong reason to want to stand in this relation and hence to give great weight to its requirements. Since this relation is not an agreement for mutual advantage, my version of contractualism does not have the implausible implications about the scope of morality that the second objection suggests. Let me now consider these matters in more detail.

First, it should be borne in mind that, as I said in the previous section, contractualism as I describe it is not meant to characterize everything that can be called "moral" but only that part of the moral sphere that is marked out by certain specific ideas of right and wrong, or "what we owe to others." The boundary of this part of morality marks an important moral distinction, but it does not mark the difference between those beings who "count morally" and the rest who are of merely instrumental value. If, as I have suggested, there are different kinds of moral values, then there are different ways of being morally significant. Much of the confusion that infects discussion of "the scope of morality" results, I believe, from a failure to recognize this plurality of moral values. We find ourselves pulled first to expand the bounds of "morality" because it is implausible to deny that certain things are "morally significant." But we are then pulled to contract this boundary again because categories appropriate to "moral" thinking (understood now as thinking about what we owe to each other) do not seem to fit the cases in question. This confusion is aided by the fact that the word 'wrong' can be used in a broad sense to express the view that some form of conduct is open to a serious moral objection of some kind. But many different things are held to constitute such objections. When someone says, for example, that it would be wrong to cut down an old forest to make millions of tacky curios, it is not plausible to suppose that they mean to be making objections based on the moral idea that contractualism attempts to characterize.

Contractualism offers an account of one particular moral idea which, it claims, plays a central role in our appraisal of our actions toward each other. The question now before us is this: if the account that contractualism offers is correct, what does this imply about the range of creatures toward whom one can behave wrongly in this central sense? Bearing this in mind, consider the following possible characterizations of the class of beings behavior toward whom is subject to such judgments.

(1) Those beings that have a good; that is, those for which things can go better or worse
(2) Those beings in group (1) who are conscious, and capable of feeling pain
(3) Those beings in group (2) who are capable of judging things as better or worse and, more generally, capable of holding judgment-sensitive attitudes
(4) Those beings in group (3) who are capable of making the particular kind of judgments involved in moral reasoning
(5) Those beings in group (4) with whom it is advantageous for us to enter into a system of mutual restraint and cooperation

Cutting across these categories, there is the question of whether morality includes within its scope all possible beings of a given kind, or only actual beings (those who do, will, or have existed), or only those beings who actually exist at the present time (the time of acting, say).

According to contractualism, the scope of the morality of right and wrong will include those beings to whom we have good reason to want our actions to be justifiable. What answers does this suggest to the questions I have just posed?

One thing it strongly suggests is that the morality of right and wrong does not cover all the beings in group (1). This group would include not only sentient creatures but also oak trees and tomato plants, and perhaps even forests and wetland ecosystems, since all these things "have a good" in the most abstract sense: that is to say, there is such a thing as events' and conditions' being good or bad for them. But these are not, intuitively, beings that one can wrong, and contractualism can explain this. In order for the idea of justification *to* a being to make sense it must at least be the kind of thing that can be conscious. This does not mean that what happens to things that are incapable of consciousness does not matter, or even that wantonly harming or destroying them would not be, in some way, morally criticizable. It might even be wrong, in the broad sense that I mentioned above, to destroy an old forest to build a parking lot. If so, this is just to say that there is a serious objection to this course of action, a moral objection in the broad sense of the term 'moral'. But this objection is not that by cutting it down we would wrong the forest or the trees that make it up. Not every entity that has a good, in the abstract sense that we are now considering, even a good that generates moral reasons for acting one way rather than another, is a being that can be wronged. This is because, I suggest, a thing's having a good in this sense is not sufficient to ground the idea of "justifiability to" that thing.

Shifting to the other extreme for the moment, it seems clear that we can make sense of "justifiability to" beings who have the capacity for moral reasoning—beings in group (4) above—and that we have strong reason to want our actions to be justifiable to them. Moreover, contractualism as I have described it provides no grounds for moving to a more restrictive conception of the scope of right and wrong. If the aim of this part of morality lay in securing the benefits of cooperation, then there might be reason to confine its scope to group (5), thereby excluding, for example, those who are incapable of being restrained by moral principles and those who could not harm or benefit us in any event and so have nothing to offer us by their restraint or cooperation. But this is not the aim I have described, and those who would be excluded by moving from (4) to (5) are still people to whom we have reason to want our actions to be justifiable.

The difference between group (3) and group (4) is in practice rather small. It is difficult to see how beings could be capable of judgment-sensitive attitudes without the capacity for language.[29] (How else are the reasons to be represented in judgment?) So group (3) seems to extend very little if at all beyond the class of human beings. There certainly could be and presumably are beings who fall within group (3) but not (4): who are capable of judgment-sensitive attitudes but not of moral reasoning. It seems to me, however, that the idea of "justifiability to" such beings nonetheless makes sense, and that we have reason to care about it. Claims about what it would be reasonable for them to accept if they were moved to find principles which others also could not reasonably reject involve a minimal counterfactual element. Moreover, their capacities for reasoning and rational self-direction call for the kind of respect that entails treating them only in ways that they could (in this minimally counterfactual sense) not reasonably object to. So contractualism gives us little reason for drawing the bounds of the morality of right and wrong more narrowly than group (3).

Should these bounds be broader? If those nonhuman animals who lack the capacity for language are therefore not capable of holding judgment-sensitive attitudes, then they will be outside the part of morality I am describing if it includes only the beings in group (3). Creatures who cannot assess reasons cannot have intentions in the strict sense in which an intention is a judgment-sensitive attitude. But nonhuman animals seem clearly to engage in goal-directed activity. In some cases this activity is the expression of biologically given instincts, as when birds migrate or when salmon swim upstream to spawn. In other cases, the goals are more idiosyncratic, as when my cat tries to get a pencil out of the crack in my desk. This makes the activity seem more like the intentional action of rational creatures, even if it is not modifiable by the assessment of reasons. It seems likely that any creature to which we can attribute pain must be capable at least of goal-directed activity, if not of judgment-sensitive attitudes, since it is difficult to see how we could attribute pain to a creature without taking it to be trying to avoid what is painful.

When we believe that a creature is in pain, we normally have an immediate sympathetic response: we see its pain as something there is reason to alleviate. Moreover, we have no reason to think this response is in general mistaken. Pain—whether that of rational creatures or nonrational ones—is something we have prima facie reason to prevent, and stronger reason not to cause. Appreciating these reasons is central to understanding the value of sentient beings (on the account of value discussed in Chapter 2). Given the plausible assumption that responding appropriately to the value of other creatures is part of morality in the broad sense, this accounts for the intuition that it is a serious moral failing to be indifferent to the suffering of nonhuman animals, and hence morally wrong in the broad sense of that term to cause them pain without adequate justification. Thus, it is not necessary to claim that nonhuman animals fall within the scope of the narrower part of morality I have been describing in order to account for the fact that there are serious moral objections to torturing animals for fun and to such practices as subjecting them to painful treatments in order to test cosmetics.

Since human beings are sentient creatures too, their pain is also something we have prima facie reason to prevent. But our moral relations with other humans involve rights and duties that go beyond this. It is this further dimension of moral relations that contractualism seeks to explain, through the idea that respecting the value of rational creatures involves not only responding appropriately to their pain but also treating them in accordance with principles that they could not reasonably reject. Since human beings have reason to avoid pain, they could reasonably reject principles that allowed others to inflict pain on them without good reason, or to fail to relieve their pain when they could easily do so. There can thus be more than one kind of reason to respond to a human being who is in pain: his pain is bad, and we may owe it to him to help relieve it.

The claim that reasons of the latter sort do not apply in the case of nonrational creatures would not imply that human pain is a worse thing to have occur than the pain of nonrational animals. The point is rather that if we have reason to care about the justifiability of our actions to other rational creatures, but not to nonrational ones, then our actions toward them are governed by a further class of reasons. Consider, then, the view that while it is morally wrong, in the broad sense of that term, to be heedless of the suffering of creatures who fall outside group (3), we do not stand in the further moral relations to them that underlie the part of morality that my contractualist account describes. Are there reasons for finding this view unsatisfactory?

It is most likely to seem unsatisfactory in cases in which we do have something like relations of this kind. With our pets, for example, we may value taking ourselves to have a relationship modeled on that between humans, a relationship involving mutual expectation, reciprocated affection, and emotions such as disappointment, anger, and even resentment. This involves attributing to the animal capacities that go well beyond those described in (2). Whether this attribution is correct or not, this kind of relationship is important to the role that pets play in our lives, and those of us who have and value this kind of relation with animals can hardly avoid applying the categories of right and wrong to our behavior toward them. This accounts, I think, for the extra degree of moral disapproval that many people feel toward the mistreatment of dogs, cats, horses, and other animals whom they see as candidates for this kind of relationship. The same can be true of some wild animals as well: much greater indignation than that provoked by the killing of just any crow or raccoon may be aroused by the death of the crow or raccoon who has become a regular visitor to one's window, or repeatedly taken food from one's hand, and has thereby become personalized and assigned attitudes and expectations.

It may seem, however, that torturing any animal, wild or tame, and whether we have any relationship with it or not, is wrong in the very same sense in which it is wrong to torture a human being. I have already allowed that there is a moral objection that applies in both of these cases: like the pain of humans, the pain of nonhuman animals is something we have reason to prevent and relieve, and failing to respond to this reason is a moral fault. But torturing an animal may seem wrong in a sense that goes beyond the idea that its pain is a bad thing: it is something for which we should feel guilty *to* the animal itself, just as we can feel guilt to a human being. This suggests that the require-

ment of justifiability to others should be extended to include all creatures in group (2). A contractualist view can accommodate this intuition if it holds that in deciding which principles could not reasonably
be rejected we must take into account objections that could be raised
by trustees representing creatures in this group who themselves lack
the capacity to assess reasons.

Once the idea of trusteeship is introduced, it would be possible to
extend the range of creatures to whom justifiability is owed even
farther, by including trustees even for objects in group (1), which
included all natural objects that "have a good." This extension is not
plausible. As I remarked above, the idea that there is a moral objection
to harming or defacing works of nature (apart from any effects this has
on human life) is adequately explained by the fact that the character of
these objects—such as their grandeur, beauty, and complexity—provides compelling reason not to harm them. Nothing would be added
by bringing in the idea of what a trustee for these objects would have
reason to reject. By contrast, in the case of rational creatures, something is added by this idea. By accepting the requirement that they
should be treated only in ways allowed by principles that they could
not reasonably reject, we acknowledge their status as self-governing
beings, not just things that can be harmed or benefited.

The question at issue is whether there is also reason to take this
requirement to apply to sentient but nonrational creatures in group
(2). We can see what this would involve by considering the grounds on
which trustees for such creatures could reasonably object to proposed
principles. One natural suggestion is that they would have at least
prima facie reason to object to principles that would permit people to
act in ways that were contrary to "the good" of the creatures in
question. This can be understood in at least two different ways. First,
the good of these creatures might be understood in the "organic"
sense, applicable to all living things, which consists in functioning well
and carrying out the life cycle typical of the kind of organism that they
are. But not everything that interferes with animals' living the kind of
life typical of their species seems to trigger even prima facie moral
objections of the kind contractualism is intended to capture. Painlessly
administering birth control medication to wild animals in order to
prevent their population from becoming an inconvenience to their
human neighbors, for example, does not seem even prima facie objectionable in this sense (assuming that it does not cause distress to
individual animals).

A second way of understanding the good of a nonrational creature is closer to the idea of well-being, discussed in Chapter 3. As I argued there, the central elements in the well-being of humans include the experiential quality of their lives and the successful carrying out of their rational aims. The beings we are now discussing do not have rational aims in this sense. They do engage in goal-directed activity, but, apart from the distress it may cause, interfering with this activity does not seem in itself to raise moral objections. So this aspect of this notion of a creature's good does not seem to provide grounds on which a trustee for nonrational creatures could object to proposed principles. By contrast, objections based on experiential harms such as pain and distress seem to have moral force that is independent of appeals to other aspects of the good of a creature. We see pain as something a trustee for a creature could reasonably object to not because it is incompatible with a creature's natural functioning, or because it is something the creature tries to avoid, but because of how we take it to feel to that creature.

It seems, then, that the objections that trustees for nonrational animals could raise to proposed principles may be limited to objections based on experiential harms such as pain and distress.[30] If this is correct, then the practical difference between the two views I have been considering may not be very great. One view holds that although it is morally objectionable, in the broad sense, to fail to take account of the pain and distress of nonrational creatures, we do not have the reason that we have in the case of rational creatures to accept the general requirement that our conduct be justifiable to them. The other view holds that we do have reason to accept this requirement, and that we can wrong nonrational sentient creatures in exactly the same sense in which we can wrong humans. But the fact that these creatures are not rational limits the ways in which they can be wronged to forms of treatment that unjustifiably cause them pain and distress. These two views may agree about which forms of treatment of nonhuman animals are morally objectionable, but they disagree about the nature of these moral objections. The second view also leaves open the possibility that there might be a wider range of duties to animals, if the line of argument I sketched in the previous paragraph turns out to be mistaken.

I myself am inclined toward the first of these views. Given the availability of the "trusteeship" interpretation, however, accepting contractualism as an account of what we owe to each other does not force one to take this alternative. While it does not settle the question of the moral status of nonhuman animals, the contractualist account does, I believe, provide a clearer account of what is at issue, and of the considerations that pull us toward different answers.

Limiting the scope of the morality of right and wrong to beings with the capacity to hold judgment-sensitive attitudes may seem too restrictive even as far as human beings are concerned. Normal adult human beings have this capacity, but drawing the boundary in this way would seem to exclude infants, even young children, and adults who do not develop normal capacities. As far as infants and young children are concerned, this objection derives its force from a misleading formulation. Infants and young children are not separate kinds of creatures. Rather, infancy and childhood are, in normal cases, stages in the life of a being who will have the capacity for judgment-sensitive attitudes. Moreover, in the case of children and infants this is already an actual being, not merely a possible one, since its conscious life has begun.

Not every human being develops normal human capacities, however, so there is the question of what this criterion implies about the moral status of those severely disabled humans who never develop even the limited capacities required for judgment-sensitive attitudes. The question is whether we have reason to accept the requirement that our treatment of these individuals should be governed by principles that they could not reasonably reject, even though they themselves do not and will not have the capacity to understand or weigh justifications. The answer is that we clearly do. The mere fact that a being is "of human born" provides a strong reason for according it the same status as other humans. This has sometimes been characterized as a prejudice, called "speciesism." But it is not prejudice to hold that our relation to these beings gives us reason to accept the requirement that our actions should be justifiable to them. Nor is it prejudice to recognize that this particular reason does not apply to other beings with comparable capacities, whether or not there are other reasons to accept this requirement with regard to them.

The beings in question here are ones who are born to us or to others to whom we are bound by the requirements of justifiability. This tie of birth gives us good reason to want to treat them "as human" despite their limited capacities. Because of these limitations, the idea of justifiability to them must be understood counterfactually, in terms of what they could reasonably reject if they were able to understand such a question. This makes the idea of trusteeship appropriate in their case, whether it is appropriate for the case of nonhuman animals or not. It also indicates a basis on which such a trustee could object to proposed principles. Severely disabled humans have reason to want those things that any human has reason to want, insofar as these are things that they are capable of benefiting from. These will include, at least, protection and care, affection, and those enjoyments of which the person is capable. So, while a large part of the morality of right and wrong, including rights and liberties that are important to us because of our interest in controlling and directing our own lives, may have no application in this case, other basic duties will have their usual force.

The answer to the first question of scope, then, is that according to contractualism the class of beings whom it is possible to wrong will include at least all those beings who are of a kind that is normally capable of judgment-sensitive attitudes, and may include nonrational creatures as well, depending on how far the idea of trusteeship is taken to apply. To turn to the second question of scope mentioned above, does the part of morality I am describing apply to all possible beings of the kinds to which it applies or only to actual beings, that is to say, to those who do, will, or have existed? Or does it apply only to those beings who exist at a certain time (say, the time of the action that is being judged)? The idea of justifiability to all possible beings (even all possible beings of a certain kind) seems impossibly broad, and barely coherent. On the other hand, a restriction to presently existing beings seems obviously too narrow. Any actual human being, or actual member of group (3), whether existing now or only at some past or future time, constitutes a point of view relative to which the question of justifiability makes sense, and we have reason to value the justifiability of our actions to these people—that is to say, to those who are already dead, or not yet born, as well as to our contemporaries.

Our duties to the dead are more limited than what we owe to our contemporaries, because of the limited ways in which their interests can be affected by what we do. But the question of these limits is a substantive question that is properly addressed within the morality of right and wrong rather than by a constraint on its scope. Similarly, there is the question, raised by Derek Parfit, of whether a course of action (such as polluting the environment or depleting its resources) can be said to have wronged people living in the future if it is also true that if a different policy had been followed those particular people would not have existed.[31] This again is a substantive question about when we have wronged someone, not a question about who can be wronged. I will discuss this question in Chapter 5, as a problem about the grounds of "reasonable rejection." Here I will only observe that contractualism provides no reason for saying that people who do not now exist but will exist in the future have no moral claims on us. It seems, then, that contractualism draws us toward the second of the three alternatives I listed: the beings whom it is possible to wrong are all those who do, have, or will actually exist.

9. Conclusion

The main aim of this chapter has been to present the contractualist idea of justifiability to others as an account of the reasons that underlie and shape a central part of our moral thinking. Contractualism offers a substantive account of these reasons: one that aims to describe them in a way that makes their appeal and significance more evident. I argued that the idea of justifiability to others has the properties that such an account needs to have. It is closely enough connected to our ideas of right and wrong to be clearly an account of *moral* reasons, but it is not so closely identified with these ideas as to amount to the trivial claim that the reason we have to avoid certain actions is just that they are wrong.

On the basis of this contractualist account we can, I argued, explain both the priority that the part of morality it describes claims over other values and the special importance we attach to being moved by it (the importance indicated by the gulf that seems to separate us from those who are not so moved). Contractualism does not provide a plausible account of everything to which the name 'morality' is commonly applied. It thus entails that morality in this broad sense is motivationally diverse, and I have maintained that this implication is, on reflection, one that we should accept.

I have not tried to show that every rational person must be committed to the aim of finding and living by principles that others, if similarly motivated, could not reasonably reject (as I might have done by, for example, trying to show that this aim follows from considerations that any rational creature must at least implicitly recognize). I myself accept contractualism largely because the account it offers of moral motivation is phenomenologically more accurate than any other I know of. It captures very accurately my sense of the reasons that ground and shape my thinking about central questions of right and wrong, and I find the distinctions that it implies—for example, between "what we owe to each other" and other areas of morality—intuitively compelling. In this chapter I have tried to present these advantages so that readers can appreciate and assess their appeal, and have tried to forestall certain natural misunderstandings and objections that might prevent them from doing so. Of course, the plausibility of contractualism depends also on its substantive implications about right and wrong. Laying these out will be the task of the next three chapters.

5

The Structure
of Contractualism

1. Introduction

The idea that an act is right if and only if it can be justified to others is
one that even a noncontractualist might accept.[1] Utilitarians, for example, who hold that an act is right only if it would produce a greater
balance of happiness than any alternative available to the agent at the
time, presumably also believe that an act is justifiable to others just in
case it satisfies this utilitarian formula, so they too will hold that an act
is right if and only if it is justifiable to others on terms they could not
reasonably reject. For utilitarians, however, what makes an action
right is having the best consequences; justifiability is merely a consequence of this.

What is distinctive about my version of contractualism is that it
takes the idea of justifiability to be basic in two ways: this idea provides both the normative basis of the morality of right and wrong and
the most general characterization of its content. According to contractualism, when we address our minds to a question of right and wrong,
what we are trying to decide is, first and foremost, whether certain
principles are ones that no one, if suitably motivated, could reasonably
reject. In order to make the content of my view clearer I need to say
more about the ideas of justifiability and reasonable rejection on which
it rests. This is the aim of the present chapter.

Many theories have been offered that are like mine in suggesting
that we can understand the content of morality (or of justice) by
considering what principles people would (perhaps under special conditions) have reason to agree to, or what principles could be willed
(from a certain point of view) to hold universally. These include, to
mention only a few well-known examples, Kant's view and the theo-

ries offered more recently by David Gauthier, Jürgen Habermas, R. M. Hare, and John Rawls.[2] Most of these theories appeal to some idea of rationality or of what it would be rational to choose (perhaps under special conditions). In Gauthier's case, rationality is identified, initially, with doing or choosing what conduces to the fulfillment of one's aims, and his aim is to show how we could have good reason to comply with principles that it would be rational, in this sense, for all to agree to. Hare identifies the rational action with the action that would maximize the satisfaction of one's present preferences as they would be if purged of logical error and modified by exposure to the facts. Since he takes moral principles to be universal imperatives (applying not only to things as they are but also to the possible worlds in which one occupies the position of any of the other people performing or affected by actions of the kind in question), a rational decision about which principles to accept must take into account not only one's present preferences but also the preferences one would have in any of these other positions. Rationally defensible moral principles will thus be those that lead to maximum satisfaction of the rational preferences of all affected parties.[3]

Kant famously held that an action is morally permissible if it would be allowed by a principle that one could rationally will to hold "as a universal law." Rawls maintains, as one part of his theory, that the principles of justice (standards for determining the legitimacy of basic social institutions) are those that it would be rational for parties to accept if they were to choose with the aim of doing as well as they can for those they represent but under conditions in which they lacked any information about their social position, their natural advantages, and their distinctive values and commitments (that is to say, if they were to choose behind a "veil of ignorance" that obscures these facts).

Each of the theories I have mentioned proposes that we can reach conclusions about the content of morality by asking certain questions about what it would be rational to do or choose or will. In each case these questions are understood in a way that requires us, in one way or another, to take the interests of others into account in answering it. In the case of Gauthier's theory, we must take account of what others have reason to do because we are trying to gain the benefits of cooperative arrangements and it would not be rational for others to accept a plan of action if doing so would not advance their interests. In Hare's theory, and in the part of Rawls's that I have mentioned, the rational choice in question is defined in a way that makes the fates of others relevant in a different way.[4] In Hare's theory this is accomplished by adding information and motivation: information about other people's preferences, which then shapes our own preferences about how we would want to be treated if we were in their position. In Rawls's theory it is done by subtracting information (imposing a veil of ignorance) and by focusing on motivation of one particular kind—the desire of mutually disinterested parties to do as well as they can for themselves and those whom they represent. Contracting parties are moved to protect the interests of the least advantaged and of cultural and religious minorities because, for all they know, they may belong to these groups themselves.

According to the version of contractualism that I am advancing here our thinking about right and wrong is structured by a different kind of motivation, namely the aim of finding principles that others, insofar as they too have this aim, could not reasonably reject. This gives us a direct reason to be concerned with other people's points of view: not because we might, for all we know, actually *be* them, or because we might occupy their position in some other possible world, but in order to find principles that they, as well as we, have reason to accept.[5] As I pointed out in Chapter 4, there is on this view a strong continuity between the reasons that lead us to act in the way that the conclusions of moral thought require and the reasons that shape the process through which we arrive at those conclusions. My version of contractualism is distinguished from these otherwise similar theories, then, by its particular motivational claim and by its appeal to the notion of reasonableness rather than rationality.

2. Reasonableness

This second feature, in particular, may seem questionable. Why speak of "principles which no one could reasonably reject" rather than "principles which no one could rationally reject"? The "reasonableness" formulation seems more obscure. Why use it, then, especially in view of the fact that I add the rider "given the aim of finding principles which others, insofar as they share this aim, could not reasonably reject"? Why not rely upon the idea of what would be *rational* for a person who has this aim?

As I mentioned in Chapter 1, "rationality" can be understood in a number of different ways. But in recent years "the (most) rational thing to do" has most commonly been taken to mean "what most conduces to the fulfillment of the agent's aims." The primacy of this usage is indicated by the contemporary theories I have just discussed, which despite their differences almost all make use of the idea of rationality in more or less this same sense. As I have indicated, I believe that this conception of rationality is mistaken, but it is so familiar that it is what any unqualified use of the term is likely to call to mind.

"Reasonable" also has an established meaning, which is much closer to what I take to be basic to moral thinking. A claim about what it is reasonable for a person to do presupposes a certain body of information and a certain range of reasons which are taken to be relevant, and goes on to make a claim about what these reasons, properly understood, in fact support.[6] In the contractualist analysis of right and wrong, what is presupposed first and foremost is the aim of finding principles that others who share this aim could not reasonably reject. This aim then brings other reasons in its train. Given this aim, for example, it would be unreasonable to give the interests of others no weight in deciding which principles to accept. For why should they accept principles arrived at in this way? This then leads to further, more complicated questions about how, more exactly, we can be asked to "take others' interests into account" in various situations.

The distinction between what it would be reasonable to do in this sense and what it would be rational to do is not a technical one, but a familiar distinction in ordinary language.[7] Suppose, for example, that we are negotiating about water rights in our county, and that there is one landowner who already controls most of the water in the vicinity. This person has no need for our cooperation. He can do as he pleases, and what he chooses to do will largely determine the outcome of the negotiations. Suppose also that while he is not ungenerous (he would probably provide water from his own wells for anyone who desperately needed it) he is extremely irritable and does not like to have the legitimacy of his position questioned. In such a situation, it would not be unreasonable for one of us to maintain that each person is entitled to at least a minimum supply of water, and to reject any principle of allocation which does not guarantee this. But it might not be rational to make this claim or to reject such principles, since this is very likely to enrage the large landholder and lead to an outcome that is worse for almost everyone. Moreover, it is natural to say that it would be unreasonable of the large landholder to reject our request for principles guaranteeing minimum water rights. What it would be rational for him to do (in the most common understanding of that term) is a different question, and depends on what his aims are.

There is, then, a familiar distinction between reasonableness and rationality. It might be objected that in calling attention to this distinction I have concentrated exclusively on what would be rational *simpliciter*, and have not considered what would be rational given the particular aim I have specified. Why not, it might be asked, take rightness to be determined by the principles no one could *rationally* reject given the aim of finding principles which others, who share this aim, could also not rationally reject? This seems to offer a way of capturing the idea that I have in mind while avoiding the obscure notion of reasonableness in favor of the clearer and better-understood idea of rationality.

My first reason for not formulating the contractualist account of right and wrong in this way is that so formulated it is most likely to be understood as a question of strategy, of how best to bring about the desired end of agreement on principles.[8] So interpreted, it is unlikely to have a determinate answer, in light of the fact, noted above, that what it is rational to do will depend on what others can be expected to do in response. If there is one principle which would make everyone better off than he or she would be under any other, then it may be obvious that it is rational for everyone to choose this principle, and the question "What principle could no one rationally reject given the aim of finding principles that others, who share this aim, could not rationally reject?" may therefore have a determinate answer. But in more common situations we must choose among principles each of which would benefit some at the expense of others. In such cases, there may be no determinate answer, in the abstract, to the question whether a given principle is or is not one that no one with the aim in question could rationally reject.

The answer to this question in a given situation may become determinate once the details of that situation—the psychologies of the individuals involved and the options open to them—are fully specified. In the water rights case mentioned above, for example, even if all of us (the large landowner included) share the aim of finding principles which no one else could rationally reject, it remains true that none of us has reason to reject the terms which he prefers. Adding the aim of rational agreement makes little difference in this case, since the landowner is in a position to make it rational for his neighbors to accept whatever principle he chooses. In this example the answer, though determinate, carries little moral weight. If we rule out the features of this example which make it morally objectionable—by requiring, for example, that there be full information and a no-agreement point which leaves everyone in a position that is at least minimally acceptable—then determinateness may be lost again, since the outcome may depend on the individual psychologies of the parties, and their relations and loyalties. One familiar strategy is to impose further constraints on the agreement in question, with the aim of preserving both determinateness and moral relevance. This strategy may well succeed in particular cases. My present aim is not to argue against theories employing this strategy but rather to distinguish it from the strategy that I am pursuing.

According to my version of contractualism, deciding whether an action is right or wrong requires a substantive judgment on our part about whether certain objections to possible moral principles would be reasonable. In the argument over water rights, for example, our judgment that it would not be unreasonable for the neighbors to demand better terms than the large landowner is offering reflects a substantive judgment about the merits of their claims. It is not a judgment about what would be most likely to advance their interests or to produce agreement in their actual circumstances or in any more idealized situation, but rather a judgment about the suitability of certain principles to serve as the basis of mutual recognition and accommodation.

If my analysis is correct then the idea of what would be reasonable in this sense is one that underlies and guides our ordinary thinking about right and wrong. It is thus an idea with moral content. This moral content makes it inviting as a component in moral theory, but also invites the charge of circularity. By basing itself on reasonableness, it may be charged, a theory builds in moral elements at the start. This makes it easy to produce a theory which *sounds* plausible, but such a theory will tell us very little, since everything we are to get out of it at the end we must put in at the beginning as part of the moral content of reasonableness. A strategy which relies on the idea of rationality (together, perhaps, with structural features of an ideal situation in which the rational choices are to be made) therefore seems to promise a more successful theory, or at least an account of right and wrong which is less threatened with circularity. Before responding to this objection, I will describe my version of contractualism in somewhat greater detail. By making clearer the ways in which judgments about reasonable rejection "have moral content" I hope to clarify both the force of the charge of circularity and my way of responding to it.

Before turning to this task, however, I want to say more about how the idea of reasonableness figures in the process of deciding whether or not an action is wrong. According to contractualism, in order to decide whether it would be wrong to do X in circumstances C, we should consider possible principles governing how one may act in such situations, and ask whether any principle that permitted one to do X in those circumstances could, for that reason, reasonably be rejected. In order to decide whether this is so, we need first to form an idea of the burdens that would be imposed on some people in such a situation if others were permitted to do X. Call these the objections to permission.[9] We then need, in order to decide whether these objections provide grounds for reasonably rejecting the proposed principle, to consider the ways in which others would be burdened by a principle forbidding one to do X in these circumstances. Suppose that, compared to the objections to permission, the objections to prohibition are not significant, and that it is therefore reasonable to reject any principle that would permit one to do X in the circumstances in question. This means that this action is wrong, according to the contractualist formula. Alternatively, if there were some principle for regulating behavior in such situations that would permit one to do X and that it would not be reasonable to reject, then doing X would not be wrong: it could be justified to others on grounds that they could not reasonably refuse to accept.

Returning to the former case for the moment, if it would be reasonable to reject any principle that permitted one to do X in circumstances C, then it would seem that there must be some principle that it would not be reasonable to reject that would disallow doing X in these circumstances. One would expect this to be true because of the comparative nature of the question of reasonable rejection. If the objections to permission are strong enough, *compared to the objections to prohibition,* to make it reasonable to reject any principle permitting doing X in C, then one would not expect the objections to prohibition to be strong enough, *compared to the objections to permission,* to make it reasonable to reject any principle that forbids doing X in C.

But it may seem that there could be cases in which this might be true.[10] Consider, for example, the case of two people swimming from a sinking ship, one of whom finds a life jacket floating in the water. May the other person take the jacket by force? It might seem that, even though any principle that permitted this could reasonably be rejected, any principle forbidding it could also be rejected, since taking the jacket is the only way for the other person to avoid drowning. Put in a general form, the idea might be that there is a threshold of reasonable rejection: a level of cost such that it is reasonable to reject any principle that would lead to one's suffering a cost that great, and reasonable to do this no matter what objections others might have to alternative principles. It does not seem to me that there is such a threshold. It does not seem, for example, that the fact that a principle would forbid one to do something that was necessary in order to save one's life always makes it reasonable to reject that principle. The reasonableness of rejecting such a principle will depend not only on the costs that alternative principles would impose on others but also on how those costs would be imposed. This reflects the general fact, which I will discuss later in this chapter, that the strength of a person's objection to a principle is not determined solely by the difference that the acceptance of that principle would make to that person's welfare. In the shipwreck case, for example, the costs of the two principles to the parties may be the same (one will drown if not permitted to seize the life jacket, and the other will drown if it is taken from him). But it may still make a difference to the force of their objections that one of them now has the jacket (perhaps he has looked hard to find it) and is therefore not now at risk.

Even if the general idea of a threshold of reasonable rejection is incorrect, however, there could still be cases in which opposing parties have strong objections that are evenly balanced. Suppose, for example, that the two swimmers, one of whom is much stronger than the other, arrive at the life jacket at the same moment. May each use force to try to seize it? It might seem that if a principle permitting this could reasonably be rejected then so too could a principle forbidding it, since the considerations on the two sides are the same. This conclusion depends on an overly simple view of the alternatives. A principle permitting each to struggle for the jacket at least has the merit of recognizing the symmetry of their claims and the need for some decisive solution. It would be reasonable to reject this principle if, but only if, there were some alternative that did this better (such as a principle requiring them to take turns or, unrealistic as it may seem, to draw lots). Similarly, a principle forbidding the use of force could not reasonably be rejected if there were some other (nonrejectable) method for resolving the matter.

It thus does not follow, from the fact that the situations of the people who would suffer from an action's being permitted and those who would suffer from its being forbidden are virtually the same, that if any principle that permits the action can reasonably be rejected then so too can any principle that forbids it. The very fact that these objections are symmetrical may point the way toward a class of principles that are not rejectable.

3. Principles

I have said that an act is wrong if it would be disallowed by any *principle* that no one could reasonably reject. The aim of this section is to explain what is meant here by a principle and to say something about the role that such principles play in our thinking about right and wrong. Taking familiar controversies about act and rule utilitarianism as a background, it would be natural to ask why justification of our actions to others should proceed by way of principles at all. Why not consider individual acts instead? Put in this way, the question is misconceived. To justify an action to others is to offer reasons supporting it and to claim that they are sufficient to defeat any objections that others may have. To do this, however, is also to defend a principle, namely one claiming that such reasons are sufficient grounds for so acting under the prevailing conditions. There is a question (corresponding to the debate between act and rule utilitarianism) as to whether the justification for an action should appeal only to consequences of that act (as compared with the consequences of alternative actions available to the agent) or whether other considerations are also relevant. I will address this question in the following section. But it is a question about the form that the relevant principles should take, not about whether justification should involve principles at all.

The emphasis that contractualism places on justification, hence on reasons and principles, captures a central feature of everyday judgments of right and wrong. Typically, our intuitive judgments about the wrongness of actions are not simply judgments *that* an act is wrong but that it is wrong for some reason, or in virtue of some general characteristic. Judgments of right and wrong are in this respect quite different from many other types of evaluative judgment such as judgments that something is beautiful, or ugly, or funny. In the latter cases the evaluative judgment comes first—we "see" that the thing is beautiful or funny—and the explanation comes later, if in fact we can supply it at all.[11] But we rarely, if ever, "see" that an action is wrong without having some idea *why* it is wrong. There may be cases in which some action "just seems wrong," even though one cannot say what the objection to it is. But these reactions have the status of "hunches" or suspicions which need to be made good: there is pressure to come up with an explanation or else withdraw the judgment if we cannot explain what our objection is.

People in different cultures regard different things as funny and have different views about what constitutes a beautiful face. They thus have "different standards" of humor and (at least some kinds of) beauty, and it is plausible to say that when a member of one of these groups makes a judgment about what is funny or good-looking, the claim that this judgment makes has to be understood as relative to the standards of that group (so that opposing assessments of the same joke, made in Omsk and Los Angeles, could both be true).[12] But even if there are, in this sense, standards of humor and beauty, these standards do not play the same role in individual judgments that moral standards generally do. A person who regards a joke as funny, or a person or scene as beautiful, may be quite unable to articulate the standards, if any, to which his or her judgment is relative. But I cannot claim that an action is morally wrong without having some idea what objection there is to it.

Contractualism offers a natural explanation of this feature of our judgments about right and wrong. In another respect, however, the claim that moral judgments involve conscious reference to principles may seem implausible. Suppose I believe that while McCormick had a legal right to build his house where he did, it was wrong of him to put it so close to the property line, thereby ruining his neighbor's view. In this example I have a definite idea what the moral objection to McCormick's action is: insufficient consideration for his neighbor's interests. But it is unlikely that I could formulate a principle to back this up, if by a principle we mean a rule specifying what weight one is supposed to give to others' interests when they conflict with one's own interests of a similar sort. So the claim I have been making may seem very implausible insofar as it is taken to suggest that we make decisions of this kind by invoking or "applying" a principle or rule.

This observation is quite correct. But the idea that it constitutes an objection to what I have been claiming rests on an overly narrow idea of what a principle is. If a principle is taken to be a rule that can be "applied" to settle quite a wide range of questions with little or no room left for the exercise of judgment, then there are very few moral principles at all, and it would certainly be false to claim that every judgment about right and wrong must be backed by one. If the claim that moral judgments must be backed by principles is to have any plausibility, the notion of a principle will have to be understood much more broadly. Principles, as I will understand them, are general conclusions about the status of various kinds of reasons for action. So understood, principles may rule out some actions by ruling out the reasons on which they would be based, but they also leave wide room for interpretation and judgment.

Consider, for example, moral principles concerning the taking of human life. It might seem that this is a simple rule, forbidding a certain class of actions: Thou shalt not kill. But what about self-defense, suicide, and certain acts of killing by police officers and by soldiers in wartime? And is euthanasia always strictly forbidden? The parts of this principle that are the clearest are better put in terms of reasons: the fact that a course of action can be foreseen to lead to someone's death is normally a conclusive reason against it; the fact that someone's death would be to my personal advantage is no justification for aiming at it; but one may use deadly force when this seems the only defense against a person who threatens one's life; and so on.

Much the same can be said of the principle of fidelity to promises. We are not morally required to keep a promise no matter what. The clearest part of the principle is this: the fact that keeping a promise would be inconvenient or disadvantageous is not normally a sufficient reason for breaking it, but "normally" here covers many qualifications. There are, for example, questions of proportionality (the kind of disadvantage that may not be appealed to in order to justify backing out depends on what is at stake in the promise) and questions about the conditions under which the promise was given (such as whether there was duress and whether crucial information was withheld).

So even the most familiar moral principles are not rules which can be easily applied without appeals to judgment. Their succinct verbal formulations turn out on closer examination to be mere labels for much more complex ideas. Moral principles are in this respect much like some legal ones. The constitutional formula "Congress shall make no law abridging freedom of speech, or of the press" may sound like a simple prohibition. But the underlying idea is much more complicated. There is of course considerable controversy about what, more precisely, this amendment covers. What is striking, however, and more relevant for present purposes, is the breadth and complexity of the area of agreement. Presented with a range of examples of governmental regulation of expression, people who understand freedom of expression will agree on a wide range of judgments about which of these involve violations of the First Amendment and which do not. These cases are sufficiently varied that it would be difficult to explain our convergent judgments as applications of any statable rule. How, then, do we arrive at these judgments? We do so, I believe, by appeal to a shared sense of what the point of freedom of expression is and how it is supposed to work: why restrictions on governmental power to regulate expression are necessary, what threats they are supposed to rule out, and what it is that they are trying to promote.[13]

Similarly, it is a familiar moral principle that promises freely made must be kept, although we must add "at least in the absence of special justification." How do we decide what forms of justification are sufficient? It is sometimes suggested that this is a matter of "balancing" the competing considerations. But this metaphor is misleading insofar as it suggests that what is involved is only a process of weighing or comparing the seriousness of conflicting interests. The costs at stake for promiser and promisee are of course among the relevant factors in deciding whether a given promise must be kept, but these must be considered within a more complex structure which the metaphor of balancing conceals. Anyone who understands the point of promising—what it is supposed to ensure and what it is to protect us against—will see that certain reasons for going back on a promise could not be allowed without rendering promises pointless, while other exceptions must be allowed if the practice is not to be unbearably costly.

For example, the point of promising would be defeated if a minor inconvenience, or even a major cost that was clearly foreseeable at the time the promise was made, counted as adequate ground for failing to perform as promised. On the other hand it would not render promises pointless to recognize, as grounds for default, a cost which is both quite unexpected and much more serious than what is at stake for the promisee. Perhaps this exception is even required in order not to make promising too risky. Factors such as whether a cost to a promisee was foreseeable, foreseen, or unexpected are made relevant by the interests to which a principle of fidelity to agreements must be responsive. But when we are deciding whether, in a particular case, these factors serve as conditions that modify the force of a given cost as a reason for not keeping a promise, rather than as further interests that are balanced against that cost.

All of this structure and more is part of what each of us knows if we understand the principle that promises ought to be kept. In making particular judgments of right and wrong we are drawing on this complex understanding, rather than applying a statable rule, and this understanding enables us to arrive at conclusions about new and difficult cases, which no rule would cover.

When we judge a person to have acted in a way that was morally wrong, we take her or him to have acted on a reason that is morally disallowed, or to have given a reason more weight than is morally permitted, or to have failed to see the relevance or weight of some countervailing reason which, morally, must take precedence. Each of these judgments involves a principle in the broad sense in which I am using that term. There may be no rule we can invoke as telling us that a certain reason is not morally sufficient (that my reason for breaking my promise is not sufficiently weighty, or that McCormick did not have good reason for disregarding his neighbor's interest in preserving his view). But we make such judgments by drawing on our understanding of why there should be a moral constraint on actions of the kind in question (why principles that left us free to do as we liked in such situations are "reasonably rejectable") and of the structure that that constraint takes (in what way we can be asked to take the relevant interests into account).[14] When, in the light of our best understanding of this moral rationale, we make a judgment about the sufficiency of the reasons for an action in a particular case, this judgment is guided by, and expresses, our understanding of a moral principle.

How many valid moral principles are there, then? An indefinite number, I would say. This, again, may seem implausible. How are we supposed to know what principles there are? By the same kind of thinking that we use to understand the content of familiar principles like fidelity to promises and freedom of speech. That is: we can see the need for limits on certain patterns of action (patterns of justification) by seeing the ways in which we are at risk if people are left free to decide to act in these ways; and by understanding the rationale for these moral constraints we can see why it is that certain reasons for action, and certain ways of giving some reasons priority over others, are morally inadmissible. Some familiar principles are generally learned through explicit moral teaching, but we can see, on reflection, that they have a basis of the kind I have just described. Other principles we may never have thought of until we are presented with a situation (real or hypothetical) to which they would apply; but when this happens we can see immediately that they are valid.

For example: we are all taught that it is wrong to break one's promises (although, as I have said, our understanding of this principle goes far beyond the content of any explicit teaching). But, as I will argue in Chapter 7, there are many other ways in which one can behave wrongly in regard to other people's expectations about what one will do: one can fail to take care about the expectations one leads others to form, fail to warn them that their expectations are mistaken, or (without promising anything) intentionally lead others to form false expectations when their doing so is to one's advantage. Not every action falling under the last two descriptions is wrong, but many are. There are no familiar and widely taught principles—analogous to "Keep your promises"—that cover these cases. Yet once the question arises we are able to see the wrongness of these actions in much the same way that we see the wrongness of breaking a promise or of making a promise that one does not intend to keep. That is to say, we are able to see that principles licensing such actions would be ones that people could reasonably reject.

4. Standpoints

The aim of finding and acting on principles that no one similarly motivated could reasonably reject leads us to take other people's interests into account in deciding what principles to follow. More exactly, we have reason to consider whether there are standpoints other than our own present standpoint from which the principles we are considering could reasonably be rejected. I want now to consider what these "standpoints" are.

According to contractualism, our concern with right and wrong is based on a concern that our actions be justifiable to others on grounds that they could not reasonably reject insofar as they share this concern. "Others" figure twice in this schema: as those to whom justification is owed, and as those who might or might not be able reasonably to reject certain principles. When we think of those to whom justification is owed, we naturally think first of the specific individuals who are affected by specific actions. But when we are deciding whether a given principle is one that could reasonably be rejected we must take a broader and more abstract perspective. This perspective is broader because, when we are considering the acceptability or rejectability of a principle, we must take into account not only the consequences of particular actions, but also the consequences of general performance or nonperformance of such actions and of the other implications (for both agents and others) of having agents be licensed and directed to think in the way that that principle requires. So the points of view that the question of reasonable rejectability requires us to take into account are not limited to those of the individuals affected by a particular action. This is so for several reasons, which are worth spelling out.

First and most obviously, widespread performance of acts of a given kind can have very different effects from isolated individual instances. Slightly less obviously, perhaps, the general authorization or prohibition of a class of actions can have significance that goes beyond the consequences of the actions that are performed or not performed as a result. This can be seen both from the point of view of agents and from that of the people who may be affected by these actions. As agents, if we know that we must stand ready to perform actions of a certain kind should they be required, or that we cannot count on being able to perform acts of another kind should we want to, because they are forbidden, these things have important effects on our planning and on the organization of our lives whether or not any occasions of the relevant sort ever actually present themselves. If, for example, I lived in a desert area and were obligated to provide food for strangers in need who came by my house, then I would have to take account of this possibility in my shopping and consumption, whether or not anyone ever asked me for this kind of help; and if I am not entitled to photocopy articles at will when they turn out to be useful in my course, then I have reason to order a more inclusive anthology to begin with, even though this may prove to have been unnecessary. The same is true from the point of view of those affected by actions. Our need for privacy, for example, is not met simply because, as a matter of fact, other people do not listen in on our phone calls and go through our personal files. In order to have the benefits of privacy we need to have assurance that this will not happen, and this is something that general acceptance of a principle can provide.

These points could be summarized by saying that general prohibitions and permissions have effects on the liberty, broadly construed, of both agents and those affected by their actions. But the acceptance of principles has other implications beyond these effects. Because principles constrain the reasons we may, or must, take into account, they can affect our relations with others and our view of ourselves in both positive and negative ways. I have already discussed some "negative" examples—cases in which principles may interfere with our entering into other relations—in Chapter 4, in connection with the problem of compatibility. The case of privacy offers a more positive example. The fact that others recognize reasons to restrain themselves so that I may be free from observation and inquiry when I wish to be is important in defining my standing as an independent person who can enter into relations with others as an equal. If the principles we all accepted did not recognize these reasons, this would crucially alter my relations with other people, and even my view of myself. (Principles defining my distinctive rights over my own body—rights to say who can even touch it, let alone claim its parts for other purposes—are an even clearer example.)[15]

As this discussion of the points of view that must be considered in deciding whether a principle could reasonably be rejected brings out, an assessment of the rejectability of a principle must take into account the consequences of its acceptance in general, not merely in a particular case that we may be concerned with. Since we cannot know, when we are making this assessment, which particular individuals will be affected by it in which ways (who will be affected as an agent required to act a certain way, who as a potential victim, who as a bystander, and so on), our assessment cannot be based on the particular aims, preferences, and other characteristics of specific individuals. We must rely instead on commonly available information about what people have reason to want. I will refer to this as information about generic reasons.

Some examples: We commonly take it that people have strong reasons to want to avoid bodily injury, to be able to rely on assurances they are given, and to have control over what happens to their own bodies. We therefore think it reasonable to reject principles that would leave other agents free to act against these important interests. Similarly, as agents we typically have reason to want to give special attention to our own projects, friends, and family, and thus have reason to object to principles that would constrain us in ways that would make these concerns impossible.

Generic reasons are reasons that we can see that people have in virtue of their situation, characterized in general terms, and such things as their aims and capabilities and the conditions in which they are placed. Not everyone is affected by a given principle in the same way, and generic reasons are not limited to reasons that the majority of people have. If even a small number of people would be adversely affected by a general permission for agents to act a certain way, then this gives rise to a potential reason for rejecting that principle. (This is a generic reason since it is one that we can see people have in virtue of certain general characteristics; it is not attributed to specific individuals.)

Whether such a reason is a ground for reasonably rejecting the principle will depend, of course, on the costs this would involve for others, and these will depend on what alternatives there are. One alternative, if a principle granting general permission to act a certain way is rejected, is a general prohibition against so acting. This may be very costly from the point of view of potential agents, and may be reasonably rejected on that account. A second possibility is a principle in which the permission is qualified, by specific exceptions or by a more open-ended requirement that there be no countervailing considerations.

There is an obvious pressure toward making principles more fine-grained, to take account of more and more specific variations in needs and circumstances. But there is also counterpressure arising from the fact that finer-grained principles will create more uncertainty and require those in other positions to gather more information in order to know what a principle gives to and requires of them. For example, the principle of fidelity to promises protects us against being bound in ways that we do not like by specifying that only voluntary undertakings are binding. But individuals differ in their ability to foresee possible difficulties and to resist subtle pressures to enter an agreement. The protection offered by the requirement of voluntariness is therefore of different value to different people. Should we have a more limited principle? That is to say, is the broader principle reasonably rejectable from the more specific point of view of those who are more easily drawn into unwelcome agreements? To argue that it is not, we need to claim that the more limited principle places an unreasonable burden on potential promisees, to ascertain the character and potential weaknesses of those with whom they are making agreements in order to know whether the agreement they have made is morally binding.

I do not mean to be deciding this substantive question here.[16] My purpose is rather to illustrate the general point that we bring to moral argument a conception of generic points of view and the reasons associated with them which reflects our general experience of life, and that this conception is subject to modification under the pressures of moral thought and argument. Some of the most common forms of moral bias involve failing to think of various points of view which we have not occupied, underestimating the reasons associated with them, and overestimating the costs to us of accepting principles that recognize the force of those reasons.[17]

It is commonly said that one important role of moral theory is to provide a way of correcting these biases. In one respect this is true. The pressure to be able to justify our actions to others, on terms that they could not reasonably reject, can help to reveal biases of this kind and press us to overcome them. But the process of doing this is one of gradually refining our intuitive moral categories under conflicting pressures of the kind I have just described, drawing on our expanding experience of others' points of view. I doubt that it is possible for theory to "correct biases" in a more radical way by specifying once and for all what the outcome of this process should be—for example, by specifying in advance the terms in which all "reasonable rejections" must be defended.[18]

5. Generality and Fairness

This description of the process of moral justification is motivated by the general contractualist framework that I am defending. I believe that it is also in accord with moral intuition. In particular, it helps to explain two familiar intuitions about the moral irrelevance of certain considerations.

If we were evaluating a moral principle simply from the point of view of a particular individual, one thing that it would be natural to take into account would be the likelihood, given that person's particular needs and circumstances, of his or her benefiting from that principle and the likelihood of his or her having to bear its various costs. For example, when we are considering a principle of mutual aid, as in Kant's famous fourth example, some people (call them the fortunate Joneses) can reliably foresee that they are not very likely to need aid themselves, or at least much less likely than others, and much more likely to be called on to give it. It might seem that this gives them less reason than others have to reject a principle that imposes no duty of mutual aid, and more reason to reject a principle requiring that we give aid when it is not too difficult to do so. So it may seem that something like a veil of ignorance is necessary in order to screen such reasons out.

There are three different responses to this question, corresponding to three ways in which the differences in the degree to which various individuals benefit from a principle might be thought relevant. First, the idea might be that those who do not expect to benefit from a principle would have no reason to take account at all of the claims of those who need its protection. So the point of imposing a veil of ignorance would be to force the fortunate Joneses to take seriously the plight of those less fortunate. But this is not necessary on the account I am offering, since the requirement of justifiability (or of nonrejectability) already requires one to take these others into account.

The second idea concerns the way in which these others might be taken into account: should the Joneses, if they are moral as well as fortunate, try to compare the net cost of this principle to them with its net costs or net benefits to various others who are more likely to need the protection it offers? The answer is that at least in most cases they should not; to do so would generally be unnecessarily complicated. At least in most cases, all we need take into account in deciding whether a principle could reasonably be rejected are such things as the following: (a) the importance of being able to get aid *should one need it*; (b) the degree of inconvenience involved in giving it, *should one be called upon to do so*; (c) the generic costs of having a standing policy of giving aid in the way this principle requires; and (d) the generic benefits of having others have this policy.

Like the degree of need referred to in (a), the burdensomeness of (b) and (c) will be specified, at least loosely, in the principle itself. That is, just as a person who understands the principle will understand how urgent a need must be in order to trigger its requirement of aid, such a person will also understand the degree to which specific performance is required, and the kinds of excusing conditions recognized (including, perhaps, the fact that one has already helped other people). In assessing the rejectability of the principle, then, we can begin by taking these values at the level specified (for example, by taking the maximum level of burdensomeness and asking whether that would give a potential agent reason to reject the principle). If even someone who was burdened to this (maximum) degree could not reasonably reject the principle, then that settles the matter.

Most of us who believe that principles of mutual aid are valid believe that they pass this test of nonrejectability. But it is at least theoretically possible that there are other principles which involve a level of sacrifice that it is reasonable to demand from a person only if he or she will also benefit from the principle, thus offsetting its high cost to them. I am not certain that there are such cases.[19] If there are, then in these cases a principle, in order not to be reasonably rejectable, would have to exempt the class of individuals who are very unlikely to benefit from it. What is at issue here is not the likelihood that any particular individual, given all that is known about him or her, will be burdened, or benefited, or both by the principle, but rather the likelihood that anyone who is burdened by the principle will also benefit from it. As in the arguments for excuses and *ceteris paribus* conditions, what would be claimed in such a case is that any acceptable principle must be made fine-grained in ways that will make this very likely.

I maintained above that in considering whether a principle could reasonably be rejected we should consider the weightiness of the burdens it involves, for those on whom they fall, and the importance of the benefits it offers, for those who enjoy them, leaving aside the likelihood of one's actually falling in either of these two classes. It might seem that setting aside probabilities in this way presents a problem, and a dilemma, for contractualism as I am describing it. If, on the one hand, the grounds for rejecting a principle are based simply on the burdens it involves, for those who experience them, without discounting them by the probability that there will be anyone who actually does so, then it would seem that there is just as strong a reason for rejecting a principle permitting people to engage in behavior that involves a small risk of bodily harm to others as for rejecting a principle that permits behavior which is certain to cause harms of this same magnitude. If, on the other hand, we take into account the probability of bearing these burdens, there seem to be two ways of doing this. One would be to allow each person to take into account, in assessing his or her reasons for rejecting a principle, the likelihood that he or she would benefit from or be burdened by it.

The alternative would be to say that what is relevant is not any particular person's actual probability of benefiting from or being burdened by a principle, but, rather, the likelihood that *someone* will do so, as represented by the percentage of the population that falls into these groups. This alternative also leads to unacceptable results. Consider any principle licensing us to impose very severe hardships on a tiny minority of people, chosen at random (by making them involuntary subjects of painful and dangerous medical experiments, for example), in order to benefit a much larger majority. A contractualist would want to keep open the possibility that such a principle could reasonably be rejected because of the severe burdens it involves. But this would be effectively ruled out on the proposal under consideration, according to which the weight given to these burdens, as grounds for rejecting the principle, would be sharply discounted because only a very small fraction of the population would actually suffer them.

This difficulty appears to be serious because it is intuitively obvious that the likelihood that a form of behavior will lead to harm is an important factor in determining its permissibility and because it is assumed that the only way to take this probability into account is as a factor that, in one way or another, diminishes the complaint of a person who suffers this harm. But this assumption is mistaken. The probability that a form of conduct will cause harm can be relevant not as a factor diminishing the "complaint" of the affected parties (discounting the harm by the likelihood of their suffering it) but rather as an indicator of the care that the agent has to take to avoid causing harm. Our reactions to the medical experiment case mentioned above, for example, depend heavily on whether the harm in question is directly inflicted on particular people or whether it occurs "by accident," that is to say, occurs despite the fact that reasonable precautions have been taken. In the latter case, permitting the experimentation that leads to the harm may be no more objectionable than allowing air travel despite the fact that some people on the ground are likely to be killed by falling planes. The difference between these two versions of the medical experiment example does not have to do with the cost to the victims: the harm is just as bad when suffered "by accident" as when it is inflicted. The difference lies rather in the cost of avoiding these ways of bringing harm. I believe that our reactions to these cases reflect the view that, except for a few very unusual kinds of cases, we can accept a prohibition against intentionally inflicting serious harm on others. But the cost of avoiding all behavior that involves risk of harm would be unacceptable. Our idea of "reasonable precautions" defines the level of care that we think can be demanded: a principle that demanded more than this would be too confining, and could reasonably be rejected on that ground.

I have been assuming so far that the candidate principles we are considering are all general in form, and the positions to which the generic reasons I have mentioned attach have all been described in purely general terms: "a person in need of help," "a person who is relying on an assurance that someone else has given," and so on. But many reasons that are important from each of our personal points of view depend on a distinction that is not describable in such terms—the distinction between ourselves and others. There are therefore cases in which each of us would most prefer principles which recognized this distinction, and singled us out for special benefits or exemption from burdens. Moreover, there would seem to be cases in which this might be done at no cost to others. Most cooperative schemes, for example, do not depend on literally *everyone's* doing her or his part, so no one would be disadvantaged if one person were exempted from the principle requiring people who voluntarily accept the benefits of such schemes to do their part in providing these benefits.

It is clear, intuitively, that this is morally ruled out, but different theories exclude it in different ways. Rawls observes that the principles of justice chosen in his Original Position will be "general" in form, by which he means that they may not include proper names or "rigged definite descriptions."[20] His explanation is that when choosing behind a veil of ignorance, the parties have no incentive to agree to principles that violate this requirement: they would have no way of knowing whether they would be favoring themselves or others. He observes, however, that while it may be clear, intuitively, what is meant by a "rigged" definite description, there are philosophical difficulties involved in spelling this out.

According to Hare, on the other hand, it is part of the concept of morality that moral principles may contain no proper names. (He calls such principles "universal," but seems to mean the same thing that Rawls means by "general.") He says, however, that there is no way of saying, on logical grounds, which definite descriptions are "rigged" and which are not. The only way to tell which descriptions may figure in moral principles is to see which principles we have reason to accept as universal imperatives.[21] Hare's discussion of "rigged definite descriptions" may sound like a criticism of Rawls, but in fact they are in agreement on the basic point that the aptness of a definite description for use in moral argument is a substantive question to be settled by asking whether principles incorporating that description would pass the relevant test of universal acceptability. (They of course have different ideas about what this test is.) Where they disagree is in the way they exclude proper names, which Hare rules out on formal grounds but Rawls treats in the same way as definite descriptions. On this point I follow Rawls. Whether or not proper names can be ruled out on formal grounds they are ruled out of moral argument on the same substantive grounds as certain definite descriptions. But I have, again, a somewhat different view of what these grounds are.

To begin with let me recall, from Section 3, that most "principles" cannot be identified with specific rules or verbal formulae which are the separable conclusions or "theorems" of moral argument. So what is presently at issue is not just a question about the logical form of such formulae (whether they can contain certain grammatical or logical elements) but rather a question about the kinds of reasons that can figure in moral argument more generally.

Proper names provide ways of picking out specific individuals. The reasons supporting principles that rely on these devices would thus be reasons for favoring (or disfavoring) particular people. Descriptions pick out specific individuals only contingently and inexactly, since it is possible that more than one individual may satisfy a given description. But descriptions strike us intuitively as "rigged" if the only reason for including them in moral argument is the belief that this provides a way of favoring (or disfavoring) certain people. In both cases, then, the question is whether the fact that a principle would help or hurt specific individuals can be a ground for preferring it, and for reasonably rejecting alternatives that would not have this effect. I believe that the answer to this question is no, and that, on the contrary, it is always reasonable to reject principles that are supported only by such "partial" reasons. The question is why this is so.

Each of us might prefer to be exempted from the requirements of any valid moral principle requiring people to help, or to take care not to hurt, others in certain ways. In most cases it is clear why principles granting one person such an exemption are not valid. *Ex hypothesi,* the generic reasons arising from the burdens that these principles involve for agents in general are not sufficient ground for rejecting a general requirement to aid (or not injure), given the reasons that others have for wanting this protection, and there is nothing special about my case: those who suffer from this person's noncompliance have no less reason to complain than any other victims, and no reason has been given for others to see compliance as being more burdensome for him or her than for anyone else.

There are other cases, however, in which exempting one person, or even a few, would not impose burdens on others, and these cases raise the question of "partial" reasons in a sharper form. Consider, for example, the question of contribution to cooperative schemes. We derive important benefits from such arrangements, and they are almost always vulnerable to the strong temptation to free-ride. It would therefore not be reasonable to reject a principle (Rawls's principle of fairness is an example) that would help stabilize cooperative schemes at tolerable cost, in favor of a principle that would leave people free to contribute or not as they wished. But many of these arrangements do not require, in order to produce the desired consequences, that everyone who benefits should also contribute. As long as most people vote, or refrain from walking on the grass, or observe restrictions during a drought, it does not matter if a few others do not do so.

Each of us has reason to want to add, to a principle like Rawls's, which requires that everyone who accepts the benefits of others' participation in a fair scheme should also comply with its requirements, a rider specifying that if the participation of all in a given scheme is not needed then he or she will be exempt from its requirements. This could be done by singling out that person by name, with a pronoun, or by some description that was tailored to include that person but very few others (so that the exemption does not threaten the cooperative arrangements). For each individual, i, there will be many ways of specifying such an exemption, and we may call a principle that incorporates one of these an "i-favoring" variant of the impartial principle. Each i has reason to prefer i-favoring principles, but, envy aside, it would seem that each i should be indifferent between a purely neutral policy and policies with "j-favoring" exemptions (where j is some other person), since these all make the same demands on i and bring the same benefits. So it might seem that while each of us has reason to prefer exemptions favoring us, none of us has reason to reject principles just because they include exemptions favoring others, since they are no worse from our point of view than a purely neutral policy.

I believe, however, that we do have such a reason, namely that these policies arbitrarily favor one person over others and are in this respect unfair. As I have said, each person has reason to prefer partial principles that would favor him or her. If one of these principles is made binding, with no further reason to support it, then one person's reason for wanting to be favored is given precedence over others' similar reasons, without justification. This is what makes such a choice arbitrary, and makes the principle rejectable. This substantive objection applies to principles that make essential use of proper names as well as to those relying on "rigged" descriptions.

Principles can of course turn out to favor one person without being arbitrary. The aims of a cooperative scheme may, for example, require that greater benefits be given to those who satisfy a certain description. More to the point, a scheme might build in some fair mechanism for deciding who should be released from contributing when contributions from all are not required. If, for example, compliance by only 80 percent of the participants is enough to keep a scheme going, then the rule might be that each person should roll a die before deciding whether to contribute, and would be excused if the die came up "six." In these cases we would not say that the descriptions picking out those who are favored are "rigged," because they are included for good reason: as a way of sharing fairly the burden of the cooperative scheme. They are thus not merely a way of responding to the understandable wishes of some people to benefit in this way while neglecting the similar claims of others.

6. Reasonable Rejection

In order to decide whether a principle could reasonably be rejected, we need to consider it from a number of standpoints. From the point of view of those who will be its main beneficiaries, there may be strong generic reasons to insist on the principle and to reject anything that offers less. From the point of view of the agents who will be constrained by it, or of those who would be beneficiaries of an alternative principle, there may be reason to reject it in favor of something different or less demanding. In order to decide whether the principle could reasonably be rejected we need to decide whether it would be reasonable to take any of these generic reasons against it to prevail, given the reasons on the other side and given the aim of finding principles that others also could not reasonably reject. What can we say, in general, about the kinds of considerations that count as generic reasons and about how conflicting reasons are to be assessed? The present section and the next three are devoted to this question.

If we were to appeal to a prior notion of rightness to tell us which considerations are morally relevant and which are entitled to prevail in cases of conflict, then the contractualist framework would be unnecessary, since all the work would already have been done by this prior notion. It may seem, then, that when we apply the contractualist test we need to set aside any claims of rights or entitlement, or to focus on cases in which no such claims exist.[22] This appears to mean that the relative strength of various generic reasons for and against a principle must be a function of the effects that that principle, or its absence, would have on the well-being of people in various positions. The crucial questions then would be how this notion of well-being is to be understood, and how the strength of a reason is related to well-being in this sense: Does the strongest objection belong to those whose level of well-being would be lowest if they lose out? or to those to whom the principle would make the greatest difference? Or does it depend on more complicated factors such as some combination of difference and level of well-being?

This is an appealing line of thought, but a mistaken one. While it would be objectionably circular to make "reasonable rejection" turn on presumed entitlements of the very sort that the principle in question is supposed to establish, it is misleading to suggest that when we are assessing the "reasonable rejectability" of a principle we must, or even can, set aside assumptions about other rights and entitlements altogether. Even in those cases that come closest to being decided on the basis of a principle's implications for the welfare of individuals in various positions, many other moral claims must be presupposed in order to provide a context in which that principle can be understood.

Suppose, for example, that we are considering a principle defining our obligations to help those in need. This would seem to be a case in which considerations of welfare are most likely to be predominant. But in order to be in a position to aid someone, an agent must be entitled to dispose of the resources that are needed, and must be free from any obligation that would prevent him or her from acting in the way required to give aid. Similarly, being in need of aid is in part a matter of not being entitled simply to take what one needs, perhaps by force if necessary. So in order to understand the scope of the proposed principle (the range of actions it might require) we need to presuppose a framework of entitlements. What this illustrates is that a sensible contractualism, like most other plausible views, will involve a holism about moral justification: in assessing one principle we must hold many others fixed. This does not mean that these other principles are beyond question, but just that they are not being questioned at the moment.

Contractualism is not based on the idea that there is a "fundamental level" of justification at which only well-being (conceived in some particular way) matters and the comparison of magnitudes of well-being is the sole basis for assessing the reasonableness of rejecting principles of right and entitlement. Even though components of well-being figure prominently as grounds for reasonable rejection, the idea of such a fundamental level is misleading on two counts. First, the claim that the possibility of suffering a loss in well-being is something that has force in moral argument is a substantive moral claim. By concealing or minimizing this fact, the idea of a fundamental level has the effect of giving these claims a privileged status over other moral considerations. In many cases, gains and losses in well-being (relief from suffering, for example) are clearly the most relevant factors determining whether a principle could or could not be reasonably rejected. And in some cases of this kind questions of responsibility—such as whether the sufferer's claim to aid might be undermined by the fact that it was his or her own fault—do not arise, either because it so obviously was not the person's fault or because it would not matter if it were. But (and this is the second way in which the idea of a fundamental level can be misleading) to identify a case as of this kind is to place it within a specific moral framework, not to view it without any moral assumptions.

It may seem that contractualism becomes viciously circular if it does not take well-being as the basic coin in which reasonable rejection is measured (if, for example, it gives independent weight to considerations such as responsibility). But this is so only if the claims of well-being are unique among moral claims in needing no further justification, and well-being is therefore uniquely suited to serve as the basis in terms of which other moral notions are explained. I believe that something like this is frequently assumed, not only by utilitarians but also by others, like me, who look to views such as contractualism specifically as ways of avoiding utilitarianism. It is therefore worth considering why this assumption should seem so plausible, especially in the context of a contractualist theory of the kind I am trying to present.

There are two directions from which one might challenge the claim that a generic reason arising from a certain standpoint is a relevant, perhaps even decisive ground for rejecting a principle. First, one might question whether the consideration in question is a generic reason at all—whether it is something that people in that situation would have reason to care about. Second, one might question whether this reason has weight in moral argument as contractualism describes it (whether it would have to be recognized as having weight by others who shared a concern with mutual justifiability).

These two challenges correspond to two possible charges of "circularity." If, for example, I were to claim that it would be reasonable to reject a certain principle because it was unfair, this might be challenged as "circular" in two different ways. One might claim that it is circular to assume that people in the situation in question would have reason to object to unfairness per se. Why should they care about it if it does not involve some loss in well-being? Alternatively, it might be held to be circular to assume that an objection on grounds of "unfairness" would have moral force—that if anyone were to have reason to raise it, then others would have reason to accept it insofar as they are concerned with mutual justifiability.

Why might it be thought that objections arising from concerns with well-being are particularly immune to charges of circularity of these two kinds? To begin with charges of the first kind, it is no doubt particularly clear that individuals typically have strong reason to want to have certain benefits, and to want to avoid pain and injury. Perhaps this claim can be generalized to cover anything that affects "how well one's life goes." But these are not the only things that people have reason to want and to object to being deprived of. I argued above, for example, that it is reasonable to object to principles that favor others arbitrarily. A principle that favors some in this way will often deprive others of benefits and opportunities they have reason to want. But why should these concrete disadvantages be the only grounds for objecting to such a principle? It would be circular for contractualism to cite, as the reason that people have for objecting to such principles, the fact that they are wrong according to some noncontractualist standard. But we need not choose between objections of this kind and objections based on loss of well-being. We have reason to object to principles simply because they arbitrarily favor the claims of some over the identical claims of others: that is to say, because they are unfair. In the process of moral reflection that contractualism describes, this provides a perfectly understandable reason for finding partial principles objectionable, a reason that does not depend on a prior idea that such principles, or the practices they would permit, are wrong.

It seems to me an important strength of contractualism that, in contrast to utilitarianism and other views which make well-being the only fundamental moral notion, it can account for the significance of different moral notions, within a unified moral framework, without reducing all of them to a single idea. What is necessary in order to do this is to show in each case why people would have reason to insist upon principles incorporating these notions (why principles that did not do this would be ones that could reasonably be rejected). I have just indicated how this can be done in the case of fairness. In Chapter

6 I will offer a similar account of the moral force of choice and responsibility.

Let me turn now to charges of circularity of the second kind. These claim that if we count generic reasons not arising from effects on well-being as relevant objections to a principle, this can only reflect a substantive moral judgment and is therefore objectionably circular. This challenge might be based on the idea that (apart from an appeal to some substantive moral doctrine) there *are* no generic reasons for objecting to a principle other than those arising from its effects on how well people's lives go. So understood, it is just a restatement of a challenge of the first kind, to which I have already responded. So I will take the challenge to be not to the existence of certain generic reasons for objecting to a principle but rather to the legitimacy of counting these reasons as morally significant—as relevant grounds for rejecting that principle.

Here my response is that, as I have already mentioned, the judgment that *any* consideration constitutes a relevant, possibly conclusive, reason for rejecting a principle in the context of contractualist moral thinking as I am describing it is a judgment with moral content. This may be easy to overlook when the reason in question is based on the impact that a principle would typically have on "how well life would go" for a person in a certain position, but it is no less true in that case than in any other. This is made even clearer once it is realized that well-being is not a well-defined notion that moral thinking can simply take over from the outlook of a single rational individual. On the contrary, as I argued in Chapter 3, from an individual's own point of view the boundaries of his or her own well-being are inevitably vague. So substantive moral choices are involved not only in giving the notion moral significance but also in defining its boundaries.

Even if it would not be uniquely immune to charges of circularity, however, a form of contractualism (what might be called "welfarist contractualism") that took a specified conception of well-being as the sole standard for assessing all putative reasons for rejecting proposed principles would represent a particularly strong claim about the nature of right and wrong. It might seem that any interesting form of contractualism would have to be similarly structured: that is, it would have to begin with a clear specification of the possible grounds for reasonably rejecting a principle (whether this is given in terms of a conception of well-being or in some other way) and with a specified method for determining the relative strength of these grounds that allow us to reach conclusions about reasonable rejectability without appeals to judgment.

The version of contractualism that I am defending does not take this form. Its first aim is to provide a unified account of the subject matter of this part of morality and of its normative basis. This account also has some clear substantive implications: the rationale it offers for taking "justifiability to others on grounds they could not reasonably reject" as the central idea of the morality of obligation supports definite conclusions about the grounds of reasonable rejection: it rules out certain considerations and identifies others as definitely relevant. I will explore these implications in the following sections. But even if they are accepted, much more is left open than under a contractualism of the kind just mentioned. Of course, even welfarist contractualism would require us to rely on our judgment as to whether a given loss of well-being would, under certain circumstances, count as grounds for reasonable rejection of a principle. On the version I am defending, however, we must sometimes exercise judgment as to whether certain considerations are or are not relevant to the reasonable rejectability of a principle, since these grounds are not completely specified in advance. There is, of course, the possibility of tightening contractualism by specifying more explicitly the grounds of reasonable rejection and the method to be used in balancing these grounds against one another. I believe that although this is a feasible aim with respect to some specific areas of morality it is not likely to succeed at the level of generality of the theory I am currently offering here—that is to say, at the level of an account that is intended to cover, if not all of "morality," then that large part of it that has to do with what we owe to each other. I will return to this question in Section 10, after the general form of contractualism that I am defending has been spelled out more fully.

7. Impersonal Values

In order for a principle to be reasonably rejectable there must be some relevant standpoint from which people typically have good reason either to refuse to accept that principle as part of their own practical thinking or to refuse to recognize it as a ground that others may use to justify their conduct. Reasons for rejecting a principle need not be based on the consequences of the actions that principle would license, or even on the consequences of those actions if performed generally. It can be good grounds for rejecting a principle that accepting it would make it impossible to recognize other values that one has good reason to recognize. For example, a principle requiring strict neutrality between friends and strangers would be unacceptable simply because it would be incompatible with the attitudes and values of friendship.

I have also argued that people's reasons for rejecting a principle need not be based on the effects that accepting it or having others accept it would have on their well-being. In discussing fairness, for example, I maintained that it is sufficient ground for rejecting a principle that it singles others out, without justification, for a privileged moral status. Even if these reasons do not have to do with well-being, however, they are still what might be called *personal* reasons, since they have to do with the claims and status of individuals in certain positions. The question I want now to address is whether a principle might also be rejected on *impersonal* grounds—that is to say, for reasons that are not tied to the well-being, claims, or status of individuals in any particular position.

It might seem that impersonal reasons for rejection must be allowed, at least in principle. For it does not seem that all the reasons we have are grounded in the moral claims or the well-being of individuals, either ourselves or others. Many people, for example, believe that we have reason not to flood the Grand Canyon, or to destroy the rain forests, or to act in a way that threatens the survival of a species (our own or some other), simply because these things are valuable and ought to be preserved and respected, and not just because acting in these ways would be contrary to the claims or interests of individuals. Whether they are correct in thinking this is not, however, a question to be settled by an account of the morality of right and wrong; it belongs to morality in the wider sense and to the broader subjects of reasons and value. But if there are impersonal reasons of this kind why should they not count as possible grounds for reasonably rejecting principles? If the value of the Grand Canyon gives me reason to want it to be preserved, for example, why does it not also give me a good reason to reject a principle that would license others to neglect this value in deciding whether or not to build a dam on the Colorado River?

In answering this question it is important to bear in mind the limited range of the part of morality we are trying to characterize. The contractualist formula is meant to describe one category of moral ideas: the requirements of "what we owe to each other." Reasons for rejecting a principle thus correspond to particular forms of concern that we owe to other individuals. By definition, impersonal reasons do not represent forms of such concern. They flow from the value of those objects themselves, not (at least in the first instance) from anything having to do with my relation to other people.

To claim this—to claim, for example, that in destroying an ancient monument or tree I do no wrong to anyone—is not to claim that we have no reason (or even no moral reason in the broadest sense) not to commit such acts. It would even be natural to say that it would be wrong to destroy these things, using 'wrong' in the broad sense in which something is wrong if there is a very serious reason against doing it. But insofar as the value of these objects provides me with a reason to preserve them, it would be a misrepresentation of this reason to say that it is grounded in what I owe to others.

Impersonal reasons do not, themselves, provide grounds for reasonably rejecting a principle. But these reasons do play a significant role in determining other grounds for reasonable rejection. This happens in a number of ways. One concerns the benefits, for individuals, of being able to engage in valuable activities. So, for example, part of what it means to say that the Grand Canyon is of value is that visiting and enjoying it is worthwhile. From the point of view of those who might engage in these activities in the future, then, there is reason to reject a principle that would allow someone to decide to flood the Grand Canyon without taking these benefits into account. These reasons for rejecting a principle are what I called above personal reasons, but their force as reasons depends in part on further judgments of impersonal value, namely the judgment that these objects are worth seeing and should be admired.

Generic reasons for rejecting a principle can also arise from the fact that the constraints that it would impose on practical reasoning are incompatible with other values that one has reason to recognize. It may seem that there is reason of this kind to reject principles that simply neglect impersonal reasons, for if I regard something as valuable and believe that its value gives people reason not to destroy it, how can I accept a principle that licenses me and others to neglect this value in deciding what to do?

But as long as a principle only *permits* one to neglect impersonal reasons, there is no ground of this kind for rejecting it. Since a principle of right and wrong specifies only those constraints on our practical thinking that are imposed by what we owe to others, the sense in which such a principle can "license" us to decide what to do in a way that neglects the value of an object is a limited one: it can say that we do not owe it to each other to take this value into account. This is something that one could well accept while regarding that value as important. Indeed, as I have noted above, it would be implausible in most such cases to hold that the reason why others should recognize an impersonal value is that they owe it to us to do so.

Genuine conflicts can arise, however, in the case of principles that do not merely license people to ignore impersonal values but forbid them from taking these values into account, or limit the role that they can have in justifying actions. For example, a principle forbidding one to interfere with other people's actions might not recognize, as a possible exception, that one could do so in order to prevent someone from destroying valuable natural or cultural objects. A second example might be a principle imposing a duty to save human lives when one can, even if the only available means would lead to the extinction of some other species. A third case would be a principle of fidelity to promises that would require one to keep a promise (even one about a relatively trivial matter) even if, in order to do so, one would have to leave a wounded animal to die in pain. It is clear that under the "trusteeship" interpretation of contractualism described at the end of Chapter 4 this principle is one that a trustee speaking for the animal could reasonably reject. But I believe that it could also be rejected even if this interpretation is not adopted, and the pain of an animal is seen simply as something that is impersonally bad.

Each of these examples involves a principle that, at least arguably, a person could not accept while also recognizing a certain impersonal value. Because of this conflict there is, in each case, a generic reason that would have to be considered in deciding whether the principle in question could reasonably be rejected. These potential reasons for rejection are personal reasons, arising from the importance, for an individual, of being able to live in a way that recognizes certain values. But these reasons depend in turn on impersonal reasons, namely on the fact that these things really are valuable.[23]

To say that these are reasons that would need to be taken into account in deciding whether the principles in question could reasonably be rejected is not yet to say that these principles could be reasonably rejected if they did not recognize exceptions of the kind these reasons call for. Whether this is so will depend on how various competing generic reasons are to be reconciled. But the strength of some of these reasons will depend on conclusions about the impersonal value in question rather than about the morality of right and wrong: conclusions about whether this is in fact something worth valuing and about the degree to which it conflicts with the proposed principle. In my third example (the one concerning promises) there is clearly a serious conflict. If the pain of an animal is something we have strong reason to prevent, then we have good reason to reject a principle that would prevent us from acting on this reason, by requiring us to give animal suffering no more weight than personal inconvenience as a factor affecting our obligations.

In the other two examples the conflict may be less clear. This is in part because, as I argued in Chapter 2, regarding something as valuable is not simply a matter of giving its survival a positive weight which is then balanced against the weight of the competing values that are at stake in each decision. Taking into account the more complex structure of values described there, it may well be, for example, that it would be incompatible with valuing certain natural objects to destroy them oneself for the sake of minor economic advantage, but not incompatible (or at least not *as* incompatible) with this value to fail to interfere physically with others in order to prevent them from destroying these objects. This is not just because the value of these objects is outweighed in the latter case by the disvalue of physically restraining another person, but rather because failing to intervene in this way is less incompatible with the value of these objects (is less of a desecration) than destroying them oneself for personal gain. Similarly, while it would be incompatible with recognizing the value of a species to think that it could be destroyed for the sake of some trivial goal, it might not be incompatible with this value to accept that the species could be sacrificed for the sake of some more important end. If so, then a principle requiring this would be one that a person could hold while still recognizing this value.

To sum up: impersonal values do not provide, in themselves, reason for rejecting principles of right and wrong. Considered in themselves, they represent a category of value, or of morality in the broader sense, that is distinct from what we owe to each other. But these values do bear indirectly, in the various ways I have mentioned, on the question of what principles we can reasonably reject, since they provide people with good reason to want to live their lives in certain ways. So, even though impersonal values are not themselves grounds for reasonable rejection, we cannot determine what we owe to each other without taking these values into account. One result is that, as we saw earlier in the case of friendship, what we owe to each other will be shaped from within to make room for the recognition of these other values. This diminishes the severity of conflict between these two categories of value, but does not ensure that conflicts will not arise. There still may be cases in which we have to choose between impersonal values and what we owe to each other.

8. Priority for the Worst Off?

Let me now focus on those personal reasons for rejection that concern components of well-being, and consider the question of priority among such reasons. In assessing the strength of generic reasons for and against a principle, should special weight be given to reasons arising from the standpoint of those who would be worst off, overall, if their claim were not accepted? It may seem, perhaps because of what is seen as an analogy with Rawls's argument for his Difference Principle, that priority of this kind is a general feature of contractualist reasoning.[24]

It is worth noting, to begin with, that there is a significant part of contractualist moral argument which is not marked by priority of this kind. Many moral principles are concerned with the provision of specific forms of assurance and protection, answering to our need to be protected against intentional harm, our need to be able to rely on assurances given us, and so on. Contractualist argument in these cases turns on comparing the generic reasons for having these protections with generic reasons for being free of the burdens imposed by the principles that provide them. The standpoints of people at different levels of well-being do not seem to be relevant. There is of course the question of whether the obligation to keep a promise should recognize some exceptions in cases of extreme need, but this is not a matter of choosing the principle that would most benefit those who are worst off. To recognize an exception (permission to break a promise or inflict harm, for example) in every case in which this would benefit the person whose overall level of well-being was lower would prevent these principles from offering the kind of assurance that they are supposed to supply. So if the claims of the worst off sometimes take priority in contractualist argument, this reflects a fact about the generic reasons for rejecting certain kinds of principles rather than a general structural feature of contractualism that holds in every case.

The idea that the complaints of the worse off have particular force has greater plausibility when we turn from principles whose aim is to create some specific form of protection or assurance to principles which tell us how we should distribute some transferable good, in cases in which the value of this good to potential beneficiaries is the dominant consideration. These cases have received a great deal of attention, and they are worth examining even though they represent a special class of cases rather than an illustration of the structure that contractualist justification always takes.

The cases in which it would most clearly be wrong not to give aid—and most clearly unreasonable to reject a principle requiring that aid be given—are cases in which those in need of aid are in dire straits: their lives are immediately threatened, for example, or they are starving, or in great pain, or living in conditions of bare subsistence. One principle stating our duties in such cases would hold that if you are presented with a situation in which you can prevent something very bad from happening, or alleviate someone's dire plight, by making only a slight (or even moderate) sacrifice, then it would be wrong not to do so.[25] It is very plausible to suppose that this principle, which I will call the Rescue Principle, is one that could not reasonably be rejected, at least not if the threshold of sacrifice is understood to take account of previous contributions (so that the principle does not demand unlimited sacrifice if it is divided into small enough increments).

This principle may not exhaust our duty to aid others when we can. There may be stronger principles requiring a higher level of sacrifice in some cases, but there are also weaker principles that apply in a quite different range of circumstances. Suppose I learn, in the course of conversation with a person, that I have a piece of information that would be of great help to her because it would save her a great deal of time and effort in pursuing her life's project. It would surely be wrong of me to fail (simply out of indifference) to give her this information when there is no compelling reason not to do so. It would be unreasonable to reject a principle requiring us to help others in this way (even when they are not in desperate need), since such a principle would involve no significant sacrifice on our part. Call this the Principle of Helpfulness.

These principles would be reasonably rejectable if they were less narrowly drawn. It would, for example, be reasonable to reject a principle that required us, in every decision we make, to give no more weight to our own interests than to the similar interests of others. From an agent's standpoint such a principle would be intolerably intrusive. This illustrates the fact that in deciding whether a principle could reasonably be rejected we do not just compare the costs, to individuals in various positions, of abiding by it, or not doing so, on a specific occasion. We have to consider also the general costs (and benefits) of its acceptance. In this case the general costs of acceptance are sufficient to support reasonable rejection. Rejecting a principle on this ground does not involve giving special weight to one's own interests. What is appealed to is not the weight of my interests or yours but rather the generic reasons that everyone in the position of an agent has for not wanting to be bound, in general, by such a strict requirement. Quite impartial reasoning about the rejectability of principles leads to the conclusion that we are not required to be impartial in each actual decision we make.

The two principles I have stated avoid this degree of intrusiveness. The Rescue Principle, for example, applies only in cases in which one can prevent something very bad from happening at only slight or moderate cost to oneself. Given the circumstances in which we live, even this constrained principle is demanding. Hardly any of us lives up to what it requires. But it is difficult to see how it could reasonably be rejected. Contractualism, as a theory, does not tell us exactly what level of sacrifice is required by this principle. I would not say, for example, that we would be required to sacrifice an arm in order to save the life of a stranger. But here a judgment is required, and I do not think that any plausible theory could eliminate the need for judgments of this kind.

We have, then, at least two principles of aid to others: a Rescue Principle and a broader principle of Helpfulness, requiring us to take others' interests into account when we can very easily do so. Both principles specify cases in which there is a duty to aid that it would be wrong to violate; these are not merely cases of charity, in which giving aid would be a good thing to do. The Rescue Principle is stronger in two ways: it is capable of requiring a higher level of sacrifice, and it presumably takes precedence in cases of conflict. This reflects the greater force of the generic reasons there would be to reject weakening of the Rescue Principle.

With these principles in hand, we can turn to the question of whether the reasoning behind them reflects some form of priority for the worst off. One way to see whether it does would be to consider how this reasoning might be extended to yield principles that would tell us what we must do in cases in which we have a duty to aid but we must choose among several possible recipients. Nagel, for example, holds that the proper principle to govern such choices incorporates a moderate form of priority for the worse off. In his view, this priority is a matter of degree: there are cases in which we should benefit those worse off even if we could confer a greater benefit on others, who are already better off, but if the difference we could make to the lives of the better off is sufficiently greater than what we can do for the worse off then the claims of the better off can have the greater moral force. In speaking of "better off" and "worse off," Nagel has in mind, he says, not appraisals of the quality of people's lives at a time but rather the "quality of their lives as a whole, from birth to death."[26]

Does contractualism support this form of priority, or something like it? This depends on whether it would be reasonable, from the standpoint of those whose level of well-being is lowest, to reject a principle of aid that required one always to give preference to helping those one could benefit more, regardless of their relative overall level of well-being. It might seem that the strength of the Rescue Principle, as compared with the weaker Principle of Helpfulness, suggests a positive answer to this question. I said above that the generic reasons for rejecting a weakening of the Rescue Principle are stronger than those against weakening this other duty. It might be suggested that this is due to the fact that a person in a position to which the Rescue Principle applies (someone who is drowning, or starving, or suffering from a terrible disease) is at a lower *level* of well-being than many of those who fall within the scope of the weaker duty. But it is also true that because they are in a worse position it is generally possible to benefit these people more. So it is not immediately apparent from this case whether the difference in level has independent weight.

As I remarked above, it is often difficult to distinguish between the moral importance of differences in the degree to which people can be helped and differences in how badly off they will be if not helped, since a given change is often a greater benefit to someone who is worse off. It is easier to draw this distinction in cases in which these differences have to do with different modes of well-being, but in such cases it is not clear that differences in level have moral force. Suppose, for example, that we must choose between preventing B from losing an arm and preventing A from suffering a broken wrist. Consider a principle according to which it is at least permissible in such a case to help B, whom we can help more, whatever his level of well-being may be. Would it be reasonable to reject this principle, on the ground that a decision in such a case should take into account such things as whether

A had had a very happy and successful life or, on the contrary, his main aims had been frustrated by bad luck? It does not seem to me that this would be reasonable, or that it would become reasonable to do this if the difference between the harm that threatened A and the one that threatened B were smaller (if, say, A stood to lose an arm and B to lose two arms). As in the case of principles discussed above, concerning promise keeping and intentionally inflicted bodily harm, these questions of overall level seem too far removed from the point of the principle at hand.

The idea of priority for the worse off has greater plausibility in cases in which the aspect of well-being in which some people are worse off is the same as the way in which they can be helped. Consider, for example, a case in which we can prevent A from suffering a month of very severe pain or prevent B from suffering similar pain for two months. Supposing that it would be wrong to help A rather than B in this case, it does seem to make a difference if we add that even if we help A she will still suffer this pain for the next five years, whereas B will be free from pain after two months, whether we help him or not. So there is generic reason, from A's standpoint, to reject a principle that directs one in such cases always to help the person in B's situation, the one to whom one can bring the greater immediate benefit. One could argue that this is not really a case of taking a person's level of well-being, as distinct from the difference one can make to her, into account, since the fact that A will be in pain for so long makes one month's freedom from pain a greater benefit to her than it would be to B. But while A's bleak future may indeed make a pain-free month more valuable than it otherwise would be, it is still doubtful that it makes one month a greater boon than *two* months is for B. So it is plausible to claim that the way in which A's situation is worse strengthens her claim to have *something* done about her pain, even if it is less than could be done for someone else.

I suggest, then, that in order for differences in level to affect the relative strength of people's moral claims to help, these differences have to be in an aspect of welfare that the help in question will contribute to. So if the claims of the worse off sometimes get priority in the way Nagel claims, what is relevant is their level in this particular aspect of well-being, not, as he says, the "quality of their lives as a whole, from birth to death." Of course, all aspects of welfare would be in the same category if we had an overall duty to bring about improvements in others' well-being.[27] But all our strong duties (ones that can demand significant sacrifices) are more narrowly tailored than this. As the contrast between the Rescue Principle and the Principle of Helpfulness indicates, being much worse off makes a difference in the strength of a person's claims if it moves that person's situation into the "rescue" category or makes it a more urgent case within that category. In order for this to happen the person must be worse off in a way that the help in question would do something to alleviate.

The conclusion that insofar as there is a "priority for the worst off" it is a feature of certain particular moral contexts rather than a general structural feature of contractualist moral argument may be surprising insofar as "priority for the worst off" is taken to play a central role in the argument for Rawls's Difference Principle, which may be seen as a paradigm of contractualist argumentation. But there are important differences between the subject of Rawls's theory and the one being considered here. To begin with, Rawls's principles of justice are not intended to guide every choice and policy. They are proposed only for the specific task of assessing the justice of basic social institutions. (A principle giving the interests of the worst off priority in every social decision would be much less plausible than one giving their interests priority in arguments about the justice of the institutions that leave them worst off.) The basic institutions of a society are the special subject of justice in part because of their pervasive effects on the life prospects of those who live under them. Consequently, the "quality of . . . lives as a whole, from birth to death" has greater significance for principles of justice than for principles of individual conduct.[28]

The argument for the Difference Principle starts from the idea that, as equal participants in a system of social cooperation, the members of a society have a prima facie claim to an equal share in the benefits it creates. The question then is whether and when departures from this equality might be justified. So the "priority" of the claims of the worst off—the reason why they are the ones to whom justification is particularly to be addressed—arises not from a humanitarian concern with the awfulness of their plight but rather from the fact that they are receiving less than equal shares of benefits to which they have a prima facie equal claim.

The case for the priority that is expressed in the Difference Principle depends, then, on a number of features that are peculiar to the particular question of the justice of basic social institutions, including an egalitarian idea that is peculiar to that case. Nagel believes that the general priority he advocates also arises from an idea of equality rather than simply from a humanitarian concern with the alleviation of suffering.[29] This is the idea that it is morally objectionable that people's overall life prospects should be very different through no fault of their own, even if the plight of those who are worse off is not particularly bad. This idea may have some force, but it is clearly distinct from the more specific idea of equality that underlies Rawls's argument and from the more general idea of reasonable rejection that underlies contractualism.[30]

9. Aggregation

All the grounds for rejecting a principle that I have so far considered arise from generic reasons that an individual would have who occupied a certain position in the situations to which that principle applies. This suggests what Parfit has called the Complaint Model.[31] On this interpretation of contractualism, a person's complaint against a principle must have to do with its effects on him or her, and someone can reasonably reject a principle if there is some alternative to which no other person has a complaint that is as strong. There are, however, two ways in which what I have already said about reasonable rejection departs from this model. First, if a principle's "effects on a person," in the sense intended in the statement of the Complaint Model, include only effects on that person's well-being, then I have departed from that model in allowing that a person could reasonably reject a principle on the grounds that it treated him or her unfairly, as I have interpreted that notion, even if this treatment did not make the person worse off. Second, the Complaint Model appears to suggest that each principle is to be tested by appealing directly to its effects on the well-being of individuals in various standpoints, leaving aside any questions of rights or entitlements, whereas I have maintained that in many cases principles must be considered within the framework of other principles which are, for the moment, being held constant, and that possible grounds for rejection are shaped by these background principles.

These departures aside, the Complaint Model calls attention to a central feature of contractualism that I would not want to give up: its insistence that the justifiability of a moral principle depends only on various *individuals'* reasons for objecting to that principle and alternatives to it. This feature is central to the guiding idea of contractualism, and is also what enables it to provide a clear alternative to utilitarianism and other forms of consequentialism. These theories are appealing partly because of their simple structure, but more because of the substantive appeal of the particular forms of value—such as the happiness or welfare of sentient creatures—on which they are based. But utilitarianism, and most other forms of consequentialism, have highly implausible implications, which flow directly from the fact that their mode of justification is, at base, an aggregative one: the *sum* of a certain sort of value is to be maximized.[32] Whether this standard is applied directly to actions or to rules governing actions, it remains true in principle that imposing high costs on a few could always be justified by the fact that this brought benefits to others, no matter how small these benefits may be as long as the recipients are sufficiently numerous. A contractualist theory, in which all objections to a principle must be raised by individuals, blocks such justifications in an intuitively appealing way. It allows the intuitively compelling complaints of those who are severely burdened to be heard, while, on the other side, the sum of the smaller benefits to others has no justificatory weight, since there is no individual who enjoys these benefits and would have to forgo them if the policy were disallowed.

The problem is, however, that contractualism appears to go too far in the opposite direction, disallowing any appeal to aggregative benefits even in cases in which the right thing to do does seem to depend not only on the impact that various actions would have on particular individuals but also on the number of individuals who would be so affected. For example, in a situation in which we must choose between saving two different groups of people from the same loss or injury, it seems that it would be wrong, absent some special justification, simply to choose the course of action that leads to more people's being killed or injured. This appears to pose a problem for contractualism, since, assuming that the losses or injuries to all the parties are the same and that their grounds for rejecting a principle depend solely on these losses, the generic reasons for rejecting a principle permitting us to save the smaller number will, it seems, be evenly balanced by the generic individual reasons for rejecting a principle requiring one to save the greater number. It therefore seems that as long as it confines itself to reasons for rejection arising from individual standpoints contractualism will be unable to explain how the number of people affected by an action can ever make a moral difference.

There are a number of possible responses to this problem. One would be to move farther away from the Complaint Model and to allow that the reasons for rejecting a principle can take into account not only generic reasons arising from the points of view of individuals but also reasons corresponding to the claims of groups of individuals. To make this move would, however, involve giving up a central and appealing feature of contractualism, and once aggregative arguments had been admitted in this way in some cases it is not clear how implausible consequences of the sort that give rise to objections to utilitarianism could be avoided.

Another response would be to hold that it would indeed not be *wrong* in the narrow sense we are presently describing to save the smaller group in a case of the kind described: doing so would be compatible with what we owe to each person.[33] Nonetheless, it would be morally objectionable to do this, in the absence of personal ties or other special reasons, since, as we have seen, morality consists of more than "what we owe to each other." This might be put by saying that recognizing the value of human life involves not only acting on principles that can be justified to others but also seeing that (within the constraints set by these principles) there is reason to act so as to minimize injuries and deaths. This approach has some appeal, but its hybrid character is unsatisfying. It is not evident that the reasons for saving the greater number are not, at least in some cases, grounded in the claims of individuals. So it is worth looking for an account in which the case for aggregation and the constraints on it are grounded in a unified conception of the consideration owed to each individual.

There does, moreover, seem to be some room for an account of this kind. The argument leading to the conclusion that aggregation presents an acute problem for contractualism relies on the assumption that the strength of individuals' complaints against a principle are a function solely of the cost to them of that principle's being accepted. But, as indicated at the outset of this section, I have already departed from the Complaint Model in this respect, by allowing that individuals' reasons for rejecting a principle can depend on factors other than effects on their well-being. We should see, then, whether this divergence provides room for an explanation of how what is right can sometimes depend on aggregative considerations.

As argued in the previous section, we can explain, on contractualist grounds, how there can be a duty in certain situations to prevent injury or loss of life. This would be required, for example, by principles of mutual aid, requiring one to prevent injury or death when one can easily do so, and also by more specific principles, such as one requiring anyone who operates an automobile, or other potentially dangerous machine, to prevent others from being injured or killed by it, insofar as he can do this. But now consider a principle which, in cases in which one has a duty of this kind and one has to choose between preventing a certain level of injury to either a larger or a smaller group of people, permits one to save either the greater or the smaller number (assuming that one is not bound by any other duties or obligations to members of either group).

What objection could be raised to this principle from the point of view of someone in the larger group? The principle would permit someone, faced with the choice between saving one stranger from injury or death and saving two other strangers from the same fate, to save only the one. In such a case, either member of the larger group might complain that this principle did not take account of the value of saving his life, since it permits the agent to decide what to do in the very same way that it would have permitted had he not been present at all, and there was only one person in each group. The fate of the single person is obviously being given positive weight, he might argue, since if that person were not threatened then the agent would have been required to save the two. And the fact that there is one other person who can be saved if and only if the first person is not saved is being given positive weight to balance the value of saving the one. The presence of the additional person, however, makes no difference to what the agent is required to do or to how she is required to go about deciding what to do. This is unacceptable, the person might argue, since his life should be given the same moral significance as anyone else's in this situation (which is, by stipulation, a situation in which no one has a special moral claim).[34]

This line of reasoning seems to me to have great force.[35] The conclusion it supports is that any principle dealing with cases of this kind would be reasonably rejectable if it did not require agents to treat the claims of each person who could be saved as having the same moral force. Since there is, we are supposing, a positive duty to save in cases in which only one person is present, this means that any nonrejectable principle must direct an agent to recognize a positive reason for saving each person. Since a second reason of this kind can balance the first—turning a situation in which one must save one into one in which it is permissible to save either of two people—the reason presented by the needs of a second person in one of these two groups must at least have the power to break this tie. The principle stated above fails to meet these requirements and is reasonably rejectable. The same objection would also apply to a principle that directed an agent faced with a choice between saving one and saving two in such a situation to decide by flipping a fair coin.

Consider, then, a principle requiring one to save the greater number in situations of the kind described. What objection could be raised to this principle from the standpoint of those in the smaller group? Such a person could not claim that his life was not taken into account in the way that those of others were. He might say that he would have been better off under a principle permitting one to save the smaller number, and might have been better off under a principle requiring the agent to flip a coin. But these are not, by themselves, grounds for reasonable rejection. It will be true of almost any principle that someone would have been better off if some other principle were in effect. And, as we have seen, these particular alternatives are subject to a strong objection that does not apply to the one now under consideration.

It would be reasonable to reject a principle for deciding what to do in these cases that did not give positive weight to each person's life. It would also be reasonable to reject a principle that did not give each person's life the same importance.[36] The principle requiring one to save the greater number in these cases satisfies these two requirements, but it might be claimed that it is not the only principle that does so. Consider, for example, the principle of proportional chances, directing one to decide which group to save by means of a weighted lottery. According to this principle, if one had to choose between saving group A, containing four people, and group B, containing five, then one should use a procedure that has a four-ninths chance of favoring A and a five-ninths chance of favoring B.[37] This principle gives everyone's life a positive weight (it would not call for the same procedure in a case of one versus one as in a case of one versus two). And although the members of the larger group have a greater chance of being saved than those in the smaller group, the presence of each person changes the procedure in the same way. Moreover, it might be argued that the strongest grounds for rejecting this principle are weaker than the strongest grounds for rejecting the principle of saving the greater number, since whoever loses out under this principle has at least been given a chance of being saved.

This argument is not persuasive, however. Whichever of these principles is followed, the ultimate stakes for the people affected are the same: some will suffer severe harm, the others will be saved. So the argument within contractualism for the principle of proportional chances is not that it makes some people better off than they would be under the alternative principle, but rather that it is a better *procedure* for deciding which people will be saved, and that the members of the smaller group could reasonably reject the alternative procedure that requires one always to save the greater number.[38] But it is not clear that they can reasonably reject this principle. In any class of cases in which we must decide between providing a good to one group and providing it to another, if a given principle would decide the matter in favor of one group, then the members of the other have a reason to prefer that the matter be settled by a lottery (even one weighted against them). They have this reason no matter how strong the case for the given principle may be, but it does not follow that they have reasonable grounds for rejecting the principle. This depends on whether there are good substantive reasons supporting that principle, and in this case it seems that there are such reasons.

As argued above, in a case in which we must choose between saving one person and saving two, a principle that did not recognize the presence of the second person on the latter side as making a moral difference, counting in favor of saving that group, could reasonably be rejected. The case for using a weighted lottery acknowledges this, since the reason for *weighting* the lottery rather than using one that gives everyone an equal chance of being saved is that this reflects the positive value of saving each person: everyone's presence makes a difference to the procedure that is followed, counting in favor of the action that would lead to his or her being saved. Why, then, doesn't this settle the matter? If there is a strong reason, other things being equal, to save this additional person, then deciding on this ground to save the two-person group is not *unfair* to the person who is not saved, since the importance of saving him or her has been fully taken into account.[39] There is no reason, at this point, to reshuffle the moral deck by holding a weighted lottery, or an unweighted one.

I conclude that it would not be reasonable to reject a principle requiring one to save the greater number in rescue situations of the kind described. The argument I have given departs from the Complaint Model, but it preserves the individualistic basis of contractualism. The principle just defended directs an agent, under the specified conditions, to choose the course of action that yields the greater benefit, but the argument for the principle considered only objections that could be raised from the standpoints of the individuals involved.[40] Admitting this argument does not, I believe, open the door to implausible forms of aggregation. To see this, we need to consider some examples.

Suppose that Jones has suffered an accident in the transmitter room of a television station. Electrical equipment has fallen on his arm, and we cannot rescue him without turning off the transmitter for fifteen minutes. A World Cup match is in progress, watched by many people, and it will not be over for an hour. Jones's injury will not get any worse if we wait, but his hand has been mashed and he is receiving extremely painful electrical shocks. Should we rescue him now or wait until the match is over? Does the right thing to do depend on how many people are watching—whether it is one million or five million or a hundred million? It seems to me that we should not wait, no matter how many viewers there are, and I believe that contractualism can account for this judgment while still allowing aggregative principles of the kind defended above.

Consider a principle requiring one to save a person in a situation like Jones's. This principle might hold that if one can save a person from serious pain and injury at the cost of inconveniencing others or interfering with their amusement, then one must do so no matter how numerous these others may be. Could this principle reasonably be rejected? I do not believe that it could. No one in the class of people whose enjoyment of the match would be interrupted could make an argument like the one I gave above against the principle allowing one to save the smaller number of people in a case in which everyone is threatened with the same serious loss. That argument relied on the fact that if one of the members of the two-person group were absent then the positive reason for saving the one person would be balanced by an identical reason for saving the remaining member of the pair, thus creating a tie, which is broken by the claims of the other member of the pair, if there is one. But when the harms in question are unequal, we cannot create such a tie simply by imagining some of the people in the larger group to be absent. To claim that there is a tie in such a case would be already to claim that the fact that there are more people in one group makes it reasonable to reject a principle requiring one to help the smaller number, each of whom would suffer the greater harm. So we cannot use this "tie-breaking" argument to justify the selection of a principle requiring one to save the greater number in such cases.

It might be claimed that my argument goes too far in rejecting aggregative reasoning. Other cases might be cited in which, it is alleged, we do or should "sum up" similar benefits and use them to offset larger costs to individuals. Suppose, for example, that we are deciding whether to build a new system of transmitting towers that will improve the quality of reception for many television viewers. It may be highly probable that in the course of this project a number of workers will suffer harms at least as great as Jones's. Yet we do not think that it is therefore wrong to go ahead. Much the same thing might be said about many other public projects, such as building a bridge, road, or tunnel that will make travel more convenient for many people. So an adequate account of the role of aggregation in our thinking about right and wrong needs to explain the difference between these two kinds of cases.

It is important in understanding our reaction to these cases to note that they involve failing to prevent accidental injuries rather than either intentionally inflicting serious harm on a few people, or withholding aid from people who need it, in order to bring small benefits to others. They differ in this respect from my original television studio example, and if they did not differ in this way our reaction to them would be very different. Our sense that it is permissible to undertake these projects also depends crucially on the assumption that precautions have been taken to make the work safe and that, in addition, workers have the choice of whether or not to undertake the risks involved. So the question in these cases is whether these precautions are adequate—whether, having taken them, it is permissible to proceed—or whether a higher level of caution is required.

This question is properly addressed in two stages. In the first, we ask what level of care is adequate; in the second, we ask whether this standard has been met in the case of a particular project. No doubt there are many actual projects in which this standard has not been met. But the question of whether it has been met (in cases in which the harms in question are serious ones and the gains to each beneficiary are small) does not depend on the number of people who will benefit. (We do not think that a higher level of safety must be provided for workers on a building that will benefit only one family as opposed to an apartment house or a public bridge.)[41]

The first question is a general one, and the answer to it affects our lives in many ways, since there are many things that we do or depend on that involve risk of serious harm to others. Suppose, then, that we are considering a principle that allows projects to proceed, even though they involve risk of serious harm to some, provided that a certain level of care has been taken to reduce these risks. It is obvious what the generic reason would be for rejecting such a principle from the standpoint of someone who is seriously injured despite the precautions that have been taken. On the other side, however, those who would benefit, directly or indirectly, from the many activities that the principle would permit may have good generic reason to object to a more stringent requirement. In meeting the level of care demanded by the principle, they might argue, they have done enough to protect others from harm. Refusing to allow activities that meet this level of care would, they could claim, impose unacceptable constraint on their lives.

My purpose here is not to argue that one or the other of these grounds for reasonable rejection should be decisive. (Since I have not stated the principle in question with any precision it is impossible to tell which side has the stronger claim.) It may be that the views we commonly hold about this matter are mistaken, because they involve exaggerating the sacrifice that would be involved if a higher level of caution were required. My present point concerns the form that such arguments should take rather than the substantive question of what their outcome should be. The contractualist argument I have just stated includes a form of aggregation, but it is aggregation *within* each person's life, summing up all the ways in which a principle demanding a certain level of care would constrain that life, rather than aggregation *across* lives, adding up the costs or benefits to different individuals. My claim is that once the arguments are properly understood it is apparent that only the first form of aggregation is needed in cases of the kind I am presently considering (that is to say, cases in which practices which benefit many people in relatively small ways will very likely involve serious accidental harm to a few). It is tempting to think that our conclusions about the moral permissibility of these practices depend on summing up the small benefits to many individuals to reach a sum that outweighs the serious losses to a few, but this is in fact an illusion.[42]

The argument just concluded relied upon "intrapersonal aggregation" of the consequences, for an individual, of a principle's being generally accepted and acted upon. This is not an ad hoc move, but is in accord with the point, made several times above, that generic reasons for rejecting a principle can include these general effects as well as the costs and benefits of someone's abiding by the principle in a particular case. Having appealed to such general consequences in this case, however, I should reexamine my television studio example to see whether a similar appeal would have led to a different conclusion in that case. The principle in question was one that required an agent to save one person from an hour of extreme pain even at the cost of inconvenience to others, regardless of the number of people so inconvenienced. The question now is whether, if that principle were generally followed, the consequences for some individuals (intrapersonally aggregated) would be so great as to make it reasonable to reject the principle. I do not believe this is so. It seems to me that we currently follow something close to this principle and that the occasions to which it applies seem sufficiently rare that the costs on each of us are not very significant. I may of course be wrong in thinking this. Perhaps if we realized how much each of us is sacrificing for rescues of this general kind we would conclude correctly that it would not be unreasonable to refuse to pay this price (even though we might want to bear it anyway, since failing to rescue such people would be inhumane even if it were not actually wrong). My point is that, whatever the correct substantive judgment may be in this case, contractualism provides a framework which allows the relevant factors to be considered and leads to plausible conclusions.[43]

I have argued that contractualism supports a principle according to which, in situations in which aid is required and in which one must choose between aiding a larger or a smaller number of people all of whom face harms of comparable moral importance, one must aid the larger number. On the other hand, contractualism does not require, or even permit, one to save a larger number of people from minor harms rather than a smaller number who face much more serious injuries. This distinction, between one class of cases, in which the number of people who can be saved is morally relevant, and all others, in which it is not, is subject to at least two objections. The first concerns the way in which a distinction is drawn between the moral significance of different harms. It seems implausible that in one case, in which we must choose between saving one person and saving ten from harms of the same degree of seriousness, we are required to save the ten, but that in a case that was otherwise identical except for the fact that the harm faced by the one was *slightly* worse we would be required to save the one instead. The proper reply here, I believe, is that the distinctions on which the principles I have argued for rely are distinctions between broad categories of moral seriousness. Slight differences in what happens, such as a pain's lasting a little longer or a person's losing two fingers rather than three, do not make the difference between a very serious loss and a moderate one, and the differences between these moral categories are not "slight."

The second objection is that although the principles I have argued for may seem correct in cases in which the harms in question are serious and all of the same degree of seriousness (as in the choice between saving one life or many) and in cases involving harms of very different degrees of seriousness (as in the television studio example), there are intermediate cases in which they lead to less plausible results. It may be clear that preventing one person from drowning takes priority over warning a whole beach full of people not to go into the water, which is polluted and will cause them several days of vomiting and diarrhea. In this case it may not matter how many people are on the beach. But this becomes less clear as we modify the example, increasing the seriousness of the harm that the many will suffer to, say, the loss of a limb, or blindness, or paralysis. On the account I have offered of how aggregative principles can be justified within contractualism, the number of people affected does not become relevant until the harm the members of the larger group suffer reaches the same degree of moral seriousness as that suffered by those in the smaller group (in this case, drowning). But it may seem that there are harms such that, although it would not be permissible to save one person from this harm rather than to save someone from drowning, nonetheless an agent would be permitted, perhaps even required, to prevent a very large number of people from suffering it, even if that meant that she would be unable to save a drowning person. As I have said, perhaps blindness and total paralysis are examples of such harms.

This might be questioned. If it is clear that, faced with a choice between saving one person's life and saving another from complete paralysis (where no other factors are relevant), we must choose the former, then is it so clear that we would be required to let one person die in order to save a very large number from being paralyzed? If, as many believe, this is clear, and yet there are other cases, such as that of Jones in the television station, in which aggregative arguments are not appropriate, then it seems that our intuitive moral thinking is best understood in terms of a relation of "relevance" between harms. If one harm, though not as serious as another, is nonetheless serious enough to be morally "relevant" to it, then it is appropriate, in deciding whether to prevent more serious harms at the cost of not being able to prevent a greater number of less serious ones, to take into account the number of harms involved on each side. But if one harm is not only less serious than, but not even "relevant to," some greater one, then we do not need to take the number of people who would suffer these two harms into account in deciding which to prevent, but should always prevent the more serious harm. Thus it might be claimed, for example, that missing half an hour of exciting television is not relevant when we are deciding whether to save a person in front of us who is in extreme pain, but that total paralysis or blindness is relevant to the even more serious harm of loss of life. So it could be wrong to save one person's life when we could instead have prevented a million people from going blind or becoming paralyzed. (Or, at least, it would be permissible to prevent this harm to the greater number of people even though it would not have been permissible to prevent this lesser harm rather than the greater if the numbers involved had been the same.)[44]

Could such a distinction be incorporated into contractualist argument? I am not certain about the answer to this question, but I will consider one possibility, drawing on some points made earlier in this section. I said earlier that a principle permitting us to save one person rather than two might reasonably be rejected, from the point of view of one of the two, on the ground that this principle did not take his or her life into account at all as a reason for choosing one course of action rather than the other. It should, I argued, at least count as a tie-breaker. The same might be said for lesser, but still serious harms, such as blindness or paralysis. It would be reasonable to reject, on this same ground, a principle that permitted one (in absence of any special justification) to save one stranger's life rather than following another course of action that would save a different life and also prevent someone from being blinded or paralyzed for life.

This is still a tie-breaking argument, but it might be extended beyond that, employing the idea of relevance just mentioned. Consider cases in which the choice is between preventing one more serious harm and a greater number of less serious ones. It might be claimed that if the less serious harms are nonetheless morally relevant to the more serious ones this means that a principle requiring (or perhaps even permitting) one always to prevent the more serious harms in such a case could reasonably be rejected from the point of view of someone in the other group on the ground that it did not give proper consideration to his admittedly less serious, but still morally relevant, loss. One might then argue that such an individual's claim to have his or her harm taken into account can be met only by a principle that is sensitive to the numbers of people involved on each side. I am not certain how such an argument would go, but it does not seem to me to be excluded in advance by the general idea of contractualism.

This rather long discussion of aggregation can be summarized as follows. The most familiar rationale for principles that make the rightness of actions depend on the number of people who will be affected by them appeals to the idea that what morality is most fundamentally concerned with is producing the greatest total benefit. On a contractualist account of right and wrong this rationale is ruled out, because the rightness of actions depends only on the rejectability of principles from various individual standpoints. This emphasis on the claims of individuals is, at least for me, one of the most appealing features of such a view, and it avoids implausible cases of aggregation in what seems, intuitively, to be the right way. But this restriction to the claims of individuals can be construed more broadly or more narrowly, depending on how these "claims" are understood. Even when this notion is construed very narrowly, contractualism can explain (by appeal to the tie-breaking argument) how the number of people affected can make a difference to the rightness or wrongness of an action in certain special cases. It is possible that a less tightly constrained version of contractualism, which gives more structure to the idea of how individuals can demand that their interests be taken into account, might yield aggregative principles that would apply to a wider range of cases, in which the harms on each side were not equally serious. I have not shown that this is the case, but my argument does not exclude it.

10. Conclusion

In this chapter I have described and defended the central elements of the account of moral thinking that contractualism presents: the idea of reasonableness that this view employs, the standpoints from which a principle can be rejected, and the idea of the generic reasons arising from such a standpoint. The considerations that count as such reasons must be ones that individuals in that position would have. They must also be personal reasons, although they need not, I argued, take the form of claims about the impact that a principle would have on such a person's well-being. To illustrate this point, I considered the way in which contractualism can explain why acceptable moral principles must be general, and showed how unfairness figures in this argument as a ground for reasonably rejecting a principle. Because grounds for rejecting a principle must come from the standpoint of some individual, contractualism rules out justifications for principles that appeal to the sum of the benefits they bring to different people. But, as I have just explained, contractualism can nonetheless account for the moral relevance of aggregative considerations in at least some cases, including those in which they have the greatest plausibility.

With regard to many of these points, my argument has proceeded in a "downward" direction: from the central motivating idea of contractualism to conclusions about what could or could not be grounds for reasonable rejection. My discussions of the grounds for excluding impersonal reasons and direct appeals to aggregative benefits, for example, took this form. In other cases, however, my arguments have contained "upward" elements: that is, they sometimes began from cases in which it seemed clear, intuitively, that a principle could reasonably be rejected and then proceeded to inquire how the grounds for this rejection should best be understood. This inquiry sometimes proceeded by considering whether a given construal of these grounds would have plausible or implausible consequences in other cases. This was the method I followed, for example, in discussing the question of priority for the worst off.

It might be maintained that a contractualist theory should avoid "upward" arguments of this kind and, if possible, avoid appealing to intuitive judgments about what is "reasonable." The point of a *theory,* it might be claimed, is to avoid such appeals. In a proper contractualist theory, it might be said, the circumstances in which agreement is to be sought should be clearly specified and the notion of reasonableness sufficiently well defined to enable us to reach a decision about whether a given principle could or could not reasonably be rejected simply by reasoning in a purely technical way, without appeals to intuitions about reasonableness. Rawls's Original Position argument might be cited as an example of how such a theory should be constructed.[45]

In response, I want to consider the prospects for extending contractualism as I have stated it into a tighter theory of the kind suggested in this criticism. I will begin by explaining why a certain general extension of this kind is not plausible and then consider what is to be learned from the example of Rawls's Original Position argument. The result, I hope, will be a clearer understanding of the relation between extended contractualist theories of the kind suggested and appeals to intuitive judgments about reasonableness.

One natural extension of contractualism would take the form of what I called above "welfarist contractualism." Such a theory would be based on a suitably chosen notion of well-being and a metric for making comparisons of well-being so understood. It would then define the reasonableness of rejecting a principle in terms of the loss of well-being that a person would experience if that principle were accepted (and perhaps also the level of well-being that would result for him or her) as compared with the well-being that that person and others would experience under alternative principles.

It does not seem likely that any form of welfarist contractualism will yield a plausible account of the morality of right and wrong. This is not likely because the justificatory force of a given increment of well-being in moral argument is not constant in all situations, but depends on other factors of a clearly moral character. I have already mentioned two factors of this kind: considerations of responsibility and considerations of fairness. Whether I have a morally forceful demand to be better off in a certain way will often depend, intuitively, on whether my fate is or is not my own doing, and on whether institutions that benefited me in the way I am demanding would be fairer, or less fair, than those presently in operation. Given this fact, it seems extremely likely that in any plausible version of contractualism the force of a given increment of well-being as grounds for reasonably rejecting a principle will be similarly dependent on, and qualified by, factors such as these.

Consider now how Rawls's Original Position argument deals with these problems. I will focus on the question of responsibility. Rawls's Original Position may seem to approximate the "technical" model described above insofar as the parties to this position are thought to choose principles of justice solely with the aim of doing as well as they can for themselves (or for those they represent), where "how well they do" is measured in terms of what Rawls calls "primary social goods."[46] (This would amount, in my terms, to saying that grounds for rejecting a principle must be stated in terms of the effect that that principle would have on the level of primary goods that they might be left with if they turned out to occupy a certain social position.)

But this description concentrates on one aspect of Rawls's construction and leaves out other assumptions which are crucial to the plausibility of having the parties concentrate exclusively on the "expectations" of representative members of society in various social positions. First, it is assumed that these positions are "open to all under conditions of fair equality of opportunity." Second, as Rawls later says, the choice of primary social goods as a measure of expectations amounts to a certain "social division of responsibility" between social institutions on the one hand and individuals on the other.[47] The idea is this. The "basic structure" of society is its legal, political, and economic framework, the function of which is to define the rights and liberties of citizens and to determine a range of social positions to which different powers and economic rewards are attached. If a basic structure does this in an acceptable way—if citizens have no reasonable complaint about their access to various positions within this framework or to the package of rights, liberties, and opportunities for economic reward that particular positions present them with—then that structure is just. It is up to individuals, operating within this framework, to choose their own ends and make use of the given opportunities and resources to pursue those ends as best they can. How successful or unsuccessful, happy or unhappy they are as a result is their own responsibility.

With these assumptions in place, it makes sense to have the parties choose principles simply with the aim of assuring for themselves as large a bundle of primary social goods as they can. But these assumptions represent substantive claims (albeit very plausible ones) about how social institutions are to be judged and about the relative roles of institutions and individuals. Three points are relevant here. The first is that although these are plausible claims about the particular case of the justice of social institutions, it does not seem likely that there are equally plausible claims about the morality of right and wrong in general, which is the subject of the contractualist theory I am proposing. It does not seem very likely, for example, that we could come up with a list of "moral primary goods" which could form the basis of a quite general "moral division of labor" between what we owe to each other and what is each individual's own responsibility. Morality (even the morality of obligation) is not "about" the provision of any such list of goods in the way that the question of the justice of social institutions can plausibly be held to be "about" the distribution of primary social goods. Within this broader area of morality issues of responsibility arise in widely varying forms. To mention just a few, there is the responsibility of an agent for wrongful conduct, responsibility for creating a situation that gives reason to break a promise, responsibility for engaging in risky conduct that has led to harm, and responsibility for misfortune that puts one in need of aid. Moreover, assessing responsibility in such cases (that is to say, assessing the moral significance of the fact that the person chose, under certain conditions, to pursue a certain line of conduct) involves assessing the significance of diverse considerations of intent, knowledge, the availability of information, and the availability and desirability of alternative courses of action.

It does not seem very likely that the significance of these diverse factors in various different circumstances can be accounted for in terms of a list of categories of liberty or opportunity, reasonably uniform across the whole range of questions of right and wrong. The conditions that would render an action "involuntary" in the sense required to absolve one of blame are different from those that make one's fate not "one's own doing" in the sense that would absolve others of any duty to aid, and these are different in turn from the conditions necessary to render a promise nonbinding because not voluntarily given. (For example, the fact that the only available alternatives led to imminent, painful death might render an act involuntary for the first two of these purposes but would not, as Hume noted, free one from a promise to pay a surgeon.)[48] What one can do at this general level (and what I will try to do in the following chapter) is to investigate what it is that gives these various elements of "voluntariness" (knowledge of circumstances, availability of alternatives, and so on) their moral significance (why they are factors that people have reason to insist that acceptable principles should take into account). But even once these reasons have been identified there remains the matter of judging what bearing they have on the rejectability of any particular principle.

The contrast I am drawing here is not between moral philosophy on the one hand and political philosophy on the other but between very general claims about morality, or about what we owe to each other, and claims about what is right and wrong in specific kinds of circumstances (claims about the justice of social institutions being one example). Rawls's Original Position argument is thus more closely analogous to an argument about one particular form of obligation (such as duties to aid others when one can) than to the general contractualist idea of reasonable rejectability that I have been describing.

This brings me to the second point about this example, which is that insofar as the Original Position does approximate the "technical" model of contractualism described above it is somewhat misleading simply to contrast it with "upward" arguments that appeal to intuitive judgments about what would constitute reasonable grounds for rejecting principles of a certain kind. This is misleading because, while the tighter character of the Original Position argument may make it possible to arrive at conclusions with less appeal to intuitive judgment, this is made possible by building into the design of the Original Position features that themselves reflect substantive judgments about the subject to which it is addressed (judgments about the proper aims of social institutions, the division of labor between institutions and individuals, and so on).[49] In Rawls's overall theory this is reflected in the fact that the Original Position itself is justified by appeal to its ability to account for our considered judgments of justice in reflective equilibrium.

The conclusion I draw is that if "tighter" forms of contractualism—ones that lead to a wider range of substantive conclusions through "downward" argument—are to be developed, this is most likely to be done through "upward" argument. Working within the framework of contractualism as I have described it, we can try to identify and describe more clearly what seem to be reasonable grounds for rejecting principles and, by doing this, to specify more fully the process of finding principles that no one can reasonably reject. For reasons given above, I believe we are more likely to arrive in this way at tighter forms of contractualism tailored to particular problems rather than at a tighter account of right and wrong in general. But this is only a guess. What progress of this kind is possible and at what level are things that can be determined only by trying.

My third and final point is that it is a mistake to think that, as the objection I have been discussing suggests, the main purpose of moral theorizing is to come up with ways of deciding moral questions without appealing to intuitive judgment, and that the viability of contractualism as a theory therefore depends on the development of tightened versions of the kind just discussed. As I pointed out earlier in this chapter, moral principles that can be stated as definite rules and applied without significant appeals to judgment are rare at best. The goal of avoiding appeals to judgment in arriving at principles seems to me a doubtful one for similar reasons. Theoretical reflection about the nature of the morality of obligation can affect our substantive moral views in other ways, however. A general account, of the kind that contractualism provides, of the process through which moral principles are justified can undermine the plausibility of some principles (such as those based on unrestricted aggregative reasoning) and enhance the plausibility of others. This may lead to the formulation of novel principles. What is more likely, however, is that by clarifying our understanding of the reasons that make familiar moral principles ones that no one could reasonably reject such an account can advance our understanding of the content of those principles and of their limits.

The next two chapters will provide examples of this kind of investigation. In Chapter 6 I will examine the generic reasons that explain the role that ideas of responsibility and choice must have in any acceptable moral principles. Chapter 7 will be concerned with the generic reasons supporting obligations of fidelity and truthfulness.

6

Responsibility

1. Introduction

Questions of responsibility, and associated questions of freedom, voluntariness, and choice, arise in a number of different ways. Questions of "moral responsibility" are most often questions about whether some action can be attributed to an agent in the way that is required in order for it to be a basis for moral appraisal. I will call this sense of responsibility *responsibility as attributability*. To say that a person is responsible, in this sense, for a given action is only to say that it is appropriate to take it as a basis of moral appraisal of that person. Nothing is implied about what this appraisal should be—that is to say, about whether the action is praiseworthy, blameworthy, or morally indifferent.

Questions of responsibility can also be asked in other senses. For example, it might be asked whether it is a father's responsibility to set up his estate in such a way as to prevent his grown son from making foolish financial decisions. Suppose that the answer to this question in a given case is no, that the money is passed on outright, and that the son, having invested it badly, complains that his father should have been more cautious. We might dismiss this claim by saying, "It was your money, and you chose how to use it. So the result is your responsibility. You have no one else to blame." These judgments of responsibility express substantive claims about what people are required (or, in this case, not required) to do for each other. So I will call them judgments of *substantive responsibility*.

As the question about the father in this example indicates, judgments about what a person's substantive responsibilities are can be used very widely, to express judgments about almost any duty, or at least the duties connected with any role. But as the question about the son indicates, what is or isn't a person's (substantive) responsibility is particularly sensitive to the choices that person makes. It is this aspect of substantive responsibility that I will be concerned with in this chapter: the way in which a person's obligations to others and his claims against them depend upon the opportunities to choose that he has had and the decisions that he has made. In order to explain this dependence I need to explain, first, why principles that no one could reasonably reject will make a person's obligations and his claims against others depend on the opportunities he has had and the decisions he has made. But this dependence also plays a deeper role in contractualist argument as I described it in Chapter 5. I said there that the force of a person's objection to a principle imposing a burden on her, or permitting others to act in a way that would impose such a burden, can be diminished by the fact that she could avoid that burden by choosing appropriately. To complete my account of contractualist argument, I therefore need to show how this can be explained without presupposing some prior moral idea about the legitimating force of voluntary choices. Sections 2 and 3 of this chapter will provide this explanation, in terms of what I will call the Value of Choice.

The distinction between responsibility as attributability and the aspect of substantive responsibility that I am focusing on (its dependence on a person's choices) is easy to overlook. It is tempting to say that the answer to the question of when a person is responsible in these two senses is the same: an action is attributable to a person just in case he or she performed it voluntarily, and a person is substantively responsible for a certain outcome just in case he or she chose, voluntarily, to bring it about. I will argue that this apparent similarity is misleading and that these two notions of responsibility have quite different moral roots. In Sections 4 and 5 I will spell out more fully the conception of moral appraisal that figures in the theory I have presented in previous chapters. This conception leads to an account of the conditions under which an action is attributable to an agent in the sense required to make moral appraisal appropriate that is quite different from the Value of Choice account, which explains the dependence of substantive responsibility on a person's choices. I will argue that it is important to distinguish clearly between judgments of responsibility of these two kinds.

Any discussion of our ideas of responsibility and the ideas of freedom and voluntariness on which they depend also needs to address the threat to these notions that goes under the heading of the problem of free will. This problem takes a number of different forms, depending on what the threat is taken to be and on which judgments are seen as being threatened. The threat is often taken to be determinism, that is to say, roughly, the thesis that there are laws of nature from which it follows, given a complete description of the world at any one time, exactly what state the world must be in at any later time. But our moral ideas also seem to be threatened by a weaker claim, which I will call the Causal Thesis. This is the thesis that all of our actions have antecedent causes to which they are linked by causal laws of the kind that govern other events in the universe, whether these laws are deterministic or merely probabilistic. I will have something to say about both of these threats, but I will be particularly concerned with the compatibility of moral responsibility and the Causal Thesis because it seems to me that the space opened up by the falsity of determinism would be relevant to morality only if it were filled by something other than the cumulative effects of indeterministic physical processes. If the actions we perform result from the fact that we have a certain physical constitution and have been subject to certain causal influences, then an apparent threat to morality remains even if the laws linking these causes and their effects are not deterministic.

The idea that there is such a threat is sometimes supported by thought experiments such as the following. Suppose you were to learn that someone's present state of mind, intentions, and actions were produced in him or her a few minutes ago by "outside forces" such as electrical stimulation of his nervous system. You would not think it appropriate to blame that person for what he does under such conditions. But if the Causal Thesis is true, then all our actions are like this. The only differences are in the forms of outside intervention and the span of time over which it occurs, and surely these are not essential to the freedom of the agent in the sense relevant to moral responsibility.

Arguments of this kind are most commonly presented as a challenge to the applicability of moral praise and blame—that is, to "moral responsibility" in the sense I have called responsibility as attributability. But the significance of a person's choices for judgments of substantive responsibility is also threatened. We would not think, for example, that a promise was binding if the act of making the promise was brought about by outside causes of one of the kinds just listed. So some response to the apparent challenge of the Causal Thesis is required to defend judgments of responsibility of both of the kinds I have listed.

One form of response would be to argue that there are mistakes in the loose idea of causality to which this challenge appeals or in the assumption it makes about the relation between mental and physical events. No doubt there is much to be said on these topics, but my response will follow a different line. It is generally assumed that when an action is caused by factors outside the agent this makes moral appraisal inappropriate, but it is seldom explained why this should be so. I will argue that once we see clearly how the freedom of a choice or the voluntariness of an action is relevant to judgments of responsibility of the two kinds I have mentioned, it becomes apparent that neither form of responsibility is threatened by the general truth of determinism or of the Causal Thesis (although it can, of course, be undermined by particular kinds of causal interventions).

2. The Value of Choice

The task of this section and the next will be to explain the role that considerations of choice and responsibility play in reasons for rejecting principles. Two things need to be explained. The first is why principles that no one could reasonably reject often must be ones that make normative outcomes sensitive to individuals' choices, or at least to their having had the opportunity to choose. The second is how considerations of responsibility can diminish a person's reasonable grounds for rejecting a principle. How can the fact that a person could have avoided a certain burden by choosing appropriately make it the case that he cannot reasonably reject a principle that makes him bear that burden? My strategy will be to derive an answer to the second question from an answer to the first. Once we understand the positive reasons that people have for wanting opportunities to make choices that will affect what happens to them, what they owe to others, and what others owe to them, we can see also how their having had such opportunities can play a crucial role in determining what they can reasonably object to.[1]

I will start, then, by examining some of the generic reasons that people have for wanting to have what happens depend on the way that they respond when presented with alternatives under the right conditions. When I go to a restaurant, for example, it is generally a good thing from my point of view to have what appears on my plate depend on the responses I give when presented with the menu. The most obvious reason for this is simply instrumental: I want what appears on my plate to be something I will enjoy eating, and I believe that this is more likely to happen if what appears depends on my responses to the menu. This reason for valuing choice is both conditional and relative. It is conditional because the value of my response as a predictor of my future satisfaction depends on the nature of the question, my capacities of discernment, and the conditions under which my response is elicited. It is relative because it also depends on the reliability of the available alternative means for selecting the outcomes in question. In the restaurant case, for example, this value depends on how much I know about the cuisine in question and on my condition when the menu arrives: on whether I am drunk, for example, or too eager to impress my companions with my knowledge of French or my ability to swallow highly seasoned food. Thus the same interest that sometimes makes choice valuable—the interest in future satisfaction—can at other times provide reasons for wanting outcomes to be determined in some other way.[2]

What I have described so far might be called the "predictive" or "instrumental" value of choice. In the example I have given, choice is instrumental to my own future enjoyment, but the class of states that one might seek to advance by having outcomes depend on one's choices is much broader. Aside from this range of instrumental reasons, however, there are other grounds for wanting to have what happens depend on my responses. One class of such reasons concerns the "representative" value of choice, which is illustrated by the example of choosing a gift.[3] On our anniversary, I want not only to have a present for my wife, but also to have chosen that present myself. This is not because I think that I am more likely to come up with a present she will like (as far as that goes it would be better to have her choose the present herself). The reason is rather that the gift has a different meaning if I choose it myself—both the fact that I chose it and the choice that I make reflect my thoughts about her and about the occasion. In other cases, for reasons similar in character but opposite in sign, I may prefer that what happens should *not* depend on my choices. For example, I would prefer to have the question of who will get a certain job (whether it will be my friend or some well-qualified stranger) not depend on how I respond when presented with the choice: I want it to be clear that the outcome does not reflect my judgment of their respective merits or my balancing of the competing claims of merit and loyalty.

The reasons we have for wanting to see features of ourselves manifested in actions and their results are of course not limited to cases in which our feelings for other people are at issue. I want to choose the furniture for my own living room, pick out the pictures for the walls, and write my own lectures despite the fact that these things might be done better by someone else. For better or worse, I want them to result from and hence to reflect my own taste, imagination, and powers of discrimination and analysis. We feel the same way, perhaps even more strongly, about important decisions affecting our lives in larger terms, such as what career to follow, where to work, and whom to marry.

These last examples, however, involve not only instrumental and representative but also what I will call symbolic value. In a situation in which people are normally expected to make choices of a certain sort for themselves, individuals have reason to value the opportunity to make these choices because not having or not exercising this opportunity would be seen as reflecting a judgment (their own or someone else's) that they are not competent or do not have the standing normally accorded an adult member of the society. For example, in societies in which arranged marriages are not the norm, people have reason to want to choose their own mates rather than have their parents do it for them, not only because they think this will lead to a more satisfactory choice (instrumental value), or because they want their choice to be an expression of their own taste and affections (representative value), but also because having their parents make the choice would be "demeaning"—that is to say, would suggest that they are not competent, independent adults (symbolic value). In a different society, in which arranged marriage was common, reasons of this last sort would be much weaker.

I am not claiming that these three categories of reasons for valuing choice are mutually exclusive (representative and symbolic value may be difficult to distinguish in some cases, for example), or that taken together they encompass all the reasons one can have for valuing choice. My aim in listing and distinguishing them is simply to illustrate the variety of ways in which choice can be important and to make clear that its value is not always merely instrumental: the reasons people have for wanting outcomes to be dependent on their choices often have to do with the significance that this dependence itself has for them, not merely with its efficacy in promoting outcomes that are desirable on other grounds. I have presented them so far simply as reasons we commonly have for wanting to have certain powers and opportunities in our lives. But I take it as obvious that these are significant classes of generic reasons that can figure as reasonable grounds for rejecting proposed moral principles.

Reasons of all three kinds would figure, for example, in determining the shape of an acceptable principle governing paternalistic interference in a person's life—that is to say, interference with a person's choices that is justified on the ground that it is "for his own good." Possible grounds for rejecting principles permitting such interference include claims that the interference they permit (a) would deprive people of the opportunity to make choices with significant instrumental value, (b) would interfere with choices that have important representative value for people as ways of shaping their lives and expressing their values, or (c) would stigmatize those who are interfered with by labeling them as immature or incompetent. Where these three values are significant (and there are no sufficiently strong countervailing ones), the principles that no one could reasonably reject will forbid paternalistic intervention, thus making it a person's own (substantive) responsibility whether to risk the harms in question.

The pejorative ring of "paternalism" and the particular bitterness that it conveys stem from cases in which it is a matter of controversy whether the loss in question is a serious one or whether choices that may lead to it are foolish. Those who are inclined to make these choices may not see them as mistaken and, partly because of the controversy, may attach significant symbolic as well as representative value to being self-determining in this way and taking these risks. Consequently, they will resent paternalistic intervention which brands them as foolish when, as they see it, they merely differ from the majority in the things they value. Such sentiments are mistaken in some cases, although in others they can be the ground of reasonable objections. But this kind of resentment has no place at all in some other cases that are commonly called paternalistic, such as wage and hour laws or compulsory contributions to Social Security. These laws can both diminish and augment workers' ability to shape their lives to suit their preferences (diminish by ruling out choosing to work longer hours in order to make more money; augment by protecting people against being forced to make this choice). But they need not involve the kind of interference with representative values that gives paternalism its bad name, nor do they involve treating the workers they protect as foolish or incompetent. So it is useful, in weighing the force of objections to policies on the ground that they are "paternalistic," to identify and distinguish between these various kinds of reasons rather than simply appealing, in a general way, to the value of making one's own choices. I believe this is true in general of arguments about principles involving responsibility and choice.

As controversies about paternalism indicate, people disagree sharply about the value of various choices and opportunities to choose. Passionate disagreements about laws regarding seat belts and motorcycle helmets, for example, reflect disagreements about the instrumental, representative, and symbolic values of "unconstrained" choices about whether to use these devices, and hence about the permissibility of various forms of reminders and constraints. In addition to mere disagreement, however, different people have good reason to attach different value to various choices and opportunities. The same form of choice can have different instrumental value for people with different levels of knowledge, self-control, and discrimination, different representative value for people with different aims and attachments, and different symbolic value for people in different groups or societies. As I pointed out in Chapter 5, insofar as argument about the justifiability of moral principles has to proceed at a high level of generality, hence in ignorance of the distinctive situations of particular individuals, it must be based on "generic reasons"—that is to say, general conclusions about the reasons that individuals in a situation of a certain kind typically have. As I remarked earlier, there is always pressure to take account of individual differences by making principles more fine-grained and counterpressure to keep these principles simpler, hence more predictable and easier to apply. As we will see below, this tension is particularly clear in cases in which the opportunity to choose under a given set of conditions has very different value for different individuals.

The reasons I have listed for preferring principles that make what happens to us depend on the ways we respond when presented with alternatives are not undermined if it turns out that these responses have causes outside us. As long as these causes affect our responses only by affecting what we are like, it will remain true that these responses can be good predictors of what will bring us enjoyment or advance our aims. Similarly, in the case of representative value, it is quite plausible to suppose that many of the tastes and capacities for discernment that we want our choices to express have a basis in our causal makeup, but this fact does not make them less a part of us and hence does not diminish the value of choices that express them. In many cases what we want our choices to reflect is not simply our instinctive reactions but rather our judgments of the relative force of competing reasons. Here again, as long as the causal processes in question do not deprive us of the ability to make such judgments at all they do not undermine the value of making choices that reflect these judgments; nor do they affect the fact that being allowed to make these judgments for ourselves is an important form of recognition as competent independent agents. So the instrumental, representative, and symbolic values of choice are not threatened by the Causal Thesis, whether the laws linking causes and effects are deterministic or merely probabilistic.

3. Responsibility and Choice

Having thus identified some of the positive reasons we have for wanting what happens to us to depend on our choices and other forms of response to alternatives, I want now to examine more fully the role that the value of choice plays in determining which principles it is reasonable to reject. It at least seems that when a person could have avoided a certain result by choosing appropriately, this fact weakens her grounds for rejecting a principle that would make her bear the burden of that result. Consider, for example, principles of the kind discussed in Chapter 5 that permit people to undertake useful projects that involve risk of harm to workers or others. It seems that the force of objections to such principles from the point of view of those who suffer this harm is significantly diminished if the principle requires that those who are exposed to this risk must be warned, in order to give them the opportunity of avoiding harm. The question to be addressed in this section is how this is to be explained.

To take a specific example, suppose that the officials of a city need to remove and dispose of some hazardous waste that has been found near a residential area. Apparently it has lain there for years, and they want to move it to a safer spot some distance away. Digging it up and moving it will inevitably release some hazardous chemicals into the air, but this is much less dangerous than leaving it in its present location, where it will in the long run seep into the water supply. Obviously they must take precautions to reduce the risks involved in this operation. They need to find a safe disposal site, away from where people normally have to go. They should build a fence around the new site, and another around the old one where the excavation is to be done, both of them with large signs warning people to keep away. They should also be sure to have the material wetted down and transported in closed trucks to minimize the amount of hazardous material released into the air. Inevitably, however, some of it will be released—enough to cause lung damage to those who are directly exposed if, because of past exposure or genetic predisposition, they are particularly susceptible, but not enough to pose a serious threat to anyone who stays indoors and away from the excavation site. Given that this is so, the officials should be careful to warn people, especially those who know they are at risk, to stay indoors and away from the relevant areas while the work is being done.

Suppose that all these precautions were taken, but that some people were nonetheless exposed and suffered lung damage as a result. Let me stipulate that the officials did all that they could be expected to do to warn and protect these people (I am assuming that evacuation of everyone in the affected area was not a reasonable option), and that a principle permitting what they have done is thus one that no one could reasonably reject. In particular, this principle could not reasonably be rejected from the standpoint represented by the people who were in fact injured. The question at issue is what role the fact that they were warned, and thus given the choice of avoiding exposure, plays in making it the case that they cannot complain of the outcome. The Value of Choice account that I am proposing explains the role of choice in the justification of moral principles by appealing to the reasons (of the kinds described in the preceding section) we have for wanting outcomes to depend on the way we respond when presented with alternatives. In the present case these reasons are purely instrumental. No one has reason to place a positive value on having the opportunity to be exposed to hazardous chemicals. So according to the Value of Choice account "giving people the choice" is, like the fences, the careful removal techniques, and the remote location of the new site, just another means through which the likelihood of injury is reduced. But this may seem not to account for the full moral significance of the fact that those who were injured "knew what they were getting into." Consider the following two cases.

Suppose that one person was exposed because, despite the newspaper stories, mailings, posted signs, sound trucks, and radio and television announcements, he failed to hear about the danger. So he went for his usual walk without realizing what was going on. A second person heard the warnings but did not take the danger seriously. Curious to see what was being done, she went to the removal site and climbed over the fence to get a closer look.

There seems to be a clear difference between these two cases. In the first case, the officials have "done enough" to protect the person simply because they have gone to such lengths to reduce the likelihood that anyone will be injured (in particular, to reduce the likelihood that anyone will fail to know of the danger). After all, there is a limit to how much one has to do to protect people. But in the case of the second person, we can say more. Since she had been warned of the danger, and chose to go to the site anyway, we are inclined to say that she is (substantively) responsible for her own injury; and it is this fact, rather than the amount that has been done to protect her or the cost to others of doing more, that makes it the case that she cannot blame anyone for what happened. By choosing, in the face of warnings, to go to the excavation site, she laid down her right to complain of the harm she suffered as a result.

This familiar and intuitively appealing idea about the moral significance of choice, which I will call the Forfeiture View, is clearly distinct from the Value of Choice account that I have presented above.[4] According to the Value of Choice account what matters is the value of the opportunity to choose that the person is presented with. If a person has been placed in a sufficiently good position, this can make it the case that he or she has no valid complaint about what results, whether or not it is produced by his or her active choice. On the Forfeiture View, on the other hand, it matters crucially whether an outcome actually resulted from a conscious decision in which the agent intentionally passed up specific alternatives. This is why that view accounts so well for our reaction to the person in the second example: not only does she have no one else to blame for her fate; she has *herself* to blame, since she chose to go to the site and climb over the fence.

This way of putting the matter can be misleading, however, insofar as it suggests that the person is responsible for her fate because she acted foolishly. What matters on the Forfeiture View is the fact of choice, not the faultiness of that choice. To see this, imagine a third person who, unlike the imprudently curious woman in my second example, did not run the risk of contamination foolishly or thoughtlessly. Suppose this person found that the day on which the excavation was to take place offered unusually good conditions for working outdoors on a scientific project to which she attached great value. Aware of the risk, she considered the matter carefully and decided that, taking into account her age and her likelihood of dying soon from an illness she already had, it was worth less to her to avoid this new risk than to advance her project in the time she was likely to have remaining to her. Surely this person is just as fully responsible for her fate, according to the Forfeiture View, as the imprudent woman is. But this conclusion does not depend on our judging her decision to be foolish or mistaken. What lies behind the Forfeiture View is thus not a notion of desert, according to which people who behave wrongly or foolishly cannot complain about suffering as a result. The idea is rather that a person who could have chosen to avoid a certain out-come, but who knowingly passed up this choice, cannot complain of the result: *volenti non fit iniuria.*

The Forfeiture View is intuitively appealing, but this appeal should be resisted. Note, first, that the Value of Choice view can account for the apparent difference between the claims of the people in the first two examples described above. We may have taken all the steps we could be asked to take to protect the person in the first example, who nonetheless failed to learn what was being done. But because we did not succeed in making him aware of the danger, we did not make what happened to him depend on his response to this information. Given that this dependence is something we all would reasonably want to have under the circumstances, we did not succeed in making this person as well off as one would reasonably want to be. The woman in the second example, however, did have the benefit of being informed, even though this turned out to be worth less as a protection than it would have been to most other people. Since it is true in both cases that we did as much as we could be asked to do to protect these people against injury, neither can "complain"—neither could reasonably re-ject a principle permitting such a project to go forward with the safeguards it involved. But it remains true that only the woman in the second example was put in the position that these safeguards aim at providing for everyone.

What is different about the second example, then, has to do with the circumstances in which the woman was actually placed by our protec-tive measures, not with the fact that she made a conscious decision to "take the risk." Consider, for example, a fourth person, who was informed of the risk of contamination but then simply forgot. As a result, when the trucks went by he was out in his yard exercising, breathing hard, with his Walkman turned up all the way. If, as in the other cases, enough was done to warn him, then this man is, like the woman in the second example, fully responsible for what happens to him, even though he made no conscious decision to take the risk.

From the fact that a person, under the right conditions, took a certain risk, we may conclude that he alone is responsible for what happens to him as a result. But this need not be seen as reflecting the special legitimating force of voluntary action, in the way that the Forfeiture View would suggest. The mere fact that he was placed in conditions in which he had the choice of avoiding the risk may be sufficient, as it was in the above examples. There are of course other cases in which it matters very much not only whether a person had the opportunity to make a conscious decision between certain alternatives but also whether he or she actually made such a decision. For example, a person is not bound by an agreement unless he or she actually consented to it. That is to say, a principle that no one could reasonably reject holds that if one has consented to an agreement under the right sort of conditions then one is bound by it; but it would be reasonable to reject any principle holding that one could be bound by contracts one had not consented to.[5] The Value of Choice account can explain why this should be so. There are solid generic reasons to want the additional degree of control over one's obligations that a requirement of explicit consent provides, and these constitute reasonable grounds for rejecting principles that do not provide it. So contractualism can explain why various conclusions that look like instances of the Forfeiture View are in fact correct. It can explain why explicit consent or a conscious decision is required in some cases but not in others. Moreover, in explaining this, it does not need to appeal to the Forfeiture View to explain why various possible reasons for rejection have force or lack it. (This was the role for which the Forfeiture View was introduced in our discussion.) The explanations provided by the Value of Choice account are sufficient.

In cases of this last kind, such as voluntary agreements, the fact that a person chose to do something, or gave his or her consent to its being done, appears to have distinctive importance in part because it is the last justifying element to be put in place. If the conditions are right, then the person's choice or consent is sufficient (and in these cases generally necessary) to make the result morally legitimate. When we focus on this last step, the fact of choice appears to have the distinctive moral force that the Forfeiture View suggests. The conditions which must already have been in place in order for the choice to have this force recede into the background, or seem important only insofar as they affect the "voluntariness" of that choice. But this way of looking at the matter is misleading, for at least two reasons. First, as we have seen, these "background" conditions are sometimes sufficient, by themselves, to determine the moral conclusion, without the occurrence of explicit choice or consent. Second, in cases in which explicit choice is important, it is unhelpful, and strains plausibility, to tie the significance of all the relevant background conditions to a notion of "voluntariness." For example, the difference between a person who entered into an unfavorable agreement because he completely ignored an alternative that was made known to him and a person who entered into such an agreement because that alternative was concealed from him does not lie in the fact that the former agreed voluntarily while the latter did not. One important virtue of the Value of Choice account is that it allows the various conditions under which a choice is (or could be) made to be taken into account separately from the fact of choice itself, and to be given the independent significance appropriate to them.

A defender of the Forfeiture View might raise a further objection at this point. According to the Value of Choice theory the moral significance of choice in cases like the hazardous waste removal example lies in its value as a protection. This is a special case of what I called, in the preceding section, the "predictive" or "instrumental" value of choice. "Having the choice"—having what happens depend on how one responds when presented with certain alternatives—is something we have reason to want because it decreases the likelihood of our suffering certain harms. But it might be objected that in the case of the imprudent woman who climbed over the fence being warned of the danger and given the choice of avoiding it turned out to have no positive value. The warning only aroused her impetuous curiosity, and she would have been better off if she had never been told at all. Yet we still feel that it is important that she was warned to stay home, and that the fact that she was warned is an important element supporting the conclusion that she cannot complain about what happened to her (and could not reasonably reject a principle permitting such a project to be undertaken). The objection concludes that since this moral significance cannot be accounted for by the positive value to her of being given this choice we need some other explanation. The natural alternative is something like the Forfeiture View.

Moreover, it may seem that if the Forfeiture View is to do the work required of it in such a case, it must rely on a more robust notion of freedom than that employed by the Value of Choice account. I claimed earlier that the Value of Choice account is not threatened by the

Causal Thesis. Choice can retain its value even if it is caused, ultimately, by factors outside us, I argued, as long as these factors operate "through us." Choice retains its instrumental and representative value, for example, if we are caused to make certain choices by the factors that cause us to be the kind of people who would so choose. But the case of the imprudent woman poses a challenge to this account. If the Causal Thesis is true, then she is caused to act as she does by factors operating "through her" in the relevant sense: she is an imprudent person. But if we accept the Forfeiture View as the right account of the moral significance of choice in her case, then we seem forced to say that she is responsible for what happens to her because she could have acted differently than she did—hence, if the Causal Thesis is accepted, differently than she was in fact caused to do. So if we accept the account of this case offered by the Forfeiture View we will need to come up with some way of understanding this "could have" and some way of explaining how it is compatible with the Causal Thesis and with the thesis of determinism.

I believe, however, that we should not accept this account. As was shown earlier by the comparisons with other examples (such as the cases of the man who did not get the word, and the one who did get it but then forgot), what is crucial in the case of the imprudent woman is not the fact of her choice but rather the circumstances in which she was placed. Moreover, an explanation that made this case turn on the fact that she "could have done otherwise" would lead to implausible results in other cases, since there are many conditions that undermine the legitimating force of choice despite the fact that a person choosing under such conditions still "could have done otherwise" in any sense that would apply in this case. It would, for example, be reasonable to reject a principle according to which a long-term contract is binding even when entered into by a fourteen-year-old without adult guidance. What is special about the case of fourteen-year-olds, however, is not that they *cannot* choose wisely (after all, many of them do), but rather that they are so likely not to do so. The same can be said, I believe, about the choices that adults make under various conditions, such as when they are drunk, or overcome with grief or fear. It is often difficult to decide whether these conditions are sufficient to render agreements invalid, but if "ability to do otherwise" were the test then it would be obvious that none of them are sufficient.

As I pointed out in the previous section, the instrumental value of choice is conditional and relative, and hence varies from one individual to another. The case of the imprudent woman illustrates this variability: an opportunity that would have great instrumental value for most people as a way of avoiding risk turns out to do her no good, and perhaps even to make her worse off. The objection asks how, in light of this fact, having given her this choice can count as improving the conditions under which she was placed and thereby helping to make it the case that she cannot complain of the result. The answer has two parts. The first lies in the distinction between the generic reasons on which the justifiability of a moral principle must rest and the reasons that a specific individual may have, given all the facts about his or her situation. The reason why it is important that this woman was informed of the danger, and thus given the choice of avoiding it, is not that this was necessarily advantageous to her but rather that it is something that people in general have reason to value and hence to demand that an acceptable principle insist on. But (and this is the second point) this is not the only thing they have reason to insist on. Because some people are likely to choose unwisely, it is not enough merely to warn people even if they could all protect themselves by taking appropriate precautions. This is why, in the example given, it was necessary to put fences around the excavations and to wet the hazardous material down and transport it carefully in order to minimize the risk to those who failed to stay indoors. If the imprudent woman has no grounds for complaint it is because adequate precautions of this kind were taken. If she does have such grounds, it is because any principle that no one could reasonably reject would require more precautions of this kind in order for the project to go forward. The Forfeiture View, by concentrating on the fact of choice and the possibility of choosing otherwise as the morally significant features of the case, focuses our attention in the wrong place.

I conclude that the Value of Choice account provides the best explanation of the significance that our choices and other forms of response have in determining what we owe to each other. This account is particularly helpful insofar as it calls attention to the variety of ways in which these responses can be significant and to the importance of conditions other than the fact of choice itself. As a further illustration of this account, and as the basis for contrasting it with the account of moral responsibility that will be the subject of the next section, consider how it would apply to the justification of criminal punishment.

I will begin with a schematic comparison of the institution of punishment and the policy of waste removal that we have just been discussing. In each case we have the following elements. First, there is an important social goal: protecting the water supply in the one case, protecting ourselves and our possessions in the other. Second, there is a strategy for promoting this goal that involves the creation of another risk: the risk of contamination in the one case, the risk of punishment in the other. Third, the effect of this strategy is that there is (literally or metaphorically) a certain affected "area" that one can no longer enter without danger. In the one case this is the area in which the excavation, transport, and disposal of the waste are being carried out; in the other case it is the metaphorical "area" consisting of the range of activities that have been declared illegal. Fourth, even if safeguards are introduced to reduce people's exposure to the risk created, it remains overwhelmingly likely that many of those who enter the affected areas, and perhaps some others, will be harmed. Some of the safeguards that are introduced (such as requirements of due process, and careful methods of excavation and transport) serve to protect those who stay out of the affected area. Other safeguards enhance the value of choice as a protection by making it less likely that people will choose to enter this area. In the example of hazardous waste these include signs and other publicity informing people of the risk, as well as fences, guards, and the choice of an obscure disposal site where no one has reason to go. Analogous features in the case of punishment are education (including moral education), the dissemination of information about the law, and the maintenance of social and economic conditions that reduce the incentive to commit crime by offering the possibility of a satisfactory life within the law. Restrictions on entrapment by law enforcement officers also belong in this category of safeguards, as do provisions which excuse from punishment those who, because of mental illness or defect, are unable to regulate their conduct in accordance with the law. Without safeguards of these kinds, the value of choice as a protection would be unacceptably low.

In each case, in order to defend the practice in question we need to argue that the importance of the social goal justifies creating the risk and making the "affected area" unsafe, and that given the safeguards that have been put in place enough has been done to protect people against suffering harm from the threat that has been created.

There are some significant differences between the two cases. First, insofar as the activities that make up the "affected area" in the case of punishment are ones that it is morally wrong to engage in, being deprived of the opportunity of "entering this area" without risk does not count as a morally significant loss. This eases the task of justification somewhat in that case. A second difference makes that task more difficult, however. It is not the aim of either policy that anyone should be harmed by the threat that is created. But in the case of punishment, when this harm does occur it is deliberately inflicted on particular people, as required by the institution itself. It is an essential part of the institution of punishment that those who violate the law should be punished, but it is no part of the waste-removal program that those who go to the excavation site should suffer contamination. Thus, since a policy of deliberately inflicting harm is more difficult to justify than a policy of creating a risk while trying (no doubt imperfectly) to protect people against it, the institution of punishment carries a heavier burden of justification than the program of waste removal.

When such an institution is justified, however, this justification entails a stronger form of "forfeiture" than we found in considering the example of hazardous waste removal. A person who knowingly and intentionally violates a justifiable law lays down his or her right not to suffer the prescribed punishment: that is to say, such a person has no legitimate complaint against having this penalty inflicted. This forfeiture is a consequence of the justification for the institution of punishment and for the particular law in question, however, not an element in that justification. More specifically, it is a consequence of the "heavier burden of justification" to which I just referred. Because the institution assigns punishment to those who fulfill certain conditions, justifying the institution involves justifying the infliction of these penalties. If the conditions for punishment include having made a certain kind of choice, then a justification for punishment justifies making that choice a necessary and, when other conditions are fulfilled, sufficient condition for punishment. No such assignment and no such forfeiture are involved in the justification of the program of hazardous waste removal. A person who recklessly chooses to enter the affected area does not lay down a right to further protection against contamination. She has, by assumption, already received all the prior protection she is entitled to, and she does not lay down her right to rescue or treatment unless this has been prescribed and the policy including this prescription is justified. Forfeiture is a creature of particular institutions and relatively specific principles such as those governing promising (provided, of course, that these are justifiable). It is not a moral feature of choice in general. As I argued above, what figures in the justification of such institutions and principles is not forfeiture but, rather, the less sharp-edged notion of the value of choice.

A justification for an institution of punishment along the lines just sketched would not be a retributivist account, since it makes no appeal to the idea that it is morally desirable for wrongdoers to suffer punishment. But the moral status of the acts for which someone can be punished would remain important in this justification, in two ways that can be brought out by considering the possibility of "strict liability" offenses. As I said above, if the actions for which punishment is prescribed are ones that it would be morally wrong to perform, then a person cannot complain of a significant loss of liberty when this "affected area" is made one that one cannot enter without fear of punishment. Systems of punishment that cover a wider range of actions could be justified, however. If, for example, a legal penalty is attached to selling contaminated milk (not merely to doing so knowingly, recklessly, or negligently), then one "enters the affected area" just by going into the milk business, and if such a law is justified then doing this involves laying down one's (legal) right not to be penalized in the event that the milk one sells turns out to be impure even though one has not been negligent in handling it. But this enlargement of the affected area to include morally unobjectionable activities (such as conscientious engagement in the milk business) makes such laws more difficult to justify.

There is also a second source of difficulty. The criminal law is not just an organized system of threats, or a system of taxes designed to encourage some activities and discourage others. It provides rules and standards that good citizens are supposed to respect—that is, to regard as norms which they accept as reason-giving. Punishment is thus in part an expression of an authoritative judgment that the criminal has not done this—an expression of "legal blame."[6] Insofar as this is so, it will seem inappropriate to punish, and hence to condemn, someone whose conduct is admitted to be blameless, such as a person who through no fault of his own has sold milk that turns out to be impure. This will seem particularly inappropriate when the punishment takes one of the forms (such as imprisonment) that has the clearest condemnatory force.

This inappropriateness remains even if the person punished had ample opportunity to avoid the sanction. After all, no one has to go into the milk business, and, we may suppose, everyone who does so knows what the penalties are for selling adulterated milk. Punishment thus has two related aspects: the penalties that are inflicted, such as fines and loss of liberty, and the condemnation that these normally express. (These are related since the unpleasantness of being publicly condemned is itself a penalty.) The schematic justification described above dealt only with the first of these aspects. It argued that, like the injuries involved in moving the hazardous waste, these penalties can be justified when certain conditions are fulfilled, prominent among which is the requirement that those who are punished should have had the opportunity to avoid punishment by choosing appropriately. As we have just seen, however, the condemnatory aspect of punishment is subject to a further requirement: the condemnation must be appropriate. What triggers this requirement is not the unpleasantness of the condemnation, but the content of the judgment expressed. Insofar as punishment involves an assertion that the agent governed him- or herself in a way that was faulty, it is appropriate only when this is true.

So an analysis of the kind presented in this section, based on the value of choice as a protection, provides only a partial account of the conditions under which punishment is justified—an account dealing only with the "penalty" aspect of punishment. Since the penalties involved in the criminal law are so severe, however, the justifiability of this aspect of punishment is by far the more important question. In the case of morality the reverse is true: moral blame is fundamentally a judgment of condemnation, not a penalty. Accordingly, as I will argue in the following section, the notion of responsibility that is a condition for moral blame is quite different from the one we have just been discussing.

4. Moral Appraisal

I turn now to the other sense of responsibility distinguished at the beginning of this chapter: responsibility as a precondition for moral appraisal, rather than as one of the ideas figuring in the principles on which this appraisal is based. The task of this section will be to spell out more fully the conception of moral appraisal that follows from the theory developed in earlier chapters. I will argue that this conception offers plausible accounts both of the range of things that can be objects of moral assessment and of the force and content of our notions of moral blame and guilt. This account will provide the basis for considering, in the following section, the conditions under which moral appraisal must be suspended—that is to say, the conditions that mark the limits of moral responsibility in the sense I am now considering. In the concluding section of the chapter I will examine some of the similarities and differences between the two notions of responsibility I have distinguished and the kinds of freedom that they require.

I have just been using the terms 'moral appraisal', 'moral criticism', 'blame,' and so on without qualifiers, and for the sake of simplicity I will continue this usage in much of what follows. In most of this section, however, I will be concerned with appraisal, criticism, and blame based on the standards of that part of morality that is the main subject of this book: the morality of right and wrong, or "what we owe to each other." Like the term 'morality' itself, however, these expressions are commonly used in a broader sense, and I will return to this question of breadth later in this section, in discussing guilt.

The part of morality with which I am mainly concerned is sometimes seen as a system of restraints which we accept in order to gain protection against the harmful conduct of others. Moral criticism (in this context, chiefly blame) is then seen as a sanction that is supposed to move people to comply with these constraints. On my view, by contrast, this part of morality is not, fundamentally, a mechanism of control and protection but, rather, what I call a system of co-deliberation, and moral reasoning is an attempt to work out principles that each of us could be asked to employ as a basis for deliberation and accept as a basis of criticism. Seeking such principles is part of what is involved in recognizing each other's value as rational creatures. Our needs for protection and for the assistance of others play a role in determining which principles it is reasonable for us to reject and which to accept, and hence in determining which actions are right and wrong. But these needs are not what underlies our concern with right and wrong at the most basic level.

On this view, moral criticism claims that an agent has governed herself in a way that would not be allowed by any principles that no one could reasonably reject. When addressed to the person in question as a fellow participant in a system of co-deliberation, this charge calls for her to explain why this claim is mistaken or to acknowledge that it is valid and that her self-governance has been faulty. I speak here of "faulty self-governance" rather than "faulty conduct" in order to encompass two different kinds of fault in the reasons a person recognizes and is moved by. First, and most obviously, if any principles that no one could reasonably reject would count certain considerations (the likelihood of harm to others, for example) as conclusive reason against a certain course of action, then a person acts wrongly when he or she decides to follow that course anyway, in full awareness of these considerations. But, second, a person also acts wrongly when he or she simply fails to take notice of considerations that these principles hold to be relevant (for example, fails to take note of the fact that his or her course of action involves a risk of serious harm to others). In order to be a ground for moral criticism, this failure need not represent a conscious choice, but it must be due to faulty self-governance. A person is not open to moral criticism for failing to take notice of the injury his action will cause if this failure is due, for example, to the fact that he is sleepwalking. But moral criticism is appropriate if he fails to notice this reason simply out of indifference or because he is very excited at the prospect of some imminent success.

Whenever a person's self-governance is faulty in one of these ways, a judgment that this is so is correct, which is to say that he or she is subject to justified moral criticism.[7] But it is a separate question, on the view I am offering, whether one should actually *express* this criticism, or do so in a certain manner. When I say that an act is wrong if it would be disallowed by any principles for the general regulation of behavior that no one, suitably motivated, could reasonably reject, the "general regulation" that is in question is, in the first instance, each person's regulation of his or her own conduct through reflective self-governance, not regulation by the application of social sanctions.

A main aim of the present section is to explain how my view accounts for the special force that moral criticism seems to have. Since this force is particularly evident from the point of view of the person criticized, I will begin by considering how the account of moral criticism and blame that I have been presenting supports a parallel analysis of guilt. No doubt, guilt is understood in different ways by different people. But it is possible to identify several clearer underlying notions with reference to which these various ideas of guilt can be understood. Having done this, I can then use these notions to characterize the idea of guilt that my account supports.

The first and broadest of these notions is the acceptance of a negative evaluation of oneself. This evaluation could be of any kind: that one is ugly, clumsy, not a good mathematician or singer, or that one's chess game is poor, as well as moral assessments such as that one is not a good friend, that one is selfish, or that one has behaved badly on some particular occasion. If shame is just a matter of feeling inferior or deficient in some respect, then self-reproach is always grounds for shame. One can feel ashamed of one's height or clumsiness as well as of one's misbehavior or one's spelling errors, mistakes in mathematics, or unwary moves in chess. But not all of these things are possible grounds for guilt.

Guilt requires negative self-evaluation of a particular kind, which I will call self-reproach. This is the attitude of taking one's rational self-governance to have been faulty, and recognizing that some judgment-sensitive attitude must be modified or taken back. Self-reproach is thus applicable only to one's judgment-sensitive attitudes, that is to say, only to things one is "responsible for" in the broad sense described in Chapter 1. I can be embarrassed about my height or ashamed of my physical clumsiness, but these are not things I can reproach myself for. Since these features of myself are not dependent on my judgment, there is nothing for me to "take back" or modify. Occasions for self-reproach are thus a subset of possible occasions for shame. The things one can properly be said to feel guilty about fall within this subset, but not all grounds for self-reproach are grounds for guilt. It would be odd, for example, to say that one felt guilty for one's errors in mathematics or one's unwary moves in chess (unless what was meant was, for example, that one felt guilty for letting others down by being insufficiently attentive).

It seems, then, that feeling guilty is a special case of self-reproach, distinguished from other cases by the grounds of the criticism involved and by its particular significance. One may have good reason to feel bad about having made a fallacious argument or a faulty calculation, but self-reproach for having done something morally wrong rests on different grounds and consequently has different significance. The question then is what the distinctive grounds are that characterize guilt as a special form of self-reproach. At this point different ideas of guilt diverge.

One answer would be to say that what a sense of guilt involves is *moral* self-reproach. If 'moral' here is understood in the narrow sense in which I have been using it in most of this section, then this yields the view that it is appropriate to feel guilt only when one believes that one has violated principles specifying what one owes to other people. This would explain the familiar fact that one rational response to feelings of guilt is a desire to acknowledge one's wrong and seek forgiveness of the person injured by it.

But, as I have stressed, people commonly use the term 'morality' in a broader sense, and the same is true of 'guilt'. Some people speak, for example, of feeling guilty for their sexual practices, and others say they feel guilty for being lazy, or for overindulging in food and drink, even when they do not believe that these things involve transgressing any duty owed to others. As I have said repeatedly, I believe that morality in this broad sense is motivationally diverse. I doubt that there is a unified account of the notion of guilt across this realm; it seems more likely that these diverse forms of self-reproach have many different grounds, and hence different kinds of significance (that is to say, there are different ways in which it is appropriate to feel bad about them). My concern here is only with guilt in the narrow sense mentioned above—the sense that is tied to violations of what we owe to each other—and with associated notions of blameworthiness, resentment, and so on. I leave it open what account might be offered of these other forms of guilt.

To see the special force of the kind of self-reproach that guilt in the narrow sense involves, on my view, consider first the significance, for other people, of the moral criticism on which this reproach is based.[8] If an action is blameworthy, then the agent has either failed to take account of or knowingly acted contrary to a reason that should, according to any principles that no one could reasonably reject, have counted against his action. So, in addition to whatever loss this action may have caused, the agent's mode of self-governance has ignored or flouted requirements flowing from another person's standing as some-one to whom justification is owed. This is what makes the action wrong rather than merely harmful, and it is what makes it appropriate for the person who was wronged to feel resentment rather than merely anger and dismay. Similarly, it is this violation of the requirements of justifiability to others that makes it appropriate for a third party to react with indignation rather than merely dismay or pity for the victim.[9]

The special force of moral criticism from the agent's own point of view is just the other side of this same coin. The realization that one has acted contrary to reasons flowing from any value that one takes seriously entails a sense of loss and regret and leaves one open to criticism by others who share this value. People can, with good reason, care about being good at chess, about not making intellectual errors, and about being responsive in the right way to works of art and other things that they see as valuable. What is special about violations of the morality of right and wrong is that the reasons one has failed to respond to are grounded not just in some value that others also recognize but in *their own* value as rational creatures. These violations therefore have particular importance for one's relations with them.[10]

The significance of these moral faults is shown in part in the ways in which others have reason to respond to them: with expressions of criticism and hurt feelings, withdrawal of friendship, and so on. But the primary significance of moral criticism lies not in what others may do in the future as a result of believing it, but rather in what is, if the criticism is correct, already the case. If I have injured someone by failing to take their interests into account in the way one should, then my relation with them is already altered by that fact, whatever they do. They may retaliate in some way, or they may forgive me. But forgiveness is merely a willingness to forgo reacting to a wrong in ways one would be justified in doing, such as by being angry or severing friendly relations. It does not alter the wrong that has been done.

This general account of moral criticism leads to several conclusions about its proper scope. It implies, first, that moral criticism applies only to rational creatures, since only they are capable of the kind of reflective self-governance in question. Second, it applies to them only in regard to their judgment-sensitive attitudes: that is, those attitudes that, in a rational creature, should be "under the control of reason." These two limitations are not peculiar to moral responsibility, but reflect limits of responsibility in the more general sense in which we are responsible for all our judgment-sensitive attitudes: that is to say, we can in principle be called on to defend these attitudes with reasons and to modify them if an appropriate defense cannot be provided.[11] According to contractualism, moral criticism is a special case of this more general rational criticism. Moral criticism claims that an agent has governed him- or herself in a manner that cannot be justified in the way morality requires, and it supports demands for acknowledgment of this fact, and for apology, or for justification or explanation. It would make no sense to criticize someone in this way, or to demand such responses, for something that is not even in principle sensitive to his or her judgment. "Why are you so tall?" cannot be a moral criticism. As I have said, however, this does not mean that moral criticism applies only to actions or attitudes that arise directly from an agent's conscious judgments. A person can be criticized, and asked to provide justification or acknowledgment and apology, for things that seem to have been done inadvertently in a situation in which advertence is called for. Being in principle "under the control of reason," and arising from conscious judgment or choice, are two different things.

It may be unclear, however, whether moral criticism is applicable or not in the case of an attitude (even a recurrent one) that is contrary to the person's settled judgment. Thomas Nagel cites such cases when he writes: "A person may be greedy, envious, cowardly, cold, ungenerous, unkind, vain, or conceited, but *behave* perfectly by a monumental effort of will. To possess these vices is to be unable to help having certain feelings under certain circumstances, and to have strong spontaneous impulses to act badly. Even if one controls the impulses, one still has the vice."[12] I take it that the "spontaneous impulses to act badly" that Nagel has in mind are not blind urges but tendencies to see certain considerations as reasons for acting in certain ways. The urges that a greedy person has to struggle against, for example, involve a tendency to see the fact that one could get more by acting in a certain way as a good reason for so acting, in cases in which, as he himself can see, it is not a good reason. Nagel's examples thus have the same structure as the case, which I mentioned in Section 8 of Chapter 1 as an example of a common form of irrationality, of a person who keeps thinking of the approval of a certain group of people as something to be sought even though he in fact judges this not to be a reason, and always dismisses it when it occurs.

The question Nagel raises is whether moral criticism is appropriate in cases of the kind he describes. On the one hand, it seems not to be: the greedy person he describes judges correctly that it would be wrong to seek his own advantage in the ways in question, and he governs himself accordingly. On the other hand, the tendency to think that seeking his advantage is what he has most reason to do is also attributable to him, even though he overrules this tendency when it occurs, and affirms the opposite judgment. (The appropriateness of this attribution is what makes these examples, like the one I cited, instances of irrationality.) It may be easier to see the moral force of this side of the problem when it is considered from the agent's point of view. The greedy person must see these tendencies as *his:* as tendencies to take certain judgment-dependent attitudes that he has to overrule and correct. (I take it as presupposed in Nagel's examples that the agents he has in mind make a "monumental effort of will" because they regard these tendencies as morally faulty, not out of, say, a concern with their reputations.)

Thus, just as the cases of irrationality I described are properly seen as involving conflicts within a person's rational capacities rather than as cases in which these capacities are overmastered by some other force, called "desire," moral examples like Nagel's should not be seen as involving a struggle between the person (identified with his considered judgment) and a psychological force that is not attributable to him and for which he therefore should not be judged. The question is not whether the tendencies to judge with which these agents are struggling arise from their conscious judgment, or whether the agent could have prevented them from occurring, but whether these tendencies are attributable to the agent in the sense that makes it appropriate to ask him to defend or modify and retract them. I take it that the answer to this question is yes: modifying or retracting is just what these agents are struggling to do (even though the "modification" that results is not as effective as it might be). This being so, the relevant question of moral assessment in such a case concerns the kind of criticism that is appropriate, taking into account both the attributability of these attitudes to the agent and his attitude toward them.[13] The answer is a boringly mixed one: the agents have governed themselves well in dealing with these tendencies, but they would be better people if they did not have them.

It is sometimes said that feeling guilty for having done something necessarily involves the belief that one should be made to suffer in some way for having done it. Similar claims are made about related notions of blameworthiness, resentment, indignation, and so on. Let me call the moral idea underlying such claims—the idea that when a person has done something that is morally wrong it is morally better that he or she should suffer some loss in consequence—the Desert Thesis. Notions of guilt, blame, and resentment that embody this thesis in the way just suggested, and the idea of responsibility that is necessary for their attributability, are what might be called desert-entailing notions.[14] Since I regard the Desert Thesis as morally indefensible, my account of moral criticism, and the notions of guilt, blame, and responsibility that it involves, are not desert-entailing notions in this sense. It may be that many people understand these terms in a desert-entailing sense, but whether this is so or not I have no interest in defending such notions.

The Desert Thesis has played an important role in debates about free will and responsibility, since moral criticism of a desert-entailing kind has seemed to many people to be clearly incompatible with determinism and with the Causal Thesis. Belief in this incompatibility has led some philosophers—J. J. C. Smart is a leading example—to recommend the adoption of what they see as a revisionist notion of moral appraisal, which lacks this connection with desert, and the adoption of what they see as a revisionist notion of responsibility, which is sufficient for the applicability of this weaker form of moral criticism but not the stronger, desert-entailing kind.[15] If the "ordinary" notions of guilt, blame, and so on do indeed have this desert-entailing character, then the account of moral criticism that I am defending is also in this respect revisionist. The reasons for my revisionism (if my view is indeed revisionist) have nothing to do with concerns about free will. To my mind, no degree of freedom or self-determination could make the Desert Thesis morally acceptable. I am claiming, however, that moral criticism as I understand it is compatible with the Causal Thesis. Moreover, my account of moral criticism differs in important respects from Smart's, which strikes me as unacceptably deflationary. I need, therefore, to make clear what this difference is, both in order to explain the kind of special force that I am claiming for moral criticism and to make clear what kind of assessment it is that I am claiming to be compatible with the Causal Thesis.

The basis of Smart's proposal is the broad class of evaluations such as "You're handsome" or "You're ugly," which merely report how a person or thing stands in regard to some standard. He refers to positive evaluation of this kind as praise and negative evaluation as "dispraise," in order to distinguish it from blame in the ordinary sense of that term, which depends, he believes, on an unacceptable metaphysics of free will. (He does not say exactly why blame in this sense presupposes free will, but it may be because he takes it to be a desert-entailing notion in the sense defined above.) Smart says that "clear-headed" people will understand moral blame in such a way that it involves only "dispraise," of the sort involved in saying that a person is ugly or inept, but with the added "proviso" that the trait being evaluated is one that is capable of being modified by the agent's exposure to unwelcome evaluations of this kind.[16] This proviso expresses what Smart means by a trait's being one for which the agent is responsible, and he believes that this conception of responsibility should replace our ordinary one.

My account of moral criticism is quite different from Smart's. In my view, moral criticism differs in two ways from other forms of unwelcome evaluation, such as appraisals of a person's appearance or talent. First, moral criticism concerns the person's judgment-sensitive attitudes and calls on that person to reconsider those attitudes and either to explain why the criticism is unjustified or to modify or withdraw them. Since a person's judgment-sensitive attitudes are often modifiable through criticism, those traits that are appropriate objects of moral criticism on my view (those that an agent is responsible for in the relevant sense) will often be ones for which the agent is also responsible in Smart's sense. But this will not always be true: some judgment-sensitive attitudes may be unmodifiable. I believe (as I will explain in Section 5) that moral criticism can still be applicable in such cases. Second, moral criticism differs from other criticism of a person's judgment-sensitive attitudes, such as criticism that points out our errors in mathematical reasoning, spelling, or chess, because the failings to which it calls attention have a particular kind of significance for the agent's relations with other people.

An agent who cares about these relations will find this kind of criticism uncomfortable, but what distinguishes moral criticism from criticism of other kinds is not, in my view, that it is a sanction whose main purpose is to modify an agent's behavior. Moral criticism differs from a sanction in several respects. First, although awareness of one's moral faults is uncomfortable, this discomfort is intrinsic to an awareness of the faults involved, not something that is assigned to them in order to serve some purpose, such as retaliation or enforcement. Second, this discomfort is not something that need be inflicted: it does not depend on what others do. People may, of course, express moral criticism with the aim of making an agent feel bad, and with the hope of thereby influencing his or her future conduct, and this may be unpleasant for the person criticized. But this unpleasantness is, as I have said, a separate matter from the force of the moral judgment itself. There are cases in which it would be wrong, because of the pain it would cause, to express moral criticism, or to do so in a certain way. But this does not mean that that criticism does not apply or that the person criticized, if he saw that it did apply, would be wrong to be distressed by this fact.

My account of the force of moral criticism thus lacks the instrumental element that makes the reinterpretation that Smart proposes seem deflationary. But while my account is closer than Smart's to what I take to be our ordinary understanding of moral criticism, it does not interpret this as a desert-entailing notion. On my view, when moral criticism applies this makes various reactive attitudes such as guilt, resentment, and indignation appropriate. But these attitudes do not, as I understand them, entail the thought that it would be a good thing, or not a bad thing, if the person to whom they are directed should suffer in some way.[17] Other reactions may also be justified by the fact that a person has behaved wrongly, such as, on the person's own part, apology, and, on the part of others, avoiding the person or severing various relations with him or her. But again, the justification for these reactions does not depend on the Desert Thesis: they are not called for because it is good that the person should suffer and these are ways of bringing that about. Rather, the reactions themselves are made appropriate by the way the person has governed him- or herself. As I will argue in the following section, these claims of appropriateness do not presuppose that the agent was acting freely in a sense that is incompatible with the Causal Thesis. It is enough that the attitudes in question be morally faulty and that they be correctly attributed to the agent.

5. Preconditions for Moral Appraisal

With this account of moral appraisal and blame as a background, I want now to consider the conditions under which these forms of appraisal are applicable. One aim, in particular, will be to determine whether the preconditions of moral responsibility include some form of freedom, and if so what form this is.

I will approach the question by considering the conditions under which a moral appraisal must be modified or withdrawn. Three categories of such conditions need to be distinguished. Conditions of the first sort show moral appraisal of an agent for an action to be inappropriate by showing that that action is not, in the proper sense, attributable to the agent. For example, it would be inappropriate to credit or blame me for a particularly offensive remark if it turned out that the remark was produced by someone else, who caused me to utter it by stimulating my brain with electrodes. The same would be true if the remark were produced by posthypnotic suggestion or uttered while sleepwalking. These conditions make moral appraisal inappropriate because they break the usual connection between the action and the judgment-sensitive attitudes of the agent, as a participant in moral relations. This break is shown in the fact that it would be pointless to ask that person for a justification of his action in such a case. Since the act is stipulated to be not under the control of his judgment-sensitive attitudes, it is not his act in the sense required in order for moral appraisal to make sense.

Under the most extreme interpretation of these cases, the electrical stimulation or hypnosis simply causes the person's limbs to move like those of a puppet or causes his mouth and larynx to produce certain words. The result thus is not even an action on the part of the agent, any more than if someone were to grab his arm and use it, like a club, to hit someone else in the face. In such cases there is obviously no point in asking him "Why did you do that?" or attributing to him the discernment or lack of discernment that would be revealed by thinking that he had good reason to do such a thing.

We can also imagine less extreme cases, in which the scientist or hypnotist produces an action or attitude by "implanting" in the agent the thought that it is warranted. The result might then be a genuine intentional action or an attitude with real content, but because of its origins this action or attitude cannot actually be attributed to the agent. These intentions are "just visiting," so to speak, and just as in the more extreme case it is pointless to expect the agent to be prepared to justify them. All he can do is to disown them.

Moral appraisal is not rendered inappropriate in such cases by the mere fact that a person's action or attitude has a causal explanation. Being a rational creature is a matter of having a coherent psychology of a certain kind: of there being the right kind of stable and coherent connections between what one says, does, and how things seem to one at one time, and what one says, does, and how things seem to one at later times. This coherence is not merely a matter of the judgments a creature makes, but also of what occurs to it and how things seem to it (what strikes it as relevant to a given question, for example). These processes presumably have some causal basis in our nervous systems, which is affected in turn by causes "outside us," through sight and hearing, for example. What distinguishes cases like hypnosis and brain stimulation is thus not that they involve causal influences but rather the fact that these causal influences are of a kind that sever the connection between the action or attitude and the agent's judgments and character. The same is true in the case of behavior induced by drugs or by sudden episodes of mental illness. Examples like these should not, therefore, be taken to support the idea that all moral appraisal is rendered inappropriate if the Causal Thesis is correct.

This category of excuses might be called "innocent agent" cases, since in these cases it is claimed that some agent, moral appraisal of whom is generally appropriate, cannot be judged on the basis of the action in question, since it does not reflect that person's judgment-sensitive attitudes. The force of these excuses depends heavily on how the agent in question is identified. Suppose, for example, that someone who has previously always been kind and considerate suddenly begins making cruel and wounding remarks to her friends after being hit on the head or given drugs for some medical condition. We would not, at least at first, take this behavior as grounds for modifying our opinion of her. The injury or the drugs constitute a break of the kind I have been discussing, which blocks the attribution of these actions to the person we have always known. But suppose that this behavior continues. If, after fifteen years, the person still behaves in this way and shows no sign of rejecting these attitudes or finding them "alien" to her, then our sense of the agent being appraised is likely to shift. Instead of disrupting the connection between the person and these forms of behavior, the accident or the drugs come to mark a change in what she is like. We may say, "She used to be so wonderful, but after her accident she became a nasty person."

The excusing conditions most often appealed to in everyday life belong to a second category, quite different from the ones just described. Rather than blocking altogether the attribution of an action or attitude to an agent, these conditions alter the character of the action that can be attributed. Ignorance and mistake of fact are typical conditions of this second type. I may think, for example, that your stomping on my foot reflects a lack of concern for my pain and for my right to be free from unwanted touching. But this appraisal of your action must be modified if I learn that you assumed that the toy spider on my boot was real and, having had experience in the tropics, you thought that you were saving my life by killing it before it had a chance to bite me. In the light of these further facts, I can still correctly attribute the action to you, but it may no longer indicate a blameworthy attitude on your part, or at least not the same attitude: your action may have been hasty, but it was not ill-intended.

In my view, coercion and duress belong to this same category of conditions: ones that do not block attribution of an action to an agent but change the character of what can be attributed. A bank teller who hands over the cash drawer when presented with a credible threat of violence is entirely responsible for this action—that is to say, it is properly attributed to him. But, although it is his action in the sense required for moral responsibility, what the teller does is not blameworthy, as it would be if he or she gave the money to a friend or negligently left it unattended. It is sometimes said of such a case that the teller should not be blamed because he or she acted "involuntarily," and this term might also be applied in the cases I discussed earlier, such as brain stimulation and hypnosis. But using the term 'involuntary' in this broad way is misleading, since it suggests that coercion, like hypnosis or brain stimulation, excuses an agent from blame by making the action "not her own." It is of course true that agents who are coerced are forced to do something that they would not otherwise have chosen to do. The same is true of the sailors in Aristotle's example, who throw their cargo overboard during a storm in order to save the ship.[18] But it remains the case that a coerced agent, like these sailors, chooses how to respond to the coercion and is responsible (even if not blameworthy) for this choice.[19] Clarity is served by distinguishing between cases in which a person is not responsible for an action (because it cannot be attributed to him or her) and cases in which the lack of eligible alternatives makes it all right, or at least less blameworthy, to do something that would normally be wrong.

The third category of cases in which moral blame is inappropriate is that in which a person lacks the general capacities presupposed by moral agency. If, as a result of mental illness or defect, a person is unable to understand and assess reasons or his judgments have no effect on his actions, then he cannot be a participant in a system of co-deliberation, and must be seen, rather, as simply a force to be dealt with, like an animal.

I believe that these three categories of conditions cover all of the cases in which we commonly say that a person is "not responsible" for some action. The idea that childhood is a state of "diminished responsibility," for example, can be understood as reflecting a combination of factors of these three kinds. First, very young children are incapable of assessing reasons and of governing their actions accordingly (an excusing condition of the third sort just considered). Second, children often cannot be expected to understand the consequences of their actions, either because they cannot foresee what the physical consequences will be or because they cannot appreciate the significance that their actions will have for the people affected. So when they do something that injures someone this may not reflect indifference to that person's pain (which could be a moral fault) but rather a non-culpable failure to foresee that pain will result. (This is an excusing condition of the second kind considered above.) Third, even when the attitude reflected in a child's action is a moral fault, moral criticism may be made inappropriate by the fact that childhood, seen as a part of a larger life, is a stage at which it is normal for moral capacities to be not yet developed. This is plausibly understood as an excusing condition of the first, or "innocent agent," type. If someone behaves in a greedy or self-centered manner at the age of three we should not conclude that he (the person whose childhood this is) is a greedy or self-centered person. The circumstances of childhood, like a blow to the head or the side effects of medication, block the attribution of these characteristics to the agent we are judging. Overcoming these effects is a process of growth, not of reform.

These explanations of how various conditions can undermine moral blame do not lead to the conclusion that blame is always inapplicable if determinism, or the Causal Thesis, is true. The mere truth of those theses would not imply that our thoughts and actions lack the continuity and regularity required of rational creatures. It would not mean that we lack the capacity to respond to and assess reasons, nor would it entail the existence of conditions that always disrupt the connection between this process of assessment and our subsequent actions. So, even if one of these theses is true, it can still be correct to say that a particular action shows a person to have governed herself in a way that is morally deficient.

This use of the word 'governed' might be held to be question-begging because it implies a dimension of freedom that determinism, or even the Causal Thesis, rules out. This is not so. A person governs herself in the sense required if she is sensitive to the force of reasons and to the distinctions and relations between them and if her response to these reasons generally determines her subsequent attitudes and actions. It might be objected that this notion of governance is too weak to bear the weight I have put on it. In this weak sense, the objection runs, a sophisticated computer that was programmed to weigh evidence and balance competing reasons might be said to "govern" its outputs (indeed, the objector might say, if the Causal Thesis is true we are such "computers"). Such a machine would be "responsible" in a causal sense for the processes it governs. We would say that errors in its program are "responsible for" defects in its output. But we would not regard it as "responsible" in the sense required for moral blame.

This objection draws its plausibility from two presuppositions. The first is that there would be no point in expressing moral indignation or blame to a computer (even a very sophisticated one of the kind imagined) or in engaging in moral argument with it. This would be like pleading with your alarm clock. But this inappropriateness derives not from the fact that a computer is a causal mechanism but rather from what are assumed to be the limited forms of interaction that we can have with it. If the Causal Thesis is true, and we are "like computers" in the very general sense that our mental lives depend on underlying causal processes, it will nonetheless remain true that we can communicate with each other in moral terms and that our behavior will be influenced by this kind of dialogue in just the way that it is now.

It might be replied that we could "communicate with" and influence a very sophisticated computer of the kind imagined above. That is to say, we could raise moral objections to its behavior, by using its keyboard or mouse, or by speaking to it. We could demand justification, explanation, or apology; and we could receive relevant responses. This would not, however, be real dialogue of the kind that moral relations involve, because computers, even very sophisticated ones, are not conscious (this is the second presupposition referred to above). Real communication must be with a party who receives—that is to say, is *aware* of—the message. (Hence the scare quotes around 'communicate with' at the beginning of this paragraph.)

Similarly, real governance, in the sense presupposed by moral interaction, requires not only the right kind of regular connection between action "outputs" and the reason-giving force of the considerations presented as "inputs" but something more, namely that these "outputs" depend at crucial junctures on the force that these considerations *seem to the agent* to have. As I emphasized in Chapter 1, being a rational creature is a matter not only of one's conscious judgments but also of what happens—mostly without our being conscious of it—to link those judgments in the right way with each other and with other states, such as perceptions and bodily movements. But it is crucial to a creature's being a rational creature that conscious judgment is one factor affecting its behavior. Computers, even very sophisticated ones, do not strike us as moral agents or rational creatures, partly because we believe that they are not conscious at all—that there is no such thing as how reasons, or any other things, seem to them. It does not matter, for present purposes, whether this belief about computers is correct or not. What does matter is that *we* are conscious and that the truth of the Causal Thesis would not alter that fact.

I will conclude this section by considering several closely related objections to the account I have been presenting. These objections are based, in various ways, on the idea that insofar as people's actions are due to causes outside them it is unfair to blame them for acting as they do, since they cannot avoid acting that way. The objections claim that this is just as true when the factors in question cause a person's deliberative processes to operate in the way that is typical of that person as it is when they disrupt these processes or interrupt the connection between our deliberative conclusions and our actions.

Many writers have identified this idea of fairness as a source of difficulty for compatibilist views.[20] Susan Wolf offers two kinds of examples in support of such an objection. In one case, a woman fails to give her friend a book that she very much wants because, as a result of her "personality and social development," she is either "too self-centered for the thought, 'My friend would like this book' to occur to her" or "so unfamiliar with examples of sincere, non-instrumental friendships that the thought 'I should buy this book, just to make my friend happy' cannot help appearing irrational to her." Another example Wolf cites is that of a person who, as a result of a terribly deprived childhood, is unable to see any reason not to exploit others and to take advantage of them whenever he can. In both of these cases, Wolf argues, the agents lack the ability to appreciate the reasons for treating others better, and they therefore cannot properly be blamed for what they do.[21]

The charge of unfairness can be understood in several ways. On one reading it is a matter of accuracy; on other readings it is a question of opportunity. Consider first the question of accuracy. It is unfair to condemn a person for a certain action if that condemnation is based on inaccurate or incomplete information, when a fuller or more accurate account would reveal that the person is not as bad as he is being portrayed. Wolf's examples can be understood in this way. The woman in the first example can be seen as someone who is trying just as hard as any of us to do the best thing, but who because of her character or lack of experience cannot see correctly what this is. Similarly, in the second case, information about the person's deprived childhood is taken as showing that he is also a victim, and that he was made into a bad person by factors beyond his control. An appraisal that looks only at his action, it might be said, does not take into account the full range of relevant information about what *he* is like.

Our moral assessment of a person can certainly be affected by additional information about his or her background and circumstances. If we imagine that the woman Wolf describes is sincerely trying to be a good friend but just cannot figure out how to do it, then we might judge her less harshly than we would if she "just didn't care." But this interpretation of the case is undermined by the suggestion that the woman cannot see a reason to buy a book for her friend because she is too self-centered. If that is the explanation, then the woman is not struggling unsuccessfully to figure out the best thing to do. Rather, she fails to think of what would please her friend because pleasing her friend does not occur to her as important. So moral criticism still seems to be warranted. The criticism in this case may be mild, since the fault she is supposed to have displayed is not all that serious. But consider instead a hardened criminal who commits terrible crimes. The fact that he fits the abstract description Wolf provides—he is someone who is unable to see the force of morally relevant reasons—does not seem, to me at least, to block moral criticism. If he commits these crimes because he does not place any value on other people's lives or interests, what clearer grounds could one have for saying that he is a bad person and behaves wrongly?

Perhaps the criminal is the way he is because of a deprived childhood. In this case we can say both that he is himself a victim and that he is not responsible for becoming the kind of person he is. One way to read this is as an appeal to excusing conditions of the first kind discussed above. The suggestion of victimhood calls our attention to the presumably innocent child that the criminal once was, and the circumstances beyond his control that corrupted him are, like the powers of the hypnotist, factors intervening between his original character and the actions and values of his later self.[22] But this interpretation is not compelling. First, it asks us to identify, as "the real agent" who is being judged, the innocent child who was corrupted by factors beyond his control. But, as I pointed out in discussing "innocent agent" cases such as that of the person who was hit on the head, once an adult has had certain characteristics for some time and shows no tendency to resist or reject them, it is appropriate to attribute those faults to him and to hold him responsible for actions reflecting them. In addition, as I observed in discussing the diminished responsibility of children, because childhood is a stage of limited and developing rational capacities, our moral assessments of agents generally give more weight to the stable attitudes they hold as adults than to what they were like as children. In both of these respects, then, the way in which excusing conditions of the "innocent agent" type work in other cases counts against the use of this model to excuse adult criminals who have had deprived childhoods. In such cases we are judging the criminal as he now is, and we are asking whether it is appropriate to take his actions as indicating faulty self-governance. In order to claim that this is appropriate we need not also conclude that he is responsible for becoming the kind of person he now is. Whether this is so—whether, for example, he has negligently allowed himself to fall into habits and associations that have undermined his character—is a separate question.

I turn now to another way of understanding the charge of unfairness: as the claim that it is unfair to blame a person for acting in a certain way if he or she has not had adequate opportunity to avoid this condemnation. As I argued at the end of Section 3, such a requirement plays an important role in explaining the limits of criminal punishment and the legitimacy of punishment within those limits. But, as I have also already argued in several contexts, moral criticism is not, like criminal punishment, a sanction—a form of unpleasant treatment introduced in order to enforce norms of behavior. In considering the conditions under which moral criticism is appropriate, what we are concerned with is the appropriateness of the judgment that a person has acted wrongly, not the appropriateness of engaging in any particular form of blaming behavior, such as admonishment, shunning, or the withdrawal of friendship. When this distinction is borne in mind, the idea that moral criticism is unfair unless the person judged has had an opportunity to avoid it is open to two objections. The first is that this requirement applies only when the criticism in question inflicts some cost on the person judged, and therefore applies more clearly to blaming behavior than to moral judgments themselves.[23] But, second, it does not generally seem unfair to react to a malefactor's actions in ways that adversely affect his interests. Imagine, for example, an incorrigible opportunist and liar who takes advantage of everyone he can, and suppose that these characteristics are due to his miserable childhood, in which everyone he encountered behaved in this way and he had little choice but to do anything he could to survive. It does not seem to follow that it would be unfair to avoid dealing with this person or entering into relations of friendship and trust with him.[24] If this is not unfair, why should there be any objection on grounds of fairness to the judgment that he has acted wrongly? Being subject to moral criticism may be unpleasant, but it is also unpleasant to have others avoid you and to be excluded from social and cooperative relations.

Insofar as it is understood as depending on the cost of being blamed, the unfairness objection appears to construe the judgment that an agent is blameworthy on the model of what I called above a judgment of substantive responsibility. In order for an action to entail the imposition on the agent of some burden, such as an obligation, two things must be true. First, the action must be attributable to the agent. Second, a principle according to which such an action generates that obligation must be one that could not reasonably be rejected. But, we may suppose, in order for such a principle to be one that could not reasonably be rejected it must hold that such an action generates this obligation only if it is an action that the agent had a fair opportunity not to perform. Similarly, it is suggested, blameworthiness requires not only that an action be attributable to the agent but also that attaching blame to the performance of such an action is justified. And, as in the previous case, this will be so only if the agent had fair opportunity to avoid blame by not performing the action.

It is true that in order for an agent to be blameworthy for a certain action that action must not only be attributable to the agent but must also be wrong. But the claim that an action is wrong should not be identified with the claim that imposing the "burden" of adverse moral judgment on the agent is justified. The "burden" of being blamed for an action plays no role in determining whether that action is wrong (in my account, in determining whether a principle permitting or forbidding that action could reasonably be rejected). This can be brought out by considering why various excusing conditions must be recognized. A principle according to which coerced promises are binding could reasonably be rejected because it would not give agents sufficient opportunity to avoid unwanted obligations. It would also be reasonable to reject a principle according to which it would be wrong to cross another person's land even when this was necessary in order to save one's life. Just as in the previous case, however, the reason for rejecting the principle appeals to the cost of abiding by it, not to the "cost" of being blamed for not doing so.

I conclude that if the claim of unfairness is to have force it must be because in cases of the kind it envisages there is something distinctively unfair about the moral judgment itself rather than about the cost, to the person judged, of that judgment's being expressed or acted upon. One response would therefore be to move back to the "accuracy" interpretation as the favored way of understanding this objection. An alternative is to see the objection as presenting a challenge to an interpretation of moral criticism, by claiming that any interpretation that can capture the special force that moral judgment seems to have will leave itself open to the charge that moral criticism is unfair unless the person to whom it applies has had an opportunity to avoid it. Applied to the account of moral criticism that I have offered, this challenge might be spelled out as follows.

I have said a number of times that moral criticism of a person's action remains appropriate as long as it is true that the process of self-governance that led to this action was both faulty and correctly attributable to the agent. This way of putting the matter may strike some as reducing moral judgments to what Smart called "dispraise"—which just tells people what people are like—thus depriving them of the special force that differentiates moral criticism from mere unwelcome evaluations such as "You're ugly." It may then seem that the only way of capturing this force is to take moral criticism to include some form of "sanction." If such a sanction brings with it a requirement that an agent who is subject to moral criticism must have had an opportunity to avoid it, then this leads us to a version of the challenge just described.

I argued at the end of the previous section that my account of moral criticism avoids this difficulty: it explains the special force of moral criticism without interpreting it as a sanction. It does this by relying on two ideas. The first is that moral criticism differs from unwelcome evaluations of a person's physical attributes because it questions the person's judgment-sensitive attitudes and calls for possible revision of them. The second is that moral criticism differs from other criticism of judgment-sensitive attitudes because of the particular significance that this form of justifiability has for an agent's relations with others.

The first of these ideas may, however, open the door to the challenge in a new form, one that is less encumbered by the difficulties about sanctions that I discussed above. On the view I propose, moral criticism presents certain objections to an agent's judgment-sensitive attitudes and calls on him or her to reexamine and perhaps reject or revise these attitudes in the light of the reasons presented. But a person who is unable to understand the force of moral reasons cannot respond in this way. It would seem to follow that moral criticism addressed to such a person is unfair, because it makes an unreasonable demand, one that the agent is unable to comply with.[25] So it appears that in characterizing the class of beings to whom moral criticism applies I should have included, in addition to the general abilities to make judgments about reasons and to govern one's actions in accord with them, the ability to understand moral reasons in particular.

This modification seems so natural that one may wonder why I did not make it in the first place. The reason derives from the second of the two ideas just mentioned: the special significance of an agent's moral failings for his or her relations with others. A plausible test for deciding whether a given condition should be taken to rule out moral criticism is to ask whether the behavior of a creature which has that condition would, for that reason, lack the distinctive significance that moral failings generally have for relations with others. The conditions that I have proposed meet this test. If a creature cannot make judgments about reasons at all, then its actions, while they may injure us, cannot reflect judgment-sensitive attitudes of the kind that challenge our moral standing and make resentment an appropriate reaction. If a creature cannot make judgments about whether anything matters, it cannot judge that harm to us does not matter, and its actions cannot reflect such judgments. By contrast, a rational creature who fails to see the force of moral reasons—who fails, for example, to see any reason for being concerned with moral requirements at all or with the justifiability of its actions to others—can nonetheless understand that a given action will injure others and can judge that this constitutes no reason against so acting. So the actions of such a creature would have implications for its relations with others that are at least very similar to (if not identical with) those of an agent who understood the relevant moral reasons but simply rejected them.

It might be urged that the objection involved an agent who did not just fail to understand moral reasons but who lacked the ability to understand them. The question is what difference this makes. When we see that a person is unable to avoid a certain action, or unable to see that that action will cause harm, this inability makes a difference because it intervenes between the agent's action and his or her assessment of the relevant reasons: because of this inability, that action need not reflect a judgment on the agent's part that the harm caused by the action did not count against performing it. But an inability to see the force of a certain reason, or of moral considerations in general, does not have this same effect.[26] A person who is unable to see why the fact that his action would injure me should count against it still holds that this *doesn't* count against it.

The objection still seems to draw force, however, from the idea that moral criticism calls upon an agent to revise his or her judgment-sensitive attitudes. Agents who are unable to see the force of moral reasons cannot be expected to revise their attitudes in response to such reasons. Therefore, it might be said, moral criticism that demands of them that they do this is unreasonable. One conclusion that might be drawn from this is that the two ideas that my account of moral criticism relies on support opposing answers to the question of whether moral criticism could properly apply to someone who was able to understand reasons in general but unable to appreciate the force of moral reasons in particular. The idea that moral criticism offers reasons on the basis of which a person is asked to reassess his or her judgment-sensitive attitudes suggests a negative answer. But the account I offered of the special significance of moral criticism (as opposed to other criticism of judgment-sensitive attitudes) suggests a positive one. One might conjecture that the strongly different intuitions that people have on this issue reflect the fact that some of them are focusing mainly on one of these aspects of moral criticism while others are thinking mainly about the other.[27]

Whatever plausibility it may have as an explanatory hypothesis, however, I believe that the first half of this claim is substantively mistaken. The idea that moral criticism offers reasons in the light of which an agent is asked to reassess his or her judgment-sensitive attitudes does not in fact lead to the conclusion that being unable to appreciate the force of a moral reason makes an agent immune from moral criticism for failing to give that reason appropriate weight in deciding what to do. The tendency to think that this conclusion does follow arises from an ambiguity in the idea of what a person can be "asked" to do. If a person holds a certain judgment-sensitive attitude, then, because this attitude is in principle sensitive to and dependent upon his judgment, it is appropriate in a general sense to ask him to defend it or to disown it. By contrast, he could not properly be asked to defend (that is to say, give his reasons for) his height or eye color. If he is unable to see the force of some reason that counts against this attitude, this does not alter the fact that the attitude and the judgment that it is warranted are properly attributable to him. Any errors involved in these attitudes are also attributable to him, and he is therefore properly criticized for holding them. (This is certainly the view we take with respect to judgment-sensitive attitudes of other kinds, such as beliefs about mathematics or strategic judgments in chess.)

As I have said several times, however, it is a separate question in all of these cases whether it is appropriate to express this criticism in any given way. In particular, it is a separate question whether it is appropriate literally to demand of him that he acknowledge the force of reasons against the attitude he holds. If it becomes clear that he is unable to see the force of these reasons then it may be unreasonable to press this demand.[28] But from the fact that such acts of criticism would be unreasonable it would not follow that the criticism they express is unreasonable or unjustified. Nor, as I have argued, does it follow that it is inappropriate or unfair to treat the person differently because of the attitude he holds (unfair, say, to avoid him because he sees no reason not to harm us when this suits him). A person's inability to see the force of reasons for modifying a certain attitude does not always make it inappropriate for us to criticize him for holding that attitude. It may do so in some cases (as in one interpretation of Wolf's example of the woman who does not buy the book for her friend), if it leads us to modify our assessment of what the person is like. But whether it does this or not depends on factors beyond the inability itself.

6. Conclusion

In this chapter I have distinguished two different notions of responsibility: responsibility as attributability and substantive responsibility. When we ask whether a person is responsible in the first of these senses for a given action, what we are asking is whether that person is properly subject to praise or blame for having acted in that way. To say that someone is responsible in the second sense for a certain outcome is, in the cases I have been concentrating on, to say that that person cannot complain of the burdens or obligations that result. These two notions have different moral roots. To understand the conditions of responsibility in the first sense we need to consider the nature of moral appraisal, praise and blame. Judgments of responsibility in the second sense, by contrast, are substantive conclusions about what we owe to each other. I have argued that a central role in supporting such conclusions is played by the Value of Choice: that is to say, the reasons that we have for wanting what happens to us to depend on the way in which we respond when presented with the relevant alternatives.

These two notions of responsibility are linked by the fact that both concern the moral significance of our judgment-sensitive attitudes and other responses. But they are distinguished by the fact that two different kinds of significance are involved. Conditions of responsibility in the first sense depend on the importance, for moral appraisal of an agent, of determining whether a given action did or did not reflect that agent's judgment-sensitive attitudes. Standards of responsibility in the second sense arise in large part from the importance, for agents themselves, of having their actions and what happens to them depend on and reflect their choices and other responses.

The difference between these two notions of responsibility is brought out in the different ways in which they depend on the freedom of the agent. Since an agent is responsible for an action in the first of these senses just in case that action is correctly attributable to her, responsibility of this kind is undermined only by those forms of unfreedom that undermine this attributability. As we saw above, however, in considering cases of coercion and Aristotle's example of the sailors who throw cargo overboard to save their ship, the absence of eligible alternatives can affect our judgments of responsibility in the second sense—our assessment of an agent's action, and of whether he should be made to bear its costs—without undermining responsibility in the first sense.

A similar phenomenon is illustrated by Harry Frankfurt's example of the "willing addict." Frankfurt considers two agents who, it is supposed, are both addicted to a drug to a degree that makes it impossible for them to resist the temptation to take it. One of them, the "unwilling addict," objects to having this addiction (in Frankfurt's phrase, he does not want the desire to take the drug to be effective in determining his action); whereas the other, the "willing addict," prefers the life of addiction, wants to act on the desire to take the drug, and would do so whether or not he was able to resist. Frankfurt says that when the willing addict takes the drug he acts freely in the sense relevant to moral responsibility, despite his inability to act otherwise. The unwilling addict, on the other hand, is not free in this sense. The account I have offered supports this conclusion, provided that by "moral responsibility" we mean the attributability of the action to an agent. Since the action of the willing addict reflects his assessment of the relevant reasons, he acts freely in the sense required by this notion of responsibility. The unwilling addict, on the other hand, does not act freely in this sense.

Both addicts are unfree, however, in the sense of freedom relevant to an assessment of the conditions in which they make their choices. It would be better for both of them to be making their choices under conditions in which they would not take the drug if they wished not to do so. As Frankfurt describes them, then, they are less free than they have reason to want to be. The sailors in Aristotle's example, and agents who are coerced, are also unfree in this sense, although the obstacles they face are of a different sort.[29] I suggested above that while the agents in these cases are responsible for their actions in the first of the two senses I have distinguished, they may not be responsible in the second sense. It is appropriate to attribute those actions to them and to praise or blame them for so acting, but it may not be proper to make them bear the consequences of these acts by, for example, requiring them to fulfill coerced agreements or making them pay for the cargo they have jettisoned.

Reaching this conclusion is made easier in these cases by the fact that, because of the lack of eligible alternatives, the actions that the agents are responsible for are blameless. It is a further question, then, whether there are cases in which agents are responsible for their actions (in the first of my two senses) and are open to moral criticism for performing them, but should not be held responsible, in the second sense, by being left to bear the burdens that result. Frankfurt's willing addict might be a case of this sort. Suppose that he grew up in an environment in which drugs were readily available. When he began to take drugs, at the age of twelve, he was aware of their dangers, in the limited sense in which anyone of that age considers future risks, but there was strong social pressure on any young male to use them. Over time, partly out of defensiveness, he developed the attitude that, contrary to what "mainstream" society claimed, a life on drugs was in fact to be preferred, and he made no serious effort to overcome his addiction, which led him consistently to violate his duties to his children and to others. Given this story, the addict is in my view open to moral criticism for taking drugs, and for becoming addicted in the first place. Nonetheless, given the pressure on a young person in his situation to take drugs and the difficulty of overcoming an addiction once it is established, it would be wrong to say that because he became and remained addicted "voluntarily" the state has no duty to provide him with drug treatment, or to ameliorate the conditions that lead to such people's becoming addicted in the first place. Similarly, we can imagine a person who, as a result of generally horrible treatment as a child and the lack of proper early training, is both undisciplined and unreliable. If this person lies to his employers, fails to do what he has agreed to do, and never exerts himself to get a job done, he is properly criticized for these actions and attitudes. But if they render him unemployable it would not be permissible to deny him welfare support on the ground that his unemployability is due to actions for which he is responsible. He is responsible (that is to say, open to criticism) for these actions, but he cannot simply be left to bear the consequences, since he has not had adequate opportunity to avoid being subject to them.

Failure to distinguish between these two notions of responsibility can have distorting effects of at least two sorts. As I argued above, understanding the conditions of blameworthiness on the model of substantive responsibility supports the idea that moral blame is a sanction, which can be applied to a person only if he or she has had a fair opportunity to avoid it. Failure to distinguish the conditions of substantive responsibility from those of blameworthiness, on the other hand, leads to the view that if people are responsible (that is to say, properly blamed) for their actions then they can properly be left to suffer the consequences of these actions, since these are "their fault." This view is frequently heard in political argument. It is said, for example, that there are two approaches to issues such as drug use, crime, and teenage pregnancy. One approach holds that these are the result of immoral actions for which individuals are responsible and properly criticized. The remedy is for them to stop behaving in these ways. The alternative approach, it is said, views these as problems that have social causes, and the remedy it recommends is to change the social conditions that produce people who will behave in these ways. Proponents of the first approach accuse proponents of the second of denying that individuals are responsible for their conduct. But this debate rests on the mistaken assumption that taking individuals to be responsible for their conduct in the sense of being open to moral criticism for it requires one also to say that they are responsible for its results in the substantive sense, that is to say, that they are not entitled to any assistance in dealing with these problems.[30]

For both of these reasons, then, it is important to distinguish between these two notions of responsibility. The account I have offered, appealing to an analysis of moral blame on the one hand and the idea of the value of choice on the other, preserves this distinction. I believe that this combined account provides satisfying explanations of our various notions of blame and responsibility. I do not, however, expect that everyone will be convinced by this. One likely source of disagreement is the fact that, as I have said above, on my account it does not follow, from the fact that a person is morally blameworthy, that it would be a good thing if that person were to suffer some loss as a result. It does follow from my account that if a person is morally blameworthy then others may have reason to treat him differently—by, for example, shunning him or suspending friendly relations. If they do this, the person is likely to be less happy as a result, but it is no consequence of my view that this unhappiness is a good thing. Nor can this conclusion be supported by the arguments I gave appealing to what I called the value of choice. Those arguments hold that if a person has had an opportunity to avoid a loss by choosing appropriately, then this diminishes the complaint that he or she could make against a principle permitting others to act in ways that lead to that loss's occurring. But it does not follow that it is a good thing for that loss to occur, or even that it is less bad for it to occur to that person than to someone who had no choice in the matter. Insofar as my view implies anything about the goodness or badness of such a loss, it is that it is a bad thing for harms to occur no matter who suffers them.

So if our ordinary notion of moral blame includes the idea that it is a good thing for those who are blameworthy to suffer, or that their suffering matters less than others', then what I am offering is in this respect a revisionist account. I am quite content with this result. The account I have offered explains the special force of moral blame, and explains how blame and indignation can be justified, without construing these reactions as sanctions designed to enforce moral requirements. It also explains how the choices people have made, and the opportunities they have had to choose, shape what they owe to others and what others owe to them. On this account, when we criticize someone who has behaved badly, or when we follow a policy that leads to some people's being injured because they have ignored the warnings they were given, we may be correct in feeling that what we do is justified. But we must also recognize that what separates us from such people is not just, as we would like to think, that we behave better and choose more wisely, but also our luck in being the kind of people who respond in these ways. In this respect our attitude toward those who suffer or are blamed should not be "You asked for this" but rather "There but for the grace of God go I."

7

Promises

1. Introduction

The aim of this chapter is to show how the obligation to keep a promise and other related obligations can be accounted for within the contractualist theory that has been set out in preceding chapters. The account I will offer describes such obligations as one special case of a wider category of duties and obligations regarding the expectations that we lead others to form about what we intend to do. These duties and obligations in turn are a special case of more general duties not to lie or to mislead people in other ways, and I will discuss these more general duties in Section 7. Even this wider category captures only some of the reasons, plausibly called "moral" in a broad sense of the term, that people may have to tell the truth and keep their word. In the final section of the chapter I will contrast my account of promises with oaths and conceptions of honor that fall in this larger class. This will set the stage for the discussion of relativism in the following chapter.

Many have argued that the wrong involved in breaking a promise is a wrong that depends essentially on the existence of a social practice of agreement-making. Hume maintained that fidelity to promises is "an artificial virtue," dependent on the existence of a convention of keeping agreements, and other accounts of this kind have been advanced in our own day by Rawls and others.[1]

On such a view, the analysis of the obligation arising from a promise is a two-stage affair. First, there is the social practice, which consists in the fact that the members of a given group generally behave in a certain way, have certain expectations and intentions, and accept certain principles as norms. Second, there is a moral judgment to the effect that, given these social facts, it is morally wrong for members of that group to violate these norms. In Hume's view this second stage takes the form of a reaction of impartial disapproval toward acts of promise-breaking, a reaction that reflects our recognition that the institution of promising is in everyone's interest. Rawls, on the other hand, invokes what he calls the principle of fairness: those who have voluntarily helped themselves to the benefits of a just social practice are obligated in turn to do their part as the rules of that practice specify. This is a general moral principle, meant to capture the wrong involved in many forms of free-riding. It applies to promising insofar as promising is seen as a just social practice that provides us with a certain good—the good of being able to make stable agreements. One of its central rules provides that a person who says "I promise to . . ." under appropriate conditions is to do the thing described. People who make promises help themselves to the benefit that the practice provides. Therefore, according to the principle of fairness, they are obligated to comply with the rules of the practice, hence to keep the promises they have made.

For many years I found this analysis quite convincing, but it no longer seems to me to provide the best account of the matter.[2] I do not doubt that there is such a thing as a social practice of promising, which consists in the fact that people accept certain norms, which they generally follow and expect others to follow. The question is what role this practice plays in generating obligations to keep one's promises. According to the standard institutional analyses, these obligations arise from a general duty to comply with just and useful social practices. I will argue, however, that the wrong of breaking a promise and the wrong of making a lying promise are instances of a more general family of moral wrongs which are concerned not with social practices but rather with what we owe to other people when we have led them to form expectations about our future conduct. Social practices of agreement-making, when they exist, may provide the means for creating such expectations, and hence for committing such wrongs. But I will argue that these practices play no essential role in explaining why these actions are wrongs. I will begin by describing some examples of one class of wrongs that I have in mind; I will then turn to the task of formulating principles that account for these wrongs and for the obligation to keep one's promises.

2. Manipulation and Regard for Expectations

Consider first a "state of nature" case. Suppose I am stranded in a strange land. In an attempt to get myself something to eat, I make a spear. I am not very good at using it, however, and when I hurl it at a deer it goes wide of the mark and sails across a narrow but fast-running river. As I stand there gazing forlornly at my spear, lodged on the opposite bank, a boomerang comes sailing across and lands near me. Soon a strange person appears on the opposite bank, picks up my spear, and looks around in a puzzled way, evidently searching for the boomerang. It now occurs to me that I might regain my spear without getting wet by getting this person to believe that if he throws my spear across the river I will return his boomerang. Suppose that I am successful in this: I get him to form this belief; he returns the spear; and I walk off into the woods with it, leaving the boomerang where it fell.

Now it seems to me that, intuitively, what I have done in this example is no less wrong than it would have been if I had promised the stranger that I would return his boomerang if he threw back my spear. Yet nothing like a social practice of agreement-making is presupposed in the example. All that appears to be assumed is that the stranger is capable of forming the belief that I have a certain conditional intention. But this appearance may be deceiving. What reason would the stranger have to believe that I have formed this conditional intention and will act on it? Here, it might be suggested, a practice of agreement-making is covertly presupposed. For in the absence of such a practice, what reason would the stranger think me to have to return his boomerang once I had recovered my spear? And how could he have a reason of the right kind? If the reason he attributes to me has nothing to do with the thought that I will be moved by a "sense of obligation," it may seem that what I have done could not be the same kind of wrong as that involved in breaking a promise. I believe that it is the same kind of wrong. To support this claim, I will consider some further examples—not, this time, "state of nature" cases, but examples that we could imagine occurring in society as we know it.

Suppose that you and I are farmers who own adjacent pieces of land and that I would like to get you to help me build up the banks of the stream that runs through my property in order to prevent it from overflowing each spring. I could get you to help me by leading you to believe that if you help me then I will help you build up the banks of *your* stream. I might do this in several ways. First, I might persuade you that if my stream is kept within its banks, then it will be worth my while to see to it that yours is too, because the runoff from the flooding of your field will then be the only obstacle to profitable planting of mine. If my stream were contained, then, simply as *homo economicus,* I would have sufficient reason to help you build up the banks of your stream. Alternatively, I might lead you to believe that I am a very sentimental person and that I would be so touched by your neighborly willingness to help me that I would be eager to respond in kind, both out of gratitude and out of a desire to keep alive that wonderful spirit of neighborly solidarity. A third alternative would be to persuade you that I am a devoted member of the Sacred Brotherhood of Reindeer, and then say, "I swear to you on my honor as a Reindeer that if you help me with my stream I will help you with yours." (It is assumed here that you are not yourself a Reindeer, and it is left open whether I am or not and whether the Sacred Brotherhood of Reindeer even exists.) Fourth, and finally, having led you to believe that I am a stern Kantian moralist, I might offer you a solemn promise that if you help me, I will help you in return.

Assume for the moment that in all these cases my intentions are purely cynical. My only concern is how to get you to help me, and I have no intention of helping you in return. Given this assumption, it seems to me that these four cases involve exactly the same wrong, and that this wrong is the same as the one involved in the "state of nature" case that I described at the outset. I will refer to this wrong as un-justified manipulation. The principle forbidding it might be stated as follows.

> *Principle M:* In the absence of special justification, it is not permissi-
> ble for one person, A, in order to get another person, B, to do some
> act, X (which A wants B to do and which B is morally free to do or
> not do but would otherwise not do), to lead B to expect that if he
> or she does X then A will do Y (which B wants but believes that A
> will otherwise not do), when in fact A has no intention of doing Y
> if B does X, and A can reasonably foresee that B will suffer
> significant loss if he or she does X and A does not reciprocate by
> doing Y.

I take this to be a valid moral principle. Considering the matter from the point of view of potential victims of manipulation, there is a strong generic reason to want to be able to direct one's efforts and resources toward aims one has chosen and not to have one's planning co-opted in the way Principle M forbids whenever this suits someone else's purposes. So it would be reasonable to reject a principle offering any less protection against manipulation. On the other side, the perfectly general generic reason for wanting to be able to manipulate others whenever it would be convenient to do so is not strong enough to make it unreasonable to insist on the protection that M provides. Of course, there are special situations in which one has particularly strong reasons for manipulating someone or in which the normally strong reasons for rejecting a principle that would permit manipulation are weakened. The existence of such situations is recognized by the limiting phrase "in the absence of special justification," and it would be reasonable to reject a principle that did not include such a phrase.

Situations covered by this phrase would include at least the following: (a) emergency cases, in which A, or someone else, is in danger, and A cannot communicate with B directly but can make it appear that it would be in B's interest to do something that will help the endangered person (or will bring B closer so that A can ask for help); (b) threat cases, such as when A (or someone else) has been kidnapped by B, and A needs to mislead B in order for the victim to have a chance to escape; (c) paternalistic cases, such as when B's capacities for rational choice are significantly diminished, and misleading him is the least intrusive way to prevent him from suffering serious loss or harm; (d) permission cases, such as when A and B have entered, by mutual consent, into a game or other activity which involves certain kinds of deception.

It would be misleading to say that these are cases in which special justifications "override" or "outweigh" the obligation specified by Principle M. Rather, they are cases in which M does not apply because the generic reasons which support it in normal cases are modified in important respects. In emergency cases, A's legitimate reasons for needing to mislead B are much stronger than normal. In threat cases, these reasons are also particularly strong, and, in addition, B's reasons for objecting are undermined by the fact that his plan involves treating A in ways that he could reasonably reject. In paternalistic cases and permission cases, B's reasons for objecting to manipulation are also weakened, but for different reasons.

This illustrates a point made in Section 3 of Chapter 5 about the open-endedness of principles. The content of Principle M reflects the balance of generic reasons in the most common range of cases. In order for M not to be reasonably rejectable, however, it must incorporate some recognition of the fact that nonstandard cases also arise; and our understanding of the case for M, and of the way this case depends on "standard" reasons, will guide us in deciding when and how it fails to apply when conditions are different.

Principle M clearly does not depend on the existence of a social practice of agreement-making. When such a practice exists, it provides one way of committing the wrong of unjustified manipulation because it provides one kind of underpinning for one person's expectation that another person will respond to his action in a certain way. But, as the examples above show, these expectations can have other bases, and manipulating others by creating such an expectation is open to the same moral objection whatever the basis of the expectation may be.

The obvious wrong of deception in all the examples I have described should not, however, obscure other respects in which these examples are morally different from one another. I have in mind here, in particular, differences in the degree and nature of the obligation to fulfill the expectation one has created, and differences in the degree to which the person who forms the expectation can be said to have a "right to rely" on it. So let me change the examples I have given by assuming that when the first farmer sets out to make the second farmer expect reciprocal help he has every intention of fulfilling this expectation. Why would it be wrong for him to change his mind and fail to perform once the second farmer has done his part? To answer this question I need to appeal to a richer set of underlying moral principles.

Principle M states one moral constraint regarding the creation of expectations about one's behavior. There are other principles of this kind, one of which is what I will call the principle of Due Care.

> *Principle D:* One must exercise due care not to lead others to form reasonable but false expectations about what one will do when one has good reason to believe that they would suffer significant loss as a result of relying on these expectations.

This principle is more demanding than Principle M since it requires a degree of vigilance beyond mere avoidance of intentional manipulation. In contrast to M, which prohibits a specific class of actions, D does not state explicitly what actions it requires. Its validity consists just in the fact that one can reasonably refuse to grant others license to ignore the costs of the expectations they lead one to form, though there is no obvious way to specify the exact nature and extent of the "due care" it is reasonable to require. The following principle of Loss Prevention is slightly more specific, and extends beyond mere care in the creation of expectations.

> *Principle L:* If one has intentionally or negligently led someone to expect that one is going to follow a certain course of action, X, and

one has good reason to believe that that person will suffer significant loss as a result of this expectation if one does not follow X, then one must take reasonable steps to prevent that loss.

The idea of "reasonable steps" incorporates a notion of proportionality between the steps taken and the magnitude of the threatened loss, as well as sensitivity to the degree of negligence involved in creating the expectation. These steps could take a variety of forms. One might avert loss by warning the person that one was not going to do X, or by doing X after all, or by providing compensation.[3] I take Principle L to be valid on the same grounds as M and D: it is not unreasonable to refuse to grant others the freedom to ignore the losses caused by the expectations they intentionally or negligently lead others to form.

Like D, this principle does not single out any particular action as the one that is required. It does not require one always to prevent others from suffering loss in such cases, and even when it does require this, the choice of means is left open: the principle is neutral between warning, fulfillment, and compensation.

But the obligation to fulfill a promise is not neutral in this way. Suppose, for example, that I promise to drive you to work if you will mow my lawn, and that you accept this arrangement. Then, a day or so later (but before the time has come for either of us to begin fulfilling the bargain) I think better of the deal and want to back out. On most people's understanding of promising, I am not free to do this. I am obligated to drive you to work unless you "release" me, even if I warn you before you have undertaken any action based on our arrangement. If I am going to break my promise then it is better to warn you than not to do so, but even if I do, this is a case of breaking a promise, not fulfilling one.

Much the same can be said of compensation. If one fails to fulfill a promise, one should compensate the promisee if one can, but the obligation one undertakes when one makes a promise is an obligation to do the thing promised, not simply to do it or to compensate the promisee accordingly. The difference between fulfillment and compensation is made particularly salient by the fact that in personal life, as opposed to the commercial transactions with which the law of contracts is centrally concerned, our main interest is likely to be in the actual performance of actions that have no obvious monetary or other equivalents, and by the fact that in the domain of informal personal morality (in contrast to the domain of law) there is no designated third party, presumed to be impartial, who is assigned the authority to make judgments of equivalence. The central concern of the morality of promises is therefore with the obligation to perform; the idea of compensation is of at most secondary interest.

So in order to explain the obligations arising from promises it will be necessary to move beyond Principle L to a principle stating a duty specifically to fulfill the expectations one has created under certain conditions. How might such a principle be formulated and defended?

3. Fidelity and the Value of Assurance

In order to assess this difficulty I need to look more carefully at the various ways in which a principle requiring only warning would be inferior to one requiring (at least some) intentionally created expectations to be fulfilled. The shortcomings of Principle L can be seen in the limitations it places on the kind of assurance one can be given—that is, on the content of the expectations it can support. In our car and lawn case, for example, the expectation you reasonably want to be able to form is the expectation that I will drive you to work *unless you consent to my not doing so*. All that Principle L will support, however, is the weaker assurance that I will drive you to work unless I warn you that I will not do so (before you have taken any further action on the basis of this expectation as a result of which you would suffer a loss if it were not fulfilled). If L is the only moral basis for our arrangement, then I cannot undertake a stronger obligation by changing the content of what I say to you (for example, by adding "and I will do it unless you release me") because L can always be fulfilled merely by a timely warning. If L were the only principle governing the fulfillment of the expectations we create, then we would be unable to give or to receive assurance of a kind that it is reasonable to want.

Consider the following example, which I will call the case of the Guilty Secret. Suppose that you are visiting for a term at a university where you know almost no one, and at a party shortly after your arrival you are surprised to encounter Harold, whom you have not seen for years. Long ago, when you were young together, Harold did something that, at the time, he regarded as perfectly all right but that he now recalls with shame and embarrassment. It was not really *that* bad (you would not be violating any duty to others by failing to tell them about it), but Harold has come to be extremely sensitive about the incident. So, when the two of you are having a brief conversation apart from the rest of the party, he brings the matter up. "Remember that awful night in Chicago?" he asks. "I'll never forget it. The thought of how I behaved that night has haunted me ever since. It would be terribly embarrassing for me if anyone here were to learn of it. I know it seems as if I'm excessively concerned with this, but will you promise not to mention it to anyone while you are here?" Suppose that you do promise, and Harold, looking much relieved, moves off in the direction of the bar. I assume that as a result of this encounter you now have two moral reasons not to tell the amusing story of that night in Chicago: you would be gratuitously injuring Harold, and you would be violating the obligation to him that you have just incurred. The question is how to account for this obligation on the basis of a theory of the kind I am trying to develop.

It seems that Harold cannot rely on the expectation you have created by taking or forgoing any action, because there is nothing he could do to shield himself from the embarrassment that would result from your telling the story. He can't leave town, and I am assuming that murder and bribery are ruled out. He's not that kind of person. So there are no options that he is passing up as the days of your visit go by. But even if there can be no reliance of either of these kinds, Harold has reason to care about whether you act as you have told him you will.

This illustrates what I will call the value of assurance. It may seem that if you were to tell the Chicago story on the last night of your visit (having promised on the first night that you would not), your overall course of action would leave Harold better off than if you had told the story without having promised not to. After all, the promise gave him fifteen weeks of peace of mind. But this is to assume that the value of assurance is purely experiential, that it consists merely in the values of freedom from worry, increased ability to sleep at night, and so on. I would maintain, however, that this assumption is false. What people in Harold's position, and in many other positions, reasonably want is not mere freedom from worry; they also want certain things to happen (or, as in Harold's case, not to happen). They want to be given assurances, and they care about whether these assurances are genuine. One reason for caring is that they may rely on these assurances in deciding what to do. This is not, however, the only reason, as Harold's case demonstrates.

Given the reasons that potential promisees have for wanting assurance, potential promisers have reason to want to be able to provide it.[4] From the point of view of both potential promisees and potential promisers, then, it is reasonable to want a principle of fidelity that requires performance rather than compensation and that, once an expectation has been created, does not always recognize a warning that it will not be fulfilled as adequate protection against loss, even if the warning is given before any further decision has been made on the basis of the expectation. Such a principle can be stated as follows.

> *Principle F:* If (1) A voluntarily and intentionally leads B to expect that A will do X (unless B consents to A's not doing so); (2) A knows that B wants to be assured of this; (3) A acts with the aim of providing this assurance, and has good reason to believe that he or she has done so; (4) B knows that A has the beliefs and intentions just described; (5) A intends for B to know this, and knows that B does know it; and (6) B knows that A has this knowledge and intent; then, in the absence of special justification, A must do X unless B consents to X's not being done.

The reasons that potential promisees and promisers have to want such a principle of fidelity are in my view sufficient to establish it as a duty unless it would be reasonable for potential promisers to reject such a principle. Would the duty described impose an unreasonable burden on those who create expectations in others? They could of course avoid bearing any burden at all simply by refraining from voluntarily and intentionally creating any expectations about their future conduct. But requirement of voluntariness would not, by itself, be enough to rule out reasonable objections. A principle according to which the only way to avoid obligations as binding as those specified by Principle F is to avoid voluntarily creating any expectations about one's future conduct would be too limiting. It would mean, for example, that we could never tell people what we intend to do without being bound to seek their permission before changing course.

Principle F does not have this effect, however, since it applies only when A reasonably believes that B wants assurance, when A has acted with the aim of giving this assurance and has reason to believe that he or she has given it, and when this and other features of the situation are mutual knowledge.[5] No one could reasonably object to a principle that, when these conditions are fulfilled, imposes a duty to provide a warning at the time of creating the expectation if one does not intend to be bound—a duty to say, "This is my present intention, but of course I may change my mind," or to make this clear in some other way if it is not already clear in the context. Since the burden of such a duty to warn is so slight, and the advantages of being able to enter into binding obligations are significant, one can hardly complain if failure to give such a warning under these conditions leaves one open to the more stringent duty to perform or seek permission to substitute. But this is just the duty stated by Principle F, since the conditions of that principle entail that no such warning has been given.[6] Indeed, quite the opposite has occurred, since A has refrained from providing such a warning in a situation in which he or she knows that the difference between an expectation qualified by that warning and one without that qualification is important to B.

When the conditions of Principle F are fulfilled, it would be wrong, in the absence of special justification, for the party in A's position not to perform.[7] In addition, the party in B's position has a "right to rely" on this performance: that is to say, the second party has grounds for insisting that the first party fulfill the expectation he or she has created. This right differentiates the case of promising (though not only that case) from some of the other examples of expectation-creation that I have been discussing.

For example, in the first version of the story about the farmers, I spoke of one farmer persuading the other that if the first farmer's stream were contained then it would be in his own economic interest to help contain his neighbor's stream as well. We could imagine this persuasion taking place in a face-to-face encounter, although it is not necessary to suppose that the encounter culminates in anything one would call an agreement. Alternatively—and this is the possibility I want to focus on—we might suppose that when the first farmer sets out to get the second farmer to believe that he will reciprocate, he does this without ever speaking to the second farmer directly. (The first farmer might drop broad hints at the feed store about the problem of the stream, and give the loquacious county agent a detailed version of the story the neighbor is supposed to hear.) In this case it would be wrong of the first farmer to fail to perform after the second had done so but all right for him to escape performance by warning the neighbor before any reliance had occurred. We would not say in this case that the second farmer had any right to rely on his neighbor's reciprocation. In performing first he "goes out on a limb" morally speaking. But in order for this not to be the case—in order for the second farmer to have the "right to rely"—it is not necessary for the first farmer to have used the words "I promise." It is enough that the conditions of intention and mutual knowledge specified in Principle F be fulfilled.

Principle F is not just the social institution of promising under another name. To begin with, the principle is not itself a social institution—its validity does not depend on its being generally recognized or adhered to. Second, the conditions of expectation and knowledge that it specifies can be fulfilled in many ways other than by making a promise. As the examples of the farmers indicate, this can be done without invoking a social institution (or by invoking a fictitious one). Promising is a special case, distinguished in part by the kind of reason that the promisee has for believing that the promiser will perform.

But what is this reason? When I promise to help you if you help me, what reason are you supposed to think I have for doing what I say I will do? This reason might stem from my desire to avoid the social sanctions that befall promise-breakers or from my personal commitment to the institution of promising. If so, promising would be like Reindeer's Honor. Recall that in that example no *moral* force was attributed to the Reindeer's code. All that was assumed was that the second farmer believed that this code was something that the first farmer cared about. Given this belief, the second farmer has reason to think that his neighbor will reciprocate if he helps build up the banks of the stream. Moral principles then explain why it would be wrong of the first farmer to induce the second to help him in this way if he has no intention of helping in return, and why it would be wrong of him not to help once his neighbor has been led to help him in the expectation of return in kind.

In this example, as in the cases of the sentimentalist and of the "economic man," the motive that the second farmer attributes to the first is independent of the moral obligation that is generated. As I have said, the same could be true in the case of promises. But there is another possibility which is more plausible. This is that when I say, "I promise to help you if you help me," the reason that I suggest to you that I will have for helping is my awareness of the fact that not to return your help would, under the circumstances, be wrong: not just forbidden by some social practice but morally wrong—disallowed by the kind of moral reasoning that lies behind Principle F and can be called upon to explain why it would be wrong for the sentimentalist, the Reindeer, and the economic man not to help the neighbor whom they had induced to help them.

Here is an analysis of how this might work. When I say, "I promise to be there at ten o'clock to help you," the effect is the same as if I had said, "I will be there at ten o'clock to help you. Trust me."[8] In either of these utterances I do several things. I claim to have a certain intention. I make this claim with the clear aim of getting you to believe that I have this intention, and I do this in circumstances in which it is clear that if you do believe it then the truth of this belief will matter to you (perhaps, but not necessarily, because you may rely upon it in deciding what to do). Finally, I indicate to you that I believe and take seriously the fact that, once I have declared this intention under the circumstances, and have reason to believe that you are convinced by it, it would be wrong of me not to show up (in the absence of some good justification for failing to appear). The function of the expression "I promise" need not be to invoke a social practice with its own special rules, but rather, like that of "Trust me," to indicate my awareness of the nature of the situation and my regard for the general moral fact that it would be wrong for me to behave in a certain way.[9] (I call this a "general" moral fact because it is not a fact peculiar to promising.)

Believing the promiser's second claim (of moral awareness and moral seriousness) gives the promisee one reason to believe that the promiser will fulfill his intention (so long as doing so is morally required). If social disapproval is attached to promise-breaking, a kind of disapproval that people generally want to avoid, then this supplies a further reason, as would the fact that the promiser is known, as a point of personal pride, to attach particular importance to keeping his or her word. I do not believe that any such additional reason is necessary to promising, but this may be doubted.

Doubts of this kind were raised by Hume, and again more recently by Elizabeth Anscombe, who has argued that accounts of promising like the one I have proposed are subject to a fatal circularity.[10] According to these accounts, saying "I promise to . . ." creates an obligation only if it convinces the recipient of the speaker's intention to do the thing in question. But it can do this only insofar as it gives the recipient reason to believe that the speaker has reason to do that thing. What is this reason? On the analysis proposed, it is the speaker's awareness of the fact that it would be wrong, having said, "I promise," to fail to follow through. But it would be wrong to do this only if saying "I promise" created an obligation, and it creates an obligation only if it gives the recipient reason to believe that the speaker has reason to do the thing promised. So there appears to be a circle here.

The difference noted earlier between promising and the other versions of the farmer example appears, here, to threaten the analysis of promising I have proposed. In those cases (of the sentimentalist, the economic man, and the Reindeer) the reason that the manipulator led the victim to believe the manipulator had for acting in a certain way was independent of the wrongness of failing to perform once the victim has been led to believe in this reason. As soon as some such independent reason for performance is assumed, the analysis I have offered of the resulting obligation goes through, and the awareness of this obligation provides an additional reason for the expected action (a kind of moral multiplier effect). But can an obligation be generated in this way without some independent source of motivation? If not, then the proposed analysis fails, and either we must suppose that the practice of promising generates obligations only because it provides a "nonmoral" motive (on the model of Reindeer's Honor) or else we must explain the moral force of promises in some entirely different way (for example, via Rawls's principle of fairness), thereby destroying the apparent symmetry between promising and the other cases I have discussed.

I believe, however, that the analysis that I have proposed can be preserved. In order to see why this "can't get started" problem is illusory, we need to distinguish between several related wrongs. The first is the wrong of which making a lying promise is a special case, the wrong described by Principle M. The second wrong is the one involved in attempting to commit the first wrong. (This would be a violation of Principle D, at least.) If you believe that I take seriously the fact that making such an attempt is wrong, then you believe that I have a significant reason not to do this. You therefore have reason to believe that (in the absence of special justifying conditions) I would not attempt to persuade you that I intended to do a certain thing (when I know that you care about and may rely upon my doing it) unless I actually had a settled intention to do that thing. Suppose, then, that I do the following:

(a) I give you good reason to believe that I am attempting to persuade you that I have the settled intention of doing X if certain conditions obtain, and that I believe that, if you are persuaded, the truth of this belief will be important to you; and

(b) I lead you to believe that I know and take seriously the fact that, under the circumstances, it would be wrong of me to attempt this unless I really had that intention.

By doing (a) and (b) I give you reason to believe that I have a settled intention to do X if the relevant conditions obtain, and hence reason to believe that I will do X under those conditions. This explains how the expression "I promise" can be used to create an expectation and thereby an obligation, and it explains this without assuming that these words trigger a nonmoral source of motivation or that they have a "special" obligation-generating force of the kind that a social practice of promising might give them.

4. The Roles Practices Can Play

Even if my analysis is correct, this does not mean that promising is not a social practice. The conditions of intention and mutual knowledge specified in Principle F are quite complex. Uttered under appropriate conditions, the expression "I promise" creates this mutual knowledge with great economy.[11] The same thing could be accomplished using other terms, but saying "I promise" does it quickly, and promising is certainly a social practice in at least this limited "linguistic" sense. But if the expression "I promise" conveys these complex conditions of mutual knowledge and intent, there is the possibility that it also conveys specific terms and conditions, which do not derive from general moral principles of the kind I have been discussing but are part of our particular social practice of promising. This would give that practice a more extensive (though still dispensable) role in determining the shape of our obligations. I turn now to an investigation of this possibility.

Saying "I promise to . . ." normally binds one to do the thing promised, but it does not bind unconditionally or absolutely. It does not bind unconditionally, because the binding force of promising depends on the conditions under which the promise is made: a promise may not bind if it was obtained by coercion or through deceit. It does not bind absolutely, because, while a promise binds one against reconsidering one's intention simply on grounds of one's own convenience, it does not bind one to do the thing promised whatever the cost to oneself and others.

It is natural to suppose that these conditions and limitations are "rules" of the practice of promising: they are part of the shared expectations that constitute that practice and are triggered by using the expression "I promise." On this way of looking at the matter, creating an obligation by saying "I promise" is like renting your house by filling in a preprinted lease form. The rules of the practice that one invokes by using this expression define the general structure and limitations of the obligation that is being incurred. All one needs to do is to fill in the blanks by specifying the thing one is promising to do and the person to whom the promise is addressed. Like the preprinted form, the social practice of promising is unnecessary. Just as one could have arrived at the same lease agreement "from scratch," starting with blank paper instead of the form, one could have generated the obligation that the promise creates by working out explicitly all the limitations and conditions specified by the "rules." But saying "I promise" does this much more quickly.

Although this "printed form" account of the role of the social practice of promising has a certain appeal, it does not seem to me to be correct.[12] Consider first what I have called the conditions (as opposed to the limitations) of binding promises. When we are trying to discover what these conditions are (for example, when we are trying to decide whether a certain form of duress invalidates a promise), is the question we ask ourselves one of social fact (what is our practice?) or is it in the first instance a more general moral question about when an obligation has arisen? It seems to me to be the latter.

This conclusion is supported by evidence of the kind I marshalled above to defend the claim that the wrong involved in breaking a promise could also occur in the absence of any social practice of agreement-making. Suppose that, under duress, I give someone reason to believe that I will do a certain thing in the future, but that I do this in some way other than by using the expression "I promise." The thought process one would go through in deciding whether the duress involved in such a case is sufficient to prevent any obligation from arising is, I believe, of the same type as the process involved in deciding whether a promise made under similar conditions would be binding. It is not, then, a matter of answering a question of social fact about what the "rules" of our social practice of promising require.

When we turn to the limitations on the obligation arising from a promise, things are slightly more complex. Just as in the case of the conditions, when I reflect on these limits—when, for example, I try to determine whether a promise to do X obligates a person to do X even at the cost of Y—it seems clear to me that I am engaging in moral reflection, not in an inquiry into what the accepted rules of our social practice of agreement-making are. It does seem, however, that a social practice could incorporate special limitations, and different practices could incorporate different special limitations, in the way that the "printed form" theory describes. For example, it might be understood that obligations undertaken by saying "Cross my heart" do not bind one to do anything that seriously inconveniences one's spouse, and obligations undertaken by using some other form of words might be understood not to require any performance on religious holidays or to lapse if they are not fulfilled within a specified period.

It is easier to explain how practices of agreement-making that generate binding obligations could differ in this way (in the limitations they incorporate) than it would be to explain how they could differ in their conditions. As long as the conditions of voluntariness specified by ordinary moral thinking are fulfilled in the making of an agreement, and the parties are aware of the limitations prescribed by the practice they are invoking, these limitations can be seen simply as part of the content of the agreement made, and as binding for that reason.[13] Although a social practice of agreement-making *could* shape the content of particular obligations arising under it in this way, I am unable to identify any such limitations built into our particular practice of promising. The "printed form" that it provides appears to be nearly blank.

5. Some Difficulties

Two kinds of situations pose potential difficulties for the account of promising that I have proposed. According to this account, the obligation generated by a promise depends on the fact that in making the promise the promiser creates an expectation that the promisee cares about. The difficulties I have in mind arise when one of these conditions fails to hold—when no expectation is created or when the thing promised is not desired by the promisee. I will examine the latter case first.

The second clause of Principle F requires that the promiser know that the promisee wants to be assured that the expected act will be performed. This condition is not fulfilled in the case of such statements as "I promise you that if you don't give me five dollars I will break your fingers," so such "promises" generate no obligations under F. The inclusion of a condition of this kind in Principle F is not ad hoc: there is no reason why potential recipients of such "threat-promises" should object to a principle that imposes on those who make them no duty to follow through.[14] The potential difficulty is that the condition as stated may be too strong. As a result of this condition, Principle F seems to imply that all undesired promises (such as a mother's promise to give her daughter a sewing machine, when in fact the daughter would not want to have such a thing in the house) are invalid. But it may seem, intuitively, that at least some such promises are binding.

A similar problem arises in cases in which no expectation is in fact created because the promisee does not believe that the promiser's declared intentions will be fulfilled. Consider the following example, which I will call the case of the Profligate Pal. Your friend has been borrowing money from you, and from others, for years, always promising solemnly to pay it back but never doing so. Finally, you refuse to lend him any more money, and others do so as well. This precipitates a crisis of shame. Your friend is humiliated by the realization that others have lost all respect for him, and he struggles to retain the last vestiges of respect for himself. He is also in great need of money. Finally, he comes to you on his knees, full of self-reproach and sincere assurances that he has turned over a new leaf. You do not believe this for a minute, but out of pity you are willing simply to give him the money he needs. You realize, however, that it would be cruel to reject his promises as worthless and offer him charity instead. So you treat his offer seriously, and give him the money after receiving his promise to repay the loan on a certain date, although you have no expectation of ever seeing your money again. Does he have an obligation to pay you back? Principle F does not generate any such obligation, but it may seem, intuitively, that there is one.

Even if there is, this would not show that Principle F is mistaken. Like Principles M, D, and L, it would still state an important part of the truth: it would still explain how obligations arise in central cases of promising. The examples just given represent "impure cases" which a complete account of the subject would have to deal with, however, so they may show that F needs to be supplemented by further principles. To see whether this is so, let me consider several forms of "impurity."

Suppose first that, contrary to clause (2) of F, the promiser has no good grounds for believing that the promisee wants X, the thing promised, or an option to have it, and that the promiser has no good grounds for believing that having X, or an option to have it, is in the promisee's interest. In particular, the promisee has not indicated, explicitly or tacitly, any desire to have X or to have the option to have it. This case resembles the case of the threat-promise considered above. What reason would there be to reject a principle that left the promiser entirely free to decide whether to fulfill such a "promise" or not? Potential promisees have no such reason. Potential promisers might, conceivably, want to be bound in this way, but in the absence of some more substantial reason for their wanting this, why should this aim count for much? Why, in particular, should it count more than potential promisees' interest in being able to control the obligations others have to them? We seem here to have at best a standoff between considerations that are all of minimal moral significance. There is thus no reason to believe in the existence of an obligation.[15]

Suppose, now, that while the promiser has no good grounds for thinking that the promisee wants to have X, or to have the option of having it (no indication of this has been given), he or she does have grounds for thinking that having X is or will be in the promisee's interest. This may be what the mother believes in the sewing-machine example. This concern with the promisee's good gives the promiser's desire to be bound more moral weight than it had in the previous case. But why should a would-be benefactor want to be bound in this way? Not, I think, as a guard against future changes of mind, but rather as a way of assuring the beneficiary that the benefit is or will be available, and that this availability is not conditional upon any future decision and will not be affected by what the beneficiary does or does not do. Would-be promisers thus have a legitimate reason for preferring a principle that would create obligations of this kind. Do potential promisees have grounds for objecting? On the one hand, they stand to benefit, since the obligations in question must be based on reasonable beliefs about their good. On the other hand, they may object to being assigned rights in this "paternalistic" way. On balance, I doubt that these considerations provide grounds for rejecting a principle, given the promiser's legitimate interest in being able to give assurance. So there is more reason to believe that there is an obligation here than there is in the previous case, although the case remains much less clear than the "pure" cases described by F.

Our sewing-machine example raises a further difficulty, however. It is reasonable to suppose, in that case, that the daughter is an adult whose values are not going to change. She knows that her mother falsely, though not unreasonably, believes that she values the assurance that she will be given a sewing machine, but out of regard for her mother's feelings (and a desire to avoid an unpleasant argument about women's roles) she does not correct this belief. Suppose for the moment that Principle F gives a complete account of the obligations in this case. The mother, then, if she relies on this principle, will falsely (though perhaps justifiably) believe that she has an obligation, when in fact she has none. This seems to me to be the correct account of the matter. For suppose that the mother were to learn the true situation. Could the daughter, or someone else, convincingly say to her, "But you *promised,* so you have to do it"? It seems to me that she could not. If not, then there is no need to supplement F in order to explain this case.

This brings us very close to the case of the Profligate Pal. Like the mother in the situation just described, the pal has reason to believe that by promising he has put himself under an obligation—in his case an obligation to repay. He surely is under *some* obligation to do this; he at least owes you a debt of gratitude. From your point of view, however, what he has received is a gift, tactfully described as a loan. So I believe that Principle F is correct in suggesting that if he fails to repay you he will not have wronged you in the way a person is normally wronged by a broken promise. In this respect his situation is like that of the mother in our last example. The two cases are different in that you, unlike the daughter, would prefer to have the "promise" fulfilled (you would have preferred making a loan to making a gift in the first place), and the pal, if he thought about it, would realize that this is what you would prefer, whatever your expectations may be. So the pal has reason to believe that either you have loaned him money on the basis of his promise to repay it or, although you would have preferred assurance of repayment, you have in fact given him money but tactfully allowed him to think of it as a loan. In either case he has an obligation to repay you, but not necessarily of the kind generated by a promise. This supports the intuition that it would be wrong of the pal not to repay you if he can, and makes it the case that this conclusion would remain true even if the nature of the situation became clear to him. Principle F requires supplementation here, but only by principles governing obligations of gratitude.

6. Summary

I have discussed three roles that a social practice of agreement-making might play in the genesis of obligations to keep agreements. First, it might serve as a mechanism for signaling our intentions and our understanding of the situation we are in. Second, it might serve as a source of motivation, and hence as a ground for expectations about what others will do. Third, the moral standing of a practice might play a crucial role in generating the obligation to keep particular agreements. That is, these particular obligations might be seen as flowing from a more general obligation to abide by the provisions of that practice.

I believe that the social practice of promising certainly does play the first of these roles. I have argued, however, that this is just a matter of convenience—the same obligations could be generated in other ways. It seems likely that the institution of promising can also play the second role of providing motivation, but I have argued that this, too, is not essential. Finally, I have argued that the institution of promising need not play the third, justifying role. When promises give rise to clear obligations, these can be accounted for on the basis of general moral principles that do not refer to the existence of social practices. There are, however, some other ways in which the obligation to keep a promise might depend on practices or conventions.

My arguments for Principles M, D, L, and F have presupposed the contractualist moral theory defended in earlier chapters, according to which the duties we have are determined by asking what principles "for the general regulation of behavior" we would agree upon under certain conditions. Since this theory makes all duties depend on the merits of general rules or practices in something like the way in which promises have been thought to do, it may seem to trivialize or at least greatly reduce the content of my claim that promises do not derive their moral force from a social institution. But the theory does not have this effect. Even if every duty depends on the possibility of hypothetical agreement on general rules of conduct, there remains a distinction between those duties that do and those that do not depend on the existence of *actual* social practices, a distinction corresponding to Hume's distinction between "artificial" and "natural" virtues. To re-confirm that the duty to keep one's promises need not fall on the former, "artificial" side of this distinction, it will be helpful to return to the question, raised at the beginning of this chapter, of how the existence of a social practice can give rise to moral duties.

When there are important effects that can be achieved only through independent action by many agents acting without direct communica-tion, the existence of an established practice coordinating these ac-tions is an important public good. Analogy with other public goods cases suggests that those who help themselves to the benefits of such a practice owe it to others to do their part to contribute to the provision of the good—that is, to support, and especially not to undermine, the practice. Thus, in the case of an established social practice of agreement-making, those who have taken advantage of the practice ought not to undermine it by, for example, violating their agreements or spreading false rumors that others are doing so. This provides *a* moral reason for keeping promises.[16] But it is not the only such reason or, I believe, the most fundamental one. As the hackneyed example of the deathbed promise indicates, the obligation to keep one's promises outruns any duty to support, and not to undermine, the practice of promising.

Rawls's more general analysis comes closer to capturing this obligation. His principle of fairness requires of those who voluntarily accept the benefits of a just scheme of cooperation not only that they support, and not undermine, that practice but more generally that they do what its rules require of them. In the case of the institution of promising, this generates a direct obligation to keep one's promises. Even on this analysis, however, the obligation to keep a promise would be derived from a general obligation owed to the members of the group who have contributed to and benefit from the practice (in my example, the members of the possibly fictitious Brotherhood of Reindeer).

But the obligation to keep a promise does not seem to have this character. Unlike an obligation to comply with a just institution that provides some of the public goods, the obligation to keep a promise is owed to a specific individual who may or may not have contributed to the practice of promising. In addition, the only expectations that are directly relevant are those created by the promiser and promisee at the time the promise is made. The behavior and expectations of third parties are of only ancillary importance—as aids in the creation of these primary expectations. I have argued that such a background of standing expectations is not necessary to generate the kind of obligation involved in a promise. And when it does play a role, this background leads to moral consequences in the case of promises in quite a different way than in the case of institutions that provide a public good—namely, in the way described by Principle F rather than that described by a principle like Rawls's principle of fairness.

There is, however, another way in which the obligation to keep a promise might, on the analysis I have offered, be regarded as arising from a "convention." In arguing for Principle F, I assumed that people have reason to attach great importance to what I called "assurance"—that is, being able to be reasonably certain that a thing will happen unless one consents to its not happening. We normally value assurance quite highly. Indeed, anyone would value it in the circumstances to which Principle F applies (this concern is built into the principle's conditions). But societies may vary in the frequency with which people find themselves in such circumstances—ones in which there is a need to work out and stabilize an ad hoc arrangement about what each of several parties is going to do. This need would be much less common in a society in which more of the situations in which important matters were at stake were governed by assigned roles.[17]

If this is correct, then not the validity of Principle F but its importance relative to other moral considerations will depend on social circumstances, and this might be regarded as a conventional element in my argument. I do not deny that obligations arising from promises are conventional in this way, and I will discuss other examples of this kind of variation in the next chapter. I mention it here chiefly in order to point out one way in which this form of dependence on "convention" differs from more familiar versions. If a convention or social practice is taken to consist in the fact that people accept certain rules or norms and typically act in accordance with them, then we need a mediating moral principle to explain how such practices can be morally binding and generate specific obligations. If, on the other hand, the conventional element in an account of a certain obligation consists in the fact that people in certain times and places have reason to value certain things, then there is no need for a mediating principle: such a fact can lead directly to moral conclusions through the standard process of moral argument with which we are already familiar.

7. Lying and Truth Telling

In this section I will consider duties not to lie and duties and obligations to tell the truth. These duties raise issues that are similar to, but also different from, the ones already discussed in this chapter, and the similarities and differences will, I hope, cast some light on both sides of the comparison.

It is important here, as elsewhere, to distinguish between the generic reasons that shape our moral principles and the structure of those principles themselves. The main generic reasons that bear on questions of lying and telling the truth are these. From the point of view of recipients, the main reasons arise from our need for information that other people can supply and, more specifically, our need to be able to rely on what other people tell us. Potential providers of information, on the other hand, have reasons arising from such concerns as preserving their own and others' personal privacy, reserving valuable information for their own exclusive use, protecting or enhancing their own reputation and that of others, protecting other people's feelings, and remaining true to their values and commitments by not aiding projects that they disagree with, disapprove of, or are in conflict with.

I will concentrate for the moment on reasons of these two kinds—roughly speaking, reasons concerned in one way or another with the value of information. Reasons of the first kind make potential recipients want principles forbidding lying and even requiring the provision of useful information. Reasons of the latter sort move potential providers to reject or at least to want to modify such principles.

A principle forbidding one to lie (or to give intentionally misleading information) is, obviously, easier to argue for than one requiring the provision of information. Potential recipients have stronger reason for wanting such a principle since relying on false or misleading information is worse than having none at all. On the other side, legitimate reasons for wanting to be free to mislead recipients are, in general, harder to come by than legitimate reasons for wanting to be able to protect one's own and others' interests by avoiding disclosure.

A principle forbidding lying would be rather similar to Principle M, which forbids lies of one particular kind: lies about one's intentions that are made for the purpose of influencing the recipient toward doing some action favorable to the agent. So a principle forbidding lying would be a generalization of M. A very general principle of this kind would take the following form. (I will call it Principle ML since it rules out intentionally misleading others.)

> *Principle ML:* One may not, in the absence of special justification, act with the intention of leading someone to form a false belief about some matter, or with the aim of confirming a false belief he or she already holds.

The case for this principle is the one I have already sketched. Potential recipients have reason to want to be informed and stronger reason to want to be able to rely on what others tell them. Potential providers of information have, in many cases, good reasons for wanting not to be required to disclose everything they know, but they do not *in general* have strong and legitimate reasons for retaining the freedom to mislead others. (I will return shortly to some of the reasons they do have.)

Principle ML forbids more than lying, since one can act with the aim of leading another to form a false belief without saying anything that one believes to be false. Indeed, one can do this without saying or writing anything at all: for example, by leaving misleading "evidence" around (an extension of the techniques used in the versions of the farmer example that I discussed in Section 3). But from the point of view of those who are misled, the reasons for insisting on at least the protection provided by ML are just as strong as the reasons for wanting the protection provided by a weaker principle forbidding only outright lies. Their interest is in not being misled; it does not matter whether this is done by saying something false, by artful and selective use of the truth, or by the planting of misleading physical evidence.

Looking at the matter from the other side, do potential misinformers have better reasons for rejecting Principle ML than for rejecting a narrower principle forbidding only outright lies? They may, but it is not clear that they do. Such reasons would have to originate from legitimate reasons for wanting to lead someone else to form, or to confirm him or her in holding, a false belief. Where there are such reasons, they may also support special justifications of the sort recognized by ML. So the most likely case for a stricter prohibition against lying would take the following form. First, there are reasons for misleading people in ways that ML would otherwise forbid, that ML must (if it is not to be reasonably rejectable) recognize as "special justifications." But, second, these reasons are not good justifications for actually *lying* to people. That is, a principle against lying would not have to recognize them as exceptions in order not to be reasonably rejectable.

A successful argument of this kind would not eliminate Principle ML as a separate requirement unless it showed that every point at which ML appeared to go beyond a prohibition against lying would actually be covered by a special justification that ML would have to recognize if it is not to be reasonably rejectable. I think this is unlikely to be the case even if there is a prohibition against lying that is more stringent than ML.

The most obvious special justifications that Principle ML must recognize fall into the same categories as those I mentioned above in discussing Principle M. (This is not surprising, since every exception to M is also an exception to ML.) These were: emergency cases, threat cases, paternalistic cases, and permission cases. In the example of an emergency case that I gave above, A needed to mislead B in order to obtain his help because there was no way to communicate with him directly to ask for it. So the question of the justifiability of lying does not even arise. It would arise if, for example, saving A (or the third party who is at risk) requires some small form of help which B refuses to provide. It seems to me that if a principle allowing A to mislead or manipulate B in a case of this kind could not reasonably be rejected, then neither could one that permitted A to lie to him. The same seems to be true of threat cases and paternalistic cases.

In permission cases, insofar as it is *actual* permission that is in question, everything depends on what permission has been given. It is quite conceivable that there could be activities and forms of competition in which it is understood, for good reason, that entry into them involves giving permission for some forms of deception but not for others (not for outright lying, for example). The more interesting class of cases for present purposes goes beyond actual consent, however. These would be cases in which there is good reason to structure certain forms of interaction (some forms of economic competition perhaps) in a way that permits some forms of deception but not others (a qualified form of *caveat emptor,* so to speak). I am not certain whether there are such cases or not. Leaving these special institutional cases aside, however, I do not believe that from a general moral point of view there is an important difference between lying and other forms of deception.

Let me turn now from the question of the wrongfulness of lying and other forms of deception to the idea of a general moral requirement to tell the truth, that is to say, not merely a prohibition against misleading others but an affirmative requirement to provide useful information when one has it. This would be a special case of a more general requirement to provide aid. As I pointed out in Chapter 5, requirements to aid can take a number of different forms, ranging from a requirement to prevent someone from suffering serious harm if one can do so without great cost to oneself, to a weaker but much broader requirement to set a positive value on helping others to advance their aims. The question presently at issue is whether requirements to provide information that others may need, or to respond to their requests for information, may be clearer or stronger than more general requirements to provide aid of other kinds.

There are at least two reasons for expecting this to be the case. First, one of the problems in formulating principles of mutual aid is that of specifying who must aid when many could equally well do so but only one is needed. This is less of a problem in information cases, in which one person may be singled out by virtue of being the only one who *has* the required information or the one who has been asked for it. Second, one of the main sources of resistance to stronger requirements to give aid is the burden that this imposes on the providers. But simply answering the question one has been asked, or passing on a piece of information in some other way, is not very burdensome; so there is less ground for resisting a principle requiring aid of this kind. (Or, to put it another way, giving this kind of aid is less likely to fall under the exclusion clauses that principles of mutual aid typically must include.)

There is an element of truth in each of these claims, but their force should not be overestimated. The first point does not mark a difference between people who are asked for information and those who are asked to provide aid of other kinds (or who are uniquely able to provide it). Second, while it is true that actually providing information is often easy, this does not mean that there are no serious costs involved in doing so. These costs are rather different from those involved in giving other kinds of aid, but they can provide good reasons, from the point of view of providers and affected third parties, for rejecting an unconditional requirement to provide information. These reasons flow from legitimate interests in such things as protecting one's own and others' privacy, preventing embarrassment or loss of reputation, and maintaining control over information that one has worked to obtain for commercial or other purposes. So any valid principle requiring one to provide information would have to recognize these interests as the basis for special justifications for not responding.

Since such a principle is not simply a requirement not to lie but a requirement to be of assistance, it requires one to provide information in an understandable and usable form. Providing so much information that the recipient will have great difficulty sorting out the relevant from the irrelevant, or giving an answer couched in impenetrable jargon, would not meet this test, even though these things (if not done with the aim of misleading) would not violate Principle ML.[18]

A principle requiring one to provide true and useful information does not correspond to any principle discussed earlier in this chapter in regard to promising. The natural correlate to such a principle would be one requiring that we inform others of our intentions when this will be useful to them. Principle ML is, as I have said, naturally seen as a generalization of Principle M, and there presumably are similar generalizations of Principles D and L, requiring us to take due care not to mislead other people and to take reasonable steps to protect them against incurring loss as a result of relying on false information that we have given them.[19]

Even if there are such principles, this still leaves us well short of anything corresponding to Principle F, on which the obligation to keep a promise was based. Thus, while one might try to explain the obligation to keep a promise by basing it on the duty not to lie or mislead, two differences seem to stand in the way of such an approach. The first is that the problem to which Principle F was addressed was how to account for an obligation to perform the promised action rather than merely to warn the promisee or to protect him or her against loss in some other way, and the notion of performance has no analogue in the case of lying. (Insofar as there is an obligation to make what one has said be true, this is a consequence of a duty, analogous to Principle L, to protect against loss, and this duty can be fulfilled by a timely warning.)

Second, promises differ from most cases of lying (or truth telling) in their reliance on a distinctive underlying motive. Typically, a promise is asked for or offered when there is doubt as to whether the promiser will have sufficient motive to do the thing promised. The point of the promise is to provide such a motive, and according to the analysis I have offered this is supplied by the promiser's awareness that, given what he or she has said, it would be wrong not to fulfill the agreement.[20] Some lies are like this. Sometimes a liar gets his victims to accept his claims by emphasizing his (supposedly) moral and honorable nature, saying such things as "I swear to you this is true. Would I lie to you about a thing like this?" And we do ask people to give testimony under oath when we want to be certain that they are telling us what they believe to be true. But most lies and, more generally, most utterances that convince their hearers do not fit this pattern. In most cases we believe what people tell us not because we think they would like to lie but are constrained by their recognition that it would be wrong to do so, but rather because we suppose that they are first and foremost moved by some motive that leads them to tell the truth: they are concerned for our welfare, or they want to help us, or they want to show off their knowledge by telling us the very best way of getting someplace or by letting us know the inside story about what *really* happened. The skillful liar generally avoids getting into a situation in which it is necessary to play "the moral card" on which promises typically depend.

My conclusion, then, is that although the moral constraints against lying and other forms of deception are closely related to the principles that led up to my analysis of promises, they differ in important respects from the principle governing the case of promising itself.

8. Oaths and Other Values

Making a promise is one way to provide assurance that one will do something when one's performance is otherwise in doubt. Taking an oath is another way of doing this, and also a way of providing assurance that one is telling the truth. I understand oaths as working in the following way. A person taking an oath says, in support of a claim to be telling the truth or to have a sincere and reliable intention to do a certain thing, "I swear to you by . . . ," naming here something to which he or she is assumed to attach great value, such as God, the Bible, or the memory of a loved one. It is not necessary that the value appealed to should itself be or involve a code of honor or convention of truth telling. The idea is just that it would be incompatible with true devotion to this value to invoke it as a sign of one's sincerity when one was making an insincere claim. Some, of course, go farther, and hold that it is incompatible with regarding something as sacred to invoke it in support of *any* claim. In some religions, for example, it is forbidden to invoke holy texts or the name of God in this way.

The reasons provided by oaths are distinct from those provided by promises and, more generally, by the various principles I have described. These reasons can, however, become intertwined in some cases. R. S. Downie cites the case of a group of Protestants who were forced by their Irish Republican Army captors to "promise on the Bible" that they would not provide information about them to the police.[21] Downie says they were advised by their minister that they had an obligation to keep this promise. What was the "obligation" about which they were advised? It might have been the moral obligation arising from a promise in accordance with the principles I have discussed. (I will return to this possibility below.) Another possibility, however, is that the minister's judgment was not about obligation in this sense but rather about what a Christian must do in such circumstances: his advice may have been that proper respect for the Bible requires that one either refuse to invoke it in this way or else do what one has sworn to do (assuming that the act is not in itself unchristian).

In the case of some oaths the value appealed to may be the agent's own sense of dignity or personal honor. The reasons invoked by these oaths can be of an amoral character and can even support immoral action, as when people give their word that they will carry out a threat or that they will take revenge. A person who makes such a threat may regard it as shameful—because weak, vacillating, or cowardly—to fail to pursue it. But the reasons provided by one's sense of honor can also have a moral character in several different ways, of which I will mention only two. These reasons can be moral in a broad sense insofar as integrity, understood as steadfastness to one's values (even one's nonmoral values), is thought of as a moral virtue.[22] In addition, they can be moral in a narrower sense, one more closely tied to the preceding discussion, if the personal value at stake is one's regard for what is morally right. This brings me back to the case of the IRA captives.

It is conceivable that the obligation by which the freed captives were bound was a moral obligation of the sort described earlier in this chapter, an obligation to their former captors. Suppose, for example, that the promise was extorted by IRA underlings so that they could then, acting out of sympathy and against the orders of their superiors, allow the captives to escape without greatly increasing the risk to themselves. Leaving this possibility aside for the moment, however, there are other moral factors that should be considered. Adam Smith, discussing a similar case of a promise made to a highwayman, says that there is no doubt that such a promise is invalid "as a matter of jurisprudence," but that things are different when the case is considered from the point of view of casuistry as a matter of what "a sacred and conscientious regard to the general rules of justice" requires. After careful discussion, in which he observes that "no regard is due to the disappointment" of the highwayman, and that considerations such as the need to provide for one's family can certainly justify failing to fulfill such a promise, he nonetheless concludes as follows:

> It may be said in general that exact propriety requires the observance of all such promises, wherever it is not inconsistent with some other duties that are more sacred; such as regard to the public interest, to those whom gratitude, whom natural affection, or whom the laws of proper beneficence prompt us to provide for . . .
>
> It is to be observed, however, that whenever such promises are violated, though for the most necessary reasons, it is always with some degree of dishonour for the person who made them. After they are made, we may be convinced of the impropriety of observing them. But there is still some fault in having made them. It is at least a departure from the highest and noblest maxims of magnanimity and honour. A brave man ought to die, rather than make a promise which he can neither keep without folly, nor violate without ignominy.[23]

Smith goes on to justify this sense of ignominy on the grounds that "fidelity is so necessary a virtue, that we apprehend it in general to be due even to those to whom nothing else is due, and whom we think it lawful to kill and destroy."[24] The "necessity" he has in mind might be the importance of fidelity for society, or it might be the central place it has in our personal relations with others. Whatever Smith may have had in mind, however, there are other grounds that might be offered, based on our preceding discussion. The puzzle is to explain how the person who fails to keep the extorted promise can be dishonored by this act even though the person to whom the promise was made is not entitled to its fulfillment either as a matter of law or as a matter of right and justice. The breach must be not with the promisee but with something else, perhaps something in the promiser himself. Here it may help to recall that a person who makes a promise, in contrast to one who appeals to other evidence of intent, makes use of his or her apparent devotion to the value of right conduct itself. Such a person claims, sincerely or otherwise, to believe that respect for this value requires fulfillment of the promise being made. A person who makes this claim, while actually believing or at least suspecting (correctly, we may assume) that the promise is invalid because coerced, and while intending to exploit this fact, is using the idea of right conduct as means of deception. No one who makes promises could hold, as some do of the Bible, that one's regard for the value of right conduct ought not to be used as a means for cementing bargains. But using one's regard for rightness as a means of deception may seem incompatible with proper regard for that value. Even when a coerced promise was made in good faith, a person who failed to fulfill it on grounds that he or she was mistaken in thinking such promises to be binding might seem to be "stained" or "dishonored" in a way that a person who disappointed a similar expectation created by other means would not: "dishonored" because, quite apart from the legitimacy of the promisee's claim, what the promiser has put on the line is his or her regard for the value of rightness itself.

This idea of "dishonor" brings out important differences in the ways in which the binding force of promises and oaths depends on their being entered into voluntarily, that is to say, without coercion. Voluntariness figured in the arguments for principles M, L, D, and F as a factor affecting the force of complaints against the burdensomeness of the obligations they describe. Potential objections to Principle F, for example, are undermined by the fact that a person can avoid the obligations it imposes simply by refraining from the creation of expectations of the particular kind described. A principle that was like F but made no exception for coercion would be open to serious objection, however, since coercion can make the alternatives to incurring obligation less eligible. It follows that coercion generally invalidates such obligations, but it does not always do so. Whether it does in a given case depends on whether the coercion removed alternatives to which the agent was otherwise entitled. Treaties entered into by defeated nations may all be coerced, for example, but this does not render them invalid when the terms are not unjust.

Things are quite different in the case of oaths. The binding force of an oath derives from the value that is invoked in making it rather than from "principles that no one could reasonably reject." If coercion undermines the force of an oath, it must do so by changing the meaning, for someone who holds this value, of invoking it in support of an act of deception. It is intelligible to claim that while it would show a lack of sincere commitment to a value to do this in the absence of coercion, using the value this way when faced with a dire threat shows no such lack of commitment. But the opposite claim is also plausible, as the advice the minister might have given the IRA captives illustrates. He might have said that, whether or not they should have "promised on the Bible," having done so it would be a desecration (or a further one) to fail to act as they said they would. Something similar may be true in the case of ideals of personal honor: it may show weakness (or a lack of integrity) to allow oneself to be coerced into giving one's word, but then to fail to keep it is a further weakness. The relevance of coercion as a factor invalidating an oath will thus depend on the value that is in question, and on what a sincere regard for that value entails.

9. Conclusion

Relying on the account of right and wrong spelled out in earlier chapters, I have defended principles that explain the obligation to keep a promise and related duties not to deceive or manipulate others. I have argued that the obligation to keep a promise need not derive its moral force from the existence of a social practice of promising, although such a practice can facilitate our obligations and help to shape their content by establishing settled expectations.

The wrongfulness of lying and other forms of deception can be explained by generalizations of the principles that forbid misleading others about our intentions and require us to take care to protect others against losses that result from relying on expectations we have created. But I have argued that the duty not to lie differs in important ways from the duty to keep one's promises (as this is described, for example, by Principle F above). In particular, the wrongfulness of lying does not play as central a motivating role in supporting our reliance on other people's utterances as the duty of fidelity plays in undergirding promises.

The case for moral principles of the kind I have described depends on what people have good reason to want, and these reasons may be different for people in different societies. I also argued, in the last section, that the principles I have defended are not the only source of moral reasons to keep one's word. Other values, moral and nonmoral, can play this role. So while the theory I have presented accounts for some of our firmest moral beliefs, it also allows for a variety of moral values and for some variability in our moral conclusions. I will explore the possibilities for variability of these kinds in the next chapter.

8

Relativism

1. Introduction

Anyone who offers an account of the morality of right and wrong is bound to be asked whether he is claiming that there are "universal" moral principles. One aim of the present chapter is to provide my answer to this question. The question is often presented as a challenge, or asked with a tone of incredulity, and the issue of relativism that it raises is one that arouses strong passions. From some, relativism provokes passionate denial, the passion and haste of which suggests an element of fear. Others are eager to affirm that they are relativists, and often do so with a particular sense of satisfaction, perhaps even of superiority. A second task of this chapter will be to examine the idea of relativism itself, with the hope of understanding, and perhaps defusing, some of the passions that attach to it.

The account of reasons, values, morality in general, and the morality of obligation in particular that I have presented in the preceding chapters allows for several ways in which defensible moral standards can vary in content, and I will describe these forms of variability below. There is an ineliminable element of vagueness about what counts as a form of relativism, but I do not believe that this term could be properly applied to the account I offer. My view does, however, explain how moral standards can vary in many of the ways that relativists have insisted upon. This is, I believe, as much variation as can plausibly be defended.

2. What Is Relativism?

Moral relativism, as I will understand it, is the thesis that there is no single ultimate standard for the moral appraisal of actions, a standard uniquely appropriate for all agents and all moral judges; rather, there are many such standards. According to relativism, moral appraisals of actions, insofar as they are to make sense and be defensible, must be understood not as judgments about what is right or wrong absolutely, but about what is right or wrong relative to the particular standards that are made relevant by the context of the action in question, or by the context of the judgment itself.[1] It is important that the standards in question here are *ultimate* standards. Any plausible moral view would allow for the fact that actions that are right in one place can be wrong in another place, where people have different expectations, or where different conditions obtain. Failing to help a person whose car has broken down, for example, would be a serious wrong in a place where someone who is stranded overnight is likely to freeze to death, but not a serious wrong in a safe country with a mild climate. A view that allows for such variations in what is right, by applying a fixed set of substantive moral principles to varying circumstances, is not relativism but rather what I will call "parametric universalism."

Moral relativism denies that there is a single set of ultimate substantive moral standards by which all actions are to be judged, but it nonetheless presupposes a single normative perspective, from which judgments can be made about which principles (including moral principles) people in various situations have reason to regard as authoritative. Recognizing such a standpoint may seem to represent normative universalism of a kind that is at odds with the spirit of relativism, but this is a mistake. Moral relativism is, after all, a thesis about what people do and do not have reason to do. It therefore cannot be intelligibly asserted without presupposing the possibility that such judgments can coherently be made and defended.

Moreover, it is by distinguishing between judgments about reasons in general (of which the thesis of moral relativism is an example) and moral appraisals (which this thesis is a judgment about) that moral relativism as I have stated it can most clearly avoid the charge of incoherence that is often lodged against it. This charge is put in its simplest form when one person says, "Every judgment is relative. What is true for you need not be true for me," and someone else replies, "So is *that* judgment just true for you?" The charge is that when relativism is understood as a perfectly general claim, it appears to undermine itself.[2] Whether it does so will depend on the kind of claim that someone who asserts this general relativist thesis is making. The charge of incoherence gets its plausibility from the supposition that, insofar as relativists assert that their thesis is correct, and that anyone who denies it is mistaken, they are making a claim to unconditional validity that is inconsistent with relativism itself, taken as a perfectly general thesis. This supposition may be challenged. It might be maintained, for example, that someone who asserts the relativist thesis should be understood as making a claim only about what is true relative to certain parameters. The charge of incoherence is thus a matter of controversy. But moral relativism as I have stated it avoids this charge altogether. As will emerge more clearly below, moral appraisals as relativists should interpret them do involve claims about reasons. For example, relativists should construe the claim that an action is wrong as, roughly, the claim that action is ruled out by principles that there is, in the context, sufficient reason to regard as having the kind of authority properly called moral. Moral relativism is the claim that there is no single consistent set of principles that people have reason to regard as having this kind of authority in all contexts. Since this thesis is not itself a principle for which the specified form of authority is being claimed (but, rather, a claim about when principles have this kind of authority), the relativist's position is clearly a coherent one.

Given this abstract account of what moral relativism is, why is it a doctrine that should be feared or resisted? There are at least three possible reasons. First, relativism can seem threatening because morality is seen as an important force for keeping people in line, and for keeping the rest of us safe from potential wrongdoers. For those who take this view, relativists will seem dangerous in something like the way that Locke thought atheists were. Near the end of his *Letter on Toleration,* after firmly condemning seventeenth-century practices of religious intolerance and presenting a stirring defense of toleration, he mentions some exceptions, and concludes by saying, "Lastly, those are not at all to be tolerated who deny the being of a God. Promises, covenants, and oaths, which are the bonds of human society, can have no hold upon an atheist. The taking away of God, though but even in thought, dissolves all."[3]

Similarly, by claiming that even what seem to be the clearest moral requirements—such as the prohibition against killing for profit—may fail to apply in some cases, relativists may seem to announce that people are free to treat others in ways that these requirements forbid. This thought would explain the element of fear in responses to relativism, and to that extent it seems to fit the facts. Philippa Foot, for example, describing common reactions to relativism, writes: "We are, naturally, concerned about the man who doesn't care what happens to other people, and we want to convict him of irrationality, thinking he will mind about that." She does not say exactly what the nature of this "concern" is, but a natural hypothesis is that it is, at base, a concern to restrain certain agents in order to protect ourselves and others. This hypothesis is supported by Foot's suggestion, later in the same paragraph, that it would be more honest "to recognize that the 'should' of moral judgment is sometimes merely an instrument by which we (for our own very good reasons) try to impose a rule of conduct even on the uncaring man."[4]

On this view, what is at stake in debates about relativism is the potential motivating power of moral judgments. Relativism is a threat because it suggests that some agents lack sufficient reason to accept basic moral principles, even those forbidding such things as murder, and that they thus would not follow these principles even if they were moved to act in the way that is most rational for them. Gilbert Harman has suggested, for example, that neither Hitler nor "a contented member of Murder, Inc." has reason to accept principles forbidding one to kill others when this would advance one's ends.[5] The prospect of people who give no weight to even this most basic moral demand is indeed a frightening one. But the acceptance or rejection of relativism, as a philosophical doctrine, does not seem to me to have much to do with the threat that they present. The people Harman describes are firmly committed to modes of life in which killing is acceptable, perhaps even routine, and are prepared to live this way whatever morality may say about it. There are probably always going to be such people, but I do not think that the spread of relativism would have much effect on the amount of violence in the world. The worst mass murderers have not been relativists, and many relativists accept, perhaps for varying reasons, the basic contents of ordinary morality. So this first reason for resisting relativism does not seem to me compelling. I mention it mainly in order to distinguish it from a second reason, which I take more seriously.

This second reason is grounded in the confidence we have or would like to have in our judgment that certain actions are wrong. When Harman says, for example, that "ought to do" judgments do not apply to people who lack relevant reasons, and that we therefore cannot say that it was wrong of Hitler to murder millions of people, this claim threatens to deprive us of something important.[6] It does this even if we believe that Hitler or others like him would not be moved by the thought that they were behaving wrongly, in the sense that we want to preserve. What relativism threatens to deprive us of in such a case is not a source of potential motivation that may help to protect us but rather, I suggest, the sense that our condemnation of certain actions is legitimate and justified.

It may of course be asked why one should care so much about such condemnations. This concern is sometimes ridiculed as an idle and self-righteous desire to be able to pass judgment on every agent, even those at great cultural or historical distance from us. So portrayed, it may seem unattractive. But if we give up the idea that an agent can be properly condemned for his action, then it seems that we must also withdraw the claim, on his victims' behalf, that they were entitled not to be treated in the way that he treated them. One need not be excessively judgmental or self-righteous to feel that conceding this would involve giving up something important, and I believe that this feeling, rather than a concern with self-protection or a self-righteous desire to pass judgment, is what lies behind most people's reluctance to accept Harman's claim about Hitler.

Relativism can also be threatening in a third way, by seeming to undermine the importance of our moral judgments even when it does not require us to withdraw them. Following Harman, I defined moral relativism as the view that there is no single ultimate standard for the moral appraisal of actions, and that if a moral appraisal of an action is to be defensible it must be understood not as a judgment about what is right or wrong absolutely, but only about what is right or wrong relative to one of many possible standards. This proposal about how moral judgments are to be understood raises several problems. Sometimes, when two apparently conflicting judgments by different speakers refer to different standards, both judgments can be true, because there is no real conflict between them. When a Sicilian tourist in Los Angeles writes, on a postcard to her family, that a person she has just met is tall, she may say something true, even though residents of Los Angeles would also be speaking the truth when they say the opposite. It might seem that if judgments of moral wrongness were understood as making implicit reference to possibly varying standards in this way, then one person's judgment that an act is wrong and another's claim that it is not wrong could both be true. Since they refer to different standards, they do not really conflict; the standards they invoke conflict in a practical sense, however, since it would not be possible to live up to the demands of both standards simultaneously.

But moral judgments do not merely refer to standards of conduct; they involve a commitment to the claim that the standards they invoke have the particular authority that morality involves. Moral standards, and the judgments that presuppose them, can therefore conflict in a deeper way insofar as these standards are rival claimants to a kind of authority that, we commonly think, at most one of them can have. Relativism, as I have interpreted it, denies that only one set of standards can have this authority. The question then is, what determines which set of standards is authoritative in a given context? One familiar relativist response is that the rightness or wrongness of an action is determined by those standards that are generally accepted in the society in question. So understood, relativism is often seen as a debunking doctrine, according to which morality is *merely* a matter of social convention—where the 'merely' reflects the assumption that being generally accepted in a society could not, by itself, confer anything like the authority that moral judgments are commonly supposed to have. This is, at least, the way relativism is frequently imagined by nonrelativists, and no doubt some relativists also have this kind of debunking claim in mind.[7]

This challenge to the importance of moral judgments is a significant threat from a nonrelativist's point of view. It is also a serious problem for those relativists who do not see their relativism as a form of skepticism. I believe that many philosophers who defend relativism take themselves to be defending a nonskeptical or, as I will call it, *benign* relativism, according to which the requirements of morality vary but are not for that reason to be taken less seriously. Philippa Foot, for example, has defended a version of benign relativism, and Michael Walzer seems also to understand his view in this way.[8] Outside of philosophy, it seems to me that anthropologists, who are some of the most common proponents of relativism, are often best understood as having this benign form of the doctrine in mind. When they urge us to see the moralities of other cultures as "just as good as ours," they mean to challenge what they see as our unwarranted sense of superiority, but not to suggest that either our standards or those of other cultures are unworthy of being taken seriously. The question that most interests me about relativism is whether and how a form of benign relativism could be correct. This will be my main concern in the next two sections.

The question is how different people could have good reason to regard different standards as having the special kind of significance that moral standards have. Of course, there is disagreement as to exactly what kind of significance this is, but it is possible to describe in general terms the kind of significance that is in question, without building in requirements that a relativist would obviously reject. Three related features of moral requirements are particularly relevant here. The first is that moral requirements are ones that an agent has sufficient reason to give the kind of importance and priority described in Chapter 4. If there are cases in which one has sufficient reason to do something that morality speaks against, these are very rare. Second, the violation of moral requirements is a proper ground for feelings of guilt, that is to say, for self-reproach of a particularly serious kind. (As I said in Chapter 6, there is some ambiguity about the basis of this reproach, and different people may understand guilt in different ways.) These two features concern the kind of reasons that moral appraisals of an action must entail for the person whose action is in question. The third feature has to do with implications that the moral appraisal of an action has for people other than the agent: moral requirements are ones whose violation gives victims and others grounds for resentment and indignation, and, conversely, if an action is licensed by the relevant moral standards then those who are affected by it have reason to accept it without protest. It is not plausible to claim that certain standards are moral standards unless one takes them to be backed by reasons that support these three features, and hence not plausible to say of others that they regard certain standards as moral standards unless one takes them to believe that they are backed by reasons of this kind.

A defense of benign relativism, then, would argue that different people can have good reasons (perhaps different reasons) for attaching this kind of significance to different standards. This leads to a problem about how relativism (at least of the benign variety) is to be distinguished from other views. If a defense of benign relativism must start from some conception of what can confer the kind of significance that marks a standard as moral, then it must start from some conception of morality. In order for benign relativism to be distinguished from parametric universalism, then, a distinction must be drawn between, on the one hand, a conception of what can confer the kind of status that moral principles have and, on the other, a substantive standard on which all other moral principles must be based. There is certainly a distinction here, but it cannot be a sharp one, since no plausible account of the considerations that can confer moral status could leave it entirely open which principles could have that status. I take it, therefore, that the boundaries of "relativism" are inevitably somewhat blurred. It is sometimes unclear whether a given view should count as relativist or not, and there is a tendency in such cases to decide the matter by asking whether the view would have the kind of debunking effect that nonrelativists have generally found shocking. This is unfortunate because, among other things, it rules out in advance benign views of the kind that I believe many relativists have wanted to defend. I conclude that the crucial question should not be whether a view is or is not properly called relativist but, rather, what kind of foundation it takes moral standards to have and how much variation in such standards it allows for.

One familiar form of benign relativism is a nondebunking version of the "social convention" view mentioned above—a version that rejects the assumption that a grounding in social convention is not sufficient to give standards moral authority. A view of this kind holds that people have reason to accept a standard as of overriding importance if it is recognized as having this status in their shared way of life, a way of life that they have reason to value and want to continue. It also holds that different people have good reason to accept different moral requirements because they have reason to value following different ways of life.[9]

The expression "a way of life" can cover many different things. With respect to some of these, which might be called "customs and traditions," an account of the kind just described is quite convincing. Suppose that I attach importance to dressing in a certain way, expressing my respect for others through certain forms of address, following the dictates of a certain conception of family relations, observing certain holidays, and being familiar with a particular history and culture, because these are elements of the life I have grown up in and want to remain a part of. This fact provides me with (at least prima facie) reason for doing these things and for preferring them to other modes of life. Perhaps I might like to think that in some way this way of life is "better than all others," but there is no need for me to think this in order to have good reasons for following it.[10] Why think that there is some notion of "getting it right" which is what we should strive for in such matters? To take this seriously would be a sign of insecurity and weakness (as Nietzscheans might say) and a foolish desire for superiority (as the relativists would add).

This is as good an example as one can imagine of a clearly benign relativism that can be accepted without undermining the judgments to which it applies. Following one "way of life" (one set of customs and traditions) is something I have reason to do only because I am a person who was brought up in this particular way and for whom these customs therefore have a particular meaning. If I had been born in a different place and had a different life, then I would not have had this reason but would instead have had other, parallel reasons for following different customs. Acknowledging this dependence does not undermine the force that these customs have for me, or make following them merely a matter of preferences that I "just happen to have," since the facts in question—being a person who has a certain past and for whom these customs therefore have a certain meaning—provide me with substantive reasons for acting in this way. In order for customs and traditions to have this kind of force it is not necessary that they be followed by every member of the group in question. To have meaning as customs of that group it is enough that they be widely shared and valued. Once this is so, the reason just described for following these customs is available to anyone in the group. Others, who do not value these customs or wish to follow them, need not take them up.

Like any relativist thesis, this one involves a general claim about what people have reason to do, namely the claim that the fact that a certain action is required by the traditions of a group to which a person belongs and values belonging can constitute a strong prima facie reason for him or her to act in that way. This is not, however, a case of "parametric universalism." The reasons that a person has to follow the traditions that are part of his or her way of life depend on the particular meaning that those actions and that history have for that person. They need not derive this importance from the value of "tradition" in general, or from a principle specifying that one ought to follow the customs of one's group. Stated in this abstract way, reasons of the kind in question largely lose their force. (When people start talking in general terms about "the value of traditions" they are often on the verge of ceasing to care about their own.)

It is easy to see why defenders of a qualified moral relativism would want to adopt an account of this kind, holding that the authority of all moral standards derives from the fact that they are part of people's ways of life. Such a view seems attractive for at least two reasons. First, since the requirements of a person's way of life can provide reasons of great importance, this view offers what I called in Chapter 4 a substantive account of moral motivation. To the defenders of such an account, reasons not grounded in a person's way of life may seem, by contrast, implausibly formal and abstract (like the abstract values mentioned in the previous paragraph). Second, since a way of life is not simply an abstract value or a personal ideal but something shared with others, an account of this kind seems to capture the essentially interpersonal nature of moral reasons, and it can explain why acting contrary to these reasons can be the occasion for feelings of guilt and of the breaking of valuable ties with others.

But there are also problems with a moral relativism of this kind. First, as I noted above, the reasons provided by those things to which the "way of life" account most clearly applies—what I called customs and traditions—seem to be in an important sense optional. People who want to live in accordance with the customs and traditions of their group can have good reason to do so, but others in the same position who do not themselves want to live in this way are not open to rational criticism for failing to follow them. So such a view seems unable to account for the special force of moral requirements.

It might be replied that when someone who is in a position to share in a way of life fails to regard himself as having sufficient reason to do so, this has a kind of importance, from the point of view of those who do share this way of life, that is similar to the importance of failures to see the force of moral reasons. Those who fail to see these reasons as sufficient will seem, to the others, to be separated from them by an important gulf. As I observed in Chapter 4, however, there are many such gulfs, and a breach of this kind is not as significant as the one that separates us from those who reject, or fail to see the force of, any reason to be concerned with the justifiability of their conduct to us.

A second problem is that a grounding in a way of life does not seem able, by itself, to account for the third feature of moral standards mentioned above, that when an action is allowed by such standards, those who are affected by it therefore have sufficient reason to accept it without protest. The fact that an action is required by standards that are part of a way of life may give those who value that way of life reason to perform it, but it does not guarantee that others (in particular, members of the same society who object to its "way of life") have reason to accept the result. Opponents of relativism thus commonly appeal to the possibility that the accepted norms of a society might license conduct which involves treating people in horrible ways.[11] In response to such objections, Walzer has argued that genuine examples of this kind are unlikely to occur.[12] Any moral view that is likely to gain wide acceptance in a society for a significant length of time, he maintains, will at least have to pay lip service to the basic interests of all its members. This is not only required to secure the compliance of dominated groups, but is also necessary in order for the moral view to serve the function, from the point of view of the dominators, of making them feel that their position is justified. As a result, Walzer claims, while isolated elements of such a view may seem to license unconscionable actions, the view as a whole will provide a basis for arguing that these actions are unacceptable.

This claim may strike some as overly optimistic. But, whether it is correct or not, the fact that some defenders of qualified relativism feel called upon to make it indicates that they do not want to claim that just any set of norms that was widely accepted in a society would have the force of morality. They are, however, drawn to the idea of basing moral requirements on the "way of life" of a society for at least two reasons. First, as mentioned above, they see ways of life as providing a clear source of motivation, in comparison with which more universal demands seem implausibly abstract. Second, they believe that the range of principles that could, under the appropriate social conditions, have moral force is wider than they take many "universalists" to allow, and they are thus drawn to a conception of morality that would permit this greater variability.

I believe that my version of contractualism goes a long way toward meeting both of these concerns. The idea of justifiability to others provides a substantive account of the basis of moral motivation, and I would argue that this idea must be recognized in, and shape, any morally defensible way of life.[13] In the following section I will address the second concern, by arguing that the ostensibly "universalist" view that I have defended in preceding chapters can allow for a wider range of variation in standards of moral appraisal than might be supposed, and that it can in fact offer all that a defensible relativism could demand.

3. Contractualism and Relativism

According to the contractualist view I am presenting, an action that would be wrong in one context might be morally unobjectionable in another. This can be so for a number of different reasons. Consider first two ways in which differences in social conventions or in "ways of life" can make a difference in what is right or wrong according to contractualism.

The first class of cases consists of those in which there is a need for some principle to govern a particular kind of activity, but there are a number of different principles that would do this in a way that no one could reasonably reject. What I will call the Principle of Established Practices holds that in situations of this kind, if one of these (nonrejectable) principles is generally (it need not be unanimously) accepted in a given community, then it is wrong to violate it simply because this suits one's convenience. I believe that this higher-order principle is one that no one could reasonably reject, given the need for some principle to govern the activities in question. By contrast, it would be reasonable to reject any principle permitting people to violate one of these established practices whenever they wished to do so or preferred some alternative. It would also be reasonable to reject a principle that would require a practice to be unanimously accepted in order to be binding, since if unanimous agreement were required, practices would be very difficult to establish and the needs they serve would be very likely to go unmet. (It is not necessary to insist on unanimity in order to prevent excessively burdensome practices from being made binding, since the Principle of Established Practices supports only practices that themselves cannot reasonably be rejected.)[14]

To see how this principle works, consider as an example the need for personal privacy. People need to be able to conduct parts of their lives protected from the scrutiny of others whom they have not chosen to admit, and people generally need to have some forms of private communication. But even within a given society there are many different ways in which these needs can be provided for—different ways of defining the boundaries between "private" and "public" spaces, and different ways of defining the forms of communication that it is wrong for others to listen to or read without explicit consent. It therefore follows from the Principle of Established Practices that when some nonrejectable rules of privacy become generally accepted in a community it is then wrong to listen to, observe, or intrude on people in the ways that these rules forbid. These rules need not be unanimously accepted in order to become binding in this way. There may always be some dissenters, including perhaps some who believe (mistakenly) that the whole idea of privacy is a bad thing. This account can thus explain, what is puzzling in some versions of relativism, how the fact that a practice is generally but not unanimously accepted in a given society can make that practice morally binding on all. Cases that can be explained in this way are not, however, examples of relativism, but only of what I called parametric universalism, since the moral force of these variable practices is explained by appeal to a single substantive moral principle.

Something closer to relativism arises from the fact that under different social conditions people will have different generic reasons for rejecting proposed principles. Here again, personal privacy provides a good example. In different societies people have different reasons for wanting to protect parts of their lives and their communications from public view. Different societies may, for example, have very different prevailing ideas of personal dignity and of the aspects of one's life it is shameful or embarrassing to have others observe. Different systems of social relations also give rise to different needs for forms of private communication. In our society, for example, the particular forms that commercial transactions take give rise to particular needs for private communication (such as being able to reveal one's credit card number to a seller without making it known to others). And the particular importance that financial matters have for us gives us reason to want facts about our finances, such as our bank balances, incomes, and levels of indebtedness, not to be public knowledge. Here again, unanimity is not required: it is not necessary that everyone agree that it is humiliating to be observed by strangers when one is in a certain position or that it is important to be able to engage in a certain kind of confidential financial transaction. What matters, in deciding whether a principle can reasonably be rejected for application to a certain society, is whether, in that society, people in the positions that the principle describes have good reason to want a certain opportunity or a certain form of protection.

This emphasis on the reasons people have differentiates the view I am defending from objectionable forms of relativism, which claim that it is permissible for people in other societies to be treated in ways that we would not accept because they do not value privacy, or individual liberty, or even life, in the way that we do. Claims about what "they" actually think (especially claims about what *all* of "them" think) are usually questionable. But such appeals to alleged differences can also be objectionable in a deeper way. It often seems evident that, whatever "they," or some of them, may actually think (they may have become accustomed to harsh treatment, for example, and think it inevitable), they in fact have the same reasons that we do for wanting not to be treated in these ways. A relativism that fails to take these reasons seriously may be put forward as broad-minded and tolerant, but it in fact shows a lack of respect for the people in question. The view I am defending allows for this counterargument, because what it takes as fundamental is not what people actually think or want, but what they have reason to want.[15] But it is also true that what people have reason to want depends on the conditions in which they are placed, and among these conditions are facts about what most people around them want, believe, and expect.

In societies which have different forms of commerce, or in which different ideas of personal dignity prevail, people will generally have different reasons for wanting forms of protection of the sort that rules of privacy provide. When this is so, the sets of rules that no one could reasonably reject, and that therefore could become binding if generally accepted, will be different. Differences in the set of possible practices that no one could reasonably reject can also lead directly to different conclusions about which actions are wrong, without appeal to established conventions. It is possible that an action that would be forbidden by any system of rules of privacy that no one could reasonably reject for use in one society might be allowed by every system that it would be unreasonable to reject for use in a different society, where people had no need for protection of the kind that that action would interfere with. The conclusion that such an action would be wrong in the first society and not in the second can thus be reached without knowing which of the nonrejectable rules has become accepted in either society, and hence without any appeal to the Principle of Established Practices.

It is worth noting that there is no need here to appeal to a universal principle holding that it is wrong to violate someone's privacy. A general statement of this kind would say something true, but its content will be indeterminate until we know which more concrete principles people in a society of the kind in question have reason to reject and, in most cases, until we know which of these principles have become accepted in the particular society that is at issue. The general statement that violations of privacy are wrong merely sums up the conclusions arrived at in these other ways, and need not be invoked in order to explain why its particular instances are correct.[16]

Variations of the kind I have just described—variations in what is right or wrong that arise from variations in what people have reason to reject in different societies—may seem more like examples of genuine relativism than the cases I previously mentioned, and many examples that are cited as instances of relativism (or at least as counterexamples to "universalism") appear to fall into this class. Walzer has argued, for example, that answers to questions of justice depend on what he calls the "social meanings" of goods.[17] As he uses this term it covers a number of different things, but in a central class of cases it refers to the way in which social factors determine the reasons that people generally have for wanting to have a certain good or to be able to use it in a certain way.[18] The idea that it is humiliating to be observed by strangers while engaging in a certain activity, or that this undermines the personal significance of that activity, would be an example of "social meaning" in this sense, as would the fact that it is embarrassing, and can put one at an economic disadvantage, to have the details of one's finances generally known. If this is correct, then what I have argued above using the example of privacy amounts, in Walzer's terms, to the claim that answers to questions of right and wrong can depend on social meanings because these meanings can affect the reasons people have for rejecting certain principles.

I am not claiming that social meanings alone determine what is right and wrong. What I have done is, rather, to explain how these meanings can have moral force by placing them within a larger contractualist moral framework. What I have offered could therefore not plausibly be called a relativist view. As I have argued above, however, any benign form of relativism must offer some explanation of how varying judgments about what is right or wrong can all have moral force. The account I have offered has the advantage of explaining how, in different societies, different conclusions about what is right can be justified as moral conclusions in the narrowest sense of that term. It does this without presenting these judgments as deriving from any substantive universal principle. It is certainly a benign account, and, though not relativist, it explains how standards of right and wrong can have a kind of variability that relativists espouse.

4. Relativism and Morality in the Broader Sense

The possibility of a broader range of variation in standards of moral appraisal emerges when we take into account the fact that the term 'moral' is commonly used to cover much more than the morality of right and wrong that contractualism seeks to characterize. Many of the forms of variation that anthropologists have studied, and that may have shocked the moral sensibilities of Europeans when they were first reported, involve such things as variations in sexual practices and in marriage and kinship structures. These are part of "morality" only in the broader sense, and some might say that they do not raise moral issues at all. But, since these practices are often cited as examples of moral relativism, it is worth examining the possibilities for benign relativism within morality in this broader sense.

As a preliminary matter, however, I should note two ways in which moral values in this broad sense are not independent of morality in the narrower sense that I have mainly been discussing. First, negatively, insofar as the forms of conduct that these values deal with involve relations with and treatment of other people, what they can require or permit is limited by morality in the narrow sense, which I have characterized as the requirements of justifiability to others. Sexual practices or family systems that involve demeaning or enslaving others, for example, are morally excluded. Second, positively, part of what moral values in the broader sense require one to do may also be required simply by the morality of right and wrong. For example, following the model provided above by the example of privacy, one could say that any society needs to have some systematic way of providing for the care, nurturing, and education of children, and for the care of the aged and infirm. There are many ways of doing this—many ways of assigning responsibility to fathers, mothers, siblings, children, teachers, and professional caregivers—that satisfy the "negative" requirements just mentioned of morality in the narrow sense.[19] If, then, one of these acceptable systems is generally accepted in a society, it follows from the Principle of Established Practices that it is wrong for members of that society to fail to fulfill the duties they are assigned by this system.

But not all the actions required by moral values in the broad sense can be derived in this way. Ideals of personal honor and excellence, for example, include more than what we owe to others. And even when what is required by one of these moral values coincides with what we owe to others, that value may not be fully accounted for by this fact. Our moral reasons for respecting other people's privacy seem to be fully explained by an account of the kind I have sketched above, but, as I argued in Chapter 4, our reasons for being a good parent or son or teacher go beyond what can be explained on this basis. The suggestion, then, is that within this broader realm there are many diverse values that are worthy of respect, and that a plurality of standards of appraisal may arise from this fact. Here are three classes of possible examples.

Different conceptions of patriotism include different ideas of the level of sacrifice that individuals are required to make for the good or the honor of their country. Patriotism can, of course, be understood simply in terms of obligations to one's fellow citizens, but what I have in mind here are conceptions that go beyond this. Someone could regard an ideal of patriotism as a moral standard, and reproach himself for not living up to its requirements, even though these requirements go beyond those of the narrower morality of right and wrong (as long, of course, as what it requires is consistent with morality in this narrower sense). People who accept such a conception of patriotism and fall short of what it demands of them may feel guilty—not for letting their fellow citizens down, but for not valuing their country sufficiently or not responding appropriately to this value.

Second, as Adam Smith's discussion of the promise to a highwayman showed, a conception of honor can require that a promise be kept even if, because it was made under duress, one would not wrong the promisee by breaking it. Similarly, an ideal of honor that emphasizes the value of personal strength could require one not to give in to threats from a blackmailer or terrorist, and a person who held such an ideal would feel morally compromised if he yielded to this kind of pressure. We can understand such an outlook, and even find it admirable, even if we ourselves hold a more pragmatic attitude that sets higher value on the protection of innocent lives.

Third, different conceptions of family ties may not only require different levels of sacrifice of one's personal goals for the sake of one's family, but may also attach different kinds of significance to particular family connections. How important, for example, is the distinction between a second and a third cousin or between a second cousin and an unrelated person, when one is deciding whether one may marry the person or whether one must make some sacrifice in order to protect him from bankruptcy? Different conceptions of the family might both be worthy of respect and adoption yet answer these questions quite differently.

The possibility of a plurality of such moral ideals raises two questions, both of which concern how someone who holds an ideal should view others who do not hold it. First, if someone who holds a certain ideal concludes that others, who have not adopted it, cannot be faulted for not doing so or for not living up to its requirements, then it seems to follow that in his own case, too, the reasons that the ideal provides must be based, ultimately, merely on his personal preference or on a choice which could, without fault, have been made the other way. This seems to trivialize the authority of an ideal. People who are committed to ideals of patriotism or honor, for example, do not normally regard these as mere matters of personal preference. While this first question concerns the implications that others' lack of reasons for adopting an ideal have for one's own reasons for following it, the second question concerns the attitude one should have toward these other people. What is the significance, for one's relations with them, of the fact that they do not share this value? The first question arises from what I called, in Chapter 1, the universality of reason judgments; the second is a question of the importance of these ideals, analogous to the question of the importance of moral reasons in the narrow sense that I discussed in Chapter 4, Section 4.

In response to the first of these questions, a defender of the kind of pluralism about ideals that I am considering could argue as follows. There are many ideals that are worthy of adoption and adherence. Sometimes a person may adopt one of these ideals rather than another because he or she finds it attractive and suitable. Some people may, for example, be more suited by temperament to ideals that emphasize personal strength and independence, others to ideals that emphasize the value of group membership and close connections with others. Often, however, the ideals that a person adopts depend on matters of chance, such as which ideal she happens to encounter or which ideal is followed in the group she grows up in or by someone she meets and particularly admires. The fact that the ideals people hold depend on factors of this kind does not trivialize their reasons for adhering to them by making these reasons merely a matter of preference or of quirks of individual psychology or of contingent social circumstances. When there are good reasons for taking one's ideal to be worthy of respect, these also provide good reasons for adhering to it even if other contingent factors determine which ideal one will adopt, and even if other ideals would also have been worthy of adherence.

Turning to the second question, how should a person who lives by an ideal regard others who give it no weight in their lives? How is someone who greatly values some particular conception of patriotism, or honor, or family ties, to regard a person who ignores patriotism or honor, so understood, or treats cousins like strangers? If, as I have argued, these others may hold equally worthy ideals of their own, we should not take them to be morally deficient because they do not follow ours. Someone who greatly values patriotism, for example, could rightly be critical of another person who, simply out of laziness or self-indulgence, cannot be bothered even to think about what is worthwhile. But he should still be able to respect another person who is not patriotic because she is strongly committed to an ideal of individual independence which she is willing to defend, for herself and others, at great personal cost. To be sure, even if such people should not look down on each other, they are still separated in an important way by their commitments. But this is, as I have argued, a different and less serious kind of gulf than separates us from those who are unmoved by the requirements of justifiability to others. People who are separated in this way value different things, but can still recognize each other as valuable.

This form of pluralism entails no suspension of judgment about the merits of others' ideals. On the contrary, it rests firmly on judgments of their worth. Much more would need to be said to defend judgments of this kind about the value of particular ideals. Some conceptions of patriotism, for example, may not be worthy of adoption because of their excessively nationalistic character, and some are even incompatible with the concern that we owe to others. Some conceptions of family ties, also, may be permissible to adopt but may not be backed by reasons that are adequate to make them moral ideals. I have not presented any ideals in sufficient detail to settle such questions. What I have been calling attention to is, rather, a possibility. It seems to me extremely likely that there are multiple, incompatible ideals that are worthy of adoption, and it is plausible to suppose that some claims often called relativist are in fact better understood on this pluralist model, as claiming that the range of ideals that are worthy of adoption and respect is wider than is usually thought.

Moral ideals of this kind are held by individuals, not groups. If we say that the members of some society—the citizens of ancient Sparta, for example—subscribed to an ideal of solidarity that required them to make great personal sacrifices for the common good, this can only be a generalization about the commitments of individual members of that society. As such, it is likely to be only roughly true. In any society of any size, over a significant period, there is bound to be some disagreement about such a question, and the fact that many, even most, members of a society hold a certain ideal provides in itself no basis for criticizing other members of that group for not living up to this standard. There are, as I have mentioned, ways in which values that are widely but not unanimously held in a given society can generate obligations binding on all members of that group. Rawls's principle of fairness provides one way: if an ideal of sacrifice for the common good is fair, then a person who has voluntarily accepted the benefits of others' compliance with this ideal can be obligated to sacrifice in turn.[20] It can also be wrong to violate the reasonable expectations of others. For example, if in my society members of a family are normally expected to support each other in certain ways then, even if I have not benefited from this practice, it could be wrong for me to allow others to suffer losses as a result of their expectation that I would follow it. I ought at least to warn them that I cannot be counted on in this way.[21] But, taken by itself, the fact that most people in a society hold a certain ideal provides no basis for criticizing other members of that society for not following it.

Facts about the ideals widely held in a group can be relevant in a different way, however, not because they establish certain ideals as morally authoritative, but because they affect the range of ideals that are available to individuals. As I have already mentioned, it would in many cases make no sense for a person to adopt a way of life shaped by a certain ideal unless there were others around who shared that ideal and formed a community within which it could be practiced. Ideals of friendship or family life, for example, cannot be realized without others who share them. In addition, the kind of society a person lives in, and the moral ideas that are recognized and embodied in that society, can make a difference in how easy or difficult it is for that person to see the force of certain reasons. This can affect the kind of criticism and blame that individuals are subject to for failing to live up to moral requirements, even if it does not alter the fact that it is wrong for them not to do so.

Consider, for example, a conscientious person living in a society of great inequality. Such a person may have sympathy for others and try hard to treat them decently, at least within the constraints of the current practices of his society, yet may fail to appreciate how wrong these practices are. He might, for example, understand, at least to some degree, the objections that the worse off have to these practices, yet believe that they could not reasonably be rejected, because he does not see what alternatives there could be, or because he overestimates the sacrifice that would be involved in giving them up.

In such a situation all of the following might be true. First, the practices in question are morally objectionable, and those who are victimized by them have a justified complaint. Second, although there may be little that an individual could do to alter this situation, if there is, nonetheless, *something* that he could do, such as making known to others that their practices are unjust, looking harder for alternatives, or modifying his personal conduct to avoid taking advantage of these unjust practices, then the person acts wrongly in not doing these things and is open to moral criticism on that account. But, third, this criticism may be qualified (though not eliminated) if a person's failure to do these things, despite conscientious efforts to "be moral," is due to the difficulty of appreciating the moral facts, given his situation. Such a case would be like that of the woman in Susan Wolf's example as I interpreted it, who fails to see a reason to buy a gift for her friend, despite conscientious efforts to understand what being a good friend involves.[22] In neither case is the fault removed by the agent's conscientiousness, but it is made into a different fault.

This line of thought may underlie the reluctance that some have to pass moral judgment on agents in distant societies, a reluctance that is sometimes taken to support relativistic views. As I have just interpreted it, however, it is not a form of relativism. In cases of the kind I have mentioned, uniform moral standards are applied to the practices of different societies and to the conduct of individuals in those societies. The only variability is in the kind of culpability that agents have for failing to live up to these standards.

This chapter began with the question of whether, on the view I am defending, moral principles are universal. My answer can now be summarized as follows. The view of morality I am presenting can be seen as including three concentric domains. The central core contains those judgments of right and wrong that hold everywhere. If a principle permitting a certain kind of action is one that people in any society could reasonably reject, then the judgment that that action is wrong falls in this central domain. The judgment that it is wrong to kill or torture someone simply because you do not like the group to which he or she belongs falls into this class, for example. Beyond this is the domain of judgments of right and wrong that depend on reasons for rejection that people have only under certain social conditions. Some judgments about the wrongfulness of invasions of privacy are examples. Judgments included in these first two domains are judgments of right and wrong in exactly the same sense. They differ only in the ways in which their grounds depend on social conditions. This does not seem to me to be an important difference; I mention it only in order to give a clear account of the ways in which my view allows moral assessments to vary.

Judgments in the third domain differ in a more significant way, since they are based not on the idea of what we owe to others but on the appeal of particular values that we may share. If, as seems plausible, there is a plurality of values within the range of morality in the broader sense that are worthy of respect and, under the right conditions, of adherence, then these values may support mutually incompatible standards of conduct.

There is, however, a question about the degree to which these standards of conduct can be called "moral." I mentioned above three features that standards properly called "moral" would have. The first two were that moral standards express requirements that agents have reason to regard as extremely important and have reason to feel guilty for violating. For those who hold an ideal of the kind I have described, the standards it entails are likely to have these features. The possible difficulty concerns the third feature, which is that the violation of moral standards provides others with reason for resentment and indignation, and that when an action is licensed by the relevant moral standards this gives others reason to accept it without protest. If someone acts contrary to an ideal that he or she accepts, but in a way that does not violate other moral requirements, this does not give others who do not share that ideal grounds for resentment or indignation (except perhaps at the hypocrisy of the agent). More important, insofar as the fact that an action is licensed or required by a person's ideal ensures that others have no ground for complaint against it, this will be so only because that ideal incorporates the requirements of morality in the narrow sense. With respect to others who share the ideal, things may be different. Perhaps they have grounds for complaint if someone who purports to share this ideal with them falls away from this commitment. If so, then the fact that an action is licensed by the standards entailed by an ideal will guarantee that others who share it will have no grounds for objection of this kind. It seems, then, that the standards entailed by ideals of the kind I have been discussing will have the third feature I ascribed to moral standards only with respect to others who share the ideal in question. This illustrates again the important difference between morality in the narrow sense and this broader range of values.

5. Disagreement about Right and Wrong

In the preceding sections, in considering possible variation in moral standards, I have treated the morality of right and wrong, understood as my contractualist theory describes it, as a fixed point. The forms of variability I have considered have been confined, on the one hand, to possible variations in what is required by the morality of right and wrong as I have described it, and, on the other, to the possibility of a variety of moral ideals that are consistent with the requirements of morality in this sense but go beyond them. In this section and the next I will consider the possibility of disagreement about this central part of morality and about the account I have offered of it. Examining these forms of disagreement will also lead to some reflections on the nature of the inquiry that I have been conducting in this book.

To claim that an action is morally wrong is to claim, at least, that it is forbidden by standards that there is good reason to regard as requirements whose violation merits serious criticism. Disagreement about right and wrong can thus take at least two forms. People can disagree about the content of the relevant standards—about which actions are right and which are wrong—and they can also disagree about the nature of the authority that these standards have—about what makes certain standards ones to which this kind of importance should be attached.[23] Often, of course, views that disagree in one of these ways will disagree in the other as well. Someone who held a teleological version of act utilitarianism, for example, might disagree in both of these ways with the contractualist view I have presented. Such a person would believe that only those actions are right that lead to at least as great a sum of happiness as any available alternative, and might hold that this is the proper standard because only the goal of the greatest happiness can provide the authoritative backing that moral principles require. By contrast, someone who thought that the act utilitarian formula was the proper standard for the appraisal of actions because it was the only principle that no one, if suitably motivated, could reasonably reject would disagree with my account of right and wrong in the first of these two ways but not in the second.

It is often unclear how much disagreement of these two kinds there actually is, since people's understanding of the moral standards they recognize is generally inchoate, and their conception of the basis of the authority of these principles may be even less clear. Some people have definite views about the ultimate ground of moral requirements—for example, that it must lie in some form of divine authority. Others, while they believe (or hope) that there are good reasons for accepting certain moral principles as overriding requirements, may be quite uncertain about what these reasons are. This uncertainty is a primary motive for philosophical inquiry of the kind I have undertaken in this book. (To those in the former group, who feel they already know what the basis of morality is, such inquiry may seem unnecessary.)

Inquiry of this kind has two potentially conflicting aims. On the one hand, its aim is interpretive: beginning from the phenomena of our moral experience, it attempts to give a clearer picture both of the values and standards that make up what we commonly recognize as morality and of the reasons that we are invoking when we regard these as authoritative. On the other hand, its aim is critical, since it must also address the question of whether these reasons have the force claimed for them and, more broadly, whether there are other reasons, perhaps better ones, on which overriding standards might be based. We may begin our inquiry with the presumption that morality, as we intuitively understand it, has something like the authority it claims, but this presumption is open to challenge. These two questions correspond to two ways in which "morality," the subject of our inquiry, can be identified. On the one hand, more concretely, we may identify "morality" with what is required by that particular source of authority that we are (perhaps inchoately) aware of as standing behind the standards of conduct we commonly recognize as moral. On the other, more abstractly, we may take morality to be what is required by those principles that there is most reason (whatever these reasons may be) to take as ultimate standards of conduct the violation of which merits serious criticism.

These two aims may seem to lead, at least potentially, in conflicting directions: one toward a careful description of what we now believe, the other toward a more critical investigation of the reasons that there are for accepting one set of standards or another. In practice, however, two facts that I have mentioned about the standpoint from which we begin our inquiry draw these two questions together. The first is that we are often not very clear about exactly what the reasons are that we take to support the moral standards we accept. The second is that we are likely, nonetheless, to be committed, at least initially, to the idea that these reasons, whatever they are, must be good ones. As a result of these two facts, the process of deciding what reasons we have in mind when we regard moral standards as authoritative is influenced by our assessments of the merits of various candidate reasons. Determining what we believe is in most cases a matter of deciding what *to* believe.[24]

Even if these questions are to a degree separable, I have tried, in this book, to address them both. The contractualist view I have presented appeals to me because it offers an account of a central part of morality that fits with our, or at least my, moral experience—that is to say, with my understanding both of the content of moral requirements and of the reasons supporting their authority. I have also argued that these reasons are good reasons—that it makes sense to give this part of morality, understood in the way I propose, the importance and the priority over other values that it is commonly supposed to have.

Such an inquiry can be seen as a quest for critical self-understanding, but it is not a solipsistic undertaking. I have started from my own moral experience, but with the presumption that there is a "we" of which it is typical—that neither the content of my ideas of right and wrong, nor my sense of their normative force, nor my judgment as to what counts as a good reason for taking them seriously, is idiosyncratic. This presumption is not unwarranted, since my ideas of the force of moral requirements and of their content have not been formed in isolation, but through interaction and conversation with many other people. On this basis, then, I offer the results of my inquiry and invite readers to conduct their own, to see whether they are led to the same results.

One always hopes that parallel investigations of this kind will lead to consensus, but it is possible that the effect will instead be to expose greater disagreement. Like the presumption that the reasons we take to support our moral principles are good ones, the presumption that when we make judgments of right and wrong we have in mind the same thing, backed by the same reasons, is rebuttable, and may be overturned by the process of making clear what these reasons are. As the idea of justifiability to others is clarified and expounded, some may recognize it as what is basic to their ideas of right and wrong, but others may become more and more convinced that what *they* regard as morality is quite different—that it must have a religious basis, for example, or be grounded in a notion of maximum welfare.

One thing that can indicate this kind of divergence is a difference in people's ideas about the unity of morality. I have mentioned repeatedly, as one conclusion of my analysis, that what we commonly call morality is motivationally diverse. I have offered an account of the motivational basis of a central part of morality, what we owe to each other, but argued that this does not include everything that might be seen as a moral requirement. Others may be convinced that morality in the broad sense has more unity than this view allows. Some may hold, for example, that sexual relations between adults of the same sex are forbidden by requirements that have the same authority as prohibitions against deception and murder. If the parties to this disagreement are not misunderstanding their own moral views, then we disagree not merely about sexual morality but also about the kind of reasons that support even those moral requirements that we both recognize. In this case, our attitudes toward these requirements will be like those of two people who agree that it would be wrong to break one's word in a certain situation but have different views about what the objection to doing this would be, one of them seeing this objection as arising from "what we owe to each other" while the other sees it as based on an ideal of personal honor.

Unlike the judgments of people who disagree about what is required by certain standards, or about which standards can claim the kind of authority that would be provided by a particular class of reasons, the judgments of people who disagree in the way just described do not make conflicting claims about a single substantive subject matter, *morality*. They disagree about morality only in the abstract sense in which 'morality' is understood to refer to those principles, whatever they may be, that there is most reason (of whatever kind) to accept as ultimate standards of conduct, the violation of which merits serious criticism.

When we find ourselves in this kind of disagreement with someone, the first question to ask is the extent to which the reasons on which their conception of morality is based are good reasons. Even if we do not have reason to accept that conception as our ultimate standard of conduct, its aspirations may be worthy of respect. A second question is the relation between the content of their moral view and that of ours. To what extent do these views overlap or converge? As I mentioned in Section 2 above, there are reasons to expect that any set of standards that are generally accepted as overriding by members of a group will at least pay lip service to the central interests of those to whom they are supposed to apply. Thus, even if a moral view is not itself contractualist, there are, as a practical matter, pressures on it that work to exclude principles that those who are supposed to accept the view could reasonably reject. In addition, since there are good reasons to value relations with others that presuppose requirements of justifiability, conceptions of how best to live are likely to recognize these requirements in some form, even if they do not take the idea of justifiability to others as basic. Many religious moralities, for example, recognize some version of the Golden Rule as a derivative principle.

Differences are likely to remain, however, and a third question, in the light of these differences, is the significance for our relations with these other people of the fact that they fail to recognize the force of reasons that we see as supporting the most central part of morality. Consider, for example, a person who does not recognize the general requirements of what we owe to each other, but who nonetheless is guided by a personal ideal of honor, and by standards of kindness, courtesy, and restraint toward us, which he regards as forms of *noblesse oblige*. Such a person might present no threat to us and might be a dependable participant in cooperative arrangements. Nonetheless, our relations with him would be affected, and some relations excluded, by this particular outlook. The question to be asked in each case is exactly what these effects would be. These questions are comparative versions of what I called in Chapter 4 the question of the importance of moral reasons. As I mentioned above, similar questions arise about the relations among people who hold moral ideals that are consistent with the morality of right and wrong as I have described it, but go beyond it in different ways. Their acceptance of different ideals marks a gulf between them. But the question is more serious in the cases presently at issue, since what is in question in these cases is whether and how we value each other, not merely what other values we agree on.

6. Disagreement and Skepticism

A further question is whether the fact that others disagree in this way should lead us to modify the claims we make for our own moral views. The fact of moral disagreement is sometimes cited in arguments for a form of relativism that is more skeptical than the ones I have been discussing in this chapter. These arguments start from the observation that serious people, who are well informed and do not appear to be making logical errors, have arrived at stable opinions about right and wrong that are incompatible with ours. What ground is there, the relativists ask, for thinking that we, rather than they, have "got it right"? It is more plausible, they say, to conclude that there is nothing there to be "right" about—that is, no "objective truth" about morality.[25]

The view I have been presenting in this book may seem particularly vulnerable to this argument. On that view, moral judgments and claims about the authority of these judgments are claims about what reasons people have. As I said in Chapter 1, the objectivity of such claims lies not in the metaphysical reality of some subject matter, independent of us, that they describe, but rather in the fact that there is such a thing as thinking about such questions in the right way—a process that yields stable results in which we have no good reason not to have confidence. But if different inquirers, who seem to be thinking about matters in the right way, arrive at incompatible, but quite stable, conclusions about the morality of right and wrong, this might seem to call that confidence into question, thus casting doubt on this claim to objectivity.

The disagreement from which this argument begins can be understood in more than one way, however. It is possible that the parties involved are best understood as having conflicting views about the same substantive question—for example, about what we owe to each other in the sense I have been describing. I will return to this possibility in a moment. Another possibility, however, is that they are best understood as valuing quite different things. This is in fact the interpretation suggested by J. L. Mackie's formulation of this skeptical argument. He writes: "In short, the argument from relativity has some force simply because the actual variations in moral codes are more readily explained by the hypothesis that they reflect ways of life than by the hypothesis that they represent perceptions, most of them seriously inadequate and badly distorted, of objective values."[26]

This interpretive hypothesis is very similar to the possibility I put forward in the previous section: that what are often described as conflicting moral views do not represent conflicting opinions about the same subject matter but, rather, commitments to quite distinct ultimate values. It is not surprising that there should be disagreements of this kind. After all, the values that people (ourselves included) hold depend to a great extent on their particular experience, history, and circumstances. All of us are likely to consider, as possible values, things that others around us value, and are likely to neglect other possibilities. Moreover, when something is of obvious value, such as human life or human freedom, we are likely to accept the interpretation of this value that others around us accept, at least until some problem or challenge forces us to question this interpretation. Custom, loyalty, and the comforting support of like-minded others direct our attention toward taking some considerations as reasons and deter us from considering other reasons that would conflict with or undermine them.

This explanation of moral disagreement does not, however, lead to a skeptical conclusion about our moral beliefs in the way that the relativist argument suggests. The major premise of that argument as I stated it is the general thesis that if well-informed, conscientious people, who inquire into a certain subject in what appears to be the right way, consistently arrive at incompatible judgments about it, then this supports the conclusion that judgments about this subject are not of a kind that can be objectively true or false. This general thesis is itself questionable, but whatever one may think about it, it does not apply to the phenomena of moral disagreement as we have just interpreted them. On that interpretation, people's conflicting moral views are not the result of sustained inquiry into the same subject matter. They represent conflicting judgments "about the same thing" only insofar as they are taken as answers to the abstract question mentioned above, namely "What principles is there most reason (of whatever kind) to accept as ultimate standards of conduct?" But this question is not one that most people have inquired into very thoroughly, for the reasons mentioned in the previous paragraph. Even people who have considered critically the reasons supporting their own values may not have considered the merits of alternatives, or even regarded them as alternatives. Since, therefore, the conditions stated in the antecedent of the general thesis are not fulfilled in most cases that are cited as examples of moral disagreement, a skeptical conclusion about the objectivity of moral beliefs does not follow.

There are, of course, some cases in which it at least appears that these conditions are fulfilled—cases in which people who seem to have much the same conceptions of right and wrong nonetheless disagree, even after careful reflection, about which things are wrong. When we are faced with such a case, there are a number of possibilities to consider, and we need to decide which of them there is most reason to believe. One possibility, which I will set aside for the moment, is that we have misdescribed the case, and it really is of the kind I have just been discussing, in which the parties are viewing the matter from the point of view of quite different moral conceptions. Other possibilities are:

(1) One party is mistaken.
(2) The other party is mistaken.
(3) Both are mistaken.
(4) Neither is mistaken, because there is nothing to be mistaken about in cases of this kind.

The plausibility of (4) depends greatly on the breadth of the category "cases of this kind." If this is meant to include all questions of right and wrong, then (4) is very unlikely to be the most plausible alternative, since there are many questions of right and wrong that seem clearly to have correct answers. There is no doubt, for example, that murder, rape, torture, and slavery are wrong. No system of rules could be a system that people had reason to accept as an ultimate, normally overriding standard of conduct if it permitted these practices. So, even if we are at present unable to decide which of the parties to some moral disagreement is mistaken, it is difficult to see how we could have reason to think that (4), understood in this broad way, was the best description of the case rather than (1), (2), or (3).

Alternative (4) may be more plausible when the class of "cases of this kind" is interpreted more narrowly. But one would then need some explanation of how this particular class of moral questions differed from others in a way that made them lack determinate answers, rather than merely being very difficult to settle. One possible explanation would be that although there are some requirements that must be included in any code of behavior that people could have reason to regard as having the importance and authority normally attached to morality, there are other standards, commonly regarded as moral, of which this is not true. These could thus be said to be matters about which there is no single morally correct answer.[27] The resulting distinction would seem to coincide with the distinction, discussed above, between what we owe to each other and other moral ideals that are consistent with but not required by it.

There are, however, many persistent disagreements about questions that at least appear to fall within morality in the narrow sense. Questions such as abortion, the treatment of nonhuman animals, standards of social justice, and the extent of our duties to aid others might be cited as examples. Some disagreements over these issues may be best understood on the model discussed above, as reflecting basically different conceptions of the basis of moral standards. (This interpretation may be particularly plausible in the case of some disagreements about abortion and about nonhuman animals.) But this is certainly not true of all such disagreements. There are bound to be persistent disagreements about what we owe to each other and, specifically, about which principles can reasonably be rejected. I do not regard this as grounds for skepticism, but I want to say something about the kind of disagreement that this is, and why it should not be surprising.

Disagreement about what we owe to each other—about the morality of right and wrong as I have described it—is disagreement about the force of certain reasons. Sometimes, as in the case of some disagreements about abortion, or about the treatment of nonhuman animals, it is disagreement about the range of cases in which we have reason to be constrained by the requirement of justifiability to others. In other cases it is disagreement about whether certain principles could reasonably be rejected—that is to say, about the strength of various generic reasons for and against these principles.

Morality is not the only subject in which there are persistent disagreements about reasons. Disagreements about which of several competing scientific hypotheses is best supported by the available evidence, for example, often persist even among inquirers who are experts in the field. Further evidence may determine which of these hypotheses was correct, but the disagreement about reasons—about which hypothesis the more limited body of evidence in fact supported—may continue, especially when the inquirers are committed to different scientific or methodological programs. Persistent disagreements about right and wrong have a similar character: they are disagreements about how complex sets of conflicting reasons should be understood and reconciled, and they are most likely to persist when people's differing interests and commitments lead them, in different ways, to concentrate on certain of these reasons (and on certain ways of understanding them) and to neglect others.

According to contractualism, disagreements about the wrongness of an action often come down to disagreements about the relative strength of the reasons that people in various positions have for rejecting principles that would license or permit such actions. Disagreement thus often arises from the fact that we often do not have, or do not bear in mind, a sufficiently clear idea of how people occupying different positions would be affected by different moral requirements. Partly as a result, we are apt to exaggerate the cost to us of departures from what we are accustomed to expect, and to minimize the costs to others that may make it reasonable to demand such changes.

This should not be taken to suggest that moral disagreement arises only, or even primarily, when our judgment is distorted by self-interest. Self-interest is an important factor, but moral disagreements persist even where people's personal interests do not seem to be at stake. Disagreement about abortion and euthanasia, for example, is intense even among people who are not themselves likely to benefit from or be harmed by these practices. Disagreement about these issues can sometimes be explained by the distorting effect of loyalties and commitments, which operate in a way that is similar to self-interest. When one has taken a position in such a controversy, one is often moved by a kind of partisanship that leads one to regard good arguments for the other side as a kind of personal defeat. This inclines one to look hardest for considerations that would support the view that one has already taken to be correct, and makes it difficult to consider in the right way all the reasons involved: that is to say, to consider them with the care that would be most likely to lead to a correct understanding of the issue.

Partisanship aside, however, disagreement is unsurprising in many cases simply because of the intellectual difficulty of the underlying issues. If our grasp of moral truths resulted from something analogous to direct perception, then disagreement among competent and un-biased moral judges might be surprising. But this is not a plausible model. Arriving at answers to difficult moral questions does not gener-ally involve the construction of long chains of complex and ingenious argument, of the kind that occur in mathematics, but it does demand both imagination and careful, sometimes subtle, analysis. It is often quite obvious that a certain consideration is morally significant, but far from clear what form this significance takes. For example, it seems clear that the number of people affected by an action is sometimes relevant in determining whether it would be the right thing to do, but also clear that some appeals to aggregative benefits are illegitimate. As we saw in Chapter 5, however, it is very difficult to find an account of the force of aggregative considerations, and of their interaction with other factors, that yields satisfactory answers in all these cases. Careful analysis is needed in such cases to identify relevant distinctions, and imagination is required in order to think of possible solutions and of cases in which these proposals can be tested.

Particularly if they have not engaged in this kind of reflection, people often have differing, and perhaps flawed, understandings of important moral notions that serve as starting points for, and fixed points within, their moral thinking. One of the main ways in which theoretical reflection can advance our understanding, and help to over-come moral disagreement, is by providing a more adequate under-standing of these notions. I argued in Chapter 6, for example, that the Forfeiture View, which I take to be widely influential even if it is not explicitly held, is an inadequate conception of how considerations of choice and responsibility figure in moral justification, and I offered what I believe is a more adequate account, based on the value of choice. Inquiry of this kind may not yield systematic theories or novel principles that give clear directives about what to do in difficult cases. It may even make some decisions more difficult, or at least more complex, by dislodging overly simple understandings of the relevant moral considerations. But it is not an insignificant form of progress, and it is, I believe, the form of progress that philosophical reflection is most likely to provide.

7. Conclusion

Many of the arguments in this book have been aimed at opening up space for this kind of reexamination of basic normative ideas. In Chapter 1, I argued that we should see reasons, rather than desires, as basic, and I called attention to the fact that practical reasoning based on reasons has a more complex structure than the ideas of desire and desire fulfillment alone can provide. In Chapter 2, taking advantage of this structure, I questioned the idea that being valuable is always a matter of being "to be promoted," and argued that values in general, and the value of human life in particular, should be understood in terms of more complex sets of reasons to act, and react, in various ways. In Part II, I have argued that what we commonly call "morality" is motivationally diverse, and I have offered an account of one central component of morality, "what we owe to each other," based on a particular idea of justifiability and reasonable rejection.

These claims are controversial. But even if all of them, including my contractualist account of the morality of right and wrong, were accepted, this would not exclude moral disagreement, since all that I have said leaves many questions unanswered. I have argued for a pluralist view of value in general, but I have not offered a full positive account of any, let alone all, particular values. To do this would require much more than one book. I have offered a very general account of one part of morality, but even this account is incomplete. I have not, for example, offered a systematic account of how reasons for rejecting proposed principles are to be formulated and their strength assessed. On the contrary, I have argued, in Chapter 5 and elsewhere, that these reasons cannot all be understood in terms of well-being, and I have expressed doubt that any systematic account of such reasons can be found.

The reasons we have to treat others only in ways that could be justified to them underlie the central core of morality, and are presupposed by all the most important forms of human relationship. These reasons require us to strive to find terms of justification that others could not reasonably reject. But we are not in a position to say, once and for all, what these terms should be. Working out the terms of moral justification is an unending task.

Williams on Internal and External Reasons

In this appendix I will discuss Bernard Williams' well-known claim that all reasons for action have subjective conditions (in his terms, that "all external reason claims are false").[1] Williams' influential arguments have been in the background of much of the preceding discussion. Considering them explicitly will provide an opportunity to draw together and illustrate some of the points made in Chapter 1, as well as to raise some issues relevant to the questions of value that are the subject of Chapter 2.

Williams distinguishes between two ways of interpreting a statement that a person "has a reason to φ" (where φ stands in for some verb of action). According to the first interpretation, the statement implies that the agent has some motive—that there is something that matters to him or her—that will be served or furthered by φ-ing. If the person in fact has no such motive, then on this interpretation the claim is false. The second interpretation includes no such condition, so on this interpretation it can be true that A has a reason to φ even though φ-ing would not serve or further any aim or value that matters to the agent. Williams refers to reason claims under the first interpretation as "internal reason statements" and refers to those under the second as "external." He illustrates this distinction with reference to the case of Owen Wingrave.

People do say things that ask to be taken in the external interpretation. In James' story of Owen Wingrave, from which Britten made an opera, Owen's family urge on him the necessity and importance of his joining the army, since all his male ancestors were soldiers, and family pride requires him to do the same. Owen Wingrave has no motivation to join the army at all, and all his desires lead in another direction: he hates everything about military life and what it means.

His family might have expressed themselves by saying that *there was a reason for Owen to join the army*. Knowing that there was nothing in Owen's [subjective motivational set] S which would lead, through deliberative reasoning, to his doing this would not make them withdraw the claim or admit that they had made it under a misapprehension. They mean it in an external sense.[2]

By a person's "subjective motivational set, S" Williams means what I referred to above as that person's desires in a broad sense, including, he says, such things as "dispositions of evaluation, patterns of emotional reaction, personal loyalties, and various projects, as they might be called, embodying commitments of the agent."[3] Williams holds that a claim that an agent has reason to φ, under the internal interpretation, can be true only if there is a "sound deliberative route" leading from elements in that agent's S to the conclusion that there is something to be said for φ-ing. His doctrine that the only valid claims that a person has a reason for action are internal reasons claims is thus naturally seen as a modified form of Hume's famous doctrine that "reason is and ought only to be the slave of the passions."[4]

Williams presents his doctrine as a modification of a simple "sub-Humean" model in two respects. First, he takes the range of possible elements of a person's subjective motivational set (indicated by the list I quoted above) to be broader than the class of desires in the normal sense of that term. Second, Williams' idea of a sound deliberative route includes more than the purely causal instrumental reasoning that Hume allowed. Deliberation as Williams understands it includes at least such things as seeing that an action "would be the most convenient, economical, pleasant etc. way" of realizing something one already cares about, as well as thinking about how the pursuit of various concerns one already has can be combined (for example, by time ordering), considering which of various conflicting aims one attaches most weight to, and "finding constitutive solutions, such as deciding what would make for an entertaining evening, granted that one wants entertainment."[5]

Williams' invocation of the idea of a "sound deliberative route" indicates that he is not a skeptic about reasons. He is quite willing to make claims about what a person who has certain elements in his or her S has a reason (in the standard normative sense) to do. He allows that such a claim can be true even if the agent in question rejects it, and he allows that an agent who accepts such claims can fail to be moved by them. Moreover, as I have indicated above, he regards a claim that an agent has reason to φ as the kind of thing that can be offered as advice. So I will assume that his claim that there are only internal reasons does not reflect skepticism about reasons in the standard normative sense, and that it is not an attempt to eliminate normative claims about reasons in favor of purely descriptive claims about motivation. Nor is he merely making the tautological claim that something can be an operative reason for a person only if that person is moved by it. So Williams seems to be offering a substantive, normative thesis about what reasons we have.

He offers two kinds of argument for this thesis. First, he takes examples like that of Owen Wingrave to show that it rings false and amounts to mere browbeating to insist that a person "has a reason to φ" if there is no basis for this reason in the person's subjective motivational set. Second, he claims that defenders of external reasons are faced with a more theoretical difficulty insofar as they maintain that the truth of external reason statements can be appealed to in order to explain how people come to have new motivations.

Suppose, for example, that I have always regarded the idea of personal honor as rather silly and old-fashioned. But then I meet, and come to admire, someone who takes this idea seriously. I see that he regards acting in certain ways as contemptible, and gradually I come to see why he does and then finally to share his reaction. Having gone through this transformation, I believe that honor is something worth caring about, and that I was mistaken before in failing to see this. A believer in what Williams calls external reasons might therefore explain the change in my views by saying that I came to see (what had been true all along) that I had reason to regard honor as a value, and reason to avoid dishonorable conduct.

Williams finds such claims mysterious: "*What* is it," he asks, "that one comes to believe when he comes to believe that there is reason for him to φ, if it is not the proposition, or something that entails the proposition, that if he deliberated rationally, he would be motivated to act appropriately?"[6] This statement, he says, is not even true until the agent has acquired the new motivation, so how could that change come about by the agent's recognizing that it was already true?

Williams does not deny that a person's S can undergo various changes, or even that one can have reasons (grounded in one's present S) for undertaking a course of action that will lead to such changes. For example, a man who finds his weekends boring may see that he has reason to develop an interest in some new activity. So he tries out a number of activities until he finds himself becoming interested in one of them (at which point a change in his S has occurred). What Williams is denying is just that a change in what one cares about can be brought about in a certain way: by coming to see that one already had a reason for caring about that thing (a reason not grounded in one's S, as it was previously constituted).

Williams is not, however, claiming that a person whose S fails to contain the motivational basis for certain reasons is never open to criticism on this ground. He writes:

> There are of course many things that a speaker may say to one who is not disposed to φ when the speaker thinks that he should be, as that he is inconsiderate, or cruel, or selfish, or imprudent; or that things, and he, would be a lot nicer if he were so motivated. Any of these can be sensible things to say. But one who makes a great deal out of putting the criticism in the form of an external reason statement seems concerned to say that what is particularly wrong with the agent is that he is *irrational*. It is this theorist who particularly needs to make this charge precise: in particular, because he wants any rational agent, as such, to acknowledge the requirement to do the thing in question.[7]

Williams seems to me to be quite right in holding that the charge of irrationality is out of place in cases of the kind he has in mind. As I argued in Chapter 1, even if an agent fails to recognize a reason that he has, even when it is clearly presented to him, it does not follow that he is being irrational. This is true even when the agent "has a reason" in the internal sense favored by Williams. Suppose, for example, that Mr. O'Brien sets great value on being a gracious host, but that he does not have very good judgment about what this involves and as a result sometimes behaves in a ridiculous manner. Given O'Brien's lack of social sensitivity, it may be that no amount of careful rethinking would get *him* to see that he has reason to change his behavior. But he does have such a reason in Williams' "internal sense," since the conclusion that there is something to be said for changing can be reached by a "sound deliberative route" from elements of his S. Nonetheless, I would not say that O'Brien is being irrational in failing to be moved by this reason; he is just insensitive.

Williams considers a different case, of a man who treats his wife badly and sees no reason to treat her any better. The supposition is that, in contrast to what I assumed about O'Brien, there is nothing in the man's "subjective motivational set" that would be served by changing his ways.[8] He is, however, the kind of person about whom Williams would allow us to say that he is inconsiderate, cruel, insensitive, and so on. These criticisms do involve accusing him of a kind of deficiency, namely a failure to be moved by certain considerations that we regard as reasons. (What else is it to be inconsiderate, cruel, insensitive, and so on?) If it is a deficiency for the man to fail to see these considerations as reasons, it would seem that they must be reasons for him. (If they are not, how can it be a deficiency for him to fail to recognize them?) Why not conclude, then, that the man has reason to treat his wife better, bearing in mind that, just as in O'Brien's case, this does not imply that he is irrational in failing to recognize these reasons?

We are pushed toward this conclusion by what I called (in Chapter 1, Section 13) the universality of reason judgments. Insofar as we do not think that our own reasons for refraining from being cruel to our spouses are dependent on our having some "motivation" that is served by so refraining, we cannot regard others' reasons as being so dependent. On this point Williams' internalist thesis seems to be in tension with the breadth he claims for the idea of a subjective motivational set. Williams' examples are all put in the third person; they concern the claims we can make about the reasons other people have. But his internalism seems to force on us the conclusion that our own reasons, too, are all contingent on the presence of appropriate elements in our subjective motivational sets. This rings false and is, I believe, an important source of the widespread resistance to Williams' claims. As I have said above, many of our reasons clearly have "subjective conditions," but there are other reasons whose normative force seems not to depend on our motivations. Williams' conception of a "subjective motivational set" is broad enough to encompass this apparent diversity, including as it does such things as "dispositions of evaluation." (He does not say exactly what these are, but it is natural to suppose that they are not just tendencies to feel approval or disapproval but, at least, tendencies to think that approval or disapproval is *merited* or *in order* because of certain features of the objects evaluated.) Broadening the class of "motivations" to include such elements makes Williams' view more plausible, but this breadth does not seem to be compatible with his internalism as applied to ourselves.

It seems, then, that by moving away from a narrow Humeanism in his conception of an agent's S, Williams makes his view more appealing but perhaps less coherent. A similar problem arises in regard to the idea of a "sound deliberative route," more specifically in regard to the distinction, if any, between the process of "deliberating from" given elements of our S and the process through which we come to recognize new reasons or values not previously included in it. The case of honor, mentioned at the beginning of this appendix, was intended as an example of the latter process, and I tried to describe this process more fully in Section 12 of Chapter 1. It consists of such maneuvers as trying to consider the right aspects of the things that others claim to value, considering helpful analogies, trying to be sure that one has not overlooked relevant distinctions (or relied upon spurious ones), and considering one's reactions to new (real or hypothetical cases) and thinking about how these reactions are best accounted for. Call this process "reflective modification" of one's reasons.

If reasoning "from" existing elements of one's S were only a matter of causal reasoning about how best to "satisfy" them, then there would be a clear difference between this kind of deliberation and "reflective modification" of one's S. But Williams rightly rejects this narrow instrumentalism. His idea of "sound deliberation" is a complex process through which we figure out what would fulfill or be true to our aims, desires, and values. It is, he says, a "heuristic process" involving the exercise of imagination and the "perception of unexpected similarities."[9] It can lead to the addition of elements to one's S and to the elimination of old ones.

There seems, then, to be no distinction between sound deliberation in Williams' sense and what I called reflective modification of one's reasons. This appears to be Williams' understanding of the matter, and it might be counted a strength of his internalism.[10] This point might be sharpened into a charge that in fact I myself turn out to be an internalist, if not about reasons then at least about practical reasoning, since all the processes I described in Section 11 of Chapter 1, through which one decides what reasons one has, depend on the reactions that the person doing the deciding has or would have to the distinctions, examples, and analogies in question. So that process is, in Williams' apt term, "controlled by" that person's S.

This term is apt because it is more plausible to claim that all practical deliberation is controlled by elements of the agent's S than to claim that all practical deliberation is directed toward "promoting" or "satisfying" elements of S.[11] But while this broadening makes Williams' internalism more plausible, it also involves a significant change in the idea of a subjective motivational set, since a person's S now includes not just the "motivations" which he or she is presently conscious of and might deliberate from (that is, take as starting points for deliberation), but also all his or her dispositions (perhaps as yet unnoticed) to respond to various experiences, exercises of imagination, and processes of analytical reflection.

This broadening brings Williams' internalism closer to what an externalist might be thought to want, but it remains "internalist" in the crucial respect, since on this view we can still give Williams' answer to the question of what it is that was "already true" when a person comes to recognize a certain consideration as a reason. What was already true was that, given the person's S (understood in this broad sense), he or she would have been moved by this consideration if he or she had gone through the right process of sound deliberation. So the difference between internalism and externalism remains. An externalist, according to Williams, wants to claim that it can be true that a person has a reason even if, because of deficiencies in that person's dispositions to respond to considerations of the relevant kind, he or she would never come to be moved by those considerations even after the most complete and careful process of reflection and deliberation. An internalist denies this.

At this point the similarity between sound deliberation about how to fulfill or live up to elements of one's S, and reflective modification of one's S, becomes relevant, since it seems that despite this similarity Williams' internalism involves treating the two differently. In cases like that of Mr. O'Brien (who was irredeemably confused about what gracious hospitality involves), internalism seems to entail that a person can have a reason even though *he* will never recognize it as such (because of deficiencies in dispositional elements of his S). For it remains true that there is a sound deliberative route from elements of his S (a concern for hospitality) to the conclusion that he should behave differently. But suppose that Mr. O'Brien's son, O'Brien Jr., is incapable (because of deficiencies in his dispositions to respond) of recognizing that there is anything to be said for hospitality in the first place. Then in his case internalism seems to be committed to a different answer, namely that he has no reason to care about it if *he* could not reach that conclusion via a sound deliberative route from *his* S. It is not clear, to me at least, why these two cases should be treated differently, given that the deficiencies involved may be quite similar. In the former, more "instrumental" case, the idea of a sound deliberative route, which determines when a person has a reason, involves a degree of idealization away from that particular person's imaginative and interpretive deficiencies. Why shouldn't the same be true in the latter case as well?

Earlier in this appendix, I used the case of coming to see the value of an ideal of personal honor as an example of what I later called reflective modification of one's reasons. I want now to return to that example to illustrate the point at which our argument has now arrived. There are, I will assume, a number of different ideals of personal honor, all of them compatible with our duties to others and each worthy of a certain respect, even though it is not incumbent on each of us to adopt any one of them. What I described in my example was a process through which, by studying and emulating a friend, I might come to see the value of one of these conceptions and perhaps even be moved to shape my life in accord with it. Let us suppose that in doing this I followed what was (given my S) a sound deliberative route. So there is a "sound deliberative route" leading to the adoption of this conception of honor, and you could follow it too, if your S were like mine. But suppose your reactions are not like mine; if this conception of honor leaves you cold as a way to live, then you do not have reason to follow it. These conclusions might be cited as showing the strength of Williams' internalism: it gives the right answer about what reasons we have because it sticks to the idea that reasons must be reachable by sound deliberative routes from an agent's *actual* S (taken to include dispositional elements).

This advantage is not, however, as great as it appears. First, the variability in our reasons can equally well be accounted for by an "externalist" view which recognizes the substantive truth that often, as in this case, reasons have subjective conditions. Second, the variability that internalism provides may be too great. If the conception of honor that I favor leaves you cold, you may not have reason to adopt it. But if it is a worthwhile conception then you do have reason not to scorn it and reason not to mock those who take it seriously. If you fail to see that you have such reasons, and would still fail to see this even after the most complete process of imaginative reflection you could manage, this indicates a kind of deficiency on your part—moral narrow-mindedness, we might call it. By contrast, a comparable failure to be sufficiently moved by this ideal to adopt it indicates no such deficiency—just normal subjective variation.

Williams' opponent could say, then, that a person has a reason to φ if there is a sound (*nondefective*) deliberative route leading from his or her S to the conclusion that there is something to be said for φ-ing, that is to say, a route through which, absent deficiencies in imagination, sensitivity, and so on, but given other elements in his or her S, the agent could be led to see this reason. This also provides us with an answer to the question of what it is that is "already true" before an agent comes to see something as a reason and could remain true even if that particular agent could never come to see it. What is already true is that the agent has a reason to φ, and this entails (as per Williams' requirement) that if the agent deliberated nondefectively (but otherwise on the basis of his or her S) he or she would reach the conclusion that there is something to be said for φ-ing.

The idea of a deficiency that is here appealed to may seem controversial. It is certainly true that our ideas about what constitutes such a deficiency are not independent of our views about which things are in fact good reasons. How could they be? But the idea that there are such failings, and that they are properly regarded as deficiencies, is not really the issue. Williams' remark about calling someone cruel, insensitive, and so on indicates that he does not reject such judgments, and I think it is reasonable to suppose that he would invoke such an idea in a case like that of Mr. O'Brien: he has a reason to behave differently because there is a sound deliberative route from elements of his S to this conclusion, even though, because of his deficiencies, he cannot see this.

The issue is not whether it can be a deficiency not to be able to see the force of certain considerations, but rather what the relation is between these judgments of deficiency and the idea of the reasons that a person has. Williams claims that a person fails to have a reason to φ if, like O'Brien Jr., his deficiency means that he or she fails and would continue to fail to see anything to be said for φ-ing. His opponents disagree.

What can be said on the two sides? The universality of reason judgments, together with the fact that some of our own reasons do not seem dependent on our own recognition of them, pushes us toward saying that a person in this situation can nonetheless have a reason. The idea that cruelty, selfishness, insensitivity, and similar faults consist in part in failing to see certain things as reasons supports the same conclusion. On the other side, there is the fact that it does seem to be browbeating to insist that a person has a reason when he denies this, and when he truly could not see the force of the consideration in question no matter how hard he tried. It *is* browbeating to go on saying this in such a case. It is generally browbeating in any argument simply to repeat in a more insistent tone the very point that your opponent has already denied, without offering any new reason for accepting it. But from the fact that it would be browbeating to go on saying something in such a context it does not follow that that thing is not true.

Is there anything more than this to be said against the idea that a person in the situation we are envisaging "has a reason"? Something more may be found in Williams' insistence that the claim that a person has a reason must be something that can be offered as advice "in the 'if I were you' mode."[12] In his view, when we speak of the reasons another person has, we are taking that person's "perspective on the situation" and pointing out what is so, given that perspective. So when, for example, ϕ-ing is what would be required by some end or value that an agent has, we can say, in the mode of advice, that he or she has a reason to ϕ. We cannot say, in this mode, that a cruel and insensitive person has reason to treat his wife better, even if we think it a failing on his part that he does not see any such reason. Cases like Mr. O'Brien's are in the middle: on the one hand, he is like the cruel person in being unable to see that he has reason to act differently, but the claim that he does at least has a foothold in his concerns.

Opposition to Williams' position arises from a different view of reasons, one that begins not from the perspective of the agent but from that of the person making the judgment. If I believe that I would have reason to ϕ in circumstances C, and that Jones's situation is no different from mine in relevant respects, then the universality of reason judgments forces me to the conclusion that this reason counts in favor of ϕ-ing in his case as well. His inability to see this makes no difference. The only way to avoid this conclusion would seem to be to accept the view that my own reason has implausible subjective conditions.

If this is the impasse, how should we react to it? The most important thing to notice, I believe, is the limited nature of the disagreement. It is, or should be, conceded on both sides that: (1) reasons very often have subjective conditions; (2) failing to see the force of a reason that applies to one need not involve irrationality; although (3) it may, as in the case of cruelty and insensitivity, involve some other failing or deficiency. Once these things are conceded, the remaining disagreement over the range of applicability of the locution "has a reason" does not seem to me to be so important.

We could resolve this remaining disagreement in either of two ways. One would be to limit the universality of reason judgments in something like this way: if C counts in favor of my ϕ-ing in conditions S, then it counts in favor of ϕ-ing for any other person whose situation is similar in relevant respects *unless some deficiency prevents them from seeing that this is so.* This will seem sensible only if we make it very clear that the locution "has a reason" is tied specifically to those things that the agent in question is capable of being moved by.

Alternatively, we could relax the requirement that in order for a person to be said to "have a reason" the argument for it must be linked to some element in the agent's current S (whether or not he or she can appreciate the force of that link). The rationale for this move would be that cases like Mr. O'Brien's are in the most essential respect like that of the person who can see no reason not to scorn and mock other people's conceptions of honor. That is to say, they are prevented from seeing the force of the reasons in question by deficiencies of the same kind. It does not matter that in O'Brien's case, but not the other, what he fails to see is a link to something he already cares about. If we are to abstract from deficiencies of this kind in deciding whether a person "has a reason" then we should do so in both kinds of cases.

As is no doubt clear, I myself prefer the latter course. But I do not think that there is any argument that would force a person who was drawn to one of these alternatives to accept the other instead. Nor do I think that it makes a great deal of difference. As long as (1), (2), and (3) above are accepted, everything really important is in place.

Notes

For full citations of the short titles given here see the Bibliography.

Introduction

1. T. M. Scanlon, "Contractualism and Utilitarianism."
2. My view is close to John Rawls's, as presented in *A Theory of Justice*. I will note some significant differences in Chapter 5, but these arise mainly from Rawls's concentration on the justice of basic social institutions. I believe that the underlying moral ideas of the two theories are very similar. David Gauthier's *Morals by Agreement* expresses a quite different moral view, but it is also sometimes referred to as "contractualist" or, perhaps more frequently, "contractarian." For a discussion of the varieties of such views see Brian Barry, *Theories of Justice*. Barry develops a view very similar to my own in *Justice as Impartiality*.
3. Robert Adams also understands the relation between rival moral theories in this way. See pp. 136–138 of "Divine Command Metaethics Modified Again," in *The Virtue of Faith and Other Essays in Philosophical Theology*.
4. See Saul Kripke, *Naming and Necessity*. My discussion draws on examples from Lecture 3 of that book. Hilary Putnam has drawn a similar distinction. See, for example, *Mind, Language, and Reality*, chaps. 8, 11. David Wong applies Kripke's and Putnam's ideas to the case of morality in *Moral Relativity*, pp. 48–51.

1. Reasons

1. See, for example, pp. 40–41 of Bernard Williams, "Internal Reasons and the Obscurity of Blame." Williams' influential views about reasons will come up frequently in the following discussion. I discuss them more fully in the Appendix.
2. A point made by Donald Davidson in a number of the essays in *Essays on Actions and Events*. See, for example, "Agency," p. 46, and "Psychology as Philosophy," p. 229. See also Allan Gibbard, *Wise Choices, Apt Feelings*, pp. 38–39.

3. Philip Pettit and Michael Smith defend a similar claim about the applicability of responsibility to beliefs as well as to actions in "Freedom in Belief and Desire." In their view, however, a person is responsible for a mistaken belief or desire only if it could, "without a total transformation of its nature," be impressed on him that it is mistaken, and if this were done he would change the belief or desire accordingly (p. 446). I defend a weaker requirement in Chapter 6, Section 5.

4. In their *reflective* character such judgments resemble what Harry Frankfurt has called "second-order desires": desires to have, or not have, other desires or for these to be, or not to be, effective in action. (See Frankfurt, "Freedom of the Will and the Concept of a Person.") The idea that a rational creature is one that is capable of making such judgments therefore resembles Frankfurt's thesis that second-order desires are the mark of personhood. For reasons I will discuss in Sections 8–10, however, I do not think that these reflective judgments are best characterized as "desires." On this see Gary Watson, "Free Agency."

5. See Gibbard, *Wise Choices, Apt Feelings,* for a wider use of 'is rational'.

6. Derek Parfit, *Reasons and Persons,* p. 119.

7. Bernard Williams, "Internal and External Reasons," in *Moral Luck,* p. 110.

8. Philippa Foot, "Reasons for Action and Desires," p. 152.

9. Parfit, *Reasons and Persons,* p. 120.

10. Robert Audi points out, in "Weakness of Will and Rational Action," that there may be cases in which what a person does is in fact rational (because it is what he has most reason to do) even though in doing it he acts against his considered (but mistaken) judgment, and thus acts irrationally in the sense I am defending. This seems puzzling only when the same word, 'rational', is taken to indicate an action's conformity with requirements of rationality of the two different kinds I have just distinguished.

11. The former labeling is very common. One recent example is Alasdair MacIntyre's thesis that "each particular conception of justice requires as its counterpart some particular conception of practical rationality" (*Whose Justice? Which Rationality?* p. 389). One of his examples is this. "Rationality requires, so it has been argued by a number of philosophers, that [in defending principles of justice] we first divest ourselves of allegiance to any one of the contending theories and also abstract ourselves from all those particularities of social relationship in terms of which we have been accustomed to understand our responsibilities and our interests." He argues that this way of proceeding is in fact partisan since it leaves out exactly those elements of tradition and historical situation that another, competing conception of rationality would deem relevant to defending claims about justice, and he says that this shows the "inescapably historical and context-bound character" which any "substantive set of principles of rationality" is bound to have. I would not deny that conclusions about justice often depend on claims about the nature of "practical rationality." Hume's account of morality and justice clearly does, for example, as do the views of theorists who reject his conclusions because they take a different view of "rea-

son." But the example just given is much more fairly described as a disagreement about the relevant grounds for defending principles of justice rather than as a case of competing conceptions of "practical rationality." MacIntyre may be correct in holding that some proponents of the views he describes try to pass off substantive views about justice as requirements of rationality. If they do, then clarity would be best advanced by calling them on this rather than by accepting their terminology. (I do not believe that Rawls, whose views MacIntyre appears to have in mind, makes such a claim.)

12. As represented, for example, in the axioms given by John von Neumann and Oskar Morgenstern. See their *Theory of Games and Economic Behavior,* appendix.

13. Daniel Kahneman and Amos Tversky describe errors of this kind in "Choices, Values, and Frames." Many of the examples they document are cases in which experimental subjects fail to see the structure of the choice facing them. Choices which violate the principle of "dominance," for example, are mentioned on p. 344.

14. As Thomas Nagel says, "To look for a single general theory of how to decide the right thing to do is like looking for a single theory of how to decide what to believe"; Nagel, "The Fragmentation of Value," in *Mortal Questions,* p. 135.

15. So rationality, as I am understanding it, requires that what Gilbert Harman calls theoretical conclusions about what reasons we have can have practical consequences by, for example, producing revisions in our intentions. See, for example, Harman, *Change in View,* pp. 77–78.

16. The general point is well made by Christine Korsgaard in "Skepticism about Practical Reason." I am much indebted to her discussion. The point has also been made by others, including Nagel, in *The Possibility of Altruism,* chap. V; by John McDowell, in "Are Moral Reasons Hypothetical Imperatives?" p. 22, and "Might There Be External Reasons?"; and by G. F. Schueler, in *Desire: Its Role in Practical Reason and the Explanation of Action.* For a statement of the contrary view, that the recognition of a reason cannot motivate except by way of something else, a desire, see E. J. Bond, *Reason and Value,* p. 12.

17. As Susan Hurley argues in *Natural Reasons,* pp. 130–135 and 260–261.

18. My view of this parallel, and of akrasia more generally, follows Donald Davidson's. See his "How Is Weakness of the Will Possible?" in *Essays on Actions and Events,* pp. 37–42.

19. Susan Hurley may have essentially this point in mind when she says that in what appear to be cases of "evidential akrasia" what the agent is moved by is a reason for action rather than a reason for belief. She also suggests that reasons for action admit of akrasia because, or insofar as, they are *pro tanto* rather than prima facie reasons (*Natural Reasons,* pp. 130–135). But this does not seem right. As the example of the pleasure of a walk shows, reasons for action can also be prima facie. I argue in the text that akrasia is possible in such cases as well as in cases of belief.

20. See Thomas Nagel, *The Possibility of Altruism,* pp. 29–30. For a systematic

examination of Nagel's distinction, and of the wider and narrower uses of the term 'desire', see Schueler, *Desire*, esp. chap. 1.

21. See Warren Quinn, "Putting Rationality in Its Place," in *Morality and Action*, pp. 236, 246–247.

22. Perhaps some compulsives have only an urge to wash, but I assume that there are others who have a desire in the sense I am describing because, for example, they are constantly thinking that their hands are dirty.

23. The insistent character that marks desires in the directed-attention sense may also be part of what Hume has in mind in speaking of "violent" passions. See *A Treatise of Human Nature*, bk. II, pt. III, secs. III, IV, and VIII. If so, then my thesis is in important respects the reverse of his. He says (pp. 417, 437) that where this character is lacking—in the case of what he calls "calm" passions—we are apt to mistake passion for the operation of Reason. I am arguing, on the contrary, that where this element is present we may mistakenly believe that the motivational force of a state lies in something other than a tendency to see something as a reason.

24. A point made by Harry Frankfurt in "The Importance of What We Care About," in his book of that title.

25. Which is not to say that such reasons do not depend on our reactions in *any* way. Our reasons can have many "subjective conditions," some of which I will discuss later in this section.

26. Quinn, "Putting Rationality in Its Place," p. 246.

27. Many people have made similar points. See, for example, Parfit, *Reasons and Persons*, p. 121; Joseph Raz, *The Morality of Freedom*, pp. 140–144; E. J. Bond, *Reason and Value*, esp. p. 31; Stephen Darwall, *Impartial Reason*, chaps. 3, 6; Michael Stocker, *Plural and Conflicting Values*, p. 191; Leonard Katz, "Hedonism as a Metaphysics of Mind and Value," pp. 41–43; and Schueler, *Desire*, pp. 91–97. In "The Authority of Desire," Dennis Stampe defends the contrary view, that desires are per se reasons for action. Stampe's position has some affinity with my own, however, since he holds that having a desire that involves its seeming to one as if *p* would be good (p. 361).

28. Parfit, for example, says: "It is seldom true that, when someone acts in some way, his reason simply is that he wants to do so. In most cases, someone's reason for acting is one of the features of what he wants, or one of the facts that explains and justifies his desire." But, he says, "Even if a reason is not a desire, it may depend on a desire," and he goes on to say that many of the reasons we have do depend on our desires. See *Reasons and Persons*, p. 121.

29. If she had decided to go to Chicago even though her better judgment was that she did not have good reason to do so, it is not clear that we would still say that she had good reason to call the travel agent.

30. See Michael Bratman, *Intention, Plans, and Practical Reason*, chap. 5, esp. p. 51.

31. See Williams, "Internal and External Reasons," pp. 106–111.

32. Taking something to be a reason in the sense I have been discussing may

count as a desire in the sense defined by Michael Smith. According to Smith, a desire is a state "with which the world must fit" rather than one which, like a belief, "must fit the world." (See Smith, "The Humean Theory of Motivation," p. 54.) In the special case of a reason to want something, taking something to be a reason appears to satisfy the first of these conditions. Whether it then counts as a desire in Smith's enlarged sense will depend on how much he intends to exclude by the contrast with belief. Does the denial that a state "must fit with the world" mean that it is open to criticism only on grounds referring to the agent's other states? If so, then even this special case of taking something to be a reason is not a desire in Smith's sense.

33. We commonly speak of desires *for* objects, such as my desire for a glass of water or for a new computer, but I take it that such desires are properly understood as desires for states of affairs in which I stand in certain relations to objects of these kinds (for example, in which I drink the water or own and use the computer). The same can be said of "wanting."

34. "Playing to win" does not mean having a reason to do just *anything* that would improve my chances of victory. But if taunting my opponent would upset him and throw him off his game, does this give me a reason to employ this strategy? This is an example of "interpreting" a maxim. How is the idea of playing to win to be understood? What kind of competition is involved? What kind does it have to be in order for me to have reason to value it in the way that I do?

35. Here I am indebted to Joseph Raz's discussion in *The Morality of Freedom*, chaps. 12 and 13. See especially his remarks on pp. 292–293 about the hierarchical structure of goals.

36. Schueler makes some similar points; see *Desire*, chaps. 1 and 3.

37. Familiar from Harry Frankfurt's well-known papers, beginning with "Freedom of the Will and the Concept of a Person."

38. Gary Watson makes a similar objection to Frankfurt's view in "Free Agency."

39. Many have pointed out these failures. They are clearly summarized by Allan Gibbard in *Wise Choices, Apt Feelings*, pp. 18–22.

40. Ibid., pp. 20–21.

41. In the sense of G. E. Moore's famous "open-question argument" in *Principia Ethica*, chap. 1.

42. Gibbard, *Wise Choices, Apt Feelings*, p. 163.

43. As John Mackie found facts about objective values. See his "argument from queerness" in *Ethics: Inventing Right and Wrong*, pp. 38–42.

44. Gibbard says, for example, that he wants to give an account which explains how normative life is a part of nature; *Wise Choices, Apt Feelings*, p. 23.

45. Even though those who offer special-attitude accounts of reasons may not intend these accounts as in any way deflationary. Gibbard, in particular, does not have such intent, I believe, but it is a matter of controversy whether his expressivist account can preserve the force of normative judgments.

46. Here there are both a similarity and a contrast between judgments about reasons and judgments about right and wrong. Judgments about right and wrong should also, I believe, be taken at face value as claims about their apparent subject matter. But in that case we can add a further characterization of that subject matter which explains the reason-giving force of these judgments. Since such an explanation must appeal to something we see as a reason, it does not seem possible to give a general explanation of this kind of the normative force of judgment about reasons.

47. See the discussion of rationality in Section 3 above. As I mentioned there, this claim amounts to saying that it is central to being a rational creature that what Harman calls one's theoretical beliefs about practical reasoning have an effect on one's practical reasoning in his sense (that is to say, on the modification of one's beliefs and intentions). The cases here discussed support the idea that one can arrive at such beliefs without modifying (or having reason to modify) one's own attitudes, but the similarity of the thought processes involved in the three cases I have mentioned seems to me to count against separating these two forms of thought more widely.

48. My thinking about this question has been helped by Christine Korsgaard's discussion of what she calls "substantive moral realism" in *The Sources of Normativity* and her arguments against "dogmatic rationalism" in "The Normativity of Instrumental Reason." I believe that my own view, even on what I have called the belief interpretation, amounts to what she calls procedural rather than substantive realism. See *The Sources of Normativity*, pp. 34–37.

49. "Need not" because the content of some beliefs, such as ordinary empirical beliefs, may at least seem to raise metaphysical and epistemological issues. It is then a matter for philosophical argument how these apparent implications are to be treated. The point is just that this need not be true in the case of everything properly called belief.

50. The analogy is complicated by the fact that the mathematics of sets appears to form a unified subject matter that might be described by a comprehensive theory. Possibly the morality of right and wrong also constitutes a domain of this kind. Given the diversity of reasons for action, however, they do not seem to form a subject in this sense, describable by a unified substantive theory. The question at issue is not, however, whether there could be such a theory but whether there are methods for settling questions about reasons that are sufficiently stable and reliable to support the idea that these are questions about which one can be correct or incorrect.

51. Gareth Evans makes parallel observations about the "seemings" that are central to perception, in particular that they are not preconceptual but are "belief independent"; that is to say, they are not dependent on and may persist in the face of my judgment (as in the case of optical illusions). See Evans, *The Varieties of Reference*, pp. 122–124. These parallels are interesting but should not, I think, lead us to construe taking something to be a reason as a kind of perception, since it lacks the crucial element of being a mechanism of representation through which

things at a distance are presented to us. We do sometimes speak of "seeing" something as a reason, but, since it is not a matter of picturing or representation, it is not a kind of perception any more than any other mode of intellectual understanding is. Mark Johnston makes the same point about judgments of value. See his "Dispositional Theories of Value," p. 142.

52. Stuart Hampshire makes a similar point in *Innocence and Experience,* chap. 3. He argues that Hume's claim that no passion can be contrary to reason derives part of its plausibility from a technique of presenting the question in isolation from any such framework.

53. Thomas Nagel describes this method as follows: "If we start by regarding appearances of value as appearances of something, and then step back to form hypotheses about the broader system of motivational possibilities of which we have had a glimpse, the result is a gradual opening out of a complex domain which we apparently discover. The method of discovery is to seek the best normative explanation of the normative appearances"; *The View from Nowhere,* p. 146.

54. Similar elements are included in Gilbert Harman's account of belief revision in *Change in View,* especially chaps. 6 ("Belief Revision") and 7 ("Explanatory Coherence"). His list of the ways in which one can make mistakes while reasoning includes such things as "One can be careless or inattentive; one can forget about a relevant consideration or fail to give it sufficient weight; one can make mistakes in long division; one can fail to see something, to remember something, to attend carefully; and so on" (p. 7).

55. Although *this* fact, about rationality, is not something an agent would refer to. Insofar as she is rational, an agent will treat her intentions as giving her reasons (unless reconsidered); she need not have the further thought that to fail to do this is irrational.

56. Since having something "catch your attention" as a potential reason for action is often a matter of having what I called above a "desire in the directed-attention sense," the selection process described here provides a sense in which it is often true that "our reasons for action depend on our desires." For the reasons I discuss in the next paragraph in the text, however, this does not make desires, any more than intentions, basic sources of reasons in the way that the desire model suggests.

57. This dependence on our acts of "selection" might be thought to mark an important difference between reasons for action and reasons for belief, since it is not at all up to us what counts in favor of something's being true. But this is only a difference in degree and should not be exaggerated. Just as it does not make sense to intend to do everything that is worthwhile, it does not make sense to believe everything for which good evidence is available, if by "believe" one means "take note of and retain for future recall, updating, and so on." Our senses bombard us all the time with evidence for more beliefs than it makes sense to form. So we are reflectively and unreflectively selective: noticing and retaining not everything but those things that have some kind of salience. There is a difference in degree between the cases of belief and action because the limits of time and energy for

action are more exigent than those of storage capacity, but an element of selection among attitudes supportable by reasons is present in both cases. Harman, for example, includes among his principles of belief revision a principle of Clutter Avoidance, and an Interest Principle directing one to add new beliefs only if one has some interest in whether they are true. See *Change in View*, p. 56.

58. One reason why it is often so taken may be the fact that it is one of the small number of classes of cases in which it is obviously *irrational* to fail to recognize something as a reason. If it is assumed that if something is a reason then it must be irrational to fail to treat it as a reason (even when it is clearly presented), then these "instrumental" reasons may seem to be the only obvious candidates. A central claim of this chapter is that this assumption should be rejected.

59. See, for example, Richard Brandt, *A Theory of the Good and the Right*, p. 22; and Gibbard, *Wise Choices, Apt Feelings*, pp. 169–170.

60. The possibility in question is that disagreements might persist even though both groups had done everything possible to check their views for errors, render them coherent, and so on. I would emphasize, however, that although this possibility may be theoretically intriguing, it is of no practical significance, since our views never meet this ideal test. So in cases of actual disagreement there is always room for further argument by appeal to inconsistencies and other inadequacies in each other's positions—room for attempts to persuade through what Gibbard calls "Socratic influence"; see *Wise Choices, Apt Feelings*, pp. 174–175.

61. Criticizing coherence accounts of justification in ethics, Brandt argues that there is no reason to think that a more coherent set of beliefs is better justified than a less coherent one "unless some of the beliefs are initially credible—and not merely initially believed—for some reason other than their coherence, say, because they state facts of observation"; *A Theory of the Good and the Right*, p. 20. This seems to me correct, but not an objection to an account of the kind I am offering. Judgments (about right and wrong, or about reasons) in which we have a high degree of confidence on reflection are *like* observations in having independent credibility even though they are not like observations in seeming to report on some physical realm that is at a distance from us. For critical discussion of Brandt's argument see David Brink, *Moral Realism and the Foundations of Ethics*, pp. 135–136.

62. In particular, it is not an instance of Kant's Categorical Imperative, since it does not require that the reasons attributed to others be ones that they could all coherently act on.

63. See Gibbard, *Wise Choices, Apt Feelings*, chap. 11.

2. Values

1. See, for example, W. D. Ross, *The Right and the Good*, p. 75.

2. Shelly Kagan, for example, in discussing what he calls the "pro tanto reason to promote the good," says that "to speak of the good is in part to use a placeholder: to say that there is a pro tanto reason to promote the good is to say that

there is a standing reason to promote those outcomes that best meet appropriate standards, whatever those standards might be"; *The Limits of Morality*, p. 60. It is assumed that whatever the good may be, it is a matter of those outcomes that are to be promoted.

3. In "Rights and Agency" Amartya Sen presents a teleological view that fully exploits the three possibilities I have just listed.

4. Thomas Nagel, *The View from Nowhere*, chap. VIII, esp. pp. 147–163.

5. Ibid., p. 178.

6. Scheffler, "Agent-Centered Restrictions, Rationality and the Virtues," in *Consequentialism and Its Critics*, p. 251. Philip Pettit makes the similar claim that, while "consequentialism fits nicely with our standard views of what rationality requires," the nonconsequentialist "has the embarrassment of having to defend a position on what certain values require which is without analog in the non-moral area of practical rationality"; "Consequentialism," p. 238. My thinking about Scheffler's argument has benefited from Philippa Foot's criticisms of it in "Utilitarianism and the Virtues." I arrive at conclusions similar to Foot's, though by a different route.

7. Scheffler, "Agent-Centered Restrictions," p. 252. Similarly, Pettit writes, "If one prognosis realizes my values more than another then that surely fixes its value"; "Consequentialism," p. 238–239.

8. For further discussion of the relevance of this structural point for moral reasoning see Chapter 4, Section 3.

9. Henry Sidgwick, *Methods of Ethics*, p. 382.

10. Nagel, *The View from Nowhere*, p. 169.

11. G. E. Moore, *Principia Ethica*, p. 187. Moore also allows that things which are not valuable in themselves, as indicated by this test, can nonetheless contribute to the value of complex wholes of which they are a part. In this case their value is revealed by considering a world in which just that complex whole existed, first with and then without the part.

12. Ross, *The Right and the Good*, pp. 134–141.

13. Moore, *Principia Ethica*, p. 188.

14. I am indebted here to Michael Stocker's discussion in "Values and Purposes: The Limits of Teleology and the Ends of Friendship." See esp. sec. III, pp. 754–758.

15. The fact that it is good that friendship should occur, but that in order for it to occur people have to be moved by reasons other than the reason of promoting the occurrence of friendship, is an instance of what might be called a "paradox of teleology." (Following Henry Sidgwick, who gave the name "the paradox of hedonism" to the fact that one often cannot promote pleasure very effectively by aiming directly at it, but must have other aims which are not seen simply as means to pleasure. See *Methods of Ethics*, pp. 48, 136.)

16. Similar accounts of value have been offered recently by Gerald F. Gaus in *Value and Justification* and by Elizabeth Anderson in *Value in Ethics and Eco-*

nomics, esp. chap. 1. I have benefited from their discussions. On the relation between "valuing" and "valuable," in particular, see Gaus, pp. 111, 156, 167; and Anderson, p. 17.

17. Moore, *Principia Ethica,* sect. 13.

18. In this respect my account of value resembles John Rawls's account of "goodness": "A is a good X if and only if A has . . . the properties which it is rational to want in an X, given what X's are used for, or expected to do and the like (whichever rider is appropriate)"; *A Theory of Justice,* p. 399. Shelly Kagan's remark about the good as a "placeholder" seems also to express what I am here calling a buck-passing account. See *The Limits of Morality,* p. 60.

19. This claim may be more plausible with respect to goodness, which is a more specific notion. I do not think that a strictly teleological account is correct in that case either, but I will not go into that question here, or into the question of exactly how goodness differs from the broader idea of value that is my main concern. For a discussion of some differences see Gaus, *Value and Justification,* pp. 118–124 and 235–241. See also Paul Ziff, *Semantic Analysis,* p. 221.

20. In his encyclopedia entry "Consequentialism," Philip Pettit observes that there are two kinds of claims one can make about any value: that it should be promoted and that it should be honored, where by honoring a value he seems to have in mind something like the range of responses I have described. Consequentialism, as he defines it, holds that "whatever values an individual or institutional agent adopts, the proper response to those values is to promote them. The agent should honour values only insofar as honouring them is part of promoting them, or is necessary in order to promote them" (p. 231). My thesis, in his terms, comes close to the reverse: that promoting a value, when it is appropriate, is properly seen as one aspect of honoring it. In addition to being in tension with "standard views of rationality," nonconsequentialism, as Pettit sees it, "is seriously defective in regard to the methodological virtue of simplicity" (p. 237). While consequentialists endorse only one way of responding to values, nonconsequentialists endorse two (p. 238). And, he might have added, the second one is extremely complex. But it is not clear why "simplicity" of this kind should be seen as a virtue. Pettit cites the general methodological practice of preferring the simpler of two hypotheses "when otherwise they are equally satisfactory." But consequentialism and nonconsequentialism are not "equally satisfactory" if, as I have argued, the former involves giving up claims about value that are at least as plausible as the ones that it retains. So the case must turn, as he later suggests, on reflection on the relative plausibility of these claims.

21. Anderson's pluralistic conception of value also emphasizes the variety of ways of valuing things. See *Value in Ethics and Economics,* esp. pp. 8–16. While I agree with Anderson's pluralism and have learned from it, I do not accept her expressive theory of rational action, according to which when we have reason to treat a valued thing a certain way this is because that mode of treatment is in accord with norms for expressing our attitude of valuing. When valuing a thing

involves seeing reason to treat it a certain way—for example, to protect it from harm—treating it this way may "express" my attitude of valuing it, and failing to protect it may express an attitude of not valuing it. But in such cases the idea of expression is secondary to and dependent on a prior idea of the reasons that the value in question involves.

22. Anderson describes a disagreement of this kind about the value of music in ibid., pp. 12–14.

23. "A simple form of hedonism" because it seems that, as I will argue below, even the value of most pleasures is not adequately captured by the idea that they are "to be sought."

24. See, for example, Samuel Scheffler's introduction to *Consequentialism and Its Critics*, pp. 1, 6.

25. A point made by Leonard Katz, in "Hedonism as a Metaphysics of Mind and Value," pp. 20–22.

26. My understanding of these issues has benefited from Ronald Dworkin's discussion in *Life's Dominion*.

27. This provides an alternative interpretation of Nagel's remark that it would be "asking too much" to claim that each person has reason to be concerned with every end another person has, an interpretation that remains at the level of reasons and value and does not invoke the limits on our obligations to others.

28. Robert Nozick offers similar descriptions of the problem of recognizing the value of human life, although he does not advocate exactly this solution. See his *Philosophical Explanations*, pp. 451–473. Nozick says, for example, that we should "treat someone (who is a value-seeking I) as a value-seeking I" (p. 462). Later he suggests that "the way to respond to the fact that these basic moral characteristics are there appears to be to follow moral principles that acknowledge these characteristics, that respond to their presence qua the characteristics they are" (470–471).

3. Well-Being

1. See John Rawls, *A Theory of Justice*, sec. 15, and "Social Unity and Primary Goods"; and Amartya Sen, *Inequality Reexamined*, chap. 3. Rawls and Sen do not intend to offer accounts of "what makes a life better from the point of view of the person who lives it." (See Rawls's statement on p. 169 of "Social Unity and Primary Goods.")

2. James Griffin, *Well-Being*; Derek Parfit, *Reasons and Persons*, app. I.

3. This is implied, for example, by Henry Sidgwick's claim that desirable consciousness is the only ultimate good. See *Methods of Ethics*, bk. III, chap. XIV.

4. It might seem that when we say this we are identifying well-being with experiential quality, and that when these two are carefully distinguished the question of well-being turns out to be the same as the question of choiceworthiness. But this is not so. A person who abandons a valued ambition in order to help

his family may have made a net sacrifice in the quality of his life, by giving up the accomplishments he would have made, even if the experiential quality of the life he chooses is no lower than that of the one he forgoes. It may, for example, involve more joy and less struggle, stress, and frustration. The life he lives could therefore be more choiceworthy and involve no loss in experiential quality while still being a worse life for him, in the sense with which I am here concerned.

5. This tripartite division follows the one Parfit gives in *Reasons and Persons,* app. I. The term "substantive good theory" is taken from T. M. Scanlon, "Value, Desire and Quality of Life." The discussion of well-being in this section and the next draws on that article but goes beyond it in a number of respects.

6. This is true even of what Parfit calls "preference hedonism," according to which the quality of a person's life is measured by the degree to which it contains experiences of the kind that that person prefers to have. See *Reasons and Persons,* pp. 493–494.

7. See John Harsanyi, "Morality and the Theory of Rational Behavior," pp. 47, 55–56; Griffin, *Well-Being,* p. 14. Griffin offers a lengthy and well-articulated defense of an informed-desire view. In his formulation, informed desires are ones that are "formed by an appreciation of the nature of [their] objects."

8. For reasons pointed out in Chapter 1, Section 11.

9. An example modeled on Parfit's case of "the stranger on the train." See *Reasons and Persons,* p. 494.

10. Confusion on this point can arise from giving the idea that a person has reason to do what will maximize her utility an "egoistic" reading, according to which 'her utility', like 'her happiness', is taken to denote some benefit to *her.* But neither the notion of preference that the formal statement of these theories employs, nor the notion of utility that results from it, is limited in the way that this reading suggests.

11. The premises of Arrow's famous Possibility Theorem, for example, can be understood either as stating conditions about how acceptable ways of making social choices must be responsive to the preferences of the members of society, or as stating conditions about how the notion of what is "good from the point of view of society" is related to what is good from the points of view of the individuals who make up that society. Amartya Sen points out the importance of distinguishing between these two interpretations in "Social Choice Theory: A Re-examination." John Broome also discusses this ambiguity in *Weighing Goods,* chap. 7.

12. The problem raised by this question has been explored at length in the literature spawned by Amartya Sen's "The Impossibility of a Paretian Liberal."

13. Harsanyi, for one, would exclude such "anti-social preferences." See p. 56 of "Morality and the Theory of Rational Behavior."

14. See Kenneth Arrow, *Social Choice and Individual Values,* esp. pp. 17–19, 106.

15. Joseph Raz emphasizes the importance of success in one's main aims as an element of well-being. See *The Morality of Freedom,* chap. 12. I am much indebted to Raz's discussion.

16. See Griffin, *Well-Being*, pp. 54–55.

17. It is plausible to hold that nothing can contribute to a person's well-being unless it affects his or her life. In "The Limits of Well-Being" Shelly Kagan describes a notion of well-being that is narrower than the one I am describing here because it is circumscribed by the stronger requirement that nothing can contribute to a person's well-being unless it benefits him or her intrinsically, where this seems to mean bringing about some change in the person's physical or psychological state. He observes in a note that a consequence of his view may be that "it might be one thing for a person to be well-off and quite another for that person's life to go well" (p. 182, n. 7). He acknowledges that there may be some question about how important this circumscribed notion of well-being is, compared with other goods. (See p. 188 and n. 10.) I would agree, and I suggest that philosophers have generally discussed the wider notion because it has greater claim to importance. I will argue later in this chapter that the importance of even this wider notion seems to me to have been exaggerated.

18. As Parfit notes in *Reasons and Persons*, p. 497.

19. The qualifier "in general" is necessary because there may be special cases in which having fulfilled an aim might be a goal worth seeking. This might be true, for example, in the case of a person who was severely depressed, whose condition would be improved by any success, however trivial.

20. See Raz, *The Morality of Freedom*, p. 293.

21. Ibid., pp. 292–293. Rawls makes a similar point about the hierarchical nature of goals in *A Theory of Justice*, pp. 408–411. As pointed out above, I am using the term 'aim' in a broad sense to include a person's values as well as specific objectives that he or she is attempting to bring about. When, following Raz, I use the term 'goals' rather than 'aims', I intend it to be understood in the same broad sense.

22. Here I rely on the point, made in Section 10 of Chapter 1, that adopting an aim or goal is not just a matter of coming to assign a positive value to certain results. When we adopt an aim or goal we give it one or another particular role in our practical thinking: the role of a temporary diversion, or of a career, or of a specific goal within a career, for example. Different kinds of reasons are required to justify adopting goals for these different roles.

23. L. W. Sumner calls this the "subject-relative or perspectival character" of the concept of welfare. See *Welfare, Happiness and Ethics*, p. 42. His requirement is obviously similar to Kagan's (discussed in note 17 above) but seems broader. I am indebted to Sumner for helpful discussion of this point.

24. A point emphasized by Raz. See *The Morality of Freedom*, p. 345.

25. Leo Tolstoy, *The Death of Ivan Ilych and Other Stories* (New York: New American Library, 1960).

26. The latter is suggested by J. David Velleman, who also suggests that one life is better than another if it constitutes "a better life story." See his "Well-Being and Time."

27. Peter Railton, for example, understands "an individual's good" in this

broader sense. It consists, he says, in "what he would want himself to want, or pursue" if he were to contemplate his present situation from a more ideal perspective. See his "Facts and Values," p. 16.

28. The two distortions I have mentioned (the transformation into apparently self-interested goals and into a teleological form) are combined in objections to deontology that interpret an agent's concern not to act wrongly as a concern with preserving his own moral purity—that is to say, with gaining for himself the good of having succeeded in conforming to his own principles.

29. David Wiggins makes a similar point about the "instability" of desire-based accounts of value. The claim that something is good because it would satisfy a person's desire should, as a claim about what is good, be endorsable from that person's own point of view. But from that point of view it is not the desire that matters ("Truth, Invention and the Meaning of Life," pp. 346–347). I am arguing that this instability is not merely a feature of desire-based views but one that will be inherited by any plausible account of well-being, since any such account must give a place to the idea of success in one's rational aims and that idea in turn captures the element of truth in desire-based views. The lesson to be drawn is that the notion of well-being should be treated with some care because, as I will argue in the next section, it is an evaluative idea that has its home in third-person perspectives but is often passed off as a central notion in first-person deliberation.

30. Stephen Darwall notes a similar divergence of points of view in "Self-Interest and Self-Concern." Darwall identifies a person's good, or interest, with what someone who cares about that person would rationally want for him for his sake (see, for example, p. 176), and he stresses the divergence between a person's good, so understood, and what that person has reason to want. Darwall suggests that "the idea of a person's good or *interest* . . . is one we need insofar as we (or he) care about him" (p. 159). As the parenthetical qualification indicates, he holds, plausibly, that the contrast in question is not, strictly speaking, one between first- and third-person perspectives, since a person can be concerned with his own interest in this sense—that is to say, can take the perspective of a benefactor toward himself. I agree that one can take this perspective, but deny that it is a perspective that has particular importance for us. For one thing, as noted above, this attitude is incompatible with the attitude that we normally take toward many of our own aims, which we value for reasons that do not refer to our interest. As I note in the text this tension is greatly reduced when the benefactor is another person.

31. Darwall considers a similar example in ibid., pp. 174–175. He suggests that in such a case a benefactor's concern for the person for her sake may be in tension with "respect and concern for her as an autonomous agent."

32. The claim that nothing is of value unless it figures in this way in people's well-being is similar to Mill's famous claim in *Utilitarianism* that "happiness is not an abstract idea but a concrete whole" with parts, each of which is desirable in itself, and that nothing is desired for its own sake unless it is desired as a part of happiness. *Utilitarianism and Other Essays,* pp. 308–310.

33. In line with the idea, argued for earlier, that the most important conceptions of well-being are moral conceptions, the claim that well-being is a "master value" might be understood as a moral claim. This claim would be that the only thing of ultimate moral importance (or of ultimate importance for the purposes of a certain kind of moral argument) is individual well-being; other things have moral importance (or moral importance of this particular kind) only by way of the contribution they make to individual well-being. So, for example, it could be claimed that individual well-being is the only thing that matters, ultimately, for the justifiability of moral principles or for the assessment of social institutions. The idea that well-being is a master *value* may derive some plausibility from being confused with one or another such moral claim, but these claims are distinct and need to be assessed on their own merits.

4. Wrongness and Reasons

1. After H. A. Prichard, who described a similar dilemma in his essay "Does Moral Philosophy Rest on a Mistake?" esp. p. 6. Prichard would not have been troubled by the dilemma as I have stated it, since he thought it was a mistake to try to explain why we should do what we are morally obligated to do.

2. Jürgen Habermas, "Discourse Ethics: Notes on Philosophical Justification," esp. pp. 90–91.

3. Alasdair MacIntyre, *After Virtue*, p. 51.

4. A similar point applies to Bernard Williams' contrast between "thick" and "thin" ethical concepts. This distinction appears at first to have an important metaphysical component. Williams says that "thick concepts" such as courage and cruelty have a great deal of empirical content and are in this respect "world guided," while more abstract "thin" concepts such as obligation and wrong are not. But the more important issue turns out, I believe, to be a matter of motivational power and reason-giving force. Williams can understand a person's being moved by, say, a conception of honor that has a central place in his way of life. Abstract notions of obligation, on the other hand, strike him as motivationally empty, and moral theory seems to him unlikely to fill this gap. See *Ethics and the Limits of Philosophy,* chaps. 8 and 9.

5. Peter Singer, "Famine, Affluence and Morality."

6. The appeal to the greatest happiness that I have in mind is Mill's "proof" of the principle of utility in chapter 3 of *Utilitarianism*. He gives a separate general account of the "sanction" in chapter 4 and a more specific account of our idea of "wrongness" in chapter 5. The aim of his "proof" is very similar to what I am calling a response to the question of importance. His discussion of the sanction could be read as a response to what I am calling the problem of priority, but is not exactly the same. One difference is that the question he appears to be addressing is purely one of motivation, whereas the question of priority, as I understand it, is a

question about what reason we have to subordinate all our other concerns to the requirements of moral right and wrong.

7. Mill, *Utilitarianism,* chap. 5, par. 14. The passage appears on p. 321 of *Utilitarianism and Other Essays.*

8. I am grateful to Derek Parfit for pointing out the advantages of this formulation over the alternative version that refers to principles "that everyone could reasonably accept" rather than principles "that no one could reasonably reject." (See "Contractualism and Utilitarianism," p. 111.) Shelly Kagan and Arthur Kuflik have argued (in correspondence) that these two formulations are in fact equivalent. Whether this is so or not, the "could not reasonably reject" formulation expresses the basic contractualist idea more directly. What is basic to contractualism as I understand it is the idea of justifiability to each person (on grounds that he or she could not reasonably reject). Unanimous acceptance is a consequence of this condition's being fulfilled, but is not itself the basic idea.

9. Mill, *Utilitarianism,* chap. 3, par. 10 (p. 303.)

10. John McDowell has defended a similar claim, put in terms of virtues. See "Are Moral Requirements Hypothetical Imperatives?" and "Virtue and Reason."

11. Habermas says something very similar about his discourse ethics in, for example, "Discourse Ethics," p. 91. On possible differences between Habermas' claim and mine, see notes 5 and 18 in Chapter 5.

12. One might, of course, try to explain the special significance of this failure by appealing to the special stringency that the requirements in question have for the agent. My strategy, however, is to explain this significance directly. The purpose of my present inquiry is not to justify morality to an amoralist but to understand and give an accurate description of our reactions to such a person.

13. Aurel Kolnai makes a similar observation, saying that although he may feel "shocked" by people whose aesthetic judgments differ profoundly from his as well as by those with profoundly different ethical views, there is a difference between the two cases: "in my first kind of reaction the sense of a gulf of alienness predominates, whereas in the second it is the sense of being challenged and outraged, and of having entered into a situation of implacable conflict"; see "Aesthetic and Moral Experience," pp. 203–204. I would add, but Kolnai perhaps would not, that this difference is clearest when the moral judgments in question concern what I am calling right and wrong. Where differing ideas of personal honor or different conceptions of friendship or family life are in question, and these do not raise questions of right and wrong, reactions of "alienness," rather than of "challenge" and "implacable conflict," may be more in order, even though these differences can correctly be described as "moral." I will return to this point in Chapter 8, in discussing relativism.

14. This gulf would of course be widest in the case of a person who saw no reason to treat us in any way other than that which best suited his private interests. My main point is that there is a significant gulf in the case of anyone who does not see us as beings to whom justification of the kind I am describing is owed. But such

a person might see other reasons to respect our interests or, at least, not to treat us in certain ways. So the full implications of this gulf for our relations with a person will vary depending on the content of his or her particular view. I will return to this question in Chapter 8.

15. See Bernard Williams, "Persons, Character, and Morality," in *Moral Luck,* esp. pp.15–19. Williams takes this example from Charles Fried, *An Anatomy of Values,* p. 227. Similar examples go back at least to William Godwin's 1793 *Inquiry Concerning the Principles of Political Justice.*

16. See Barbara Herman, "Integrity and Impartiality."

17. Williams, "Persons, Character, and Morality," p. 18.

18. The latter point is emphasized by Ronald Dworkin in "Foundations of Liberal Equality."

19. Judith Thomson discusses this phenomenon in *The Realm of Rights,* pp. 25–29.

20. A point emphasized by Joseph Raz in *The Morality of Freedom,* chap. 13. The nature of one's society can of course affect the strain between moral demands and personal relations in other ways as well; for example, by affecting the degree of sacrifice we are required make to help those less well off. These strains are discussed by Thomas Nagel in *Equality and Partiality,* chap. 10.

21. The importance of this challenge has been pressed on me by Frances Kamm, among others. Judith Thomson has raised a very similar objection. "For my own part," she writes, "I cannot bring myself to believe that what *makes* it wrong to torture babies to death for fun (for example) is that doing this 'would be disallowed by any system of rules for the general regulation of behavior which no one could reasonably reject as a basis for informed, unforced general agreement.' My impression is that explanation goes in the opposite direction—that it is the patent wrongfulness of the conduct that explains why there would be general agreement to disallow it"; *The Realm of Rights,* p. 30, n. 19. The contractualist formula that Thomson quotes is intended as an account of what it is for an act to be wrong. What *makes* an act wrong are the properties that would make any principle that allow it one that it would be reasonable to reject (in this case, the needless suffering and death of the baby).

22. This depends, of course, on what "our" ideas of right and wrong are. As we search for an explanation of the importance and priority of right and wrong it may emerge that different people, who have quite similar views about the content of right and wrong, nonetheless have rather different ideas about the nature and source of the authority of these concepts. I will discuss this possibility further in Chapter 8.

23. Immanuel Kant, *Grounding for the Metaphysics of Morals,* Ak. 430. W. S. Gilbert put much the same point more entertainingly:

> When a felon's not engaged in his employment
> Or maturing his felonious little plans,

His capacity for innocent enjoyment
Is just as great as any honest man's.
Our feelings we with difficulty smother
When constabulary duty's to be done:
Ah, take one consideration with another,
A policeman's lot is not a happy one!

Pirates of Penzance (or, The Slave of Duty), act II; *The Complete Annotated Gilbert and Sullivan,* ed. Ian Bradley (Oxford: Oxford University Press, 1996), pp. 249–251.

24. I will discuss these matters in more detail in Chapter 5.

25. Many have noted this divergence, with varying reactions to it. James Griffin, for example, observes that the current use of the word 'moral' is narrower than past uses, applying to the question "How must I accommodate the interests of others?" rather than the broader "How should I live?" He does not believe that we should regret the change. See *Value Judgment: Improving Our Ethical Beliefs,* pp. 126–127 and 167–168, n. 9. Bernard Williams, on the other hand, deplores the tendency in contemporary philosophy to concentrate on the narrower notion, for which he reserves the terms 'morality' and sometimes (more pejoratively) 'the morality system', in contrast to 'ethics', which refers to answers to the broader question "How to live?", which he believes should be the focus of our attention. See *Ethics and the Limits of Philosophy,* chap. 1 and passim.

26. Thomas Nagel defends a similar thesis, but the distinctions he proposes are somewhat different from mine. See "The Fragmentation of Value," in *Mortal Questions,* pp. 128–141. Alasdair MacIntyre also argues that our current conception of morality is a collection of fragments without an overall rationale, but he takes a more negative view of this situation. See *After Virtue,* chap. 1.

27. This distinction, between those categories of value that do, and those that do not, arise out of the ideal of justifiability to others, captures one of the things that might be meant by the distinction between "the right" and "the good." So understood, this distinction marks a deep difference in the motivational basis of these values, not a difference in their form ("the good" does not, for example, correspond to a realm of goals and "the right" to a realm of constraints on their pursuit).

28. It is not clear exactly how the boundaries of "morality" in the broader sense would be drawn. Perhaps moral criticism in this sense is generally understood to apply to all matters of character having to do with a person's appreciation of and response to important values. If this is correct, then all the examples I listed at the beginning of this section could plausibly be said to involve moral issues. But on this understanding the category of the moral would be very wide indeed: would a failure to see the value of art count as a moral fault?

29. But for an argument that there can be sensitivity to reasons without the capacity for language, see Merlin Donald, *Origins of the Modern Mind: Three Stages in the Evolution of Culture and Cognition,* chap. 3. This possibility calls

attention to the fact that the divisions between the groups I have listed may not be sharp, but a matter of degree. I am grateful to Leonard Katz for helpful discussion of this point.

30. There is, of course, the possibility that trustees for nonrational creatures could raise objections based on their reasons for wanting to have certain experiential goods, as well as to avoid experiential harms such as pain and distress. This does not seem plausible to me, but I will not explore the question here.

31. What Parfit calls "the non-identity problem." See *Reasons and Persons,* chap. 16.

5. The Structure of Contractualism

1. Judith Thomson, for example, suggests that this biconditional "is arguably a necessary truth," hence one that any theorist must accept. What is not in her view a necessary truth, and what she denies is true at all, is that an act is wrong *because* it meets this condition. See *The Realm of Rights,* p. 20, n. 15, and p. 30, n. 19. In regard to Thomson's latter claim, see Chapter 4, note 19, above.

2. David Gauthier in *Morals by Agreement;* Jürgen Habermas in many works, including *The Theory of Communicative Action* and the essays collected in *Moral Consciousness and Communicative Action;* R. M. Hare in a series of works beginning with *The Language of Morals* and including, most recently, *Moral Thinking;* John Rawls in *A Theory of Justice.* There are of course many others who employ one or another version of the contractual idea, such as Bruce Ackerman in *Social Justice and the Liberal State* and G. R. Grice, *The Grounds of Moral Judgment.*

3. Hare, *Moral Thinking,* chap. 5, esp. pp. 105–106.

4. Since Kant's view raises interpretive problems that would take me too far afield I will concentrate here on Hare and on this portion of Rawls's theory.

5. In this respect my view has more in common with Habermas'. He holds that in order for a practical norm to be valid "the consequences and side effects of its general observance for the satisfaction of each person's particular interests must be acceptable to all"; "Morality and Ethical Life," in *Moral Consciousness and Communicative Action,* p. 197. Insofar as my view, like his, interprets moral judgments as involving claims about the justifications that some agents could ask others to accept, rather than claims about what a single agent would have reason to want under specified conditions, it avoids in at least one way the charge of being "monological," which Habermas levels against some similar views. (See "Discourse Ethics," in *Moral Consciousness and Communicative Action,* pp. 66–68.) But he also says that "the justification of norms requires that real discourse be carried out, and thus cannot occur in a strictly monological form, i.e., in the form of a hypothetical process of argumentation occurring in the individual mind" (p. 68). In my view, while interaction with others plays a crucial role in arriving at well-founded moral opinions (see note 13 below and the accompanying text), reaching a conclusion about right and wrong requires making a judgment about

what others could or could not reasonably reject. This is a judgment that each of us must make for him- or herself. The agreement of others, reached through actual discourse, is not required, and when it occurs does not settle the matter. In this respect my account may remain, in his terms, "monological."

6. For discussion of this claim about 'reasonableness', in its epistemological as well as moral uses, see Chapter 1, Section 3.

7. As is pointed out by W. M. Sibley in "The Rational versus the Reasonable."

8. Thus, for example, what Richard Miller calls "formal contractualism" assigns to each individual an equally intense desire to achieve the goal of regulation by principles all agree on. This is then balanced against individuals' other (actual) desires in order to determine what principles they have reason to reject or to accept. I agree with Miller's rejection of contractualism, so understood. See *Moral Difference*, pp. 354 and also 355–364.

9. I will say more in Sections 4 and 6 of this chapter about how these objections are to be understood.

10. Thomas Nagel discusses this possibility in *Equality and Partiality*. I am grateful to him for helpful discussions of this issue, and also to Shelly Kagan.

11. I am indebted to Donald Davidson and Hannah Ginsborg for a conversation in which they called my attention to this contrast. See also Aurel Kolnai, "Aesthetic and Moral Experience," pp. 202–203.

12. As Philippa Foot has argued in "Morality and Art" and *Moral Relativism*. I will discuss this kind of relativity in Chapter 8.

13. I have defended this view in more detail in "Freedom of Expression and Categories of Expression."

14. This structure is more complex in some cases than in others. It may be more complex in the case of promises and of rights such as freedom of expression than in such principles as ones requiring us to be sensitive to our neighbors' interests. But even in cases like McCormick's, our sense of the relative strength of the claims that various interests make on other people depends not only on what those interests are but also on our assessment of what constitutes a workable principle specifying the ways in which we can be asked to take others' concerns into account.

15. The last two factors I have mentioned, the importance of assurance and the significance of the reasons people recognize, may bear on the interpretation of a somewhat surprising statement by J. S. Mill in "Remarks on Bentham's Philosophy." In this unsigned essay of 1833, Mill criticizes Bentham for confusing utilitarianism with what Mill calls "the doctrine of specific consequences," by which he means the doctrine that "an act is to be judged right or wrong on the basis of its consequences or the consequences of similar acts if performed generally." The brief explanation that Mill goes on to offer is somewhat enigmatic, but it seems that he may have in mind factors like those I have just mentioned. According to Mill, in judging whether an act is wrong we are judging whether people should be blamed for so acting, and in deciding whether they should be blamed we need to take into account the reasons that we would like to inculcate in people and have

them be animated by. Here we must take into account not only the consequences of the actions that certain reasons would lead people to perform but also what it would mean to have people be motivated in this way. Robert Adams also stresses the fact that the consequences of motives are not limited to those brought about through the actions they motivate; see "Motive Utilitarianism." See also Henry Sidgwick, *Methods of Ethics*, pp. 405–406, 413.

16. In fact I believe that we generally overestimate the value of the voluntariness requirement and the burden of taking the weaknesses of our bargaining partners into account. I will return to this question in Chapter 6.

17. Feminist writers have called attention to important biases of these kinds. See, for example, Catharine MacKinnon, "Sex Equality: On Difference and Dominance."

18. Here I am in agreement with one interpretation of Habermas' insistence that moral judgment depends on "a real process of argumentation." As he says, "nothing better prevents others from perspectivally distorting one's own interests than actual participation" ("Discourse Ethics," p. 66). But while one's understanding of the generic reasons arising from various standpoints depends in this way on one's experience, including the experience of hearing and discussing the claims that people actually in these standpoints advance, it also remains true that decisions about which actions are right require judgments about what others could or could not reasonably reject. Information about what they do or do not actually reject may be useful in arriving at such judgments but is not sufficient for them.

19. I am unable to think of a general moral principle of which this seems to be true. It is more plausible to think that particular cooperative arrangements, such as a practice among neighboring farmers to help one another with their harvests, might make demands that would be too onerous to be required of any except those who can expect to benefit in their turn from the contributions of others.

20. Rawls, *A Theory of Justice*, p. 131.

21. Hare, *Moral Thinking*, p. 41.

22. See David Brink, "The Separateness of Persons, Distributive Norms, and Moral Theory." On p. 253 Brink writes: "Because these different moral theories and distributive norms provide accounts of the foundations of moral and political entitlements, we must examine their implications for contexts in which entitlements do not already exist. To do this, we must focus on macro issues of just institutional design, because this will explain how particular entitlements are generated, and micro questions of allocation among individuals none of whom has a prior claim of special entitlement or desert."

23. As I argued in Chapter 3, well-being is not a master value: the value of other things does not always derive from the fact that they make individuals' lives better. But if these things are valuable, then recognizing them does contribute to the quality of people's lives. From an individual's point of view, what is primary in most cases is the (impersonal) value of these aims and pursuits. In determining

what we owe to each other, however, what matters is the contribution that these values make to individual lives.

24. Thomas Nagel has argued for a qualified version of this priority thesis, and I have suggested something like it myself in earlier writings. In "Contractualism and Utilitarianism" (p. 123) I wrote: "Under Contractualism, when we consider a principle our attention is naturally directed first to those who would do worst under it." The issue has also been discussed by Parfit and by Brink. See Nagel, *Equality and Partiality*, esp. pp. 65–74; Derek Parfit, *Equality or Priority?*; Brink, "The Separateness of Persons, Distributive Norms, and Moral Theory."

25. Peter Singer argues for such a principle, but without the qualification I go on to state, in "Famine, Affluence and Morality."

26. Nagel, *Equality and Partiality*, p. 69.

27. It is perhaps significant that one of Nagel's intuitively forceful examples concerns what he suggests are a parent's stronger reasons for benefiting one child, who is in general worse off, rather than another who can be benefited more. As I argued in Chapter 3, the idea of overall well-being plays a more significant role in the concern of parents for their children than it does in the duties owed to others more generally. Some of Nagel's other examples move from individual morality to questions of social justice, where again considerations of overall well-being have greater significance.

28. This is not to say that generic reasons for rejecting principles of individual conduct never depend on effects over a whole life. Effects over a whole life are relevant, for example, when the overall burdensomeness of living under a certain principle is taken into account. But what is relevant in such cases is the *difference* it would make, over a whole life, for someone to have to live up to that principle, not a comparison of different people's overall levels of well-being.

29. Nagel, *Equality and Partiality*, p. 69.

30. As Nagel notes, ibid., p. 70, n. 19. While Nagel's egalitarian ideal has some force, I believe that the considerations that pull us most strongly toward greater equality are of a different, and more specific, character. I defend this view in *The Diversity of Objections to Inequality*.

31. Parfit, *Equality or Priority?*

32. Some forms of consequentialism seek to avoid these implications by including not only the sum of individual benefits but also other values, such as equality, as part of the good that is to be maximized. I do not think that bringing in equality in this way, as a separate good that can be balanced against benefits to individuals, provides an adequate response to what is intuitively objectionable about sacrificing the interests of a few in order to bring small benefits to a large number of others. But I will not explore these possibilities here.

33. A position defended by G. E. M. Anscombe in "Who Is Wronged?"

34. Frances Kamm considers a similar argument for aggregation in *Morality, Mortality*, chap. 6, esp. pp. 116–117. I have learned much from Kamm's discussion.

35. It is important here not to rely on the slippery metaphor of "weight." As Shelly Kagan has pointed out, from the fact that a certain consideration is morally relevant it does not follow that its moral significance takes the form of a reason that is "added to" the force of other reasons (see "The Additive Fallacy"). But there are grounds for thinking that in this case the significance of saving the additional life does take this form. First, it is part of the definition of the case that there are no relevant factors other than each person's need to be saved. Second, if there were only two people, and only one could be saved, then the reasons for saving them would be equivalent, so it is very plausible to suppose that (other considerations being excluded) if there is a third person then the positive reason for saving him or her should be the deciding factor.

36. I should emphasize that the cases in question here are ones that do not involve special ties. As I have said, I think that it would be reasonable to reject principles that required us always to give the same weight to the lives and interests of strangers as to those of our loved ones or, for that matter, our own.

37. This principle is advocated by John Broome in "Selecting People Randomly."

38. There are cases in which it could be argued that a lottery is to be preferred because, over time, it leads to a different, and fairer, outcome. For example, in an electoral district with a permanent minority it might be argued that a weighted lottery in which everyone votes and the decision is made by choosing one of the votes at random is fairer than majority rule as a method for making political choices. Majority rule could be reasonably rejected, according to this argument, because under it the minority will never have any influence on political choices. I will not try to assess this argument here. My point is that this case is different from the one considered in the text. The electoral example concerns a method for making many decisions over time, in which the same people will be involved and will be in the same positions. I have assumed in discussing the Rescue Principle that the case in question is not of this kind: the members of the smaller group should not expect, over time, to find themselves repeatedly in this minority position. In special cases that were of this kind the case for weighted lottery would be stronger. John Taurek considers such a case in "Should the Numbers Count?"

39. If a decision is based on consideration of the relevant reasons, then it is not unfair in the sense I specified in Section 4 above. For Broome, however, this does not guarantee fairness, which he understands more narrowly. For him, a decision to send a particular person on a dangerous mission because her skills make the mission more likely to succeed would be unfair. Since this person's claim to safety is just as strong as that of the others, fairness would require a lottery. He acknowledges that it may be right to make the assignment on the basis of talent instead, but if so this is because the value of efficiency outweighs fairness. See Broome, "Fairness" and *Weighing Goods,* pp. 193–196.

40. This distinction is made very clearly by Rahul Kumar in "Consensualism in Principle," p. 99.

41. Perhaps there are cases (such as protecting a town from being washed away

by a flash flood) in which the urgency of the project is so great as to justify risks to workers that would normally not be allowed. But the urgency of these cases is a matter of the greater costs or benefits that are involved for individuals, not simply of the fact that greater numbers are affected.

42. Even if I am right in holding that we do not need to appeal to interpersonal aggregation in order to explain why the accidental injuries that such projects are likely to entail do not make it wrong to undertake them, this does not rule out the possibility that this form of aggregation might be relevant to other questions. For example, even if the likelihood that, despite all reasonable precautions, some workers will suffer serious injury does not make it impermissible to build a large building that few will use, it still might be *better* not to build it. It might also be argued that interpersonal aggregation of benefits is called for in order to decide whether a given project represents a proper use of public resources.

43. There may be some interaction between this principle, allowing (or requiring) certain forms of rescue, and the principle I discussed earlier, permitting projects that involve risk of injury or death. A policy of rescuing people like Jones, even at the cost of inconvenience to many, is one of the things that reduce the likelihood of serious injury to those who do dangerous work. So it may be that the cost of the former principle is a crucial element in making it unreasonable to reject the latter.

44. In *Morality, Mortality*, vol. 1, Frances Kamm formulates a view of this kind (her Principle of Irrelevant Utilities, p. 146) and examines in detail (chaps. 8–10) various reasons that could be offered for it.

45. I will use Rawls's Original Position argument as an example, since it is likely to come to many readers' minds as fitting this model. Some remarks in *A Theory of Justice* suggest an argument of this kind. On p. 119, for example, Rawls says: "That is, a simplified situation is described in which rational individuals with certain ends and related to each other in certain ways are to choose among various courses of action in view of their knowledge of the circumstances. What these individuals will do is then derived by strictly deductive reasoning from these assumptions." I do not think, however, that this model is an accurate characterization of the argument of *A Theory of Justice* taken as a whole, or even, as I have argued in "Contractualism and Utilitarianism" (pp. 123–128), the most plausible interpretation of Rawls's Original Position argument in particular. But I will leave this interpretive question aside.

46. The primary social goods include rights and liberties, powers and opportunities, income and wealth, and the social bases of self-respect. See Rawls, *A Theory of Justice,* pp. 62, 92 and 142.

47. See John Rawls, "Social Unity and Primary Goods," pp. 168, 169, 170.

48. David Hume, *A Treatise of Human Nature,* bk. III, pt. II, sec. V (p. 525 in the Selby-Bigge edition).

49. So, for example, I argued in Section 6 above that it would be reasonable to reject principles that rely on pronouns, proper names, or "rigged descriptions" because they arbitrarily favor some over others. In Rawls's theory, by contrast, the

parties have no reason to propose or agree to such principles because they have no way of knowing whether they or those they represent would be favored by them. But the reason for imposing this veil of ignorance lies in the judgment that people would have reason to accept principles of justice that emerge from the Original Position only if it is a fair process in which "no one is able to design principles to favor his particular condition" (*A Theory of Justice*, p. 12). So Rawls's argument and my own rely on the same judgment, made in my case as part of the "contractual" process and in his as part of the rationale for its design.

6. Responsibility

1. This is basically the strategy set out by H. L. A. Hart in "Legal Responsibility and Excuses," and I am indebted to his account. Since Hart's article, many others have written in a similar vein although, like Hart, they have been concerned mainly with the theory of punishment. See, for example, John Mackie, "The Grounds of Responsibility."

2. Gerald Dworkin calls attention to the variability of the value of choice in "Is More Choice Better than Less?"

3. Earlier, in "The Significance of Choice," I called this "demonstrative" value. This term, especially in conjunction with the example of the gift, had the disadvantage of suggesting that what is in question is the value of demonstrating *to others* certain aspects of one's self. As I hope the examples in the next paragraphs make clear, what I have in mind is broader than this. I am grateful to John Roemer for calling this problem to my attention.

4. The idea expressed in the Forfeiture View is stated with particular clarity by Carlos Nino in "A Consensual Theory of Punishment."

5. The obligation to keep a promise is, however, an instance of a more general form of obligation for which explicit consent is not always a precondition. I will discuss this matter more fully in the next chapter.

6. Joel Feinberg calls attention to this aspect of punishment in "The Expressive Function of Punishment."

7. This does not mean that what the person did is necessarily wrong and that he should have done something else. There is such a thing as doing the right thing for the wrong reasons, in which case a person is open to moral criticism for the way in which he decided what to do even though the proper way of deciding would have led to the same action.

8. Here I return to matters discussed in Sections 4 and 5 of Chapter 3, under the headings "Importance" and "Priority."

9. The importance of such "reactive attitudes" was emphasized by Peter Strawson in "Freedom and Resentment." These attitudes also play a central role in Jay Wallace's account, *Responsibility and the Moral Sentiments,* esp. chap. 3. Strawson's understanding of these attitudes differs from mine, however. See note 17, below.

10. This is the kind of importance described in Chapter 4, Section 4, with the slight difference that what was discussed there was the importance of a person's being concerned at all with the requirements of justifiability to others, whereas what is at issue here is the importance of living up to these requirements.

11. See Chapter 1, Section 2. We can "in principle" be called on to defend our judgment-sensitive attitudes: asking for such a defense is not inappropriate in the way that it would be inappropriate to ask someone to justify his height or the size of his feet. But the appropriateness of actually asking for such a defense on any particular occasion is of course another matter, and depends on many factors such as the subject matter of the attitude, the grounds of one's interest in it, and one's relation with the person in question.

12. Thomas Nagel, "Moral Luck," in *Mortal Questions,* pp. 32–33.

13. For another defense of the view that people can be responsible, and blameworthy, for mental states that are not under their voluntary control see Robert Adams, "Involuntary Sins."

14. I take the term 'desert-entailing' from Galen Strawson, "On 'Freedom and Resentment,'" p. 90. See also his book *Freedom and Belief.*

15. See J. J. C. Smart, "Free Will, Praise, and Blame."

16. Ibid., p. 212.

17. Here my understanding of these attitudes differs from Peter Strawson's, since he takes them to entail a "partial withdrawal of goodwill" and a "modification of the general demand that another should, if possible, be spared suffering"; "Freedom and Resentment," p. 78. Thus on his understanding, but not mine, these are desert-entailing notions.

18. *Nicomachean Ethics* 1110a9–19. Aristotle says that such actions are "mixed" because they are in some ways like voluntary actions and in others like involuntary ones. But he comes down on the side of calling them voluntary since "the origin of the action is within" the agent. Bernard Williams emphasizes that the sailors in this example *choose* to throw the goods overboard, but that they nonetheless do not "act freely"; *Shame and Necessity,* pp. 153–154. For more on this question of freedom, see note 29 below.

19. In Harry Frankfurt's view, this would not count as coercion but only as duress. He writes: "A person who is coerced is *compelled* to do what he does. He has *no choice* but to do it. This is at least part of what is essential if coercion is to relieve its victim of moral responsibility—if it is to make it inappropriate either to praise or to blame him for having done what he was coerced into doing." Frankfurt's analysis is that "a coercive threat arouses in its victim a desire—i.e., to avoid the penalty—so powerful that it will move him to perform the required action regardless of whether he wants to perform it or considers that it would be reasonable for him to do so." See Frankfurt, "Coercion and Moral Responsibility," in *The Importance of What We Care About,* pp. 26–46. The quoted passages occur on pp. 36–37 and 41, respectively. What Frankfurt calls coercion is certainly a loss of control akin to those in my first category, hence another way in which threats

can absolve a person of responsibility. If cases of this kind are the only ones properly called "coercion," however, then coercion is very rare. I therefore think that what we commonly call coercion does not "relieve its victim of moral responsibility" in the radical way Frankfurt suggests. But this disagreement with Frankfurt is largely terminological. We appear to agree on the important point that the relevant conception of moral responsibility here is what I called above responsibility as attributability.

20. See, for example, Jonathan Glover, *Responsibility,* pp. 70–73; Jay Wallace, *Responsibility and the Moral Sentiments,* esp. chap. 4; and Ferdinand Schoeman, "Statistical Norms and Moral Attributions," esp. p. 311. For a critical discussion of this idea see Gary Watson, "Two Faces of Responsibility."

21. Susan Wolf, *Freedom within Reason,* pp. 37, 77, 85–86. The quoted passages occur on p. 85. She does not mention the idea of fairness, but her objection is nonetheless similar in spirit to those just mentioned.

22. On this reading, the general conclusion that because people cannot control the development of their character they can never be blamed for what they do might be named the Doctrine of Original Innocence. It does not seem likely, however, that Wolf intended her examples to be understood in this way, since she distinguishes her account from what she calls "The Real Self View," according to which a person is properly blamed for an action if and only if it reveals her true self. She criticizes this view in *Freedom within Reason,* chap. 2.

23. Gary Watson puts the point more strongly. He writes: "[It is] only insofar as and because blaming responses (at least potentially) affect the interests of their objects adversely that moral accountability raises the issues of avoidability that have been central to the traditional topic of moral responsibility"; "Two Faces of Responsibility," p. 239.

24. It would be unfair to withdraw all sympathy or to respond to his faults with gratuitous unpleasantness. Useless moral lectures might fall into the latter category. But these forms of ill treatment would not be licensed simply by the moral judgment that he is a nasty person who has treated others in indefensible ways.

25. This form of the appeal to unfairness is endorsed, and discussed in detail, by Jay Wallace in *Responsibility and the Moral Sentiments,* esp. pp. 108–111.

26. At least it need not do so. Perhaps it might in a case like that illustrated by the interpretation of Wolf's example that I suggested, according to which the woman who sees no reason to get the book for her friend is seen as struggling sincerely to discover the best thing to do. This would, however, be a rare case at best.

27. This might explain the divergence between, on the one hand, theorists such as Wolf and Wallace, who in different ways support the idea that agents who cannot appreciate the force of moral reasons cannot properly be blamed, and writers such as Watson and I, who take the opposite view. Bernard Williams might also be counted in the former group.

28. This could be browbeating in the sense discussed in Chapter 1, in connection with Williams' use of the case of Owen Wingrave.

29. It is sometimes suggested that it makes a difference to the assessment of an agent's freedom whether eligible alternatives are removed by the conscious intervention of other agents (as in cases of coercion) or by forces of nature (as in the case of the sailors). Bernard Williams says, for example, that while it is quite reasonable to say that the sailors in Aristotle's example act freely in throwing the goods overboard, "it would be a great paradox to say that someone acted freely if forced to surrender his goods in a holdup" (*Shame and Necessity,* p. 153). He goes on to say that "even the case in which my choices are limited by others' intentional actions is less obviously a limitation of my freedom if the intentions are not directed against me. The reason for this is that being free stands opposed, above all, to being in someone's power" (p. 154). From one point of view this seems mistaken. When we are simply assessing an agent's situation it often does not matter whether the alternatives available to that agent have been restricted by nature or by other agents. Being deprived of desirable alternatives in either of these ways is a bad thing. (Here I agree with Frankfurt; see "Coercion and Moral Responsibility," p. 45.) But the distinction Williams mentions can also be important, for at least two reasons. First, even if we are simply assessing an agent's situation from his or her point of view, being under the control of others can have a special disvalue (an example of what I called "symbolic value" in Section 2 above), although not every case of being deprived of alternatives by the action of others involves being "under their control" or is objectionable in this way. Second, when questions of freedom are raised, what is often at issue is not just an assessment of an agent's situation but a question of whether an agent is being treated properly by other agents or by the social institutions of his society. When this is what is at issue, restrictions that result from alterable human actions or institutions obviously have greater significance than those due to unalterable forces of nature. But this reflects the particular question that is being asked rather than a general fact about what diminishes a person's freedom.

30. The prevalence of this mistake may lend support to the opposite tendency: people may be reluctant to say that someone who behaves badly as a result of a deprived childhood can nonetheless be blamed for what he does, because this seems to imply that such people are not entitled to our help. No doubt many others have pointed out the error in the political argument I have just discussed. One that has come to my attention is Lynne Sharp Paine, "Managing for Organizational Integrity."

7. Promises

1. David Hume, *A Treatise of Human Nature,* bk. III, pt. II, chap. V. See John Rawls, *A Theory of Justice,* pp. 344–350.

2. Neil MacCormick expressed similar misgivings in "Voluntary Obligations

and Normative Powers I." He goes on to offer an account based on a general obligation not to disappoint the expectations of others whom we have knowingly induced to rely upon us (p. 68). I will set out the moral foundations of a similar account that I hope will avoid objections such as those raised by Joseph Raz in his contribution to that same symposium ("Voluntary Obligations and Normative Powers II") and in his "Promises and Obligations." In the latter article, Raz distinguishes between the "intention" conception of promises, according to which the essence of a promise lies in the communication, under the proper circumstances, of a firm intention to act in a certain way, and the "obligation" conception, according to which the essence of a promise lies in the intention to undertake, by that very act of communication, an obligation to perform a certain action. In my view, which lies in the common ground between MacCormick's account and Raz's, the elements of intention and obligation are interdependent: promises are distinguished by the fact that the intention expressed is supposed to be made credible by appeal to a shared conception of obligation, but the grounds of this obligation lie in a principle very close to the one which MacCormick states. Judith Thomson presents an account of promises that is similar to mine in *The Realm of Rights*, chap. 12.

3. In "Promises and Practices" I wrote: "or by providing compensation—that is, by doing something else 'just as good'" (p. 204). This now seems to me mistaken. If no assurance of the kind (described later in the text in Principle F) has been given, then the *most* that could be required would be to compensate the person for any loss suffered as a result of relying on this mistaken belief. In fact I am inclined to say that the most that could be required would be the lesser of the following two things: *either* the level of compensation required to make the person as well off as he or she would have been without having so relied *or* the level of compensation required to make the person as well off as he or she would have been as a result of this reliance if the other party had performed as he expected.

4. The importance of promisers' interests in being able to bind themselves is pointed out by Joseph Raz, *The Morality of Freedom*, p. 173. It seems to me, however, that the interests of promisees are primary here and provide the clearest grounds of obligation. The interests of promisers have real force only when linked to them.

5. In the absence of these conditions there could still be *some* obligations, but they would be of the weaker sort specified by Principles D and L.

6. They entail this since A has led B to believe that he or she will do X *unless B consents to A's not doing* X. This is the assurance that A is said to know that B wants and that A intends to provide. But A would not have provided this assurance if A added the rider, "But of course I may change my mind and reserve the right to do so." I am grateful to Michael Bratman for pressing me to clarify this point.

7. As I indicated in the case of Principle M, this justification need not take the form of considerations that *override* the obligation specified by Principle F. But

there are cases in which this term may seem more appropriate than in the four examples I listed in discussing manipulation. For example, if the thing one has promised to do would be improper or wrong, it may be that one should not do it despite having promised to do so. (This could be accounted for by the fact that the promisee's interest in having the thing done is not legitimate.) In such cases there may remain an obligation, of the kind specified by Principle L, to warn the promisee that one will not perform or, if he has performed first, to compensate by repaying the cost of that performance.

8. Páll Ardal notes this "emphasizing" role of the words "I promise" in the opening paragraphs of "'And That's a Promise.'"

9. By contrast, a person who says, "I firmly intend to do X, but I don't *promise* to," gives the kind of warning which makes Principle F inapplicable, and expresses the judgment that, having given this warning, he or she is free to decide not to do X.

10. G. E. M. Anscombe, "Rules, Rights, and Promises."

11. As noted by MacCormick ("Voluntary Obligations and Normative Powers I," p. 72) and by Raz ("Promises and Obligations," p. 214).

12. I once held such a view myself (see "Liberty, Contract, and Contribution"), but it no longer seems to me to be correct. My thinking on this topic was aided by very helpful discussion with Christopher McMahon. The idea that promising should be seen as a practice with specific rules is criticized by Stanley Cavell in *The Claim of Reason*, p. 293. Cavell also stresses the continuity between promises and other ways of making a commitment (p. 298).

13. At least this is so as long as the special limitations are a restriction, not an extension, of the "normal" limits and as long as only the parties to the agreement are affected by them in a material way.

14. The fact that those who make such threats would like to be able to "bind themselves" by "promising" in order to make their statements of intent more convincing carries no weight. Analogous desires of would-be benefactors, however, are a different matter.

15. This reflects the fact that the interest of potential promisers in being able to provide assurance retains little moral weight when it is separated from promisees' interest in having assurance provided.

16. B. J. Diggs has argued that the obligation to keep a promise is best accounted for in this way.

17. Here I am indebted to a helpful comment from Geoffrey Hawthorn.

18. The question of what to say about such cases is raised by Alan Ryan in "Professional Liars." Ryan's discussion of lying and of obligations to tell the truth is concerned with the special duties of people such as doctors, public officials, and politicians. These include not only duties not to lie but also special duties to provide patients, clients, constituents, and colleagues with true and useful information.

19. The parallel between these two sets of principles characterizes the close relation between the moral objections to lying and to faithless promises. This

parallel explains why it is natural to say, as Charles Fried does, that "every lie is a broken promise," even though, as I will go on to argue, the obligation to keep a promise in fact differs in important respects from the duty not to lie. See Fried, *Right and Wrong*, p. 67.

20. This dependence of the efficacy of promises on the moral prohibition against breaking them (and against making them in bad faith) is what underlies the plausibility of Kant's claim that a maxim according to which one will make a "lying promise" whenever it suits one's convenience could not even *be* a universal law, let alone be willed to be one (*Grounding for the Metaphysics of Morals*, sect. 2 [Ak. 422]). Promising is a way of getting someone to loan you money, who is otherwise unwilling to do so, only because it is generally regarded as wrong to fail to fulfill a promise and people are generally influenced by this fact. So if it were a universal law that anyone may make a promise, with no intention of fulfilling it, when this is the only way to get the money he or she needs, then promising would not in fact be a means of getting money under such circumstances. (As Kant says, people would laugh at promises as a vain pretense.) But things are crucially different in the case of lying, since the efficacy of most lies does not depend on the idea that those who tell them are constrained by a moral prohibition against lying. So it is not true in general that if it were permissible to tell a lie whenever this was supported by the balance of one's nonmoral reasons then these lies would not be believed. Christine Korsgaard has pointed out that a lie told to a murderer who comes to the door asking whether his intended victim is in the house could remain efficacious even if its maxim were made a universal law, because the murderer, who supposes that his intentions are not known, does not know that he is in a situation of the kind to which this law would apply. (See Korsgaard, "The Right to Lie: Kant on Dealing with Evil.") If what I have been saying is correct then something similar is true of lies in general, since those to whom they are told often have no reason to believe that they are in a situation in which the person speaking to them would lie unless constrained by a duty not to do so.

21. R. S. Downie, "Three Concepts of Promising."

22. See Lynne McFall, "Integrity." But I doubt that integrity in this sense could provide a reason to *carry out* an immoral threat. Simply to forget that one had made the threat, or to abandon it out of fear, might show a lack of integrity; but to renounce it on grounds of immorality would not.

23. Adam Smith, *The Theory of Moral Sentiments*, pp. 330 ff. Downie cites Smith in "Three Concepts of Promising."

24. Smith, *The Theory of Moral Sentiments*, p. 332. Kant also, in discussing the case of lying to a murderer who comes to the door looking for his intended victim, says that such a lie would be wrong even though it would not be a wrong to the murderer. See "On a Supposed Right to Lie Because of Philanthropic Concerns" (Ak. 426), p. 163. On this general point I am indebted to Sally Sedgwick's "On Lying and the Role of Content in Kant's Ethics."

8. Relativism

1. Here I follow Gilbert Harman's account in "What Is Moral Relativism?" and in his contribution to Gilbert Harman and Judith Jarvis Thomson, *Moral Relativism and Moral Objectivity*, p. 5.

2. This problem is forcefully presented by Hilary Putnam in *Reason, Truth, and History*, chap. 5.

3. John Locke, *Letter on Toleration* (1689). Quoted from the Library of Liberal Arts edition (Indianapolis: The Bobbs-Merrill Company, 1950), p. 52.

4. Philippa Foot, "Morality and Art," p. 143.

5. Gilbert Harman, "Moral Relativism Defended."

6. Ibid. Harman does allow that we can condemn Hitler in other ways, for example by saying that he was evil.

7. The relevant response to this form of relativism is to offer a positive account of the grounds of moral requirements, as I have done in the preceding chapters.

8. See Philippa Foot, "Morality and Art" and *Moral Relativism*; Michael Walzer, *Spheres of Justice, Interpretation and Social Criticism*, and "Moral Minimalism." Gilbert Harman also sees the relativism he defends as a nondebunking view. See Harman and Thomson, *Moral Relativism and Moral Objectivity*, pp. 5–6.

9. Michael Walzer defends such a view in the works cited in the preceding note.

10. A point emphasized by Stuart Hampshire. See, for example, "Morality and Convention."

11. It seems that those who defend relativism generally focus on how moral requirements could give agents reason to act, while those who oppose it focus on how these requirements could ensure that the victims of these actions have reason to accept their results (a characterization of the motives of anti-relativists that might have made Nietzsche smile, even though he did not consider himself a relativist).

12. Walzer, *Interpretation and Social Criticism*, pp. 40–48. For a similar use of an empirical claim about the content that any institutions (in this case legal institutions) must have if they are to be generally accepted, see H. L. A. Hart's discussion of the "minimum content of natural law" in *The Concept of Law*, pp. 189–195.

13. Walzer appears to accept at least an explanatory, if not necessarily a normative, role for this idea. See *Interpretation and Social Criticism*, p. 46.

14. As I have stated it, the Principle of Established Practices differs from Rawls's principle of fairness in not requiring, as a condition of being bound by a practice, that one have willingly accepted its benefits. In this respect it is more like what Rawls calls the natural duty of justice. The argument I have offered for it is similar to the reasoning Rawls presents for this natural duty, although his discussion concentrates on the case of political and economic institutions, which are the main concern of his theory. See *A Theory of Justice*, secs. 51–52, pp. 333–350.

15. This is not to say that it would be permissible to intervene, against their wishes, in the name of their true interests. Since, as I noted in Chapter 6, one of the things people have reason to want is to be able to control their lives in certain ways, what people actually want makes a difference to how they may be treated. But this is compatible with the fact that actual wishes are not what is fundamental: what people have reason to want determines how and when what they actually want makes a moral difference.

16. It may therefore count as what Walzer calls a "reiterative" principle rather than a free-standing universal norm. See "Moral Minimalism," pp. 6–9.

17. See Walzer, *Spheres of Justice,* esp. pp. 6–20. In Walzer's discussion it sounds as if moral consequences can be read off directly from the "social meanings" themselves. By contrast, I am trying to show how what he would call differences in social meaning can have moral significance within the framework of a larger (contractualist) account of right and wrong.

18. I discuss the variety in Walzer's examples of "social meanings" in "Local Justice."

19. For reasons like those mentioned in the case of privacy, these negative requirements will not be the same in every society. For example, the kind of preparation that children need to become self-sufficient adults will not always be the same.

20. See Rawls, *A Theory of Justice,* p. 112.

21. It might seem that the Principle of Established Practices could also bind people to abide by a widely held ideal, but this will not be so if there is no need to have one of these ideals rather than another established.

22. See Chapter 6, Section 5.

23. The latter would be one version of the phenomenon David Wong describes by saying that the term 'adequate moral system' may have different extensions as used by different people. See his *Moral Relativity,* p. 45.

24. On the transparency of first-person attributions of mental states, see Richard Moran, "Making Up Your Mind: Self-Interpretation and Self-Constitution."

25. See J. L. Mackie, *Ethics: Inventing Right and Wrong,* pp. 36–38.

26. Ibid., p. 37.

27. Philippa Foot draws a distinction that can be interpreted in this way in "Moral Relativism." I discuss her distinction and its interpretation in "Fear of Relativism."

Appendix

1. Bernard Williams, "Internal and External Reasons," in *Moral Luck,* p. 113.

2. Ibid., p. 106.

3. Ibid., p. 105.

4. At least as that doctrine is commonly understood. I take Williams to be making a claim about reasons in the "standard normative sense," so he is generalizing Hume's doctrine only if Hume is also making such a claim. I believe that he

is commonly so interpreted, but I will not go into the question of whether this interpretation is correct. Hume's famous remark is from *A Treatise of Human Nature*, bk. II, pt. III, sec. III (p. 415 in the Selby-Bigge edition).

5. See Williams, "Internal and External Reasons," p. 104.

6. Ibid., p. 109.

7. Ibid., p. 110.

8. Bernard Williams, "Internal Reasons and the Obscurity of Blame," p. 39.

9. The first two observations are from "Internal and External Reasons," p. 110; the last from "Internal Reasons and the Obscurity of Blame," p. 38.

10. "There is an essential indeterminacy in what can be counted a rational deliberative process. Practical reasoning is a heuristic process, and an imaginative one, and there are no fixed boundaries on the continuum from rational thought to inspiration and conversion"; Williams, "Internal and External Reasons," p. 110.

11. The importance of this distinction is pointed out by John McDowell in "Might There Be External Reasons?" p. 70.

12. Williams, "Internal Reasons and the Obscurity of Blame," p. 36. Williams goes on to say: "Taking other people's perspective on a situation, we hope to be able to point out that they have reason to do things they did not think they had reason to do, or, perhaps, less reason to do certain things than they thought they had."

Bibliography

Ackerman, Bruce. *Social Justice and the Liberal State*. New Haven: Yale University Press, 1980.

Adams, Robert. "Involuntary Sins." *Philosophical Review* 94 (1985): 3–31.

—— "Motive Utilitarianism." *Journal of Philosophy* 73 (1976): 467–481.

—— *The Virtue of Faith and Other Essays in Philosophical Theology*. New York: Cambridge University Press, 1987.

Anderson, Elizabeth. *Value in Ethics and Economics*. Cambridge, Mass.: Harvard University Press, 1993.

Anscombe, G. E. M. "Rules, Rights and Promises." In *Ethics, Religion, and Politics: Collected Philosophical Papers*. Minneapolis: University of Minnesota Press, 1981. pp. 97–103.

—— "Who Is Wronged?" *Oxford Review* 5 (1967): 16–17.

Ardal, Páll. "'And That's a Promise.'" *Philosophical Quarterly* 18 (1968): 225–237.

Aristotle. *Nicomachean Ethics*. Translated by Terence Irwin. Indianapolis: Hackett, 1985.

Arrow, Kenneth. *Social Choice and Individual Values*. 2d ed. New York: John Wiley & Sons, 1966.

Audi, Robert. "Weakness of Will and Rational Action." In *Action, Intention, and Reason*. Ithaca: Cornell University Press, 1993. Pp. 319–333.

Barry, Brian. *Justice as Impartiality*. Oxford: Clarendon Press, 1995.

—— *Theories of Justice*. Berkeley: University of California Press, 1989.

Bond, E. J. *Reason and Value*. Cambridge: Cambridge University Press, 1984.

Brandt, Richard. *A Theory of the Good and the Right*. Oxford: Clarendon Press, 1979.

Bratman, Michael. *Intention, Plans, and Practical Reason*. Cambridge, Mass.: Harvard University Press, 1987.

Brink, David. *Moral Realism and the Foundations of Ethics*. Cambridge: Cambridge University Press, 1989.

———— "The Separateness of Persons, Distributive Norms, and Moral Theory." In *Value, Welfare, and Morality*. Edited by R. G. Frey and Christopher Morris. Cambridge: Cambridge University Press, 1993. Pp. 252–289.

Broome, John. "Fairness." *Proceedings of the Aristotelian Society* 91 (1990): 87–102.

———— "Selecting People Randomly." *Ethics* 95 (1984): 38–55.

———— *Weighing Goods*. Oxford: Blackwell, 1991.

Cavell, Stanley. *The Claim of Reason*. New York: Oxford University Press, 1979.

Darwall, Stephen. *Impartial Reason*. Ithaca: Cornell University Press, 1983.

———— "Self-Interest and Self-Concern." *Social Philosophy and Policy* (1997): 158–178.

Davidson, Donald. *Essays on Actions and Events*. Oxford: Clarendon Press, 1980.

Donald, Merlin. *Origins of the Modern Mind: Three Stages in the Evolution of Culture and Cognition*. Cambridge, Mass.: Harvard University Press, 1991.

Downie, R. S. "Three Concepts of Promising." *Philosophical Quarterly* 35 (1985): 259–271.

Dworkin, Gerald. "Is More Choice Better than Less?" In *Midwest Studies in Philosophy*. Edited by Peter French, Thomas Uehling, and Howard Wettstein. Minneapolis: University of Minnesota Press, 1982. Pp. 47–62.

Dworkin, Ronald. "Foundations of Liberal Equality." In *The Tanner Lectures on Human Values*. Vol. 11. Edited by Grethe B. Peterson. Salt Lake City: University of Utah Press, 1990. Pp. 1–119.

———— *Life's Dominion*. New York: Alfred A. Knopf, 1993.

Evans, Gareth. *The Varieties of Reference*. Edited by John McDowell. Oxford: Oxford University Press, 1982.

Feinberg, Joel. "The Expressive Function of Punishment." In *Doing and Deserving*. Princeton: Princeton University Press, 1970. Pp. 95–118.

Foot, Philippa. "Morality and Art." *Proceedings of the British Academy* 56 (1970): 131–144.

———— *Moral Relativism*. The Lindley Lecture. Lawrence: University of Kansas, 1979.

———— "Reasons for Action and Desires." In *Virtues and Vices*. Berkeley: University of California Press, 1978. Pp. 148–156.

———— "Utilitarianism and the Virtues." In *Consequentialism and Its Critics*, Edited by Samuel Scheffler. Oxford: Oxford University Press, 1988. Pp. 224–242.

Frankfurt, Harry. "Freedom of the Will and the Concept of a Person." *Journal of Philosophy* 68 (1971): 5–20.

———— *The Importance of What We Care About*. Cambridge: Cambridge University Press, 1988.

Fried, Charles. *An Anatomy of Values*. Cambridge, Mass.: Harvard University Press, 1970.

———— *Right and Wrong*. Cambridge, Mass.: Harvard University Press, 1978.

Gaus, Gerald F. *Value and Justification*. Cambridge: Cambridge University Press, 1990.

Gauthier, David. *Morals by Agreement*. Oxford: Clarendon Press, 1986.

Gibbard, Allan. *Wise Choices, Apt Feelings*. Cambridge, Mass.: Harvard University Press, 1990.

Glover, Jonathan. *Responsibility*. London: Routledge and Kegan Paul, 1970.

Godwin, William. *Inquiry Concerning the Principles of Political Justice*. Edited by K. Codell Carter. Oxford: Clarendon Press, 1973.

Grice, G. R. *The Grounds of Moral Judgment*. Cambridge: Cambridge University Press, 1967.

Griffin, James. *Value Judgment: Improving Our Ethical Beliefs*. Oxford: Oxford University Press, 1996.

—— *Well-Being*. Oxford: Oxford University Press, 1986.

Habermas, Jürgen. "Discourse Ethics: Notes on a Program of Philosophical Justification." In *The Communicative Ethics Controversy*. Edited by Seyla Benhabib and Fred Dallmayr. Cambridge, Mass.: MIT Press, 1990. Pp. 60–110.

—— *Moral Consciousness and Communicative Action*. Cambridge, Mass.: MIT Press, 1990.

—— *The Theory of Communicative Action*. 2 vols. Boston: Beacon Press, 1987.

Hampshire, Stuart. *Innocence and Experience*. Cambridge, Mass.: Harvard University Press, 1989.

—— "Morality and Convention." In *Morality and Conflict*. Cambridge, Mass.: Harvard University Press, 1983. Pp. 126–139.

Hare, R. M. *The Language of Morals*. Oxford: Oxford University Press, 1952.

—— *Moral Thinking*. Oxford: Oxford University Press, 1981.

Harman, Gilbert. *Change in View*. Cambridge, Mass.: MIT Press, 1986.

—— "Moral Relativism Defended." *Philosophical Review* 84 (1975): 3–22.

—— "What Is Moral Relativism?" In *Values and Morals*. Edited by Alvin Goldman and Jaegwon Kim. Dordrecht: D. Reidel, 1978. Pp. 143–161.

Harman, Gilbert, and Judith Jarvis Thomson. *Moral Relativism and Moral Objectivity*. Oxford: Blackwell, 1996.

Harsanyi, John. "Morality and the Theory of Rational Behavior." In *Utilitarianism and Beyond*. Edited by Amartya Sen and Bernard Williams. Cambridge: Cambridge University Press, 1982. Pp. 39–62.

Hart, H. L. A. *The Concept of Law*. Oxford: Clarendon Press, 1961.

—— "Legal Responsibility and Excuses." In *Punishment and Responsibility*. New York: Oxford University Press, 1968. Pp. 28–53.

Herman, Barbara. "Integrity and Impartiality." In *The Practice of Moral Judgment*. Cambridge, Mass.: Harvard University Press, 1993. Pp. 23–44.

Hume, David. *A Treatise of Human Nature* (1739–40). Edited by L. A. Selby-Bigge. Oxford: Oxford University Press, 1888.

Hurley, Susan. *Natural Reasons.* Oxford: Oxford University Press, 1989.

Johnston, Mark. "Dispositional Theories of Value." *Proceedings of the Aristotelian Society,* supp. vol. 63 (1989): 139–174.

Kagan, Shelly. "The Additive Fallacy." *Ethics* 99 (1988): 5–31.

——— *The Limits of Morality.* Oxford: Oxford University Press, 1989.

——— "The Limits of Well-Being." *Social Philosophy and Policy* 9 (1992): 169–189.

Kahneman, Daniel, and Amos Tversky. "Choices, Values, and Frames." *American Psychologist,* April 1984, pp. 341–350.

Kamm, Frances. *Morality, Mortality.* 2 vols. Oxford: Oxford University Press, 1993.

Kant, Immanuel. *Grounding for the Metaphysics of Morals.* In *Kant's Ethical Philosophy.* Translated and edited by James Ellington. 3d ed. Indianapolis: Hackett, 1993.

——— "On a Supposed Right to Lie Because of Philanthropic Concerns." In *Kant's Ethical Philosophy.* Translated and edited by James Ellington. 2d ed. Indianapolis: Hackett, 1994.

Katz, Leonard. "Hedonism as a Metaphysics of Mind and Value." Ph.D. diss., Princeton University, 1986.

Kolnai, Aurel. "Aesthetic and Moral Experience." In *Ethics, Value, and Reality: Selected Papers of Aurel Kolnai.* Indianapolis: Hackett, 1978.

Korsgaard, Christine. "The Normativity of Instrumental Reason." In *Ethics and Practical Reason.* Edited by Garrett Cullity and Berys Gaut. Oxford: Clarendon Press, 1997. Pp. 215–254.

——— "The Right to Lie: Kant on Dealing with Evil." *Philosophy and Public Affairs* 15 (1986): 325–349.

——— "Skepticism about Practical Reason." *Journal of Philosophy* 83 (1986): 5–25.

——— *The Sources of Normativity.* Cambridge: Cambridge University Press, 1996.

Kripke, Saul. *Naming and Necessity.* Cambridge, Mass.: Harvard University Press, 1972.

Kumar, Rahul. "Consensualism in Principle." D.Phil. thesis, Oxford University, 1995.

Locke, John. *Letter on Toleration.* Indianapolis: Bobbs-Merrill, 1950.

MacCormick, Neil. "Voluntary Obligations and Normative Powers I." *Proceedings of the Aristotelian Society,* supp. vol. 46 (1972): 59–78.

MacIntyre, Alasdair. *After Virtue.* Notre Dame: University of Notre Dame Press, 1981.

——— *Whose Justice? Which Rationality?* Notre Dame: University of Notre Dame Press, 1988.

Mackie, John. *Ethics: Inventing Right and Wrong.* Harmondsworth: Penguin Books, 1977.

——— "The Grounds of Responsibility." In *Law, Morality and Society: Essays in Honour of H. L. A. Hart*. Edited by P. M. S. Hacker and Joseph Raz. Oxford: Clarendon Press, 1977. Pp. 175–188.

MacKinnon, Catharine. "Sex Equality: On Difference and Dominance." In *Toward a Feminist Theory of the State*. Cambridge, Mass.: Harvard University Press, 1989. Pp. 215–234.

McDowell, John. "Are Moral Reasons Hypothetical Imperatives?" *Proceedings of the Aristotelian Society* 52 (1978): 13–29.

——— "Might There Be External Reasons?" In *World, Mind and Ethics*. Edited by James Altham and Ross Harrison. Cambridge: Cambridge University Press, 1995. Pp. 68–85.

——— "Virtue and Reason." *The Monist* 62 (1979): 331–350.

McFall, Lynne. "Integrity." *Ethics* 98 (1987): 5–20.

Mill, J. S. "Remarks on Bentham's Philosophy." In *Essays on Ethics, Religion and Society. Collected Works of John Stuart Mill*. Vol. 10. Edited by J. M. Robson. Toronto: University of Toronto Press, 1969. Pp. 5–18.

——— *Utilitarianism and Other Essays*. Edited by Alan Ryan. London: Penguin Books, 1987.

Miller, Richard. *Moral Difference*. Princeton: Princeton University Press, 1992.

Moore, G. E. *Principia Ethica*. Cambridge: Cambridge University Press, 1903.

Moran, Richard. "Making Up Your Mind: Self-Interpretation and Self-Constitution." *Ratio*, n.s. 1 (1988): 135–151.

Nagel, Thomas. *Equality and Partiality*. New York: Oxford University Press, 1991.

——— *Mortal Questions*. New York: Cambridge University Press, 1979.

——— *The Possibility of Altruism*. Oxford: Clarendon Press, 1970.

——— *The View from Nowhere*. New York: Oxford University Press, 1987.

Nino, Carlos. "A Consensual Theory of Punishment." *Philosophy and Public Affairs* 12 (1983): 289–306.

Nozick, Robert. *Philosophical Explanations*. Cambridge, Mass.: Harvard University Press, 1981.

Paine, Lynne Sharp. "Managing for Organizational Integrity." *Harvard Business Review*, March–April 1994, pp. 106–117.

Parfit, Derek. *Equality or Priority?* The Lindley Lecture. Lawrence: University of Kansas, 1991.

——— *Reasons and Persons*. Oxford: Oxford University Press, 1984.

Pettit, Philip. "Consequentialism." In *Blackwell's Companion to Ethics*. Edited by Peter Singer. Oxford: Blackwell, 1992. Pp. 230–240.

Pettit, Philip, and Michael Smith. "Freedom in Belief and Desire." *Journal of Philosophy* 93 (1996): 429–449.

Prichard, H. A. "Does Moral Philosophy Rest on a Mistake?" In *Moral Obligation*. Oxford: Clarendon Press, 1949. Pp. 1–17.

Putnam, Hilary. *Mind, Language, and Reality: Collected Philosophical Papers.* Vol. 2. Cambridge: Cambridge University Press, 1975.

—— *Reason, Truth, and History.* New York: Cambridge University Press, 1981.

Quinn, Warren. *Morality and Action.* Cambridge: Cambridge University Press, 1993.

Railton, Peter. "Facts and Values." *Philosophical Topics* 24 (1986): 5–31.

Rawls, John. *Political Liberalism.* New York: Columbia University Press, 1996.

—— "Social Unity and Primary Goods." In *Utilitarianism and Beyond.* Edited by Amartya Sen and Bernard Williams. Cambridge: Cambridge University Press, 1982. Pp. 159–186.

—— *A Theory of Justice.* Cambridge, Mass.: The Belknap Press of Harvard University Press, 1971.

Raz, Joseph. *The Morality of Freedom.* Oxford: Oxford University Press, 1986.

—— "Promises and Obligations." In *Law, Morality and Society: Essays in Honour of H. L. A. Hart.* Edited by P. M. S. Hacker and Joseph Raz. Oxford: Clarendon Press, 1977. Pp. 210–228.

—— "Voluntary Obligations and Normative Powers II." *Proceedings of the Aristotelian Society,* supp. vol. 46 (1972): 79–101.

Ross, W. D. *The Right and the Good.* Oxford: Clarendon Press, 1930.

Ryan, Alan. "Professional Liars." *Social Research* 63 (1996): 619–641.

Scanlon, T. M. "The Aims and Authority of Moral Theory." *Oxford Journal of Legal Studies* 12 (1992): 1–23.

—— "Contractualism and Utilitarianism." In *Utilitarianism and Beyond.* Edited by Amartya Sen and Bernard Williams. Cambridge: Cambridge University Press, 1982. Pp. 103–128.

—— *The Diversity of Objections to Inequality.* The Lindley Lecture. Lawrence: University of Kansas, 1996.

—— "Fear of Relativism." In *Virtues and Reasons: Philippa Foot and Moral Theory.* Edited by Rosalind Hursthouse, Gavin Lawrence, and Warren Quinn. Oxford: Clarendon Press, 1995. Pp. 219–246.

—— "Freedom of Expression and Categories of Expression." *University of Pittsburgh Law Review* 40 (1979): 519–550.

—— "Liberty, Contract, and Contribution." In *Markets and Morals.* Edited by Gerald Dworkin, Gordon Bermant, and Peter Brown. Washington, D.C.: Hemisphere, 1977. Pp. 43–67.

—— "Local Justice." *London Review of Books,* September 5, 1985, pp. 17–18.

—— "Promises and Practices." *Philosophy and Public Affairs* 19 (1990): 199–226.

—— "The Significance of Choice." In *The Tanner Lectures on Human Values.* Vol. 8. Edited by Sterling McMurrin. Salt Lake City: University of Utah Press, 1988. Pp. 149–216.

—— "Value, Desire and Quality of Life." In *The Quality of Life.* Edited by

Martha Nussbaum and Amartya Sen. Oxford: Oxford University Press, 1992. Pp. 185–200.

Scheffler, Samuel. *Consequentialism and Its Critics*. Oxford: Oxford University Press, 1988.

Schoeman, Ferdinand. "Statistical Norms and Moral Attributions." In *Responsibility, Character and the Emotions*. Edited by Ferdinand Schoeman. Cambridge: Cambridge University Press, 1987. Pp. 287–315.

Schueler, G. F. *Desire: Its Role in Practical Reason and the Explanation of Action*. Cambridge, Mass.: MIT Press, 1995.

Sedgwick, Sally. "On Lying and the Role of Content in Kant's Ethics." *Kant-Studien* 82 (1991): 42–62.

Sen, Amartya. "The Impossibility of a Paretian Liberal." *Journal of Political Economy* 78 (1970). 152–157.

—— *Inequality Reexamined*. Cambridge, Mass.: Harvard University Press, 1992.

—— "Social Choice Theory: A Re-Examination." In *Choice, Welfare, and Measurement*. Cambridge, Mass.: MIT Press, 1982. Pp. 158–200.

—— "Rights and Agency." *Philosophy and Public Affairs* 11 (1982): 3–39.

Sen, Amartya, and Bernard Williams, eds. *Utilitarianism and Beyond*. Cambridge: Cambridge University Press, 1982.

Sibley, W. M. "The Rational versus the Reasonable." *Philosophical Review* 62 (1953): 554–560.

Sidgwick, Henry. *The Methods of Ethics*. 7th ed. Chicago: University of Chicago Press. 1907.

Singer, Peter. "Famine, Affluence and Morality." *Philosophy and Public Affairs* 1 (1972): 229–243.

Smart, J. J. C. "Free Will, Praise, and Blame." In *Determinism, Free Will, and Moral Responsibility*. Edited by Gerald Dworkin. Englewood Cliffs: Prentice-Hall, 1970. Pp. 196–213.

Smith, Adam. *The Theory of Moral Sentiments*. Edited by D. D. Raphael and A. L. MacFie. Oxford: Oxford University Press, 1976.

Smith, Michael. "The Humean Theory of Motivation." *Mind* 96 (1987): 36–61.

Stampe, Dennis W. "The Authority of Desire." *Philosophical Review* 96 (1987): 335–381.

Stocker, Michael. *Plural and Conflicting Values*. Oxford: Clarendon Press, 1990.

—— "Values and Purposes: The Limits of Teleology and the Ends of Friendship." *Journal of Philosophy* 78 (1981): 747–765.

Strawson, Galen. *Freedom and Belief*. Oxford: Oxford University Press, 1986.

—— "On 'Freedom and Resentment.'" In *Perspectives on Moral Responsibility*. Edited by John Fischer and Mark Ravizza. Ithaca: Cornell University Press, 1993. Pp. 67–100.

Strawson, Peter. "Freedom and Resentment." In *Free Will*. Edited by Gary Watson. New York: Oxford University Press, 1982. Pp. 59–80.

Sumner, L. W. *Welfare, Happiness and Ethics*. Oxford: Clarendon Press, 1996.

Taurek, John. "Should the Numbers Count?" *Philosophy and Public Affairs* 6 (1977): 293–316.

Thomson, Judith. *The Realm of Rights*. Cambridge, Mass.: Harvard University Press, 1990.

Velleman, J. David. "Well-Being and Time." *Pacific Philosophical Quarterly* 72 (1991): 48–77.

von Neumann, John, and Oskar Morgenstern. *Theory of Games and Economic Behavior*. 3d ed. Princeton: Princeton University Press, 1953.

Wallace, R. Jay. *Responsibility and the Moral Sentiments*. Cambridge, Mass.: Harvard University Press, 1994.

Walzer, Michael. *Interpretation and Social Criticism*. Cambridge, Mass.: Harvard University Press, 1987.

——— "Moral Minimalism." In *From the Twilight of Probability*. Edited by William Shea and Antonio Spadafora. Canton, Mass.: Science History Publications, 1992. Pp. 3–14.

——— *Spheres of Justice*. New York: Basic Books, 1983.

Watson, Gary. "Free Agency." *Journal of Philosophy* 72 (1975): 205–220.

——— "Two Faces of Responsibility." *Philosophical Topics* 24 (1996): 227–248.

Wiggins, David. "Truth, Invention and the Meaning of Life." *Proceedings of the British Academy* 62 (1976): 331–378.

Williams, Bernard. "Ethical Consistency." In *Problems of the Self*. Cambridge: Cambridge University Press, 1973. Pp. 166–186.

——— *Ethics and the Limits of Philosophy*. Cambridge, Mass.: Harvard University Press, 1985.

——— "Internal Reasons and the Obscurity of Blame." In *Making Sense of Humanity*. Cambridge: Cambridge University Press, 1995. Pp. 35–45.

——— *Moral Luck*. Cambridge: Cambridge University Press, 1981.

——— *Shame and Necessity*. Berkeley: University of California Press, 1993.

Wolf, Susan. *Freedom within Reason*. New York: Oxford University Press, 1990.

Wong, David. *Moral Relativity*. Berkeley: University of California Press, 1984.

Ziff, Paul. *Semantic Analysis*. Ithaca: Cornell University Press, 1960.

Index